ALL·IN·ONE

CHFI™ Computer Hacking Forensic Investigator Certification

EXAM GUIDE

Charles L. Brooks

New York • Chicago • San Francisco
Athens • London • Madrid • Mexico City
Milan • New Delhi • Singapore • Sydney • Toronto

Cataloging-in-Publication Data is on file with the Library of Congress

McGraw-Hill Education books are available at special quantity discounts to use as premiums and sales promotions, or for use in corporate training programs. To contact a representative, please visit the Contact Us pages at www .mhprofessional.com.

CHFI™ Computer Hacking Forensic Investigator Certification All-in-One Exam Guide

Figure 4-2 courtesy of ErrantX.

Figure 6-3 courtesy of Evan-Amos with permission granted under the terms of the Creative Commons Attribution-Share Alike 3.0 Unported license, http://creativecommons.org/licenses/by-sa/3.0/legalcode.

Figure 10-6 courtesy of Viljo Viitanen.

Figure ll-5 courtesy of Ale2006-from-en with permission granted under the terms of the Creative Commons Attribution-Share Alike 3.0 Unported license, https://creativecommons.org/licenses/by-sa/3.0/legalcode.

2 3 4 5 6 7 QVS/QVS 21 20 19 18 17

ISBN: Book p/n 978-0-07-183153-6 and CD p/n 978-0-07-183154-3
of set 978-0-07-183156-7

MHID: Book p/n 0-07-183153-3 and CD p/n 0-07-183154-1
of set 0-07-183156-8

Sponsoring Editor Meghan Riley Manfre	**Technical Editor** Bobby E. Rogers	**Production Supervisor** George Anderson
Editorial Supervisor Patty Mon	**Copy Editor** Lisa McCoy	**Composition** Cenveo Publisher Services
Project Manager Raghavi Khullar, Cenveo® Publisher Services	**Proofreader** Paul Tyler	**Illustration** Cenveo Publisher Services
Acquisitions Coordinator Mary Demery	**Indexer** Karin Arrigoni	**Art Director, Cover** Jeff Weeks

This book is dedicated to my wife, Helyn Pultz.

ABOUT THE AUTHOR

Charles Brooks, MsCIS, CISSP, CEH, CHFI, CTT+, CCNA, CWNA, CWSP, is a writer and educator with a background in IT that spans 30 years, with the last 15 years in information security and education. Since 1998, he has been involved in information security, first as a technical lead for the VPN Advantage IPsec-managed service at Genuity, Inc., and then as overall software architect for the project. At EMC, Charles developed and delivered computer-based and instructor-based training in general information security and storage security. At RSA, Charles developed courses in cloud security fundamentals, network analysis, and advanced analysis and forensics. He has written and contributed to several technical training books, as well as continued to develop graduate-level courses in network security, secure software development, software security testing, and securing virtualized and cloud infrastructures. Charles has taught at several colleges and technical institutes in the Greater Boston area, and currently teaches at Brandeis University in the Rabb School/GPS MSIS program, as well as facilitating online courses at Boston University. Charles is currently the owner/principal consultant at Security Technical Education.

About the Technical Editor

Bobby E. Rogers is an information security engineer working for a major hospital in the southeastern United States. His previous experience includes working as a contractor for Department of Defense agencies, helping to secure, certify, and accredit their information systems. His duties include information system security engineering, risk management, and certification and accreditation efforts. He retired after 21 years in the United States Air Force, serving as a network security engineer and instructor, and has secured networks all over the world. Bobby has a master's degree in information assurance (IA), and is pursuing a doctoral degree in IA from Capitol College, Maryland. His many certifications include CompTIA A+, CompTIA Network+, CompTIA Security+, and CompTIA Mobility+ certifications, as well as CISSP-ISSEP, CEH, and MCSE: Security.

CONTENTS AT A GLANCE

CONTENTS

ACKNOWLEDGMENTS

First of all, thanks to Carole Jelen, my literary agent at Waterside Productions, for putting me in contact with Meghan Manfre, my acquisitions editor at McGraw-Hill Education, and to Meghan for getting this process started and bringing me up to speed. Mary Demery, my acquisitions coordinator, kept me on the straight and narrow and offered guidance and encouragement throughout the project. Thanks as well to Raghavi Khullar, associate project manager at Cenveo Publisher Services, who shepherded this book through copy editing and production, and to Lisa McCoy for copy editing the manuscript and making my tortured prose less so. I'm sure that there are others at McGraw-Hill Education who have worked on this book, and I thank them for their contributions as well.

A huge measure of thanks is due to my technical editor, Bobby Rogers. Bobby provided a wealth of constructive criticism and suggestions on how to improve the material, as well as pointing out areas that I needed to clarify and expand. The book is better because of his contributions, and I'm a better writer for having worked with him. I won't forget the three-sentences rule!

A nod and a tip of the hat to my friend and colleague, Ric Messier, for commentary, perspective, and "talking the talk *and* walking the walk" when it comes to digital forensics.

Finally, all credit goes to my beautiful and talented wife, Helyn Pultz, for encouragement, speaking the truth to me with love, and understanding when I vanished upstairs to my office in the evening for too many nights in a row. This book would not have been possible without her love and support.

INTRODUCTION

Congratulations! By picking up this book, thumbing through it, and starting to read the introduction, you've taken your first step toward a deeper understanding of computer (digital) forensics, and perhaps a career in this field. Before we dive into the details, I want to make one thing clear. *This book will help you pass your test.* It will help you do so by teaching you what you need to know to pass this certification exam. It will not tell you how to pass the certification exam. To be blunt, this book alone will not allow you to pass this exam; no single source could. You'll need to supplement this book with other texts that deal with digital forensics, Internet research, and getting some hands-on practice by downloading some of the software mentioned in this book and experimenting with it.

How to Use This Book

This book covers the exam objectives for EC-Council's Computer Hacking Forensic Investigator (CHFI) v8 certification examination. Each chapter covers specific objectives and details for the exam. EC-Council has defined 22 areas of study for this exam, and the book is divided into 12 chapters. I've consolidated certain areas where they made sense to me. For example, the last chapter in the book covers the objectives for writing a report and for acting as an expert witness. If you're engaged as an expert witness, you are going to need to write a report.

Each chapter has several features designed to communicate effectively the information you'll need to know for the exam:

- The **Certification Objectives** covered in each chapter are listed first. These identify the major topics within the chapter, and help you to map out your study. Since several chapters cover information in multiple areas, some of the objectives have been combined into a single sentence. Fear not: The information is there.

- **Sidebars** are included in each chapter and are designed to point out information, tips, and stories that will be helpful in your day-to-day responsibilities:

  - **Exam Tips** are exactly what they sound like. These are included to point out a focus area you need to concentrate on for the exam. No, they are not explicit test answers. Yes, they will help you focus your study.

  - Specially called out **Notes** are part of each chapter too. These interesting tidbits of information are relevant to the discussion and point out extra information. Don't discount them.

  - You should pay attention to the notes labeled **Caution**, as they point out areas when you can go very wrong.

This book is divided into two general sections. The first three chapters address meta-issues in computer forensics, and propose a process for performing an investigation. Chapter 4 talks about what you need to do to set up a forensics lab, and offers good advice about what you need to consider if you're thinking of going into business for yourself. The rest of the chapters go through this process in more detail, from the initial involvement with a case through writing a report and perhaps acting as a witness. Along the way, the book covers what I think of as "traditional" forensics, including evidence acquisition from disk drives and computer memory. The book also covers forensics as applied to other digital communications, including mobile devices, network-based attack and defense, and attacks against e-mail and web-based applications.

The Intended Audience

There a couple of groups of people who will benefit from this book. The first are people who are interested in having a career in the field of digital forensics, or are just interested in the topic. Unfortunately, this book doesn't provide all the information that you need to start your career. EC-Council recommends that people who wish to obtain this certification should have already obtained the Certified Ethical Hacker (CEH) certification. This book assumes that you have a background in how computers are actually built (CPU, memory, persistent storage, and so on) and that you have some familiarity with current operating systems such as Linux, Microsoft Windows, Mac OS X, and Oracle Solaris. Without this background, I think you'll find this book rather tough sledding. Remember, though, that I wrote this book for beginners in the field of digital forensics, so you will gain valuable information from reading this book.

The second group of people who will benefit from this book are those who have this basic knowledge already, as well as some knowledge and experience in the material covered in the CEH certification (the *CEH Certified Ethical Hacker All-in-One Exam Guide* is a good place to start). These folks may be looking for a career change or simply expanding their knowledge and expertise. If you're one of those people, I think that this book will offer you a good resource to come up to speed quickly in the basics of digital forensics.

Next Steps

Where do you go from here? One thing to consider is gaining expertise in the "big two" of forensic software suites: AccessData's Forensic Toolkit (FTK) and Guidance Software's EnCase. Both of these vendors offer training and certification for these products. Other professional certifications include the Certified Forensics Examiner (CFE) from the International Society of Forensic Computer Examiners (ISFCE) and the Certified Forensic Computer Examiner (CFCE) from the International Association of Computer Investigative Specialists (IACIS).

You may also encounter a set of certifications and tools that are reserved for people in law enforcement. Frankly, there are elements of digital forensics that you will probably never get to do unless you are in law enforcement. However, the principles and processes that we cover in this book are appropriate for those of you who will be involved in incident response or internal investigations, since forensics techniques and technology are increasingly a part of incident response.

The Examination

Before you take that next step in your career, you need to pass the CHFI certification examination. Passing this exam is complicated because of the breadth of the material covered (EC-Council lists 22 different subject areas). Nevertheless, take heart! This book will help you gain the knowledge needed for you to pass the exam. Read on!

Exam Details

The exam itself is computer-based and contains 150 multiple-choice questions with a few true/false questions thrown in. You have four hours to complete the exam. That's a little under 40 questions an hour, or 1 question every minute and 30 seconds. Go ahead, take a deep breath, and count from 1 to 90 slowly (one thousand one, one thousand two…). That's how long you could spend on every question and still complete the exam in the allotted time. Since there are some questions you can answer immediately, within five seconds or so, you don't need to worry about running out of time. A passing score for the exam is 70 percent. For the mathematically inclined, that means that you need to answer 105 questions correctly to pass. Not quite as daunting as 150 questions, is it?

How to Register for the Exam

You will need to register for the exam at the EC-Council web site (www.eccouncil.org). The first step in the process is to apply to actually take the exam. Once you've been approved, you can purchase an exam voucher at the EC-Council online store, after which you can schedule your exam at a Prometric or VUE testing center.

Preparing for the Exam

I want to be very clear about this. This book will help you pass the exam. It will provide you with information you need to know to pass your exam, but it will not give you all the information and experience you need to pass the exam. Instead, it should help point you toward areas where you need more study or background. Take the practice exams included on the CD-ROM. EC-Council also offers an online assessment that will give you a feel for the actual exam. Be tough on yourself while practicing with these exams. If you get a question right and you guessed the answer, you need to know what the correct answer is and why the other answers aren't correct.

Exam Strategies

I've sat for a number of examinations, and I've developed a personal strategy that works for me. First, arrive early for the examination. Take a bio break and drink some water. Get loose. Walk around, shake your fingers, do whatever you like to do and need to do to loosen up. Don't try to cram until the last minute. If you have a "cheat sheet" (a quick summary of important points), review that. A school of thought says you'll remember the last thing you put into your head. Your moment of exam Zen: Remember everything and nothing. For most tests, you'll be provided with an erasable pad and a marking pen. If you need to write down some information, write it on the pad before you even start the exam. This can save you time later and increase your accuracy, since you won't have to rack your brains trying to remember details after you've been staring at a computer screen for an hour or so.

While you're taking the exam, answer the question if you can. If you're in doubt, mark the question and skip it. The answer may come to you as you proceed, or another question later in the exam may jog your memory or start you thinking in the right direction. Make sure that you read the question and all of the answer choices! If you choose the first answer choice that "looks right," you may ignore a better answer choice following it.

After you've completed 30 questions or so, force yourself to stop, relax, take a deep breath, stretch, and look away from the screen. Moreover, blink! These exercises will keep you from tightening up, and blinking will prevent developing dry eye from staring at the screen for too long. The point is to keep yourself mentally and physically relaxed and loose.

When you've completed the exam, take a minute or three to relax before you start reviewing the questions you've marked. Then go back and look at the questions you marked. If you're still unclear, leave the question marked and proceed to the next question you've marked. If you can eliminate one or two of the answer choices, you'll have a better chance of narrowing the choice between the other two. As far as I know, there is no penalty for wrong answers, so, if worse comes to worst, choose the answer that "feels" correct. Remember, everything you read or studied in the course of preparing for this exam is stored in your memory, and although you may not be able to recall it, you may do so subliminally—the answer just "feels right" or "looks right." Trust me: It works. When you've answered the question, unmark it. Repeat until you have no marked questions, you run out of time, or you can't stand to look at the screen any longer.

Thank you for picking up this book and reading. I truly hope that this book will help you along your career path, as well as helping you fulfill your dreams and ambitions. Digital forensics is a fascinating, constantly changing, constantly challenging endeavor. You may become frustrated, but you won't be bored! The work that you do can help catch the bad guys and exonerate the good guys. Moreover, at the end of the day, that's not such a bad way to occupy your time.

Objective Map

The following table has been constructed to allow you to cross-reference the official exam objectives with the objectives as they are presented and covered in this book. References have been provided for the objective exactly as the exam vendor presents it, the section of the exam guide that covers that objective, and a chapter and page reference.

CHFI v8 312-49

Computer Forensics Today

In this chapter, you will learn how to
- Define computer forensics
- Describe the objectives and benefits of computer forensics
- Discuss the meaning of cybercrime
- Explain the role of the forensics investigator
- Distinguish between corporate and criminal investigations
- List important events in the history of computer forensics
- Describe important computer forensics–related laws and regulations

"May you live in interesting times," or so says an ancient curse. I myself am astonished at how much computing technology has changed in the last decade (post–September 11, 2001). Apple's iPod classic contains a 160GB drive. You can purchase a solid-state drive (SSD) for about U.S. $1.00 per gigabyte. Virtualization technology (VMware, Hyper-V, Xen, and VirtualBox) is increasingly widespread in the data center, with businesses reporting that over 50 percent of their servers are virtualized. Advances in virtualization technologies have enabled Cloud (with a capital C) computing, the ability for vendors to offer software (SAAS), platform (PAAS), or infrastructure (IAAS) as a service. Amazon introduced its Amazon Web Services (AWS) in 2006; today, anyone with a credit card can rent a high-powered Amazon virtual machine image (VMI), and you pay based on use. Microsoft's BitLocker software (full disk encryption) was available in the Ultimate and Enterprise versions of Vista and continues in Windows 7 and Windows 8. All of the things I've mentioned represent profound changes as to how we practice computer forensics. Interesting times, indeed.

So What Is This Computer Forensics Business Anyway?

While computers are a relatively new addition to the world, the practice of forensics had been going on long before the UNIVAC 1101 ever saw the light of day. The actual scientific discipline of forensics has existed for a long, long time and has multiple areas of practice, while computer forensics is relatively new. Today, computer forensics is a subset of the larger category of digital forensics that also includes forensic data

1

analysis, database forensics, network forensics, mobile device forensics, and video and audio forensics. We'll be covering four out of the seven topics listed here in upcoming chapters.

For the purposes of this book, we'll define computer forensics as "the discipline that combines elements of law and computer science to collect and analyze data from computer systems, networks, wireless communications, and storage devices in a way that is admissible as evidence in a court of law."[1]

One of the many complexities of computer forensics is determining the role of the computer in the particular incident we're considering. A computer can play one of two roles: a tool that was used to support the activity we're investigating, or the target for that particular activity. Consider an incident when an attacker has illegally gained control of a user's computer within an organization. The attacker then uses that computer and others to make their way to the server that contains the information they seek. In the first case, the computer is used as a tool; in the second instance, the computer (server) is the target of the attack. If the attacker had gained access to a single computer and had taken information stored there, then the tool and the target would be identical.

There is a third aspect regarding how a computer might be used in the commission of a crime. We can view the computer itself as a digital crime scene, containing evidence that helps us determine when and how the attack took place (as well as the who, the what, and maybe the why).

The History of Computer Forensics

When it comes to computer forensics, separating the legal from the technical can be difficult. Technical advances alter the kinds of evidence we can collect; changes in laws affect how we collect that evidence and whether that evidence will be admissible.

Technical

In the beginning, there was forensics. Table 1-1 shows a much-abbreviated set of significant dates from a technical perspective. Forensics has been around for a long, long time in many different areas.

One of the most significant development in forensics was a principle formulated by Edmond Locard, who built the first police laboratory in Lyon, France, in 1910. His principle was succinct: "Every contact leaves a trace." Practically, this means that the criminal always leaves some bit of evidence at the crime scene and always take some bit of evidence from the crime scene, no matter how small. Consider the following description of fiber analysis:

> Cross-transfers of fiber often occur in cases in which there is person-to-person contact, and investigators hope that fiber traceable back to the offender can be found at the crime scene, as well as vice versa. Success in solving the crime often hinges on the ability to narrow the sources for the type of fiber found.[2]

So there it is. Physical actions leave physical evidence in the physical world; digital actions leave digital evidence in the digital world (cyberspace), as we will see in later chapters.

Date	Event
1910	Albert Osborn creates guidelines for documenting crime scene evidence. Edmond Locard opens the first police forensic laboratory in Lyon, France.
1932	FBI establishes regional labs to provide forensic services.
1984	FBI forms the Computer Analysis and Response Team (CART) to support field offices.
2000	FBI opens the Regional Computer Forensics Laboratory (RCFL) to support cybercrime investigations.
2001	VMware offers the first x86 server virtualization product. Memory and disk contents are now files in a file system rather than part of the computer hardware.
2003	First open-source hypervisor (Xen). Virtualization technology is now available for free.
2006	Windows Vista Enterprise and Ultimate editions released with BitLocker full-disk encryption. Any use of encryption adds to the complexity and difficulty of a computer forensics investigation.
2006	Amazon offers Amazon Web Services (AWS), including the Simple Storage Service (S3) and the Elastic Compute Cloud (EC2). Storage and computing resources (servers) are now available for rent simply by charging the cost to your credit card: You can release these resources back to the provider, making forensic analysis of these resources difficult or impossible.
2009	Solid-state drives (SSDs) offered in laptops. SSDs function very differently than their mechanical counterparts with respect to the treatment of deleted files.

Table 1-1   Significant Dates in the History of Computer Forensics (Adapted from EC-Council. Computer Forensics: Investigation Procedures and Responses (MA: Cengage, 2010), p. 1:2.)

NOTE   I sometimes think of this as the "Tommy Boy" principle from the movie of the same name. In it, Chris Farley plays Tommy, a character who is accident-prone. His standard exclamation after running into something was "OWWW! %^&*@#!! *That's going to leave a mark!*"

Although there were advancements in forensics techniques in the early years of the 20th century, it wasn't until 1932 that the Federal Bureau of Investigation (FBI) set up a laboratory to provide general forensic services. As we can see from Table 1-1, formal recognition at the national level of the importance of forensic examinations of computers starts in 1984, when the FBI developed the Computer Analysis and Response Team (CART) to support computer forensics investigations, which was furthered by the Regional Computer Forensics Laboratory (RCFL).

Several events in the first decade of the 21st century altered the state of the art in computer forensics. Consider that in 2001 VMware created the first x86 server virtualization product. The open-source hypervisor Xen was introduced in 2003. The introduction of these technologies introduced a new file system (VMFS for VMware), as well as a new model of computer storage: Everything (including computer memory) was now represented as a file stored in a file system. Access to machine memory no longer required access to the actual machine; access to a file server—whether it be network attached storage (NAS) or storage area network (SAN)—was enough.

In 2006, Amazon introduced Amazon Web Services (AWS) that included their Simple Storage Service (S3) and the Elastic Compute Cloud (EC2). Anyone within reach of a credit card could store files in Amazon's Cloud or could rent a virtual service, called an Amazon Machine Instance (AMI), and pay based on use and the relative power of the virtual machine (disk space, memory, CPU). Microsoft offered BitLocker (full-disk encryption) in the Ultimate and Enterprise versions of Windows Vista, thereby making full-disk encryption widely commercially available to desktop machines and laptops.

Solid-state drives started to appear in netbooks in 2007 and in laptops in 2009. We'll go into more detail in the chapter on disk drives about the differences between SSDs and hard disk drives (HDDs). For the moment, however, we will note that SSDs have very different internal mechanisms for allocating and de-allocating physical sectors on the device, and this has profound implications for creating forensic copies of these drives, as well as the ability to reassemble physical sectors to recover a file's contents (called "carving").

In 2003, H. D. Moore and his colleagues released the original Metasploit framework. What is more significant for us is the incorporation of Vincent Liu's *Timestomp* program into that distribution around 2005. Timestomp is an antiforensics program that overwrites the MACE file system attributes—the time when the file was Modified, Accessed, or Created, or the information about that file was modified (Entry Modified).

Legal

Table 1-2 shows another abbreviated set of dates regarding the enactment of significant laws.

As we mentioned earlier, no bright line separates the legal and the technical. Advances in technology allow us to gather and analyze evidence that would be very difficult for a human being either to see or to collect (think of fiber analysis from rugs, clothing, etc.). On the other hand, technology (like computers) creates other legal issues that need to be addressed. Resolution of these issues may require a change to existing laws or the creation of new laws that specifically address the use of computers in the commission of a crime. Consider one of the earliest instances of a law aimed at the use of a computer for fraudulent purposes. In 1978, a group of criminals used computers to print out fake winning tickets at the Flagler Dog Track. In response, the state of Florida passed the Florida Computer Crimes Act, which made any intrusion of a computer system a crime, regardless of intent.

Looking at the laws currently in place, the Fourth Amendment addresses protection from unreasonable search and seizure by the government. The Fifth Amendment

Table 1-2	Date	Law Passed
Significant	1791	Bill of Rights (Fourth and Fifth Amendments)
Dates for Laws	1934	Federal Communications Act
Affecting	1967	*Katz v. United States*
Computer	1968	Omnibus Crime Reporting Act
Forensics	1986	Computer Fraud and Abuse Act
	2008	Identify Theft and Restitution Act

provides for protection from self-incrimination. The Katz case resulted in the Supreme Court decision that stated that physical conversation is protected from unreasonable search and seizure under the Fourth Amendment if it is made with a "reasonable expectation of privacy." We'll discuss in more detail in a later chapter what a "reasonable expectation of privacy" might mean to a forensics investigation.

Three statutory laws affect how you might conduct an investigation. These are the Wiretap Act (18 USC 2510-22), the Pen Registers and Trap and Trace Devices Statute (18 USC 3121-27), and the Stored Wired and Electronic Communications Act (18 USC 2701-120). Although originally written for telecommunications, the first two laws reflect how and what can be collected. These laws also address the issue of content of these communications as opposed to non-content. Both of these laws apply to real-time communication. We will have more to say about these laws when we talk about network forensics; for now, be aware that these laws apply to different protocols that make up data communications.

Stored communications (e-mail, for example) is covered under the Stored Wire and Electronic Communications Act that distinguishes between an "electronic communication service" and a "remote computing service." The law differs for each of these services and considers whether the e-mail has been opened or not and whether it has been stored for over 180 days. If you are contemplating using the data you collect as evidence in a courtroom, you need to understand the U.S. Federal Rules of Evidence. The U.S. Constitution and U.S. statutory laws govern the collection process; the Federal Rules of Evidence cover whether the evidence is admissible.

TIP Even though your evidence may be admissible in a courtroom, it may not be introduced into evidence, depending on the judgment of the attorney and whether or not it is ruled to be allowed to be admitted into evidence. As the investigator, you're responsible for making sure that policies and procedures are followed such that the information collected won't be judged inadmissible solely based on the way that it was collected.

Objectives and Benefits

Computer forensics has two main objectives. We have already discussed one objective: to collect, protect, and store potential evidence such that we could present this evidence in court. The second objective is related closely to the first: This collection, preservation, and analysis must be completed in a timely fashion. We do this to determine the extent of the damage done to the victim of the crime, as well as the identity of the attacker and their intentions.

TIP Always remember this from our detective friends: who, what, when, where, why, and how (5WH is a handy acronym). The Vocabulary for Event Recording and Incident Sharing project (VERIS) incident analysis method uses four of these elements to analyze an attack: assets (what was the goal of the attack), who was the actor (attacker), which actions affected the asset, and attributes (how the asset was affected in terms of confidentiality, availability, and integrity).

The ability quickly to determine the impact of the attack, the identity of the attacker, and their possible goals illustrates the benefits that a computer forensics capability provides for an organization. Other benefits to an organization that result from developing a computer forensics capability are the ability to maintain the operational status of computer systems and networks, as well as providing information to law enforcement concerning illegal activities undertaken by an employee using the organization's computers and network.

Cybercrime Investigations

What exactly is cybercrime? How does it differ from regular, non-cybercrime?

I have a simple criterion for determining whether the term cybercrime is appropriate. Let's take the example of cyberstalking, usually understood to be using computer and data communications to harass and follow someone. In this case, however, these activities would have been stalking, regardless of whether or not a computer was used. Other crimes that follow the same pattern are fraud, identity theft, theft of intellectual property, extortion, and embezzlement. There are crimes, however, that could only have been committed if computer or digital communications were involved. These include hacking/ cracking into a computer system, the spreading of malware (viruses, worms, adware, spyware), manipulation of a computer program, fraud at online auctions, denial-of-service (DoS) attacks, webjacking, password trafficking, and illegal use of telecommunications equipment against networked computers (eavesdropping, creating false communications, etc.) The attacker could have used a computer as a tool to commit the crime (logging in to a remote system, sending e-mail, using a chat or video-chat service). The computer itself may be the target of the attack (as in the case where information is obtained from a server). Or the computer can be a crime scene in the sense that there is evidence on that computer that needs to be preserved (log files, software, timeline of activities). So in general, cybercrime relates to criminal activities that occur in the digital world as opposed to the physical world (think about cyberbullying). As a result, some of the traces that are left by these activities are transient (volatile): If they're not recorded and captured in a very short time, they're gone. Others are more permanent, such as modification to a file, update to a database, or modification of a web page.

Given that, what might constitute a cybercrime investigation? Very simply, a cybercrime investigation occurs when computer systems have been utilized as a tool, a target, or as part of the crime scene. This definition demonstrates that recognizing cybercrime and initiating an investigation are not something to start only after the crime has been committed (this is called "locking the barn after the horse is out"). Hence, the need for cybercrime readiness planning within an organization. Cybercrime readiness planning implies that a team exists with the skills and resources necessary to respond to a particular incident. As Nelson indicates, this notion of incident response, in conjunction with network intrusion detection, is one side of a triangle of computer security in general, the other two sides being vulnerability assessment and computing investigations.[3]

Intrusion detection, vulnerability assessment, and computing investigations directly relate to various security controls that an organization can implement. Vulnerability assessment identifies flaws that can be corrected or mitigated, intrusion detection and response represent detective and compensatory controls, and investigations aim at root-cause analysis and the institution of preventive controls.

Corporate vs. Criminal Investigations

It's important to differentiate between criminal and corporate investigations. Criminal investigations are those that occur within the context of a crime: a violation of state, federal, or international law. Violating the law is either a civil or a criminal case. In civil cases, punishment is usually financial. On the other hand, conviction of a criminal offense can result in financial penalties, imprisonment, or both.

Corporate investigations usually involve a violation of corporate policy. A classic example is running your own business using the resources of the company where you're currently employed. Spending most of your working hours surfing gambling web sites is another example that will at least get you a stern reprimand, but in some cases, may also be illegal in the state you reside in.

Corporate investigations can often turn into criminal investigations. An investigation into heavy use of computer networks might result in the discovery of an employee sending the company's intellectual property (such as product plans) to a competitor. Now we move from questionable corporate behavior to a case of theft. Whether this case could end up in court depends in part on the nature of the evidence gathered concerning the use of the network and how investigators handled this evidence during the investigation. We'll discuss this further in future chapters.

Given that a corporate investigation may turn into a criminal investigation, it's always a good strategy to inform and involve your human resources (HR) team and your legal team from the start of the investigation, assuming that they weren't the source of the request for an investigation. A general rule of thumb for all investigations is that you must be authorized to perform that investigation. Who provides that authorization will vary, depending on the nature of the investigation: We'll discuss this in more detail in a later chapter.

Another factor to consider in any investigation is a process known as the Enterprise Theory of Investigation (ETI). This process looks at each separate incident as part of an ongoing series of activities by a particular enterprise or organization (for our purposes, this could be a criminal gang, a loosely organized team of cyberthieves, or a large business such as Enron). A good example of applying this process is the story of how Clifford Stoll discovered and traced the actions of an East German hacker, as told in the book *The Cuckoo's Egg* (Doubleday, 1989). An accounting error of a few cents led to the discovery of unauthorized access to a computer account, which in turn led to the discovery of additional hacking activity at various universities and military computer sites.

The Forensics Investigator

What is the role of the forensics investigator? Given what we now know, we could start by saying that the role of the forensics investigator is to act as the expert in detecting evidence, preserving evidence, analyzing evidence, and reporting the findings. A useful acronym for this activity is PIEID (pie-eyed?): Preservation, Identification, Extraction, Interpretation (Analysis), and Documentation (Reporting). The forensics investigator is expected to preserve the evidence at the crime scene. Based on information received about the particular incident, the investigator identifies which evidence is most relevant and begins the chain-of-custody procedures. Once identified, the evidence must be extracted from the device. The original data are stored and protected from access: All investigation and interpretation must be performed on a copy of the data. Once the investigation is complete, the forensics investigator needs to assemble the documentation recorded for each step into a final report. We'll cover this process in more detail in future chapters.

 EXAM TIP There are two great laws of forensics investigations. The first is always work with a copy of the data, never with the original. The second is leave the device in the state that you found it. If it's on, leave it on. If it's off, leave it off.

The role of the forensics investigator overlaps with that of an incident responder. Although the same tools may be used in both roles, the goal of the exercise is very different, and each activity has its own set of processes and procedures. We'll cover this in more detail in the chapter on the investigation process.

Chapter Review

Computer forensics is only one branch of forensics science in general, and can be described as "the discipline that combines elements of law and computer science to collect and analyze data from computer systems, networks, wireless communications, and storage devices in a way that is admissible as evidence in a court of law."

The objectives of computer forensics are to collect, protect, and store potential evidence such that we could present this evidence in court, and to perform these activities in a timely manner. Organizations that develop a computer forensics capability can more quickly determine the impact of the attack, the identity of the attacker, and their possible goals.

A forensics investigator acts as the expert in the detecting of evidence, preserving that evidence, analyzing that evidence, and reporting on the findings. Cybercrime refers to criminal activities where a computer or a computer network is used in the commission of a crime. A major distinction between criminal investigations and corporate investigations is that the former involves laws being broken, whereas a corporate investigation may be the result of a violation of company policy. Forensics science predates computer forensics, as do various applicable laws and regulations, such as the Fourth and Fifth Amendments to the U.S. Constitution. Computer forensics is viewed now as a subset of digital forensics.

Questions

1. What are three technological advances that have proved challenging to forensics investigators? (Choose all that apply.)

   A. Solid-state drives (SSDs)

   B. Cloud

   C. Virtualization

   D. 1TB disk drives

2. Computer forensics can best be described as:

   A. The analysis of computer software to determine flaws that could be exploited by an attacker

   B. The application of forensic science to the collection and preservation of evidence from computers or computer networks

   C. Gathering physical evidence from computers, such as DNA or fingerprints

   D. Statistical analysis of crimes utilizing a computer or computer network

3. Which of the following is an example of cybercrime? (Choose all that apply.)

   A. Denial-of-service attack

   B. Online auction fraud

   C. Software piracy

   D. Cyberstalking

4. How are solid-state drives (SSDs) different from hard disk drives (HDDs)?

   A. No difference. File system information can be retrieved from both.

   B. File systems on SSDs are different from traditional file systems.

   C. No difference. The same forensics information can be retrieved from both.

   D. The design of SSDs results in overwriting interesting forensics information.

5. The most significant aspect(s) of the forensics investigator role is/are:

   A. Discovery of malware on the target machine

   B. Documentation of the crime scene

   C. Collection and preservation of evidence

   D. Testifying in a court of law

6. John has been asked to investigate an employee's excessive use of the Internet during business hours. In the course of the investigation, he discovers that the employee is downloading copies of pirated software. This is an example of a:

   A. Corporate investigation

   B. Criminal investigation

   C. Both

   D. Neither; excessive use of the Internet is neither a crime nor a violation of policy

7. Edmond Locard's _____ principle states that every contact leaves a trace.

   A. Exchange

   B. Location

   C. Evidence

   D. Extrinsic

8. Any law regarding the search and seizure of computer evidence by the government must be formulated within the bounds laid out by the:

   A. Fourth Amendment of the U.S. Constitution

   B. Fifth Amendment of the U.S. Constitution

   C. Federal Rules of Evidence

   D. Katz doctrine

9. Whenever you are asked to investigate the actions of an employee, best practices indicate that you always should involve:

   A. The human resources department

   B. Your organization's legal department

   C. A and B

   D. Neither; you can proceed on your own as long as you are authorized to do so

10. You've been asked to investigate a break-in that resulted in confidential data being stolen from a server. It appears that the attacker has spent a lot of time logged in and searching the server. How was the server used in this scenario? (Choose all that apply.)

    A. Tool

    B. Target

    C. Crime scene

    D. Launchpad

11. The primary objective of computer forensics is:

    A. The preservation of computer records in order to return the machine to its original state

    B. The preservation of evidence for presentation in a court of law

    C. The discovery and attribution of attacks to a particular individual or organization

    D. The identification and removal of compromised or unauthorized software from the target machine

Answers

1. **A, B, and C.** Solid-state drives (SSDs), cloud, and virtualization represent fundamental changes and challenges to how information has been handled in the past. D increases the time to search and analyze the data, but it doesn't represent a fundamental change.

2. **B.** "The application of forensic science to the collection and preservation of evidence from computers or computer networks" is the definition of computer forensics.

3. **A, B, C,** and **D.** Denial-of-service attack, online auction fraud, software piracy, and cyberstalking all represent activities that utilize a computer or a computer network, and therefore are considered cybercrimes.

4. **A.** The file systems created on SSDs are identical to those created on HDDs, but block acquisition of the device doesn't produce the same results as with HDDs because of the way blocks are allocated to individual files.

5. **B, C,** and **D.** Discovery of malware on the target machine, documentation of the crime scene, and collection and preservation of evidence all reflect aspects of the forensics process, but they are useless as evidence if the data are not properly preserved.

6. **C.** The scenario given is an example of a corporate investigation (policy based) transitioning into a criminal case (theft).

7. **A.** It is Locard's exchange principle that states that every contact leaves a trace.

8. **A.** The Fourth Amendment of the U.S. Constitution protects a citizen from unreasonable search and seizure.

9. **C.** You should always involve both HR and the legal department since each function will be aware of the specifics concerning the rights of the employee and the laws applicable to such an investigation.

10. **B** and **C.** In this scenario, the server was a target of the attack, and may well be a crime scene in that the attacker has left evidence of the attack on the server.

11. **B.** The main focus of the forensics investigator always should be to preserve evidence.

References

1. *Computer Forensics* (Washington, DC: CERT, 2008). Retrieved from www.us-cert .gov/sites/default/files/publications/forensics.pdf.

2. Bardsley, M. and Bell, R. *The Atlanta Child Murders: Fiber Analysis.* Retrieved from www.trutv.com/library/crime/serial_killers/predators/williams/33.html.

3. Nelson, W. et. al. *Guide to Computer Forensics and Investigations,* Fourth Edition, (MA: Cengage, 2010), pg. 5.

The Nature of Digital Evidence

In this chapter, you will learn how to

- Define digital evidence and explain its role in the case of a computer security incident
- Discuss the characteristics of digital evidence and the various types of digital data
- Discuss Federal Rules of Evidence (FRE) and articulate the best evidence rule
- Summarize the international principles for computer evidence
- Differentiate between the Scientific Working Group on Digital Evidence (SWGDE) and the International Organization on Computer Evidence (IOCE)
- List the considerations for collecting digital evidence from electronic crime scenes
- Explain electronic crime and digital evidence consideration by crime category

The term *evidence* is another one of those slippery terms whose meaning depends on context, which is another way of saying that your definition of evidence may not be my definition of evidence. In this chapter, we will focus on the definition of "digital evidence" and how that evidence needs to treated in order for it to be suitable for admission in court.

What Is Digital Evidence?

We spent a good deal of time in the previous chapter talking about computer forensics. Early on, "computer forensics" seemed to be a good description for the application of forensic science to these particular devices (recall, too, that the definition of forensics is "presenting to a court"). As the types of devices that utilized digital communications and digital data increased, the phrase "digital forensics" became more popular, as it more precisely captured what the forensics investigator faced during an investigation. Consider that smart phones, tablets, laptops, netbooks, music players, and other devices are capable of using and generating digital data.

We represent digital data by a sequence of binary digits (a one or a zero), frequently abbreviated as bits: 8 bits are a byte; 4 bits are a nibble (seriously). These bits are only intelligible to us when we impose an agreed-upon structure (format) on that data and we interpret data under the rules of that structure. Figure 2-1 shows a screen capture of a file containing ASCII text, with the binary values expressed in hexadecimal notation on the left and the ASCII representation on the right (hexadecimal notation is base 16, with values running from 0 to F; conveniently, a single hexadecimal character reflects 4 bits). Some of the bytes in the file don't have a printable representation, so we divide these characters into printable and nonprintable. Usually, the interpretation of digital data is done via a computer program, itself a collection of bits. Virtually anything can be represented digitally: audio, video, text, graphical images, and computer programs. Any and all of this information can be transmitted and stored as a collection of bytes, commonly referred to as a file.

Digital data are quite different from what we are used to in the physical world. Digital data are ephemeral: They can be present one moment and gone the next. They are fragile; they are easily damaged or destroyed, but at the same time, they are very easy to copy.

 EXAM TIP Know the characteristics of digital data, especially that they are fragile and easily damaged, but easy to copy and transmit.

Now that we have a working definition of digital data, we'll define a *digital investigation* as an effort that requires examination of a digital device because that device has been involved in a particular incident, which may be a crime. Our need to understand and explain a series of digital events motivates us to perform this investigation. We do this by developing a hypothesis regarding what might have happened and then searching for evidence that would refute that hypothesis.

Digital evidence is a digital object that contains reliable information that supports or refutes a hypothesis. This definition of evidence reflects its use in scientific investigations.

![Hex Edit screen capture showing hexadecimal and ASCII representation of All26.txt file]

```
Hex Edit - [All26.txt]
File   Edit   View   Operations   Template   Aerial   Tools   Window   Help

                                              47          71             ASCII default

  All26.txt

       00 01 02 03  04 05 06 07  08 09 0A 0B  0C 0D 0E 0F 0123456789ABCDEF
00:    46 6F 72 20  6E 6F 77 20  69 73 20 74  68 65 20 74 For now is the t
10:    69 6D 65 0D  0A 66 6F 72  20 61 6C 6C  20 67 6F 6F ime..for all goo
20:    64 20 6D 65  6E 0D 0A 74  6F 20 63 6F  6D 65 20 74 d men..to come t
30:    6F 20 74 68  65 20 61 69  64 0D 0A 6F  66 20 74 68 o the aid..of th
40:    65 20 70 61  72 74 79                              e party

                                        0              47h   71   Length: 47
```

Figure 2-1 Hexadecimal and ASCII representation

In the legal arena, digital or electronic evidence is "any probative information stored or transmitted in digital form that a party to a court case may use at trial."[1] Digital forensics investigations thus are a "process that uses science and technology to analyze digital objects and that develops and tests theories which can be entered into a court of law to answer questions about events that have occurred."[2]

Figure 2-2 shows the relationships between digital objects, digital investigations, and digital forensics investigations. Digital forensic investigations are a subset of digital investigations, with more constraints added by the forensic process itself. It follows that investigations and forensics investigations use digital objects, but how they use these objects will differ, depending on the type of investigation.

This helps to explain why you must take care in collecting, processing, and storing digital objects. Unless you're very sure that the evidence you collect will not be used in court, it's a very good idea to exercise due caution and care with the evidence such that you don't do anything to preclude using that digital evidence in a courtroom. It's certainly possible that an investigation that starts out as purely information gathering may turn into a criminal investigation.

What kind of digital objects might we encounter? The document "Electronic Crime Scene Investigation: An On-the-Scene Reference for First Responders"[3] lists 14 different crime categories and 60 different kinds of electronic crime and digital evidence. Of these 60 items, 43 of them are either digital devices or the input or output of digital devices. Financial records appear in 11 instances of criminal activities, while identity theft and prostitution are associated with 13 of the digital objects used in the commission of these crimes. Other potential sources of evidence include answering machines, audio recorders, external data storage devices, MP3 players such as the Apple iPod, multifunction machines, and pagers, among others. A quick rule of thumb is that if it's an electronic device that can store information (even an electric alarm clock can do that), then it's a potential source of evidence.

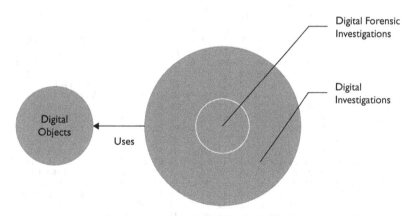

Figure 2-2 Digital objects, digital investigations, and digital forensic investigations (Adapted from Carrier, B. File System Forensic Analysis (NJ: Pearson Education, 2005), p 4.)

Anti-Digital Forensics

The worst mistake an investigator can make is to underestimate their adversary. Perhaps the best position to take is to assume that she is smarter than you are, has better equipment, and has more time and patience to commit the crime than you have to gather and analyze the available evidence. As in chess, don't depend on your opponent making the wrong move. But if they do, be prepared to capitalize on it.

Anti-digital forensics is a set of methods and tools that are used to destroy or obfuscate digital objects such that they cannot be used as digital evidence. We'll cover some of these techniques in future chapters, such as encryption, steganography, packing, compression, compression and encryption (in that order), the modification of file metadata (such as the MAC time—when the file is created, accessed, or modified), file erasure, and hidden file systems (such as those created by the *TrueCrypt* software). The results of using these techniques can result in no evidence that the file existed, the file existed but was erased (not just deleted), or the file exists but the content is inaccessible. Figure 2-3 shows the contents of a *TrueCrypt* file (container.dat) that has been formatted as a FAT32 file system protected by a password and has a second password-protected file system contained within it. Notice how the file appears to be random characters—exactly what you would like an investigator to see.

Take note that the previously mentioned anti-forensics techniques include techniques for ensuring privacy as well as personal information security. One provocative question is: Can you be forced to give up an encryption key? Or is it your Fifth Amendment right not to divulge this secret? In one case, the court ruled that if you had written down the password, you must reveal it, but if you had memorized the password, you did not have to reveal it.

```
Container.dat

Offset     0  1  2  3  4  5  6  7   8  9 10 11 12 13 14 15
00000000  54 FC 72 02 3D D7 1A F4  C8 3C AE C4 A8 AC C8 07   ôür ·=x ôÈ‹®Ä¨¯-È
00000016  00 3B D0 D7 40 F8 C2 01  7D 20 35 21 6B 09 71 48   ;Đ×@øÂ } 5!k qH
00000032  F8 E3 D4 3B C2 E9 BF 39  85 3E E0 D6 C7 B5 CC 27   øãÔ;Âé¿9|>àÖÇµÌ'
00000048  34 09 4D E9 26 5A BD 19  77 76 59 2E CE 28 ED 80   4 Mé&Z½ wvY.Î(í
00000064  BC CD 87 51 63 8F F6 F2  BB 43 71 20 41 06 A3 E6   ¼Í‡Qc öò»Cq A £æ
00000080  FC 91 D3 3F C1 82 BD 9B  27 9B FB 62 C9 0B 89 B0   ü'Ó?Á½› 'ûbÉ ‰°
00000096  32 4F 2B 5C 6C 54 75 32  EE 7E FE 25 3B AD D9 00   2O+\lTu2î~þ%;-Ù
00000112  FE 5F BA 86 EF 42 B1 C7  BB 35 BB 83 C5 D4 96 AE   þ_º†ïB±Ç»5»ƒÅÔ–®
00000128  58 A3 E0 7C 81 E1 DF 69  0E 47 5F 0C 94 07 57 1B   X£à|áßi G_ ” W
00000144  3D 62 91 E7 9F 96 C7 50  19 11 2A EF 17 79 EF A1   =b'çŸ–ÇP *ï yï¡
00000160  57 9E 34 2E B4 30 EE 28  E5 EE F9 9B ED 7C 73 C2   Wž4.´0î( åîù›í|sÂ
00000176  25 62 17 05 EF D7 BB 17  CA 34 BD C8 D5 B4 96 4B   %b ï×» Ê4½ÈÕ´–K
00000192  19 FC 44 7C 55 26 4A 34  68 D1 6A 8C BB D5 69 77   üD|U&J4hÑjŒ»Õiw
00000208  8D DC 8B 2D CB 21 5A EB  3D 02 D0 86 46 01 A6 FE   Ü‹-Ë!Zë =Đ†F ¦þ
00000224  F9 EB 53 5F 5C 8E 52 3B  DE 55 D1 50 30 7A E6 CC   ùëS_\ŽR;ÞUÑP0zæÌ
00000240  48 31 D5 A2 84 20 E3 73  8A 0D C0 64 47 02 1E 4B   H1Õ¢„ ãsŠ ÀdG K
00000256  B5 3E 06 04 F6 D3 3C 04  66 05 77 31 69 D2 D7 35   µ> öÓ< f w1iÒ×5
00000272  FA 1D 65 37 B2 97 F3 84  D8 0E 77 41 D9 95 83 68   ú e7²—ó„ Ø wAÙ•ƒh
00000288  05 F3 99 CB 91 1A 48 D6  12 D0 CF F5 1A 21 A9 49   ó™Ë' HÖ ĐÏõ !©I
00000304  1D 45 C2 08 BA CA 9F B7  4C 01 97 C9 17 CB 90 54   EÂ ºÊŸ· L —É Ë T
00000320  60 92 DB BC 8B 6E F7 6A  2A 11 E3 B4 F2 B5 A8 14   `'Û¼‹n÷j * ã´òµ¨
00000336  6E 61 D3 0B 16 C0 68 6E  52 9C FA 48 10 AF 77 25   naÓ ÀhnRœúH ¯w%
00000352  2F A1 60 3B FA 9B E4 1F  1F 1C C0 A4 D9 1D 2A 14   /¡`;ú›ä À¤Ù *
00000368  98 35 A6 35 5A 65 58 12  9E ED 54 62 E8 30 26 3F   ˜5¦5ZeX žíTbè0&?
00000384  E7 A2 4F 0A 17 35 DC 93  39 85 E4 56 A5 0B 96 F3   çoO 5Ü“ 9 äV¥ –ó
00000400  2C E9 A0 62 E7 6E 65 2E  E3 ED 8A E2 94 50 7B 17   ,é bçne.ãíŠâ”P{
```

Figure 2-3   Contents of a *TrueCrypt* container

Locard's Exchange Principle

You were introduced to Locard's exchange principle in Chapter 1: Every contact leaves a trace. How might this work in a crime scene that involves a computer? Consider this paragraph from Paul Kirk's *Crime Investigation* regarding Locard's exchange principle applied to a physical crime scene:

> Wherever he steps, wherever he touches, whatever he leaves, even without consciousness, will serve as a silent witness against him his fingerprints or his footprints, but his hair, the fibers from his clothes, the glass he breaks, the tool mark he leaves, the paint he scratches, the blood or semen he deposits or collects. All of these and more bear mute witness against him. This is evidence that does not forget. It is not confused by the excitement of the moment. It is not absent because human witnesses are. It is factual evidence. Physical evidence cannot be wrong, it cannot perjure itself, *it cannot be wholly absent* [my italics]. Only human failure to find it, study and understand it, can diminish its value.[4]

Imagine the following: We walk into a crime scene as presented in Figure 2-4. As a computer forensics investigator, we see several possible sources of digital evidence. DVDs, a printer, a desktop computer, and a cell phone. What about a network connection? Is the desktop computer powered on or powered off? Before we start collecting this evidence, we need to ensure that we don't disturb any physical evidence that is left

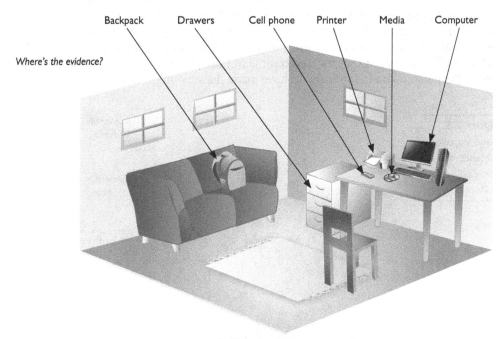

Figure 2-4 Our imaginary crime scene

here, such as fingerprints, fiber evidence from a coat, or hair on the chair. And let's not forget what might be in the drawers or in the backpack on the sofa. The harder we look, the more we see potential sources for evidence that is either related to or generated by a digital device.

Federal Rules of Evidence (FRE)

The Federal Rules of Evidence (FRE) are a collection of laws that determine what can or cannot be admitted into evidence in a federal courtroom. States are not required to use the same standards as presented in the FRE, but they are encouraged to do so, and many do. As always, as a digital investigator, you should know the rules of evidence for your local state or province. Copies of the FRE can be obtained from many locations; one such location is from the web site www.uscourts.gov.

Let's assume that we've done our very best and collected all possible evidence found at our imagined crime scene as shown in Figure 2-4. We've done due diligence: We've been authorized to collect everything we've collected, we've worn gloves so as not to contaminate physical evidence, we've made a sketch, we've labeled everything appropriately, and we've photographed everything within the room. So we have everything we need, right?

Not necessarily. Figure 2-5 illustrates that only a subset of our evidence may actually be admissible, even though it's relevant, while some relevant evidence may not be admissible. One reason for this is Rule 802 from the FRE that states: "hearsay is not admissible unless any of the following provide otherwise: a federal statue, these rules; or other rules prescribed by the Supreme Court."[5] Hearsay is defined in Rule 801 as "a statement, that the declarant did not make while testifying at the current trial or hearing, and a party offers in evidence to prove the truth of the matter asserted in the statement."[6] It turns out that the declarant is not the person on the witness stand, but rather, the person who is supposed to have made the statement. Using a familiar poem

Figure 2-5
Evidence, relevant evidence, and admissible evidence

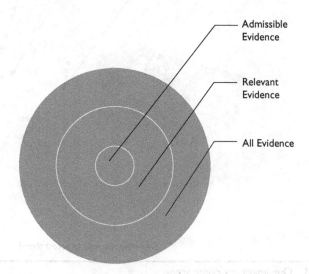

as an example, the speaker in "'Twas the Night Before Christmas" is not the declarant, but rather Santa Claus, who exclaimed (as he drove out of sight) "Merry Christmas to all, and to all a good night."

Computer-Generated vs. Computer-Stored Records

When it comes to computers, it's not possible to present the actual information stored on the computer. Instead, we need to generate some tangible output based on the information, such as a printed document or a picture. This leads us to the difference between computer-generated records and computer-stored records. According to the U.S. Department of Justice (DOJ), computer-generated records are those records produced by a running computer program, while computer-stored records are records or documents (files) containing information created by a human author.[7] Computer-stored records are generally considered hearsay; computer-generated records, however, are increasingly likely to be recognized as acceptable, especially if they are produced as part of "regularly conducted business activity (FRE 803(6))." A good example of this is logging, whether it be at a system-wide level, as would be the case with a Security Information and Event Management (SIEM) installation, or on a local workstation, such as the various Windows event logs. A word of caution, however. Logging that takes place only when an event is observed or log levels are increased may not be admissible since it isn't part of "normal business processes." However, if increased logging is part of a standard, documented process for incident response, then the evidence may be admissible.

EXAM TIP Know the difference between computer-generated records and computer-stored records. Computer-generated records have been created by a running software program; computer-stored records have been generated by a person. An easy way to remember the difference between the two is that only people go to the store.

Computer-generated records must be authentic, or identified.[7] The authenticity (identification) of that computer-generated record can be established by the testimony of the individual who caused that record to be created. For example, a systems administrator could testify that she had initiated packet capture on the computer's Internet-facing network interface and had captured this information to a file on a RAID 1 storage array. Chain of custody contributes to the authenticity of these records as well. Chain of custody is a documented record of who had possession and control over a particular piece of evidence at every moment until that object is entered into evidence in the courtroom. It is critical that this chain of custody be documented by a relevant form (the chain-of-custody form). Standard formats exist for these kinds of forms. The primary details are the date and time of transfer, who provided and who received the evidence, and the purpose of the transfer (for example, Dick transferred the CD-ROM containing the log files to Jane on January 3, 2013, at 3:00 PM EST for the purpose of analysis). Chain of custody is a significant portion of the entire chain of evidence. A chain-of-evidence form includes the search and seizure of that evidence and the cataloging of that evidence, as well as the chain of custody of that evidence once it has been obtained. Figure 2-6 is an example of a chain-of-custody form. Take particular notice of

Property Record Number:
_____

Anywhere Police Department
EVIDENCE CHAIN OF CUSTODY TRACKING FORM

Case Number: _____ Offense: _____

Submitting Officer: (Name/ID#) _____

Victim: _____

Suspect: _____

Date/Time Seized: _____ Location of Seizure: _____

Description of Evidence		
Item #	Quantity	Description of Item (Model, Serial #, Condition, Marks, Scratches)

Chain of Custody				
Item #	Date/Time	Released by (Signature & ID#)	Received by (Signature & ID#)	Comments/Location

APD_Form_#PE003_v.1 (12/2012)   Page 1 of 2 pages (See back)

Figure 2-6 Chain-of-custody form (Source: "Sample Chain of Custody Form," NIST. Retrieved from http://www.nist.gov/oles/forensics/upload/Sample-Chain-of-Custody-Form.docx.)

the information at the top of the form, items like property record number, case number, date and time seized, location of the seizure, and the list and item numbers of this evidence. All of this information provides us with the ability to trace a particular piece of evidence within the criminal justice system.

After all that, is our evidence reliable? That is, does the software that generated the evidence produce evidence that can be relied on? An example of that is data that are generated by a program that is part of ongoing business processes and that are utilized for other purposes within the organization. Consider an event file that records time of user login and logout, which in turn is processed to generate usage reports for particular individuals for charge-back purposes. If this event file were used as evidence, the fact that it had been used as part of normal business purposes for a second purpose would indicate that the information contained within that file was considered reliable. Proving that the program produces accurate results can also improve the chances of admission of computer-generated records that aren't usually collected as a part of normal business processing.

Essential Data

Another characteristic of computer information is that the data that we gather and use must be essential. Essential data are digital data we can trust. Brian Carrier, in his book *File System Forensic Analysis*, uses the example of a file content address.[2] We can trust that data because if they were not true (accurate), then neither we nor the suspect could have accessed that digital object. Nonessential data simply are data that we can't trust because they may have been modified, or they may have never been created in the first place. Reconsidering our example of modifying MAC times on a file, we realize that these values represent nonessential data because we ultimately can't trust these values (it may be true that our adversary is clever enough that the times have been changed such that they seem plausible but completely hide the exact order of events). Nonessential data may be correct most of the time, but it's worth looking for other evidence that supports that assessment (corroborative evidence).

One last complication: We may trust a piece of essential data (a file content address) but we may not trust the data referenced by a file content address. Metadata for a deleted file may indicate that the file contents were located at file content address 3589, but the data that reside there may now be part of a different file because the file blocks associated with the address have been assigned to another file.

Best Evidence

When presenting evidence in court, you're required to present the best evidence. FRE 1001 defines the best evidence for a computer thusly: "For electronically stored information, any 'original' means any printout—or other output readable by sight—if it accurately reflects the information."[8]

The best evidence rule applies when a party wants to admit as evidence the contents of a document at trial but the original document is not available. In this case, the party must provide an acceptable excuse for its absence. If the document itself is not available and the court finds the excuse provided acceptable, then the party is allowed to use secondary evidence to prove the contents of the document and have it admissible as evidence. The best evidence rule only applies when a party seeks to prove that the contents of the document ought to be admitted as evidence.[9]

Think about the case when we have created a memory dump from a suspect's computer. In this case, the best evidence would be the actual contents of the computer memory at the time of capture. Failing that, however, we can use the contents of our memory dump as secondary evidence. Likewise, we can introduce a listing of network connections as evidence even though we lost the actual connections once the computer shut down. There are simply times when providing the original of the evidence is impractical, such as a rack of blade servers, or a series of disk tray cabinets in large storage array networks (SANs). Since seizing the physical devices is impractical, a forensic copy of that device must be created as a bit-for-bit forensic image, and this requirement has a specific impact on how the copy is made, as we'll see in our chapter on acquiring evidence.

International Principles of Computer Evidence

As the number of PCs and workstations in use increased during the 1990s, so did the recognition that standards should be developed internationally in order to facilitate communication and sharing of information, as well as to standardize procedures. We'll focus on two organizations in this section: the International Organization on Computer Evidence (IOCE) and the Scientific Working Group on Digital Evidence (SWGDE).

International Organization on Computer Evidence

The IOCE was organized in the mid-1990s in order to develop international standards regarding computer evidence. By the time the group produced the document "Guidelines of Best Practice in the Forensic Examination of Digital Technology" in 2002, the notion of computer evidence had already been replaced with the more generic category of digital evidence. The guidelines cover a range of best practices for implementing a forensics capability, and include equipment, training, and organizational needs.

Scientific Working Group on Digital Evidence

The SWGDE was organized in 1999 to act as the U.S. representative of the IOCE. By the time the SWGDE came into existence, the notion of computer evidence had been subsumed by the notion of digital evidence. SWDGE published their first document in 2003 and has been active since then. They have published papers on audio forensics, cell phone forensics, and general digital forensics. Table 2-1 lists a selected set of publications that are available on their web site (www.swdge.org).

Date	Title	Purpose
02-11-2013	SWGDE Best Practices for Computer Forensics V3-0 (released for public comment)	Preferred methods for conducting the computer forensics process
02-11-2013	SWGDE Best Practices for Mobile Phone Examinations V2-0	Preferred methods for conducting forensics investigations of mobile phones
02-11-2013	SWGDE Best Practices for Vehicle Navigation and Infotainment System Examinations V1-0	Preferred methods for extracting information from navigation, information and entertainment system
02-11-2013	SWGDE Core Competencies for Mobile Phone Forensics V1-0	What mobile phone DFIs need to know to perform their duties
04-08-2013	SWGDE-SWGIT Glossary V2.7	Definitions for image, video and forensic audio analysis as well as computers
06-04-2012	SWGDE Best Practices for GPS Devices V1.0	How to examine global positioning systems (GPS) devices
09-15-2011	SWGDE Core Competencies for Forensic Audio V1.pdf	Skills and information needed by forensic audio investigators.
05-15-2010	SWGDE Technical Notes on Microsoft Windows 7	How XP, Vista, and Windows 7 differ
01-28-2008	Capture of Live Systems V1.0	How to capture live data from computers

Table 2-1   Selected Publications (Available from SWGDE. Adapted from "Public Documents," Scientific Working Group on Digital Evidence. Retrieved from https://www.swgde.org/documents/Current%20Documents.)

Evidence Collection

We spent the beginning of this chapter discussing the nature of digital evidence and how that evidence can be admitted into a courtroom. The first thing that has to be done is that the evidence (by which I mean the sources of the evidence) must be handled in a particular way. We'll go into the mechanisms of this in our next chapter, but for the moment, let's consider some general rules for actually collecting the evidence.

There are two ways to acquire evidence: via a live collection or a dead collection. Live collections occur when the computer in question is running the operating system (OS) installed on that computer. This means that data collection goes on using the resources of the computer itself (memory, the network, etc.) and that the investigator is logged in to machine, either via the console or remotely using remote login software. Dead collections, on the other hand, utilize an OS that is not running on the machine in question; rather, the OS has been started from a floppy disk, or more likely these days, from a live CD-ROM or a universal serial bus (USB) thumb drive. In this case, we can access the persistent storage of the computer, but we've lost the volatile information such as the contents of memory, network connections, running processes, etc.

Let's add another dimension to this activity, namely the role of the forensic investigator versus the role of the incident responder. We've already learned the difference between them. In the case of incident response, we're looking for digital evidence that can help us determine the root cause of the event that concerns us.

> **NOTE** I think of this as the "stop the bleeding" approach. What's of greater concern: terminating the attack or finding evidence with which to prosecute and ultimately convict the attacker? In the case of discovering an ongoing attack, the initial impulse usually would be to terminate that attack to minimize the loss to the business. And in so doing, the investigator may modify the data such that they no longer have value as forensic evidence. The first responder must weigh the cost of allowing the attack to continue versus the collection of critical evidence.

Whether you are acting as a forensic investigator or as an incident responder, your first rule is to be circumspect in what you're doing. In other words, don't make a mess at the crime scene by acting like a bull in a china shop. Understand your role as part of the forensics team that will be examining the crime scene. Be careful that you don't destroy latent evidence or contaminate the evidence by adding your own physical traces to the scene (remember, Locard's principle applies to you as well). As Eoghen Casey notes, the evidence we collect must be relevant, authentic, and integral, and must have been collected and stored in a forensically sound manner.[1] Evidence is relevant if it has probative value, that is, a direct bearing on the incident in question. It must be authentic: We have to ensure that it hasn't been tampered with, and integral to that, the integrity of the evidence cannot have been compromised. We do this by following specific procedures to seize and collect that evidence, documenting those efforts, and recording our efforts in chain-of-evidence forms and chain-of-custody forms. Simply speaking, a chain-of-evidence form reflects the entire history of a piece of evidence, while the chain-of-custody form documents who has had possession of the evidence at every moment since it was "bagged and tagged" until the evidence is entered into the courtroom proceedings.

IOCE Guidelines for Recovering Digital Forensic Evidence

The IOCE Guidelines outline the following general principles for recovering digital forensic evidence:

1. The general principles, that have been adopted as G8[9] recommendations relating to digital evidence, that should be followed by forensic laboratories are as follows:

   a. The general rules of evidence should be applied to all digital evidence.

   b. Upon seizing digital evidence, actions taken should not change that evidence.

   c. When it is necessary for a person to access original digital evidence that person should be suitably trained for the purpose.

d. All activity relating to the seizure, access, storage, or transfer of digital evidence must be fully documented, preserved, and available for review.

e. An individual is responsible for all actions taken with respect to digital evidence whilst the digital evidence is in their possession.

2. All activity relating to the seizure, examination process, and presentation of evidence access, storage, or transfer of digital evidence must be documented, preserved, and available for review.

3. Responsibility for maintaining evidential value and provenance is a personal, not corporate issue. If an individual has acknowledged responsibility for an item by signing an access log they are responsible for all actions taken in respect of that item until such time as it is returned to storage or formally transferred to another individual.[10]

No surprises here.

NOTE G8 is the Group of Eight, an organization consisting of eight countries with the largest economies.

The Scientific Method

Motivating the underlying principles for collecting digital evidence is a process of discovery labeled the scientific method. Remember that the scientific method is a way by which we can test out our ideas of why and how a particular event occurred. There are a number of definitions of the scientific method, and while they may vary in terminology, most definitions will include most if not all of the steps listed here.

1. Define a question/accept a question. Gather information and resources (observe). Some people consider gathering information to be a separate step.

2. Form an explanatory hypothesis.

3. Test the hypothesis by performing an experiment and collecting data in a reproducible manner.

4. Analyze the data.

5. Draw conclusions. These may support or contradict your original hypothesis. If the data and your conclusions do not support your hypothesis, go back to step 2.

6. Communicate results (report).

We will go into more depth regarding the scientific method in our chapter on the forensic investigation process and show how forensics investigations mirror the steps outlined here.

Consider a Scenario

Consider an incident response scenario that illustrates these steps. Joe Sample has been called in to investigate a possible compromise of a critical server. The immediate question is was this server compromised, and, if so, what was the attack vector (how did the attacker gain access to the server?). Joe isolates the server from the rest of the network while still permitting network communications and begins a live analysis of the running machine, making sure to document any action that would change the state of the machine.

Joe's initial hypothesis is that access to the machine was via the network. His first action, however, is to examine the login history via the console. He notes that there are no recorded logins for the past several weeks, and he then checks to see if anyone has tampered with the logs on the server. They have not, so Joe discards the alternative hypothesis that the machine was compromised via console access.

Joe examines the list of running processes and sees nothing amiss. He continues to search the log files for login attempts (successful or unsuccessful) and discovers that an SSH (secure shell) session had been initiated three days ago from one of the internal networks that had access rights to the server. Joe is surprised to see the login name, as he knew all of the other employees who were authorized to access that server, and this individual wasn't one of them. He checks the /etc/password file (yes, the server is a Linux machine) and discovers that this user does indeed have a valid account that has been created with group membership that provides extended administrator privileges.

Joe stops for a minute to catch his breath and take stock. Given the configuration of the server, access had to come from either the console or from the network via an SSH session. No logins via the console were recorded during the period he was investigating, so the access had to be from the network. Joe has discovered that there was a suspicious login (an unauthorized user) from an internal machine.

Joe considers his options. He can turn his attention to what had occurred during that login session on the server. He could investigate the machine that was the source of the login. Or he could report back to his manager that the machine does appear to have been compromised (unauthorized access) and they should reimage the machine.

As an investigator, are you going to follow each of the previous steps in exact detail? Probably not. Remember that your investigation is in response to a question and that you are investigating a specific hypothesis (a hypothetical explanation) of what occurred. Remember our old friend 5WH.

Exculpatory Evidence

Evidence takes on two forms: inculpatory evidence and exculpatory evidence. Inculpatory evidence is evidence that tends to show that the defendant is guilty or had criminal intent, and supports our initial hypothesis about what may have happened. On the other hand, exculpatory evidence is "evidence, such as a statement, tending to excuse, justify, or absolve the alleged fault or guilt of a defendant" (www.law.cornell.edu/wex/exculpatory_evidence). Applying this to our scientific method, exculpatory evidence would be evidence that disproves or fails to support our current hypothesis (although an absence of evidence doesn't necessarily mean that the hypothesis is wrong). In the previous example, the absence of log records for a console login during a given time period disproves (fails to support) the hypothesis that the server was compromised via a console login. This isn't always easy to do in the heat of an investigation. We all tend to look for evidence that supports our current notion of what is happening or has happened (otherwise known as confirmation bias).

Chapter Review

Digital evidence refers to digital objects that help an investigator support or disprove a hypothesis. Digital evidence is easily modified, easily copied, very volatile (consider computer RAM), and can come in many forms: images, video, audio, documents, databases, etc. Certain types of digital evidence are often associated with particular types of crime. According to the National Institute of Justice (NIJ), the most popular piece of digital evidence across all crime categories is financial records, while prostitution and identity theft utilize the most number of digital materials. It's a wired, wired world we live in!

The Federal Rules of Evidence (FRE) are a set of criteria that determine what things can be admitted as evidence in a federal court. The best evidence rule simply states that the original evidence is preferred over a copy unless a copy is specifically allowed. The international principles for computer evidence, as established by the IOCE, establish a framework for each member state to develop standard operating procedures (SOPs) for the entire digital forensics process. The Scientific Working Group on Digital Evidence (SWGDE) is the U.S. representative to the IOCE and is charged with disseminating best practices for the collection and protection of digital evidence.

When collecting digital evidence from electronic crime scenes, take care not to destroy physical evidence associated with the digital equipment, have a plan regarding which evidence should be seized, and try to preserve the digital device in the state it was found.

Questions

1. Digital evidence is best described as:

   A. The entire contents of the physical recording medium (disk, USB stick, floppy disk, etc.)

   B. Any binary data file

   C. A digital object that supports our investigation and can either support or disprove our original hypothesis

   D. A digital object generated by systems software

2. During a security incident, digital evidence helps in determining:

   A. How a system was compromised

   B. What data was compromised

   C. When the system was compromised

   D. All of the above

3. Which is *not* an instance of digital evidence?

   A. Audio files

   B. Image files

   C. System software

   D. Microsoft Word documents

4. True or false: The presence of financial records at a crime scene means that they were used in committing the crime.

   A. True

   B. False

5. The best evidence rule intends to:

   A. Eliminate all copies as possibly forged

   B. Only allow a single piece of evidence that demonstrates the defendant's guilt or innocence

   C. Provide the original item if at all possible

   D. Prevent contamination of evidence while in custody

6. True or false: In the United States, the Federal Rules of Evidence are required to be used by the states.

   A. True

   B. False

7. Which of the following is *not* a consideration when collecting digital evidence from a crime scene?

   A. Preservation

   B. Documentation

   C. Transfer

   D. None of the above

8. What is the difference between a computer-stored record and a computer-generated record?

   A. Computer-stored records are always readable text files.

   B. Computer-generated records can be interpreted only by another computer program.

   C. A computer-generated record is generated by normal business processes and not directly by a person.

   D. Computer-stored records are created on one computer and then moved to another.

9. What is the first step of any digital investigation?

    A. Turn all machines off that may contain digital evidence.

    B. Plan your strategy based on the information that you've been provided concerning the case.

    C. Assign different people responsibilities for collecting data from different digital devices.

    D. Allow the physical forensics team to transport the digital devices to the lab to search for physical evidence.

10. What is the difference between a live investigation and a dead investigation?

    A. Live investigations require the presence of an investigator, while dead investigations can be automated such that no investigator needs to be present.

    B. Live investigations only consider evidence that is transient and may be destroyed when the computer is turned off.

    C. A live investigation collects evidence from a running computer. A dead investigation collects evidence from persistent storage associated with that computer when the computer isn't running.

    D. Live investigations require the consent of the owner; dead investigations do not.

11. John logged in to a running compromised server and began recording open files, users logged in, network connections, running processes, etc. Once he had satisfied himself that the machine was locked down and no longer under attack, he shut down the machine and rebuilt the machine from backups. What was John doing during that time?

    A. Performing a digital forensics investigation

    B. Performing a digital investigation

    C. Standard system maintenance

    D. None of the above

12. After determining that an attack was in progress, John, in accordance with the company's incident response policy, turned up the logging level on the network in order to collect extra information. Is this information admissible in court?

    A. Yes. All log records are admissible, regardless of when or how they are collected.

    B. No. Information collected in special circumstances that is not part of standard business activities is never admissible.

    C. Maybe. The evidence could be admitted if the collection method was used as part of an incident response action.

    D. Not enough information to tell.

Answers

1. **C.** Digital evidence is any digital object that we can use to support our investigations.

2. **D.** Digital evidence could supply information leading to the determination of what data was compromised, how access was obtained, and when it happened.

3. **C.** System software would not be considered digital evidence, since it has no probative value with respect to a potential incident.

4. **B.** These financial records would have to be tied to the crime itself; the presence of such records doesn't mean that they are always related to a crime.

5. **C.** The intent of the best evidence rule is to provide the original item if at all possible.

6. **B.** In the United States, it is highly recommended, but not required, that the states use that same standard for evidence.

7. **D.** Preservation, documentation, and transfer are all considerations when collecting digital evidence.

8. **C.** Software running on a particular machine can produce computer-generated records and these records can be introduced as evidence, provided they are part of normal business processing. Computer-stored records, on the other hand, can be denied based on the rule of hearsay.

9. **B.** The first step in any investigation is to plan and prepare your strategy based on the information provided to you about the incident.

10. **C.** We perform live investigations on a running computer that is running the OS native to that given machine. Dead investigations do not utilize the OS installed on the computer, but instead use an OS that is loaded from an external data source, like a live CD, floppy disk, or USB stick.

11. **B.** John was performing a digital investigation, since there was no effort made to collect the information using sound forensics procedures and the machines were wiped and rebuilt immediately thereafter.

12. **C.** The evidence may be admissible, given that turning up the logging level on the network is part of a defined business process (the company's incident response policy).

References

1. Casey, E., *Digital Evidence and Computer Crime*, Third Edition (MA: Academic Press, 2011).

2. Carrier, B., *File System Forensic Analysis* (NJ: Pearson Education, 2005), pp. 4–5.

3. "Electronic Crime Scene Investigation: An On-the-Scene Reference for First Responders, Second Edition," National Institute of Justice (NIJ). Retrieved from www.nij.gov/pubs-sum/227050.htm.

4. Kirk, P. L., *Crime Investigation*, Second Edition (NY: Wiley, 1974), p. 2.

5. "Rule 802: The Rule Against Hearsay," Cornell University Law School. Retrieved from www.law.cornell.edu/rules/fre/rule_802.

6. "Rule 801: Definitions that Apply to this Article; Exclusions from Hearsay," Cornell University Law School. Retrieved from www.law.cornell.edu/rules/fre/rule_801.

7. Searching and Seizing Computers and Obtaining Electronic Evidence in Criminal Cases, Washington, DC: USDOJ, 2009), p. 192. Retrieved from http://www.usdoj.gov/criminal/cybercrime/docs/ssmanual2009.pdf.

8. "Require the Original," Cornell University Law School, accessed July 2013 at www.law.cornell.edu/rules/fre/rule_1002.

9. "Best Evidence Rule," Cornell University Law School. Retrieved from www.law.cornel.edu/rules/fre/rule_1001.

10. "Guidelines for Best Practices in the Forensic Examination of Digital Technology," International Organization on Computer Evidence. Retrieved from www.ioce.org/fileadmin/user_upload/2002/ioce_bp_exam_digit_tech.html.

The Investigation Process

In this chapter, you will learn how to

- Provide an overview of the computer crime investigation process and its methodology
- Prepare for an investigation, including obtaining the necessary warrants and evaluating and securing the scene
- Collect and secure the evidence in a forensically sound manner
- Explain different techniques for acquiring and analyzing the data
- Summarize the importance of evidence and case assessment
- Prepare the final investigation report and testify in court

Regardless of whether you're conducting a digital forensics investigation or a digital investigation as either a digital forensics investigator (DFI) or an incident responder (IR), you need to follow a process. The process is crucial to success. Tools come and go, or are replaced with new versions that have enhanced capabilities but sometimes lose other capabilities in the name of progress. Training and a process are the keys to success, regardless of the tool. The process transcends the tool, and a "fool with a tool is still a fool."

Your process will tell you what needs to be done first, will serve as guidance for what you should do next, and will tell you when you're done with a particular phase, as well as what you'll need to successfully enter the next stage. After you've completed your investigation, the process serves as a checklist to ensure that you've completed everything and that you have the appropriate documentation for each step.

The Process Is Key

Your process is more than just the individual steps. Instead, it reflects an abstraction of the steps that you might take at present. Consider the following activity: Collect the data in a forensically sound manner. Today, that would mean creating a forensic image of persistent storage or generating a memory dump from a running computer. However, it might also mean making a forensically sound copy of a set of files comprising a VMware virtual machine. While the process remains the same, the actual step performed will vary, depending on the technologies available when you actually perform that step.

Overview

Many organizations and individuals have defined their own forensic process. Much like the scientific method, the phases of these processes will differ. Some definitions will combine steps; others may break a phase into multiple steps. Figure 3-1 uses an HIPO (Hierarchical Input-Process-Output) diagram to illustrate the process we'll be using as a series of input-process-output phases.

We've synthesized this process model from several sources. Casey[1] has defined five different models, including his own, but they all share the steps of preparation, survey/identification, preservation, examination and analysis, and presentation. Analysis is the step where we apply the scientific method to answer our 5WH questions.

 NOTE Remember our 5WH questions: who, what, when, where, why, and how.

Before the Investigation

You need to do several things before you ever actually participate in an investigation. These include getting your equipment in place, reviewing relevant laws and policies, and ensuring that you have authorization from the appropriate authorities, whether they're a judge who grants a search warrant or a member of senior management who identifies you as a digital forensics investigator within your organization. Last, make sure that your forensics toolkit is packed and ready to go.

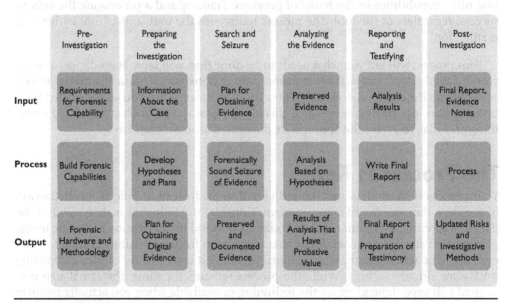

	Pre-Investigation	Preparing the Investigation	Search and Seizure	Analyzing the Evidence	Reporting and Testifying	Post-Investigation
Input	Requirements for Forensic Capability	Information About the Case	Plan for Obtaining Evidence	Preserved Evidence	Analysis Results	Final Report, Evidence Notes
Process	Build Forensic Capabilities	Develop Hypotheses and Plans	Forensically Sound Seizure of Evidence	Analysis Based on Hypotheses	Write Final Report	Process
Output	Forensic Hardware and Methodology	Plan for Obtaining Digital Evidence	Preserved and Documented Evidence	Results of Analysis That Have Probative Value	Final Report and Preparation of Testimony	Updated Risks and Investigative Methods

Figure 3-1 Defining a forensic process

TIP Replace any disposable items that you've used during an investigation immediately after that investigation concludes. That way, you'll know that you're stocked up and ready to go. Also, ensure that any reusable digital media has been forensically wiped clean of any data.

Buying or Building a Forensics Workstation

At one time, choosing Windows versus Linux versus Mac would have been a much greater issue than it is today. Now you simply need to choose a platform that runs one of the virtualization platforms: VirtualBox, QEMU, VMware, or Citrix. In this case, you can create virtual machines that can support multiple operating systems. Alternatively, you can choose a hardware platform with sufficient disk space and a central processing unit (CPU) that you can boot into the operating system (OS) of your choice.

It's normally a good idea to be versatile and have multiple available operating systems for your evidence collection and analysis, as you don't necessarily know what kind of operating system you'll encounter in the field. Some operating systems are better for collecting and analyzing data in specific field situations, so it's good to have a variety in your toolset!

Your workstation should have as much hardware as you can afford: at least 8GB random access memory (RAM) (16 is better), multiple universal serial bus (USB) and serial advanced technology attachment (SATA) ports, a terabyte (TB) of local data, and the most powerful multicore CPUs that are within your budget (and you will have a budget).

Consider the specification for Digital Intelligence's Forensic Recovery of Evidence Device(FRED)SR.[2] These are the specifications for one particular product. There are many others on the market, and depending on your budget, you might need to repurpose other equipment and create your own forensic workstation.

- Dual(2) Intel Xeon E5-2609 CPU, (Quad Core) 2.4 GHz, 10MB Cache, 6.4 GT/s Intel QPI
- 16GB PC3-12800 DDR3 1600 MHz ECC Memory
- 1 × 300 GB 10,000 RPM SATA III Hard Drive – OS Drive
- 1 × 2.0 TB 7200 RPM SATA III Hard Drive – Data Drive
- 22″ Widescreen LCD Monitor with Built-in Speakers

Why these particular features? As I mentioned earlier, a forensics workstation needs to be powerful. The processing speed of the Quad Core Xeon processor, combined with the 10MB cache, ensures quick CPU performance, while 16GB of memory provides storage for examining large files or running a virtual machine with a different OS using VMware or VirtualBox. The OS drive spins at 10,000 RPM, which should ensure rapid transfer speed. The 2TB data drive provides room for digital evidence at a reasonable transfer rate. Last, a 22″ screen lets you look at two documents side by side, or read a document displaying two pages at once. This saves time by not requiring you to switch from window to window. Finally, built-in speakers save desk real estate, and between manuals, cables, disks, paper, and others, space will be at a premium.

In instances where you need forensics capabilities on site, a laptop computer provides a more portable solution. Consider Digital Intelligence's FRED-L (FRED Laptop),[3] which has the following features:

- Intel Cori7-4800MQ Quad Core Processor, 2.7 GHz, 6MB L3 Cache
- 8GB DDR3 1600 PC3-12800 Memory
- 256GB Solid-State Internal SATA Drive
- Intel HM87 Express Chipset
- 15.6" Full HD (1920 × 1080) LED Backlit Display
- nVidia GeForce GTX 770M With 3GB GDDR5 VRAM
- Internal 6× BD-R Blu-Ray Burner /8× DVD ± R/2.4× +DL Super Multi Combo Drive
- Integrated Components:
  - 10/100/1000 Mbps Ethernet LAN
  - 802.11a/b/g/n Wireless LAN + Bluetooth (Intel 6235AGN)
  - Card Reader 9-in-1 (MMC/RSMMC/MS/MS Pro/MS Duo/SD/Mini-SD/ SDHC/SDXC)
  - 2.0 Megapixel Digital Video Camera

Once again, these specifications provide a great degree of capability in the portable (luggable?) package. I/O is covered by supporting up to Gigabit Ethernet on the local area network (LAN) card and 802.11n on the wireless card. Sufficient CPU power, memory, and a solid-state drive (SSD) for the OS provide snappy response. A separate graphics card doesn't steal cycles and memory from the CPU. The built-in card reader, combined with the optical burner, lets you capture the contents of memory cards to a read-only medium. Finally, a 15.6" screen at 1920 × 1080 pixels is a good compromise between portability and size. Simply put, you cannot have too much power or too much speed when it comes to outfitting a forensics workstation.

The kinds of equipment that you need and the kind of environment that you need for your forensics workspace depends on the kind of work you're doing. You may be an independent consultant, one of a team of consultants, or the owner of a digital forensics business. At the very least, you need a workspace where you can securely store evidence, prevent access to that evidence by outside parties, and an environment that won't corrupt the evidence or cause your equipment to malfunction. We'll go into much more detail in our chapter on building a forensics lab.

Reviewing Policies and Laws, Including Forensics Laws

We will come to see in our chapter on searching and seizing evidence how various laws affect the collection of particular kinds of evidence. As a DFI, you need to know how the laws affect your conducting the investigation. If you're working on a corporate investigation, you need to know what policies are in effect at that organization, as well as what laws would be in effect, regardless of the organization's policies. The following should be emblazoned on a plaque on the wall of your office, and while it was originally for government agencies, it applies equally well to any forensic effort.

Work within the parameters of the agency's policies
and applicable federal, state, and local laws.[4]

Notifying Decision Makers and Acquiring Authorization

Making yourself known to decision makers is always a good idea. In most instances, as a DFI, you won't be making a final determination regarding the ultimate disposition of a particular case. Your primary responsibility is to report the facts of the case as clearly and as accurately as possible.

In all cases, you will need to acquire authorization to perform your investigations. This might be blanket authority granted to a forensics organization within an enterprise, or it could be on a case-by-case basis, depending on whether the case is important enough to deserve an investigation. Regardless, you must ensure that the appropriate levels of management in your organization have signed off on your activities and that the scope of your investigation is well defined. Overstepping the bounds of an investigation may result in evidence being disqualified or a case being dismissed because of an error in conducting the investigation.

Building a Computer Investigation Toolkit

When I used to travel quite a bit on business, I had an "essentials" kit already packed and ready to go. This kit included personal items, over-the-counter medications, an emergency $100, spare glasses, sunglasses, headphones … you get the idea. When something ran out, I replaced it immediately. When it was time to leave on a business trip, I'd pack my essentials kit. No worries, no last-minute panic about whether I did or didn't or should or shouldn't bring a particular item. The same strategy applies for your forensics investigation toolkit. The DoJ suggests that your kit should include such items as[4]

- Cameras (still and video)
- Boxes
- Notepads
- Gloves
- Evidence inventory logs
- Evidence tape
- Paper evidence bags
- Evidence stickers
- Labels or tags
- Crime scene tape
- Antistatic bags
- Permanent markers
- Nonmagnetic tools
- Frequency-shielding material
- Blank CDs or DVDs
- Spare USB drives, sticks, or writeable media

You need to pack radio frequency–shielding material such as Faraday isolation bags or aluminum foil to wrap various kinds of mobile communication devices.[5] You want to keep these devices incommunicado and unable to receive a text, a call, or any other communications. Why? Many commercial smart phones include the capability of remotely "wiping" (expunging) data on the device.

Preparing the Investigation

So, you've been contacted to initiate an investigation. Your involvement with the investigation begins when you first pick up the phone, read the text, silence your pager, or read the e-mail. Regardless of how you're notified, you should have a preliminary discussion with the client who contacted you. The point of this discussion is to establish the 5WH for this particular investigation:[6]

Who: Who is the incident manager? Is there a case name or title?
What: What happened?
When: Am I needed right now? Tomorrow?
Where: Where is the incident scene located? What jurisdiction is this?
Why: Is this engagement going to be covert (undercover)? Or is it going to be overt (out in the open)? Is this a corporate investigation or a criminal investigation?
How: What exactly is going to be seized? Do we have make, model, location, ID number? How much work is this engagement going to require?

Creating an Initial Plan/Case Assessment

You need to have performed several tasks before you grab your gear and head for the door. Spend some time creating your initial plan. Creating such a plan is often described as a case assessment. Given the information that you've received from the client, and given what you already know from research and experience, what initial hypotheses have you developed? A significant portion of your case assessment is a risk assessment. When considering your plan of action, you should assess what kinds of issues you've faced in other investigations. As an example, consider the computer skills of the suspect. Might they have created a start-up process that would delete and overwrite files if the computer wasn't started with a particular account? How do you assess the computer skills of the suspect? Are they sophisticated enough to hide data in the host-protected area (HPA) of a local disk?

Getting Permission: Do You Need a Warrant or Not?

Regardless of the nature of your investigation, you need authorization to perform that investigation. We've already mentioned being authorized by a member of senior management in the case of an internal investigation. If you'll be part of a criminal investigation, you will need a search warrant that details the scope of the search and the items that are included in that search. We'll go into more detail on warrants, subpoenas, and various exceptions to these laws in a later chapter, but for now, realize that you will need authorization as well as a statement as to what is considered in scope for your investigation.

On the Scene: Preparing for Search and Seizure

One of the first things you should do after arriving on the scene and making sure that the digital evidence is preserved is to make a sketch of the scene. A few years ago, creating a hand-drawn sketch of a crime scene would have been standard practice. Even though smart phones have changed the game (software apps exist that act as a voice recorder, a camera, and allow you to annotate a photograph), creating a sketch on paper is still a good idea. Electronic instruments can be fragile things: Dropping the phone on a concrete sidewalk, into a puddle of water, or into a toilet (yes, it happens to the best of us) can cause notes and documentation to be lost very quickly. So take along a pad of paper to do your initial sketch by hand as well.

EXAM TIP   You must document every step of the investigation process.

At this point in the investigation, start practicing case management. This is where recordkeeping comes into play. The professional DFI needs the imagination of a computer hacker and the organizational skills and attention to details of a certified public accountant (CPA). You'll need to assign a case number, investigator name, and other identifying labels to the evidence that you collect. If you're working independently, create a case number according to a standard format. Ultimately, the format itself is less important than maintaining consistency.

Let's distinguish between the information that you are recording as part of case management and the notes you are taking as part of your investigation. There will be overlap, but your notes should be more than just factual: Instead, they should provide clues and ideas that may influence choices made later on in your investigation.

TIP   Keep your factual details and your speculation separate; if not physically separate, then annotate your observations such that you can tell one from the other.

When you arrive on the scene, make sure that you secure the scene, if it hasn't been done already. Securing the scene can involve taping or roping it off to limit access, identifying all those who were at the crime scene, and ensuring that the digital equipment present is handled appropriately. If other law enforcement officers are already present, determine their level of training with respect to digital forensics and introduce yourself as the digital forensics expert. We'll go into more detail in Chapter 5.

Labeling Everything and Taking Pictures

You may think that you have an excellent memory, and you very well may have. Nevertheless, in the noise and hustle and bustle of the investigation, you may forget exactly which port was connected to what device. First, take a picture of the device before touching it; then focus on labeling the device and its connections. Physically labeling everything (input ports, cables, devices, and others) along with a description of what that item is will make the job of actually filling out chain-of-evidence forms that much easier. Take another set of pictures of all the evidence with labels attached. Figure 3-2 shows a desktop computer after you've applied the labels.

Figure 3-2
Desktop
computer
with labels
(Source: Electronic
Crime Scene
Investigation,
Second Edition
(Washington, DC:
USDoJ, 2008),
p. 34.)

If the computer is running, you need to capture an image of what is on the screen. Either the screen will displayed, in which case you should capture which applications are running, or the screen may be blank. If the screen is blank, move the pointing device (mouse, trackpad, or trackball) sufficiently to terminate the screen saver or cause the machine to wake up from suspension.

Seizing the Evidence

At this point in the investigation, you're ready to actually start seizing the evidence. We're skipping over the details of what evidence you've decided to collect, but one thing is clear: Whatever evidence you identified and mean to collect must be in accordance with local, state, or federal search and seizure laws, using forensically sound processes and procedures. You may have encountered evidence at the scene that wasn't anticipated when you initially became part of the investigation. If so, make sure you are within your legal rights to collect that evidence; our chapter on search and seizure provides those details.

Identifying Sources

You will have done some of this work during your pre-planning for the site visit, in that you will have determined what digital containers exist based on the description of the crime and the crime scene. Nonetheless, when you arrive on the scene, be prepared to amend your initial list based on what is actually present. Yes, there may be a desktop computer, but also there may be an external disk drive, a USB stick, a network connection, and so forth. Make sure you identify other digital containers, such as music players, tablets, smart phones, answering machines, and audio recorders (yes, they still exist). Carefully examine the area around all digital equipment for notes, notebooks, DVDs (especially ones that have been used for backups), and sticky notes (these may contain a password outright or a hint—for example, "Call 7-277-9673" are the keys that, when pressed, spell "password").

Even in a home, look for various networking equipment, such as routers, wireless access points (WAPs), and switches. Depending on the sophistication of the networking devices, they may have log files and trace files that recorded network activity. No network gear? Remember that cell phones can be used as wireless access points to send data over cellular networks. Recall, too, that there are devices that store data even though that isn't their primary function—some copiers will store the number of documents already printed; fax machines will have a list of the last numbers called.

Finally, but perhaps more importantly, look for things that should be there but aren't. Consider what particular kind of cable attached to a computer can mean: What if it's a printer cable, but no printer is in sight? Where is it? What about an owner's manual for an absent piece of equipment? Are there SD cards labeled as photographs, but no camera is visible?

Seizing the Evidence

You now are in a position to actually confiscate the evidence. We'll go into detail in Chapter 5 on how you would go about doing this. Remember, though, that the goal of seizing the evidence is to preserve the evidence. Store the digital devices and digital information in appropriate evidence storage bags, and start the chain of evidence. You now have the evidence "bagged and tagged." Start documenting the 5WH. Figure 3-3 shows an example of a chain-of-evidence form.

From this moment on, the movement of the evidence between individuals must be documented via a chain-of-custody form (see Figure 3-4). Maintaining these two forms is absolutely critical to ensure that the evidence will be admissible in court.

Differentiating between the chain of custody and the chain of evidence can be difficult sometimes, in that certain organizations will call the chain of custody the chain of evidence. I think that it's worth distinguishing between the two by noting that the chain of custody helps establish the chain of evidence, which starts a bit earlier than the chain of custody when you assign a case number and an evidence number to a particular object. The chain of custody will then refer back to that object you originally documented. The objects will be identified in part by the labels that you attached earlier to the digital equipment.

Creating and initially filling out the chain-of-custody form isn't a one-time event. You will need to create an entry in the chain-of-custody form every time the evidence is moved, stored, transferred, or received. Any gaps in the chain of custody will call into question the integrity of that evidence.

EXAM TIP The chain-of-custody records everyone who accessed the evidence from the time it was put into an evidence locker to the time that it was brought to the courtroom. It's important to prove that you can account for the evidence for the entire time that it was held and that no unauthorized or unidentified individual had access to the evidence.

Computer Evidence Worksheet

Case Number:_____   Exhibit Number: _____

Laboratory Number: _____   Control Number: _____

Computer Information

Manufacturer: _____   Model: _____

Serial Number: _____

Examiner Markings: _____

Computer Type: Desktop ☐   Laptop ☐   Other: _____

Computer Condition: Good ☐   Damaged ☐ **(See Remarks)**

Number of Hard Drives:_____   3.5" Floppy Drive ☐   5.25" Floppy Drive ☐

Modem ☐   Network Card ☐   Tape Drive ☐   Tape Drive Type: _____

100 MB Zip ☐   250 MB Zip ☐   CD Reader ☐   CD Read/Write ☐

DVD ☐   Other: _____

CMOS Information	Not Available ☐

Password Logon: Yes ☐   No ☐   Password = _____

Current Time:_____   AM ☐   PM ☐   Current Date: _____ / _____ / _____

CMOS Time: _____   AM ☐   PM ☐   CMOS Date: _____ / _____

CMOS Hard Drive #1 Settings	Auto ☐

Capacity: _____   Cylinders: _____   Heads: _____   Sectors: _____

Mode: LBA ☐   Normal ☐   Auto ☐   Legacy CHS ☐

CMOS Hard Drive #2 Settings	Auto ☐

Capacity: _____   Cylinders: _____   Heads: _____   Sectors: _____

Mode: LBA ☐   Normal ☐   Auto ☐   Legacy CHS ☐

Computer Evidence Worksheet	Page 1 of 2

Figure 3-3   Chain-of-evidence form (Source: Forensic Examination of Digital Evidence, (Washington, DC: USDoJ, 2004), p. 44.)

Environmental Impact

Think about what changes in the environment might do to digital media. If I have a computer that has been operating at 68°F, and I take that machine into the open air, where the temperature may be 104°F in the shade, with humidity at 97 percent, will the digital equipment suffer any ill effects? Consider things like condensation. Very dry

Property Record Number:
_____

Anywhere Police Department
EVIDENCE CHAIN OF CUSTODY TRACKING FORM

Case Number: _____ Offense: _____
Submitting Officer: (Name/ID#) _____
Victim: _____
Suspect: _____
Date/Time Seized: _____ Location of Seizure: _____

Description of Evidence		
Item #	Quantity	Description of Item (Model, Serial #, Condition, Marks, Scratches)

Chain of Custody				
Item #	Date/Time	Released by (Signature & ID#)	Received by (Signature & ID#)	Comments/Location

APD_Form_#PE003_v.I (12/2012)   Page I of 2 pages (See back)

Figure 3-4   Chain-of-custody form (Source: Evidence Chain of Custody Tracking Form, NIST. Retrieved from www.nist.gov/oles/forensics/upload/Sample-Chain-of-Custody-Form.docx.)

climates may increase the risk of static discharge. Devices that are used to sitting quietly on a table in a rack may react badly to jouncing over a road full of potholes.

Analyzing the Evidence

We'll assume that all the evidence you've collected has been stored, secured, and labeled appropriately and that all the initial documentation has been completed. Now it's time to begin analyzing the evidence. Before we fire up our favorite forensics analysis toolkit, however, we need to ensure the preservation and integrity of the original evidence. The chain-of-custody form attests to the integrity of the data, meaning that only known and authorized individuals had access to that evidence. In order to preserve the evidence, however, we need to work from a copy of the evidence and not the original. The less we need to actually handle the original digital evidence, the better.

 NOTE "Fat fingers" or "slip of the keyboard" have bitten all of us at one time or another. I recall attempting to format a USB thumb drive and mistakenly typed "sdb" instead of "sdc," thereby wiping out the master boot record on my USB backup drive (which took the partition table with it). Needless to say, I lost a few hours of work as well as a few handfuls of hair from my head getting that repaired.

Making a Copy

At this point, you have the evidence in a place where you can create a copy of it such that environmental conditions won't contaminate the copy or the original. This copy must be forensically sound—that is, it must faithfully represent an exact duplicate of the original. How do we know that we have a forensically sound copy of the digital evidence? We confirm this by performing a mathematical computation called *hashing* on the data. Hashing algorithms read the data and produce a numeric value called a hash value with a length of 128 bits (16 bytes) (MD5) and 160 bits (20 bytes) (SHA-1). These algorithms give us the ability to determine if any changes have been made to data. This is why hashing is used to ensure data integrity. If a single bit in the file has been changed at all, the changed file will produce a different hash value, given the same hashing algorithm. If the copy of the evidence and the original evidence result in the same value when hashed, then we can say with a high degree of certainty that the copy is a forensically sound duplicate of the original.

SHA-1 is one of four families of secure hashing algorithms: SHA-0, SHA-1, SHA-2, and SHA-3. One of the desirable properties of a hashing algorithm is that it is "collision free," meaning that two dissimilar documents will never produce the same hash value. Collision attacks have been demonstrated for SHA-0, and are theoretically possible for SHA-1, so current wisdom (and the mandate for the U.S. government) is that SHA-2 should be used. SHA-2 has several flavors: SHA-224, SHA-256, SHA-384, and SHA-512. Each of these versions will produce a digest (hash value) of 224, 256, 384, or 512 bits (28, 32, 48, and 64 bytes), respectively. As an aside, SHA-3 was developed and accepted as the winner of a competition sponsored by the National Institute of Standards (NIST) in 2012. SHA-3 has the advantage in that it is not derived from the SHA-0, SHA-1, and SHA-2 algorithms, which minimizes the chances that it is subject to the same flaws in the other three algorithms.

 TIP Consider making a copy of the copy as your original working copy. Should you need to start over, having the original copy can save you the time and effort of creating that copy again from the original evidence.

Performing the Analysis

We now have our working copy of the original evidence. What we do next will depend on what we had planned to do prior to collecting the evidence. Given what you first learned in the original case assessment, what is your hypothesis or hypotheses? What kind of evidence would support your hypothesis? Where might this evidence be located? What would change your mind and cause you to reject your hypothesis? (Since the network was unavailable during the time the incident occurred, the document was not exfiltrated via e-mail at that particular time.) What would make you say, "Okay, the subject didn't perform this action, because if she had, I would have expected to find this, and I didn't"?

There are multiple ways of analyzing the evidence. Physical analysis looks at the actual disk blocks; logical analysis examines the data via the file system that has been created on that disk. Physical analysis can produce information that's not accessible via logical analysis. You can perform keyword searches across the physical disk blocks, extract files from the disk using a technique called "file carving," and retrieve free space on the disk. Logical analysis is useful for retrieving information like filenames and sizes, file types, and other metadata stored concerning the state of the file system (file slack space, unallocated space, and more).

The EC-Council[7] cites four ways that a DFI can analyze the evidence. Time-frame analysis determines what file activity occurred on the computer during a particular time and examines various system log files to correlate file system activities with other activities. Data-hiding analysis looks for ways that information may be hidden either within the file system or in portions of the disk that are normally inaccessible to standard file system access. Application and file analysis looks at the contents of files, maps files to applications, and maps application activity to file creation and deletion (one such example is mapping e-mail messages to file attachments). Last, ownership and possession analysis can help identify activities tied to a particular login account, such as file deletion, modification, or attempts to change the owner of a particular file.

These activities aren't mutually exclusive. In fact, you will probably perform each type of analysis during an investigation.

Finding the Unexpected

You may find something unexpected in the course of your investigation, as was true in *United States v. Carey* in 1998.[8] In this case, the investigator was searching the computer for evidence of drug trafficking. In the course of this investigation, the investigator discovered what appeared to be evidence of child pornography and began to pursue an investigation into whether there was more evidence of this activity. The result was that the evidence concerning child pornography was ruled inadmissible, since this information was not part of the original warrant.

 CAUTION If you are focused on a particular line of investigation and you discover evidence of other criminal activity, you should stop your analysis at once and obtain authorization to pursue this line of inquiry as well.

Reporting and Testifying

Once you've completed your analysis, and sometimes during your analysis, you'll need to write a report. This report could be a threshold assessment or a final investigative report. The final investigative report will be more complete based on all the evidence that has been collected and analyzed. The threshold assessment, since it's preliminary, will only include the evidence discovered when the assessment is written.

Threshold reports will usually include a summary of conclusions to date and examinations performed, as well as a detailed case background. The report may include an analysis of previous investigations with respect to missing information or faulty conclusions drawn and investigative suggestions. Threshold reports are very much like progress reports, and the findings may point to other aspects of the investigation that should be pursued or indicate that the investigation can be concluded.

Preparing the Final Report

You will base your final report on the documentation that you created at each step of the process. This is true for any phase of the actual investigation, including the analysis phase. Make sure to document each step in your analysis and the results, time- and date-stamping each entry in your log. An entry might look like the following:

```
7/27/2013 300 PM EDT. Performed a keyword search on the contents of USB
drive ZZZ. Discovered the name of a primary client of QQQ company. Further
investigation discovered that the name was in a deleted file labeled
thoughts.txt. Contents of the file appeared to be a letter to the head of
sales of QQQ, introducing the suspect and making an offer to the head of
sales concerning supplying contract details for other clients of company
QQQ. Analysis of mail log files indicated that this file was included as an
attachment e-mailed to the head of sales five minutes prior to file deletion.
```

Prior to actually writing your final report, ask yourself some questions. Who is your audience? Will others receive the report in addition to your primary contact? Will the report delivery be oral or written? Will it be a formal or informal report? Regardless of the answers to these questions, it's wise to prepare your report for a nontechnical audience. Second, who is your customer (client)? This may be the same person or persons who will be receiving the report, but it may be someone else, perhaps a third party. Understanding their perspective will help you tune your message appropriately.

Your report must provide a systematic, thorough, and unbiased presentation of your findings. Ultimately, the format of the report is not as important as demonstrating a deliberate, thoughtful, and organized approach to writing the report.

Testifying in the Courtroom

There is a very good chance that you will be called to testify in court. Depending on your background, experience, and qualifications, you may be called either as an evidentiary witness or as an expert witness. As an evidentiary witness, your testimony will be restricted to the facts of the case. As an expert witness, you may be asked to testify regarding your opinions about the evidence in the case. Testifying as an expert witness requires special qualifications and job history. We'll go into more details in our chapter on report writing and testifying.

Closing the Case

Finally, this particular case is over. Or is it? In some ways, information about the case lasts forever in terms of your professional conduct. If you have testified as an evidentiary witness, continue to keep the case confidential.

Always perform a postmortem analysis of the case and how you conducted your investigation. What did you learn? What might you have done to be more effective? What new risks did you encounter? What might you do to avoid them in the future? Answers to these questions will feed into your next case assessment.

Last, replenish your forensics toolkit. Send all the evidence, reports, and other artifacts results to archival storage, as required by your organization. Forensically sterilize any secondary media that you used as part of the investigation.

Chapter Review

The computer crime investigation process and its methodology involve preparation, survey/identification, preservation, examination and analysis, and presentation. In our model, we divided our process into six phases: pre-investigation, preparing the investigation, searching and seizing, examination and analysis, reporting and testing, and post-investigation. Preparing for an investigation includes obtaining the necessary warrants, as well as performing a case assessment to understand the risks surrounding the investigation and establishing a plan to mitigate these risks.

When collecting and securing the evidence, start the chain-of-evidence and chain-of-custody procedures as soon as you have labeled the items you'll be seizing. Make sure that you prepare the evidence for transport back to the lab for analysis. Consider environmental factors such as temperature, humidity, vibration, and others.

Different techniques are used to acquire and analyze the data. These include time-frame analysis, data-hiding analysis, file and application analysis, and ownership and possession analysis.

Preparing the final investigation report requires understanding your audience and ensuring that you report the facts of the case without bias and without forming an opinion. This report will be the basis of your testimony if called as an evidentiary witness, and as the grounds for forming an opinion if you are called as an expert witness. After the case is closed, maintain a professional distance, and conduct a postmortem for "lessons learned" from this case that can make you a more effective investigator.

Questions

1. Which is the proper order of steps shared by all digital forensics process models?

   A. Preparation, survey/identification, preservation, examination and analysis, and presentation

   B. Preparation, preservation, search and seizure, examination and analysis, and presentation

   C. Preparation, survey/identification, preservation, examination and analysis, and testify

   D. Preparation, search and seizure, examination and analysis, presentation, and testify

2. True or false: Search warrants are required in criminal cases prior to seizing evidence.

   A. True

   B. False

   C. Usually true

   D. Usually false

3. When should a chain-of-evidence form be started?

   A. As part of preparing for the investigation

   B. After the evidence is stored and tagged

   C. As part of the case management procedure

   D. After the chain-of-custody form has been started

4. A forensically sound copy is:

   A. A copy that can be analyzed using forensic analysis tools

   B. A copy that has been recorded in the chain of evidence

   C. Any copy of an original that requires a chain-of-custody record

   D. A bit-for-bit image of the original evidence

5. Which kind of digital devices should be stored in a Faraday bag or aluminum foil?

   A. All digital devices

   B. Mobile communications devices

   C. Only devices equipped with either Bluetooth or near-field communication (NFC) radios

   D. Devices capable of transmitting a wireless signal

6. What is the purpose of conducting a case assessment?

   A. Prepare an initial plan for conducting the investigation

   B. Estimate the time commitment to determine your billing rate

C. Give the investigators time to collect the physical evidence

D. Determine the level of certainty regarding the suspect's guilt

7. What might you do if you learned that the suspect is a famous computer hacker?

    A. Turn off any computers immediately upon arrival

    B. Perform a risk assessment

    C. Plan to perform a dead analysis of all computer systems

    D. Plan a series of questions to be asked during the interview

8. You've just discovered that the suspect has reassigned the owner ID of several of his files to his wife's account. What kind of analysis is this?

    A. File and application

    B. Time-frame

    C. Ownership and possession

    D. Data-hiding

9. When writing your final report as a DFI, you should always:

    A. Only relate facts that are relevant to your particular audience

    B. Utilize a systematic approach

    C. Add your own interpretation and opinion to your report

    D. Exclude details such as where and when a particular event occurred

10. As an evidentiary witness, you will be expected to:

    A. Explain the relevant details of a digital forensics examination

    B. Testify as to the facts of the case

    C. Provide an opinion based on the evidence collected

    D. Present your technical report

11. The primary objective of a post-investigation analysis is to:

    A. Detail the mistakes made during the investigation

    B. Report additional information to the attorney who hired you

    C. Improve your risk analysis and planning skills

    D. Add skills gained to your professional resume

Answers

1. A. The correct order is preparation, survey/identification, preservation, examination and analysis, and presentation.

2. C. Usually true. One extenuating circumstance is if there is reason to believe that critical evidence will be destroyed prior to being able to obtain the warrant.

3. **C.** You should start your chain-of-evidence form as part of your initial case management actions.

4. **D.** A forensically sound copy is a bit-for-bit image of the original evidence.

5. **B.** Mobile communications devices should be stored in Faraday bags or aluminum foil to prevent reception of over-the-air transmissions.

6. **A.** The purpose of performing a case assessment is to help create a plan for conducting the investigation.

7. **B.** Knowing that the suspect is a skilled computer user would be input to the risk assessment portion of your case assessment.

8. **C.** Discovering that a suspect had changed ownership of a file is an example of ownership and possession analysis.

9. **B.** Writing a final report requires a systematic approach to recounting the facts of the case.

10. **B.** As an evidentiary witness, you relate the facts of your investigation.

11. **C.** The underlying reasons for doing a postmortem analysis of a case is to improve your ability to ascertain risk and to improve your investigative abilities.

References

1. Casey, E. *Digital Evidence and Computer Crime*, Third Edition (MD: Academic Press, 2011), p. 189.

2. Digital Intelligence. Specifications for FRED SR platform. Retrieved from www.digitalintelligence.com/products/fredsr.

3. Digital Intelligence. Specifications for FREDL platform. Retrieved from www.digitalintelligence.com/products/fredl.

4. *Electronic Crime Scene Investigation*, Second Edition (Washington, DC: USDoJ, 2008), pp. 13–14, 17.

5. National Institute of Justice. *Electronic Crime Scene Investigation: A Guide for First Responders*, Second Edition (Washington, D.C.: National Institute of Justice, 2008), p. 13.

6. EC-Council. *First Responder Procedures: Computer Forensics Investigation Procedures and Response* (NJ: Cengage Learning, 2009), pp. 4–9.

7. EC-Council. *Examining the Digital Evidence: Computer Forensics Investigation and Procedures* (NY: EC-Council, 2010), pp. 3–20.

8. *U.S. v. Carey*, 172 F.3d 1268 (10th Cir. 1999).

Computer Forensics Labs

In this chapter, you will learn how to
- Set up a computer forensics lab
- Discuss the investigative services in computer forensics
- Define the basic hardware requirements in a forensics lab
- List and summarize various hardware forensics tools
- Discuss the basic software requirements in a forensics lab
- List and summarize various software forensics tools

In the previous chapter, we discussed a process to follow before being called out on an investigation, and we talked about the kind of equipment you needed to bring to the crime scene.

If you're a digital forensics investigator (DFI), you will need a workspace to perform your data extraction, your analysis, and your reporting. You'll need a place to store your gear while you're performing your analysis and a place to secure the evidence once you've taken custody of it. This workspace may be your own place of business, such as your home or a one-person office, or it may be one workspace among several others at a large firm. Regardless of the size of the organization and number of coworkers, both of these situations have much in common. We'll talk about these commonalities in the rest of this chapter, as well as the differences.

Regardless of your role in the organization, the same two basic principles apply:

- You are responsible for the preservation and protection of evidence when it is in your custody; that is, you must prevent it from becoming "lost, stolen, or strayed." In addition, avoid contamination of the evidence from environmental factors (smoke, dust, and others).
- You will maintain professional standards.[1] Among them are standards that apply to lab accreditation, minimal education, experience and certification requirements, insurance, bond and liability standards, lab equipment, and software certifications. We'll address some of these later on in this chapter.

There are two primary roles within a forensics laboratory. The lab manager is responsible for the operations of the lab itself, while the forensics scientist or the forensics examiner actually performs the analysis, writes the reports, and provides testimony if needed. A third role associated with the lab is that of the forensics investigator. The forensics investigator is usually a member of law enforcement who is initially responsible for securing the crime scene and acquiring the evidence. The role of the DFI as we have defined it combines the roles of the forensics examiner and the forensics investigator. A good DFI needs to understand how these two roles complement each other. In some organizations, a single person may act in both roles (this may be the case in corporate investigations). In larger organizations, these roles may be split out into separate organizations: Law enforcement collects the evidence, and the forensics examiners actually analyze the evidence.

What Services Are You Offering?

If you anticipate forming your own digital forensics business, you'll have to decide on what services you are going to offer. Chances are that they will be forensics investigative services, analysis, and expert testimony.

Investigative services is the actual retrieval of digital evidence. If you're not a member of law enforcement, you will be doing this within a corporate environment. In either case, however, you will need to maintain proper procedures for searching, acquiring, and extracting information. We'll have more to say on this in another chapter; for the moment, let's just say that there are laws governing what you can get without a search warrant and what you can get without violating the suspect's right to privacy. Recall that a warrant is only necessary for agents of the government or law enforcement, and doesn't usually apply in a corporate environment unless the corporate investigation reveals that a crime was committed.

Examination and analysis services should remain the same whether this is a civil, criminal, or enterprise case. The best course to assume in all instances is that your actions and the evidence you extract will be presented in court. Moving from an enterprise investigation to a criminal investigation requires you involve the proper legal authorities immediately.

 TIP Know who your external contacts are: local police, state police, and Federal Bureau of Investigation (FBI). Make a point of reaching out to them at the earliest possible moment to establish a working relationship.

If you believe that you might be called as a witness during a trial, make sure that you have documented everything. There are many ways to do this: pen and paper, creating a text note on a smart phone, taking a picture, creating a video, creating an audio note, or a mixture of these. Regardless of how you've chosen to record your initial notes, recapture them in a standard format as soon as possible to keep your memory fresh.

 EXAM TIP Presenting evidence in an organized, structured manner is more important than the actual format of the document.

You might also wish to offer forensic deletion of data. As mentioned earlier, you will need a "forensically sterile" media to receive the copy of your digital data, and creating this "sterile" media means that you need to be familiar with data deletion standards. This "forensically sterile" media means that there are no data remaining from any previous use of that medium (usually referred to as data remanence). Data remanence can compromise security by leaving portions of files on a previously written disk; in the case of forensics, data remaining from a prior investigation could compromise the integrity of the data used for analysis in a current case.

Each country has its own data deletion standards. In the U.S. government, the old standard was DoD 5220.22-M, the National Industrial Security Program Operating Manual (NISPOM). The first version of this document described an algorithm for overwriting files multiple times with a random selection of characters. The latest version, however, doesn't include any particular methods, but instead refers to standards for individual branches of the government, known as the "cognizant security agency." The more general case is addressed by the National Institute of Standards (NIST) special publication 800-88, "Guide to Media Sanitization, Revision 1."[2]

The original algorithm documented in NISPOM was to make three passes over the data. Each pass over the data would perform a different write operation, specifically writing a character (for example, 0x00), verify the write, write the character's complement (0xFF in our example), verify the write, and then write a random character (0 × 97, for example) and verify the write. You may hear this described as "the DoD three-pass wipe" and sometimes as "the DoD seven-pass wipe." The prevailing wisdom as of 2013 is that given today's disk technology (especially for multigigabyte drives), one pass is sufficient. Take note that this doesn't address issues with wiping a solid-state drive (SSD). For the latest recommendations, the NIST document is probably the most up-to-date.

 EXAM TIP DOD 5220.22-M is often referred to as a source for standards for data destruction, although it no longer contains detailed instructions on how to destroy digital data.

Staffing Requirements and Planning

Of the two main roles within the forensics laboratory, the lab manager is responsible for the overall operations of the lab. This includes staffing needs, workload estimates, arranging training for technical staff (recall that the SWDGE—Scientific Working Group on Digital Evidence—recommendations indicated requirements for training), and determining needs for accreditation. Technical staff includes anyone and everyone who actually accesses or handles the evidence. Your staffing needs will be determined in part by your anticipated workload for the coming year. As a lab manager, planning doesn't stop once the facility is built and everyone moves in. Prior to moving in to the new facilities, a lab manager needs to have a business continuity/disaster recovery (BC/DR) plan in place. This is even more critical if the lab is going to handle dangerous materials (flammable, explosive, or biological). Disaster recovery is one aspect of business continuity and occurs during and immediately after the disaster. Business continuity itself is focused on how the company can continue to operate after the immediate effects of the disaster have ceased.

Becoming Certified

If you will be building a large forensics laboratory, you will need to be certified. The organization that provides that certification is the American Society of Crime Laboratory Directors (ASCLD)—their site is www.ascld.org—although the actual organization performing the certifications is ASCLD/LABS (www.ascld-lab.org). Their certification process is based on the ISO 17025:2005 standard, *General Requirements for the Competence of Testing and Calibration Laboratories,* and demonstrates that the lab's technical and management systems meet the requirements established by that standard. Labs can apply for accreditation as either Forensic Science – Testing or Forensic Science – Calibration. A computer lab would fall under the Forensic Science – Testing category for Digital and Multimedia Evidence.[3]

 EXAM TIP   The ASCLD/LABS organization oversees the certification process.

Setting Up Your Lab

If you're starting out in business on your own, your choice of laboratory space may be straightforward. You may be setting up a home office, or you may be renting office space. If the actual space you'll be using already exists, then you will need to evaluate this environment based on physical security needs. Figure 4-1 lists physical, technological, and administrative considerations for setting up your computer lab (as well as any other space where security is required—it's not really a question of whether it's required or not, but rather what are the appropriate levels of security given the assets you need to protect). You'll notice that many of these considerations are exactly the same as for other kinds of enterprises. Information is information security after all, and the same principles apply when you have information such that you would incur a substantial loss (reputation, economic) if you lost the confidentiality, integrity, and availability (CIA) for that information.

On the other hand, if you're responsible for building a large laboratory facility from scratch, such as a Regional Computer Forensics Laboratory (RCFL) for law enforcement, you will have a lot of work ahead of you. Typical administrative activities will include planning, generating a budget, determining the number of clients, and understanding the kinds of investigations you'll be asked to perform. The document "Forensic Laboratories: Handbook for Facility Planning, Design, Construction, and Moving"[4] lists multiple considerations; we'll address a few of them here that are applicable to a computer forensics lab.

Physical Location Needs

There is a truism in the real estate industry that states the value of a piece of property is dependent on three things: location, location, and location. The actual location of your lab requires careful planning, and considerations include access to emergency services (ambulance, fire, police), access to electrical power, and Internet communications.

Figure 4-1

Types of security considerations (Source: Harris, S. *CISSP All-In-One Exam Guide, Second Edition* (CA: McGraw-Hill Education, 2003), pp. 256–257.)

Physical Controls	Administrative Controls	Technical Controls
Fencing	Facility management	Access controls
HVAC	Facility selection or construction	Instrusion detection
Bollards	Personnel controls	Firewalls
Locks	Training	Auditing
Fire detection and suppression	Emergency responder and procedures	Identify and access management
Power supply	Security policies	Backups
Monitoring (CCTV)	Security procedures	File permissions
Lighting		

At the heart of information security are mechanisms that we use to protect our assets: physical security (gates, locks, cameras, and dogs), logical security (passwords and others), and administrative (policies, background checks, and more). We can further categorize these mechanisms as to their intended purpose:

- **Preventive**   Prevents a security incident from happening
- **Detective**   Discovers if a security event is in progress or has already occurred
- **Corrective**   Aimed at fixing the root cause of the vulnerability that gave rise to the incident
- **Recovery**   Restores the computing environment back to a "good known state"

Other categories that are sometimes included are

- **Deterrent**   Keeps an event from happening by creating an obstacle for the attacker
- **Compensating**   A control inserted to compensate for lack of a permanent control

Some authors only list the first four, although all these types are used in information security design.

We can categorize a particular technique based on its category and its mechanism. For example, guard dogs might be considered as a preventive, deterrent, or compensating physical control. A popular overall strategy is to focus on preventive controls. Detective controls mean that you have discovered a security violation of some kind (either in progress or sometime in the past). Recovery and corrective controls are meant to stop the bleeding.

Physical security is the first consideration when constructing a forensics laboratory or when obtaining space for a lab. Two principles apply, regardless of whether you are setting up a home office or constructing a large regional forensics investigation center:

- Ensure the physical security of the lab.
- Ensure the physical security of the evidence within the lab.

One question you might well ask regarding the first principle is: What might destroy the entire facility? Some answers that come to mind are fire, flood, and explosion. A compensating control for those threats would be a location close to emergency services: a fire station, police, hospital, and ambulance service.[5]

The next step is to consider the physical security of the building itself and its employees. Make sure that lighting is sufficient (people can see and be seen). Don't provide places for an intruder to conceal themselves (bushes close to an outside wall, clumps of bushes or evergreen trees).[5] Parking is another concern: The NIST document "Forensic Laboratories: Handbook for Facility Planning, Design, Construction, and Moving" lists the following recommendations:

- **Level 1**   Insecure. Close to visitor entrance.
- **Level 2**   Partially secure. The lot should be fenced in. The lot provides controlled access to the facility by service people.
- **Level 3**   Secured. Restricted to staff parking. Gaining access to the parking facility requires some form of identification (perhaps a proximity key or a card-key).
- **Level 4**   High security. Restricted to specific individuals; access may require a thumbprint or palmprint reader or at least a combination lock.

Higher-security areas may require an intrusion alarm (this is true inside and outside the building). Guards can patrol the premises; guard dogs often act as a deterrent control. Closed-circuit TVs (CCTVs) can observe areas that aren't physically visible to guards or other employees. Access to the laboratory proper should be via a single entrance that can be monitored. This doesn't mean that there can't be multiple exits from the lab (as would be the case for fire regulations), but these doors would probably be locked and alarmed. Last, windows should be kept closed, removing them from consideration as a way of entering the premises (but remember to add increased costs for heating, ventilation, and air conditioning—HVAC—into your budget). All access to the lab by nonemployees should be recorded in a log book: who they are, the reason for the visit, the time of day in and out, whom they are representing, and whom they are visiting.

Our second principle is protecting the evidence and the work products that are stored at the lab. Of all the disasters that can strike a laboratory, the most common and the most devastating is probably fire. Something as simple as the freezing of a disk actuator can start a fire due to overheating. Fire suppression systems are a necessity for a laboratory, especially class C fire extinguishers (dry chemical) for electrical fires and sprinkler systems according to building codes (don't forget to include water damage as part of your disaster recovery plan).

EXAM TIP Know your fire extinguisher classification! Only certain kinds of fire extinguishers are suitable for electrical fires (water isn't a good idea for obvious reasons).

Evidence storage (the evidence locker or fire-rated safe) should address both unwanted illegal access and damage by fire or water. These lockers should be constructed of steel, should always remain locked, and must be monitored closely. Access to the evidence locker must be limited to authorized personnel. How far you want to go depends on the kind of forensics investigations you're doing, but you might want to consider recording all access to the locker, regardless of what evidence is actually accessed (and recorded in a chain-of-evidence form).[6]

The size of your workspace again will depend on your place and kind of employment. As a sole employee, you might have two separate tables: one with two forensics workstations that usually aren't connected to any network and one with two plain workstations that have Internet connectivity. This is probably the safest configuration but begs the question whether remote access is needed to the forensics workstations. If remote access is required, consider the bandwidth requirements, not only for software performance but also for the transfer of data. Compute the bandwidth needed internally and externally. Other communications considerations include dial-up access (perhaps your site won't be reachable via the Internet), disconnection from the network (in the case of forensics workstations), and relationships with your Internet service provider (ISP).

 NOTE Consider this quick heuristic: Assume 10 bits per byte (this makes the math easier). A data rate of 16 Mbits/second is 1.6MB/second, or 96 Mbytes/minute, or 10.5 minutes to copy a 1GB file. That assumes you're getting all the bandwidth on the line, and your drive can sustain that data rate, and on and on. It's still true, at least in this case, that bigger and faster are better.

Why two instances of a forensics workstation and two instances of a plain workstation? We've already mentioned Internet connectivity—forensics workstations should only connect to the corporate local area network (LAN) or the Internet when absolutely necessary. A second instance of the forensics workstation can run certain forensics software that you can use to validate the results of other forensics software. Remember that you should be able to get the same results when different analysis tools claim to offer the same functions—a good case in point is disk imaging. Having two plain workstations allows you to perform updates and upgrades on one while still having the other as backup if the changes result in the first workstation becoming unusable.

Otherwise, planning for a forensic lab is much like planning for any other technical office space. A workspace should be large enough to allow collaboration with a colleague, and space enough for reference materials, lab manuals, and so on. Locking storage is another good thing to have, good for storing tools and any work in progress that shouldn't be left lying around. You'll need space for printers, scanners, extra hard-drives, and backup storage (disk or tape). Some of the material can be shared, but remember that some cases may require physical separation of materials. Don't forget about conference rooms, large enough for your entire staff, and smaller conference rooms for working and discussion groups. You'll need to stock other materials as well: cables, power cords, network interface cards (NICs)—all the incidentals that are required to support local and remote connectivity.

How much power do you need? If you're running a large lab, you'll want an uninter-ruptable power supply (UPS). How much amperage do you need? You'll need power for lighting, both emergency and regular; all evidence sections (segregated by type of investigation, determining the kind of clearance needed); all the security devices; work-stations; storage systems; and possibly such equipment as X-ray processing rooms and photo-processing rooms. Make sure that each workspace has sufficient power outlets (extension cords stretched throughout the workplace is an accident waiting to happen).

Software Requirements

The software that you need in your lab requires you to be able to process information from old hardware and old operating systems (OS). These operating systems include multiple versions of Windows, Linux, various flavors of UNIX (Sun/Oracle Solaris), Apple Macintosh systems with OS X, and antiquated systems such as Commodore. More gen-eral applications include software to display graphical images (QuickView and IrfanView are examples of this software), accounting software (Quicken QuickBooks), personal databases (Microsoft Access, LibreOffice database), and video players (VLC, RealPlayer, Windows Media Player). For some of these applications, a full-featured demo version might suffice for a short investigation. That said, many demo versions will not allow results to be saved, or will print reports with the word "DEMO" conspicuously displayed on every page. Consider, too, that paying the license fee gets you updates and mainte-nance. Imagine the impact on your workload if you are stymied by a software bug and you have to wait for your HR and legal departments to negotiate and sign a maintenance contract. Equally important is the necessity of legally licensed software if your investiga-tion should go to court. In some cases, an investigator may be subpoenaed to provide a list of software used in the analysis and investigation along with proof of license. Failure to do so may call into question the integrity of the investigator and the results of the tool.

Along with commercial software, you need to build up your forensics software toolset. Your toolset should support the following general activities:[7]

- Acquisition
- Validation and discrimination
- Extraction
- Reconstruction
- Reporting

How you go about obtaining these tools depends on your client base and how well your chosen tools are recognized throughout the forensics industry and by the courts. Guidance Software's EnCase product and Accessdata's FTK are both widely recognized and extensively used. Brian Carrier's The Sleuth Kit and the Autopsy browser are freeware tools that provide many of the same capabilities (we'll see a comparison of these three products in Chapter 8). Another well-established tool that I've used is X-Ways WinHex

Forensics. Guidance Software and AccessData both offer training and certifications in the use of their tools. Becoming certified in the use of a tool is a good idea if you're planning on standardizing on one or the other.

 NOTE Ultimately, EnCase, FTK, or The Sleuth Kit should provide the essential capabilities to support an investigation. Your decision may rest on personal preference, the choice of your employer, or the standard used by your colleagues in law enforcement or security services.

How do we make a choice regarding what other tools to acquire? The NIST Information Technology Laboratory (www.nist.gov) runs the Computer Forensic Tool Testing (CFTT) project. The project is described as follows:

Overview: The CFTT project provides a measure of assurance that the tools used in the investigations of computer-related crimes produce valid results. It also supports other projects in the Department of Homeland Security's overall computer forensics research program, such as the National Software Reference Library (NSRL).

Industry Need Addressed: There are approximately 150 different automated tools routinely used by law enforcement organizations to assist in the investigation of crimes involving computers. These tools are used to create critical evidence used in criminal cases, yet there are no standards or recognized tests by which to judge the validity of results produced by these tools.

Impact: The implementation of testing based on rigorous procedures will provide impetus for vendors to improve their tools and provide assurance that their results will stand up in court. […]. Law enforcement and other investigatory groups can use results as a basis for deciding when and how to use various tools.[8]

NIST publishes a catalog of tested software: "The Computer Forensics Tool Testing Handbook."[9] The most recent version is dated 2012, and the versions tested are not the most current. Regardless, the test results are useful for differentiating among the various tools and should prepare you to ask probing questions of the vendors when it comes time to actually write the check. NIST's Computer Forensic Reference Data Sets (CFReDS) provide a baseline for tool testing by "[providing] to an investigator documented sets of simulated digital evidence for examination."[10] Each data set is documented as to its contents and its structure so you can tell, for example, that the tool found a particular byte offset at a particular byte location with the file.

Hardware Requirements

Your hardware requirements will be dictated by whether you are performing searching and seizing in the field or whether you will be performing examination and analysis in the lab. One aspect of your choice is portability of hardware if you're going to be carrying it into the field. In either case, common activities need to be done when acquiring evidence, regardless of where you're doing the acquisition.

Field Tools

You need a well-stocked field toolkit when you go out on an investigation. You essentially need to prepare for any eventuality when you arrive at the crime scene, as demonstrated by the items in the accompanying list:[6,11]

- Faraday isolation bags or aluminum foil to block wireless communication, including 3G and 4G phones as well as Wi-Fi (802.11), Bluetooth, and near-field communication (NFC).
- Cardboard boxes (or original packaging if available at the scene) and cable ties.
- Notepads.
- Gloves.
- Various sizes of evidence bags: paper, antistatic, and so forth.
- Write-blocker (in case you have to perform a data acquisition on site). Some tests have indicated that a journaled file system, such as NT File System (NTFS), may actually write journaled information back to the device even if the device is mounted read-only. Figure 4-2 shows a typical attachment of a write-blocker between the disk and the acquiring device.
- Various kinds of cables (printer, USB, power).
- SIM card reader.
- Camera (photo and video capture) for capturing screen images as well as the crime scene itself.
- Remote chargers for your equipment and other digital devices found on the scene.
- Permanent markers (different colors).
- Evidence tape, crime scene tape, evidence stickers and tags.

Figure 4-2
Write-blocker

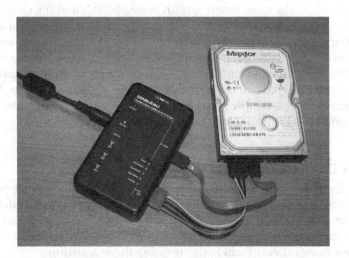

- Nonmagnetic tools.
- Flashlight (torch for our UK readers).
- Your fully charged cell phone, which can double as a camera and a note-taking device (written or audio).

Lab Hardware

Every lab needs some kind of device that quickly can make copies of large disks. Time is your enemy here: The more time you spend moving bits around is time taken away from the timely resolution or determination of the extent of a criminal act. Once you have captured the device image, you will need hardware and software to archive and restore these images to your working storage, whether it be physically attached to your workstation or accessible via your LAN. Other hardware can include photographic hardware for still photographs (color and black and white) and video equipment.

We've already discussed mobile forensics laptops and forensics workstations in a previous chapter. It bears repeating that if you are buying a commercial product, you should buy the biggest iron you can afford. Load up on memory, disk interfaces (IDE, SCSI, US), and a SAN card (ISCSI or Fibre Channel) if you're using a storage area network (SAN) for file storage. If you decide to build your own forensics workstation, obtain a write-blocker, a data acquisition tool, and a data analysis tool, and build your own custom hardware. However, building your own forensics workstation requires a degree of comfort and familiarity with computer hardware that is greater than a DFI has to know in order to perform an acquisition.

Other Considerations

Make sure that lab procedures are documented and that lab staff is familiar with these procedures and actually follows them. Having this information readily available will be a big help when it comes time to get certification.

Depending on the sensitivity of an investigation, an investigator may need a private room such that no one else can observe the evidence collected. Private rooms will require additional hardware if physical isolation is needed. It's possible that access to a virtual machine that accesses the data may be acceptable, but the use of virtualization technologies within the practice of digital forensics is still a work in progress.

Chapter Review

Determining which computer forensics investigative services you wish to offer will determine what kind of hardware and software you will need, as well as the physical workspace you will need to support those services.

Setting up a computer forensics lab requires that you plan for the physical security of the building and for the lab itself, as well as protecting the evidence you have within the lab from loss or destruction.

Hardware requirements for your lab include hardware that will quickly create an image of a disk drive; photographic and video hardware; write-blockers for data acquisition; and all the cables, power supplies, power cords, and device readers that are needed to collect and transfer digital evidence.

Software requirements for your lab include software tools that support acquisition, validation and discrimination, extraction, reconstruction, and reporting. Examples of this kind of forensics software include EnCase, FTK, The Sleuth Kit and Autopsy, and WinHex Forensics.

Questions

1. Landscaping, lighting, and parking lot security are all examples of _____ security.

   A. Technical

   B. Physical

   C. Logical

   D. Administrative

2. True or false: DoD 5220.22-M is the final authority on data destruction techniques.

   A. True

   B. False

3. Which of the following is a characteristic that does not belong in a computer forensics lab?

   A. Windows that open

   B. Secured single entrance

   C. Visitors logbook

   D. Locking evidence (cage)

4. Which standard is often referred to as the source for data sanitization?

   A. ISO 27001

   B. NIST SP800-88r1

   C. NAVSO P-5239-26 (MFM)

   D. DoD 5220.22-M

5. What is the purpose of a write-blocker when used with digital imaging? Choose all that apply.

   A. Prevent changes to the metadata of the device performing the capture

   B. Avoid updating the last accessed timestamp on the captured files

   C. Prevent changing the data on a drive being captured

   D. Reads from the capturing machine will occur more quickly if writes are blocked

6. True or false: SIM card readers are general-purpose devices that can read data from a number of different device types.

   A. True

   B. False

7. Which of these would *not* provide shelter for an intruder?

   A. Bushes

   B. Clumps of bushes

   C. Evergreens with low-hanging branches

   D. A grove of maple trees

8. Which of these capabilities is a secondary requirement for investigative software?

   A. Search

   B. Cryptanalysis

   C. Data recovery

   D. Bit-stream copy

9. What are the reasons that you would use well-known forensics commercial tools? Choose all that apply.

   A. Results judged acceptable in court

   B. Well established in the industry

   C. More capable than freeware tools

   D. Commercial support and updates

10. The _____ project at NIST has the goal of evaluating forensics software against a set of criteria.

    A. CFTT

    B. FSTE

    C. ESET

    D. CERT

Answers

1. **B.** Landscaping, lighting, and parking lot security are all examples of physical security.

2. **B.** DoD 5220.20-M once specified a particular erasure algorithm, but now refers to different policies that apply to different government branches.

3. **A.** Windows that open are not a characteristic of a forensics laboratory since they may provide a way of forcibly entering the building.

4. **D.** DoD 5220.22-M (NISP Operating Manual) NISPOM.

5. **A, B,** and **C.** Write-blockers prevent any changes to the data on the drive from being captured. They do not increase the copying speed.

6. **B.** False. SIM card readers are meant specifically for mobile phones.

7. **D.** Maple trees are deciduous (lose their leaves in winter) and don't provide low-hanging cover.

8. **B.** Cryptanalysis isn't always needed in a forensics tool.

9. **A, B,** and **D.** Well-known commercial forensics toolkits have been proven within the industry, are more likely to have results accepted in court, and come with updates and support.

10. **A.** The Computer Forensics Tool Testing (CFTT) project tests multiple products in several categories according to a defined set of testing criteria and a standard set of test data.

References

1. ASCLD/LAB. "Guiding Principles of Professional Responsibility for Crime Laboratories and Forensic Scientists" (NC: ASCLD/LAB, 2013.)

2. Kissel, R. et al. "NIST SP800-88 Rev1: Guide to Media Sanitization" (MD: NIST, 2012). Retrieved from http://csrc.nist.gov/publications/PubsSPs.html.

3. ASCLD-LAB. "International Program Overview 2010 Edition" (NC: ASCLD/LAB, 2010), p. 5.

4. "Forensic Laboratories: Handbook for Facility Planning, Design, Construction, and Moving" (MD: NIST, 1998). Retrieved from http://www.crime-scene-investigator.net/forensiclabdesign.pdf.

5. "Forensic Laboratories: Handbook for Facility Planning, Design, Construction, and Moving" (MD: NIST, 1998), p. 20.

6. EC-Council. *Computer Forensics: Investigation Procedures and Reponses* (MA: Cengage, 2010), p. 2, 4–6.

7. Nelson, B. et al. *Guide to Computer Forensics and Investigations* (MA: Course Technology, 2010), p. 261.

8. CFTT Project Overview. Retrieved from http://www.cftt.nist.gov/project_overview.htm.

9. Computer Forensics Tool Testing Handbook (MD: NIST, 2012).

10. The CFReDS Project. Retrieved from http://www.cfreds.nist.gov.

11. *Electronic Crime Scene Investigation*, Second Edition (Washington, DC: USDoJ, 2008), pp. 13–14.

## CHAPTER 5

Getting the Goods

After completing this chapter, you should be able to

- Summarize the steps involved in searching and seizing computers, with or without a warrant, under the tenets of the Fourth Amendment and the Privacy Protection Act
- Define consent and voluntary disclosure, and discuss the scope of consent
- Describe drafting the warrant and affidavit, basic strategies for executing computer searches, and explain post-seizure issues
- Describe the Electronic Communications Privacy Act and its effect on electronic surveillance in communications networks, and the differences between content and addressing information
- Describe the role of first responder, the first responder's toolkit, and provide an overview of how to collect and store the electronic evidence at the crime scene
- Articulate how to get the first response from laboratory forensic staff, conduct preliminary interviews, and document the crime scene
- Explain how to collect and preserve electronic evidence, how to package and transport electronic evidence in a forensically sound manner, and how to prepare a report on the crime scene
- Justify providing a checklist for the first responders, and discuss common mistakes made by first responders
- Define data acquisition and explain the various types of data acquisition systems, data acquisition formats and methods, and how to determine a best acquisition method
- Describe static and live data acquisition, how to acquire RAID disks, and define contingency planning for image acquisition
- Explain the various types of volatile information, provide an overview of volatile data collection methodology, and articulate best practices for acquisition
- List the requirements of disk imaging tools, list various data acquisition software and hardware tools, and demonstrate how to validate data acquisitions on Windows and Linux

This chapter covers activities required in order to seize potential evidence from a crime scene.

Similar activities and techniques may be used during incident response. The incident responder needs to have authorization to perform actions on the possibly compromised machine. Likewise, an incident responder needs to be careful to maintain the state of the compromised machine. Same tools; different objectives.

Searching and Seizing Computers

We've been playing a little fast and loose with the sequence of events that you would encounter as a digital forensics investigator (DFI). In a criminal case, the search and seizure phase will take place in several subphases. The phase we're interested in here is obtaining the permission to search. Earlier, we talked about your arrival at the crime scene and completing your initial evaluation: You have sketched and photographed everything, labeled connections, labeled each piece of electronic equipment, and so on. With respect to authorization to search, four possible situations exist prior to your actual arrival at the crime scene. You have a warrant that covers everything, or you have no warrant at all. Here the issues are relatively straightforward. Two problematic situations arise when you have a warrant, but you've discovered a digital device that isn't explicitly named in the warrant, or you don't have a warrant and yet you and others believe that there is valuable evidence contained within a particular piece of electronic equipment. Table 5-1 illustrates these decision points.

Remember that when we're talking about warrants, we're specifically talking about a criminal investigation. In an enterprise investigation, a different set of rules apply. In some organizations, there is no expectation of privacy. This can arise either because of a company policy that you probably were required to sign and acknowledge, or because of a banner that is displayed as part of a logon process that indicates that anything you do can be recorded or investigated. The human resources and legal departments of your organization are much better prepared to debate the fine points of what is acceptable and what is legal.

 EXAM TIP Never proceed in any investigation unless you are sure that you have proper authorization.

Is Your Search and Seizure Unwarranted?

Let's consider the situation where you don't have a warrant at all. We need to go back to the Fourth Amendment to the Constitution, which states

> The right of the people to be secure in their persons, houses, papers, and effects, against unreasonable searches and seizures, shall not be violated, and no Warrants shall issue, but upon probable cause, supported by Oath or affirmation, and particularly describing the place to be searched, and the persons or things to be seized.

		Device Listed in Warrant?	
		Yes	No
Do You Have a Warrant?	Yes	Okay to seize and search	Maybe
	No	N/A	Maybe

Table 5-1 Seizing Devices With or Without a Warrant

The Fourth Amendment and the Right to Privacy

The Fourth Amendment is the foundation of the idea of a right to privacy. The Supreme Court has held that a "'search' occurs when an expectation of privacy that society is prepared to consider reasonable is infringed."[1] If you don't have a warrant, then you must take into account whether the search violates an assumed protection of privacy, and if it does, does the search fall under the provisions of one of the exceptions that exist when a computer is involved? If the search does not violate an assumed protection of privacy, then you have one less obstacle to overcome.

When determining if a computer search is justified, remember that computers usually are considered "closed containers" (such as a briefcase or a file cabinet or a suitcase). This means that you can seize the computer itself, but you will probably need a warrant to actually search the contents of the computer.

TIP A helpful way to determine if a search of a computer is justified is whether the search would be acceptable if you were searching a footlocker, backpack, or briefcase. If it wouldn't be justified in those cases, you'll need a warrant.

The Privacy Protection Act

The courts have ruled that searches can be carried out if there is probable cause to believe that the search would provide evidence of a crime or contraband. However, the Privacy Protection Act (PPA) states that search and seizure must be authorized by the Justice Department if there is a chance that materials could be seized that are protected under the First Amendment, and the person is not suspected of participating in criminal activity for which the materials are sought. When applied to the search and seizure of digital devices, however, issues can arise if the computer is used for the publishing of protected speech, and because evidence may be commingled with other items that are protected.

There are several exceptions to the rule of privacy violation. First is the issue of consent. You can ask the suspect for consent to search their computer or other electronic device. Alternatively, you may conduct a search if someone in authority has given consent, although this consent may limit the scope of your investigation. Consent of a third party occurs when someone gives consent and is considered a partial owner or user of the digital advice. Based on the Matlock decision,[3]

> [...] a private third party may consent to a search of property under the third party's joint access or control. Agents may view what the third party may see without violating any reasonable expectation of privacy so long as they limit the search to the zone of the consenting third party's common authority.[4]

You may also mount a search if there are "exigent circumstances." These exigent circumstances occur under the following conditions:

- There is an immediate danger that the evidence can be destroyed.
- A threat exists that puts the police or the public in danger.
- The police are in "hot pursuit" of a suspect.
- The suspect is likely to flee before the authorities can get a search warrant.

The first circumstance is usually the most compelling when applied to computer searches because computer data is extremely perishable: Digital data can be encrypted, and whole drives can be deleted with a single command ("rm -rf /"). Electronic components can be damaged by water, heat, magnetism, or blunt objects. Information could be lost due to the lack of battery power, or because new data may overwrite old data. An interesting issue surrounding exigent circumstances is that you can seize a device because of exigent circumstances, but you may not be justified to search it later. In this instance, a DFI would need to actually obtain a search warrant.

The "plain view" doctrine holds that if something is clearly visible (sitting out in plain sight), then you are able to access that digital device without consent of the owner. Two conditions must apply, however: You must be in a lawful position to observe and access the evidence, and the fact that it is incriminating evidence must be readily apparent. You can't use the plain view doctrine to open a container that you wouldn't have been allowed to open otherwise.

Finally, after a lawful arrest, you can search the arrested person and search the surrounding area. The courts have generally ruled that a search incident to a lawful arrest applies to portable electronic devices, such as pagers, cell phones, personal digital assistants, and others.

Inventory searches occur after law enforcement has seized a particular digital device. Law enforcement officers routinely inventory the items they have seized. These searches are considered reasonable if the search serves a legitimate, noninvestigatory purpose (such as protecting an owner's property when in custody), or to keep the police from danger. For this reason, searching computer disks or files is not usually covered under this exception, and a warrant is required.

Border searches have become quite contentious of late. In some instances, travelers have had electronic equipment seized and searched without their explicit permission and in the absence of a specific warrant. Although this may be something of a surprise, the courts have found that border searches are exempt from Fourth Amendment protection. This applies to U.S. citizens as well as foreign nationals.

Finally, international searches will require the participation and consent of the appropriate authorities in the country where the computer is located or where it is believed that the crime has occurred. Contacting a foreign Internet service provider (ISP), for example, might require prior permissions of the foreign government, the approval of the Department of Justice's (DOJ's) Office of International Affairs (OIA), and with clear indications that such contact would not be objectionable in the country in question.

Workplace Searches

Workplace searches have their own set of constraints, depending on whether the workplace is part of the private sector or the public (government) sector. Private sector searches without a warrant are usually acceptable if you've obtained consent from the employer or the employee who has authority over the area to be searched. In the public sector, a government employee has a reasonable expectation of privacy in their workplace, unless the searches are "work-related, justified at their inception, and permissible in scope."[5] However, searches may raise issues under the Stored Communications Act, 18 U.S.C. §§ 2701–2712 or Title III, 18 U.S.C. §§ 2510–2522. More on these later in this chapter. Take note, however, that official policy or a login banner may alleviate the expectation of privacy.

> **TIP**   If you're acting in a security role at an organization, establishing that the employee has no reasonable expectation of privacy up front can make your life easier when it comes time to perform forensic analysis or mount an investigation. It's better to establish this at the onset rather than try to implement this after the fact.

You Have a Warrant

If you are on the scene and you have a warrant, you needed to go through several steps prior to this. In order to get the warrant, you had to appear before a judge and assert that there is probable cause to search a particular person or location and to seize certain kinds of property.

When drafting the warrant, make sure that the property to be seized is described accurately and with enough detail that the property can be distinguished from other kinds of property. A "laptop computer" might not be specific enough, while "a dark-blue MacBook Pro with a sticker on the front that says 'Apple Rules!'" probably would uniquely identify a particular device. You can specify the property within the warrant itself, or as an attachment to the warrant. The more specific you are, the better your ability to defend against courtroom challenges based on the description of "things to be seized."

The place to establish probable cause is in the affidavit written in support of the warrant. In the affidavit, include an explanation of your search strategy and the details of the practical and legal considerations that will govern the actual search.

There are three general strategies for performing a computer search when you have a warrant. The first strategy is when the digital device is itself contraband—such as when the computer stores child pornography or the computer itself is stolen property. The second strategy is when the digital hardware is just a storage device for the evidence of a crime, as evidenced by documents, log files, or browsing history. Last, as described by the U.S. Office of Legal Education, a computer can be an "instrumentality of the crime"[4]: the computer was used as a tool in carrying out the crime, such as distributing illegal materials, hacking into a company's computers, or spying on someone without their consent.

Computer searches aren't always about the documents stored on the computer. In some instances, the search may attempt to demonstrate that a particular individual was using the machine at a particular time or shortly thereafter to check the results, such as a bank balance. It may be necessary to indicate that no viruses or malware were present on a computer and couldn't have performed actions on the network of which the user was unaware. Finally, the search may attempt to show that the user had knowledge of a particular subject based on browsing history or on materials downloaded and then deleted.

If you need to search various network locations, you may need multiple warrants in order to achieve this. Jurisdiction comes into play depending on if the data are stored locally, within the United States, or outside the boundaries of the United States. In the first two instances, you should try to get a warrant to search the machine where the data are stored. Things become much more complicated, however, if the data are stored remotely outside of the United States. If you didn't know and couldn't know that the machine was physically located outside of the United States, you may still be able to present the evidence in court.

Once we move into the area of network searches, we run full-tilt into a different set of privacy concerns.

Electronic Surveillance

The Electronic Communications Privacy Act (ECPA)—sometimes referred to as the Stored Communications Act (SCA) [18 U.S.C. §§ 2701–2712]—sets up regulations concerning how the government can obtain stored account information from network service providers.

 EXAM TIP Know that the ECPA (18 U.S.C.) regulates what the government can obtain from network service providers.

The Electronic Communications Privacy Act

In the case of Internet communications, ISPs provide a local connection to the Internet. One way to classify providers is whether they provide "electronic communications services" or "remote computing services." An electronic communications service (ECS) allows its users to send or receive wire or electronic communications. A remote computing service (RCS) provides computer storage or processing services to the public via an ECS. Information stored by an ECS or an RCS is of three kinds: contents, non-content records about the subscriber or customer, and basic subscriber and session information. Subscriber and session information contains information that you would normally associate with billing information (name, address, length of service, and payment information). Records or other information about the customer is information that is neither subscriber information nor contents. Examples of this would be e-mail addresses of people with whom the customer has communicated and account usage records. Finally, contents are the actual data (files) stored in the account. As you might suspect by now, contents can be either "electronic storage" or content stored by an RCS, where electronic storage refers to temporary storage of information about the transmission of data and not the stored content of that communication.

 NOTE However, the courts have ruled that e-mail that is stored by a mail server prior to its being accessed by the recipient is "electronic storage." Remember that this isn't about technology; it's about the law.

Under the SCA, providers can be compelled to disclose the contents of electronic storage and stored records. This usually means that you need a subpoena, a court order, or a search warrant. However, if the service provider doesn't provide services to the public, then that provider can freely disclose contents and other records. For a provider of public services, if the provider is willing and able to voluntarily disclose this information, then there is no need for law enforcement to compel that disclosure.

When working with network providers, communicate often and early, and understand how that particular provider operates. As a member of law enforcement, you can order the provider to preserve existing records before actually getting the legal authority to seize those records. Nevertheless, you can't ask a provider to preserve records that haven't yet been created, and it may be the case that collecting these records may warn a suspect—hence, the need for often and early communication with that provider.

Electronic Surveillance in Communications Networks

We've already mentioned the Wiretap Statute (Title III) 18 U.S.C. §§ 2510–2522 and the Pen Registers and Trap and Trace Devices of Title 18 (the pen/trap statute) 18 U.S.C. §§ 3121–3127. Recall that the pen/trap statute regulates the collection of addressing and noncontent information, while Title III regulates the collection of actual content.

The key issue that all these statutes address is the difference between content or addressing information, also called metadata. Consider monitoring telephone traffic. Addressing (metadata) information would include the calling number, the called number, and the duration of the call. The actual conversation is content. In the case of Internet communications, the source IP address, the source port, the protocol, the destination port, and the destination address would be considered addressing information; the actual data portion of the communication (the payload) would be considered content. Figure 5-1 shows the

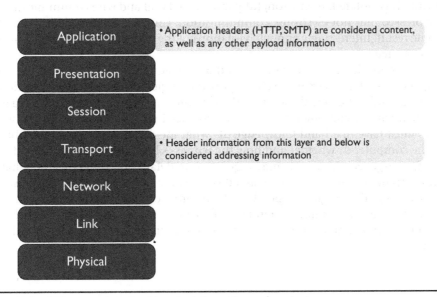

Figure 5-1 OSI protocol stack: addressing information and content

different layers of the seven-layer Open Systems Interconnection (OSI) network model that would be considered content as opposed to addressing information.

You can apply this distinction at higher levels in the protocol stack as well. When doing e-discovery on e-mail messages, header information such as the sender, the recipient, the length of the message, and the time the e-mail was sent is addressing information. The actual body of the e-mail is content, as is the subject line. Similar provisions apply for Short Message Service (SMS) messages, text chat, and others.

 NOTE In a potentially landmark case ruling in September 2013, a federal judge, Judge Lucy Koh of the Northern District Court of California, "ruled that Google [the search engine enterprise] may be violating wiretap law when it scans the e-mails of non-Gmail users, allowing a lawsuit against the company to move forward."[6]

Title III uses a broad brush to prohibit the interception, use, or disclosure of communications, unless a statutory exception applies. As you might expect, there are a number of statutory exceptions. One such exception is "bannering and consent." If you present a network banner to a user upon access to the network that informs the user that using the network means they consent to having their traffic monitored, then there is no violation of Title III. The provider exception says that an employee or agent of communication services can disclose communication if the provider's rights and properties are in jeopardy. Finally, the "extension telephone" allows a company that provides an employee with a telephone extension for remote work to monitor that line without violating Title III. Other exceptions affecting computer crime and evidence are the "computer trespasser" exception, the "inadvertently obtained criminal evidence" exception, and the "accessible to the public" exception.

If Title III is violated, then wrongfully intercepted oral and wire communication can be suppressed, but not electronic communication. Constitutional violations can have the same result. Interestingly enough, violations of the pen/trap statute provide no suppression remedy.

A major consideration for evidence is that it is authentic, which is a short way of saying that it is what it says it is. When applied to digital devices, authentic evidence is the same as authenticity with other kinds of records. A witness who testifies regarding the authenticity of computer records does not need special qualification; rather, the witness must have first hand knowledge of "what the data is and how it was obtained from the computer or whether and how the witness's business relies upon the data."[4]

Computer-generated records may require more detail, but, generally, the reliability of the computer program that generated those records can be shown by demonstrating that the users of the program depend on the records so generated in the normal course of business. Once a minimum standard of trustworthiness has been established for the computer program, the focus is on the weight of the evidence and not whether the evidence is admissible.

Post-seizure Issues

Let's assume that the searching and seizing portion of the investigation completed successfully. You will still need to address several post-seizure issues. One of these issues is the return of property, as established in Rule 41(g) in the Federal Rules of Criminal Procedure (FRCP).

The Return of Property

Seizing someone's computer equipment may hurt that individual's legal and legitimate business, so you won't have infinite time to investigate. In addition, you may only have one chance to actually collect information from that device, so it's a good idea to take what you need in the beginning because that may be your only chance.

This leads us to the question of how long you can take to examine a seized computer. In essence, there is no upper limit and no explicit limit on how long it can take to perform the search, although the Fourth Amendment does imply that the search must be performed within a "reasonable" time.

First Responder Procedures

Beginnings are always difficult. Some people say that your first five seconds create an initial impression that's difficult to shake. The same principle still applies when you arrive on the crime scene as the DFI. Getting things right from the beginning is critical to collecting the right evidence and preserving it for investigation, and mistakes that you make then will linger throughout the investigation.

First on the Scene

Who exactly is the first responder? One candidate is the first person to arrive on the scene, who may not be a member of law enforcement. The other candidate for the role of first responder is the first DFI on the scene, who is qualified and trained in gathering electronic evidence. In the rest of this chapter, you can assume that the first responder is the first DFI on the scene. The goal of any effort prior to the arrival of the DFI is to protect the digital evidence, which means that other members of your law enforcement team or your systems and network administrators in an enterprise need to be trained on what to do and what not to do when confronted with sources of digital evidence.

The first response rule is to preserve the crime scene and the evidence, regardless of who actually discovered the incident. If we are working on an enterprise investigation, a system administrator may be one of the first people to notice that a breach or questionable activity is occurring. System administrators should be trained to contact your organization's Computer Security Incident Response Team (CSIRT) or the Computer Emergency Response Team (CERT).

Regardless of affiliation, a first responder should perform the following tasks as suggested by NIJ:[7]

- Secure all electronic devices, including personal devices.
- Prevent unauthorized individuals from accessing any electronic device.

- Refuse help or assistance from any unauthorized person.
- Remove everyone from the area where evidence will be collected.
- Maintain the state of any digital device: If it's on, leave it on; if it's off, leave it off.

Incident Response

Non-law enforcement cases usually take the form of an incident response. Someone, either from the organization's CSIRT or from senior management, will decide how to respond to this particular incident. At this time, nonforensic corporate staff may arrive to take over the scene. If an attack has occurred, it's time to initiate an attack response, which has four phases: mitigation, notification, investigation, and resolution.[8] As a DFI, we'll be most involved in the mitigation and investigation phases. If law enforcement is going to be involved, then our job as a forensics specialist is to protect the digital evidence from destruction. If law enforcement or outside professionals won't be involved, then it will fall to us to collect the evidence from memory and from disk in a forensically sound manner. As usual, be sure to document your actions and the results. This would be true regardless of whether we are performing as a forensics expert or as a member of an incident response team. Remember, though, that a full incident response will also involve notification of required parties or involved parties, and mitigation will fall to systems administrators and network and systems security professionals within your organization. This leads us back to the difference between a forensics investigation and incident response. Recall from our first chapters that incident response and digital forensics investigations may use the same tools, but the aims of each activity are different.

 NOTE The lines between incident response, digital forensics, and malware analysis are blurred. For me, I distinguish among them as follows. If I'm determining if there has been a security breach, I'm performing incident response. If I'm collecting persistent data and transient data on a particular device, I'm performing digital forensics. If I've determined that the incident involved downloading malware, and I'm investigating how that malware operates, I'm doing malware analysis. You may take on all these roles in the course of the computer hacking forensics investigation.

First Things First

When you arrive on the scene as a DFI, have a quick conversation with the people who first arrived on the crime scene. Assure yourself that all efforts have been made to secure the crime scene and preserve the evidence. After you've completed this initial conversation, take a moment to capture the details. Given what you've learned, review your risk analysis findings and your notes on what to look for and what to do with it… memory joggers are always beneficial, and they will help you complete your checklist. Make sure you bring the results of your risk analysis. Knowing what to do in the event you have to make choices about what evidence to collect first can save valuable seconds. Finally, a checklist like this lets you know when you're done.

CAUTION   Don't let a checklist blind you to other possible sources of information or activities warranted due to special circumstances.

Managing the Crime Scene

Once you've made sure that the evidence has been preserved, you can now begin the process of actually searching or seizing the evidence. The first step to take is to conduct preliminary interviews with people on the scene, including witnesses and possibly the suspect as well. Any adult present at the crime scene should be isolated for further questioning after recording their location at the crime scene when you arrived.

TIP   It's worth repeating: No one should be allowed to access any digital device at the crime scene except an authorized professional. Period.

Before beginning the interview, quickly review your agency's policies regarding interviews, as well as local, state, and federal laws. Within these parameters, gather the following information:[7]

- Names of all users of the computers and devices.
- All computer and Internet user information.
- All login names and user account names, and all passwords, including systems administrator or application administration accounts.
- Purpose and uses of computers and devices.
- Any automated applications in use. This can include remote services that may back up and delete material from the computer or scheduled tasks on the computer itself.
- Type of Internet access (LAN, WAN, dial-up).
- Any offsite storage, including cloud accounts such as Box, Dropbox, and others.
- Internet service provider. This is especially important if you anticipate that you will need to subpoena the ISP for traffic records.
- Installed software documentation. This can aid in your investigation, especially if the software in use is specific to a particular occupation or industry.
- All e-mail accounts used locally.
- Security provisions in use. Is the device running an antivirus product (including malware detections), a local firewall, a proxy server, or other software?
- Web mail account information, both personal and business.
- Data access restrictions in place. Are certain data storage areas restricted to the computer owner?

- All instant-message screen names. Remember that many instant messaging clients also support file transfer.

- All destructive devices or software in use. Does the owner have access to programs that can wipe the disk in the computer?

- MySpace, Facebook, Tumblr, or other online social networking web site account information.

- Any other relevant information that you've identified as part of your preliminary investigation.

In the case of the suspect, one of the first tasks is to gain consent from the suspect for the search itself. This is especially important if there's a piece of evidence that's not covered by the warrant. If the suspect agrees, have them sign a consent form. Figure 5-2 is an example of such a form.

In the case of witnesses, make sure you ask them in a preliminary interview details about the digital equipment and its use. Was the computer turned on? Could they see what was on the screen? Was the printer active? Was the suspect using a scanner? Was the suspect removing or moving portable storage devices (USB thumb drives, USB external drives)? Make sure that you have the witness sign their description after you've completed the interview.

Documenting the crime scene will take several forms. I think of this as the "helicopter zoom." First is the "30,000 foot view"; in this case, you might use a video camera to do a 360-degree view of the crime scene, or at least a series of overlapping still photographs. These should be taken from the perspective of someone entering the room. After doing that, however, create a hand-drawn sketch of the crime scene as well, both as a check on the video and as a backup should the video be unwatchable (remember the cell phone in the toilet scenario). After documenting the overall crime scene, create still photographs of each piece of digital equipment, including the tags that you've already placed on various cabling and external devices. At the end of this process, you should have the following:

- A 360-degree video of the crime scene, accompanied by a hand-drawn sketch of the entire crime scene with appropriate handwritten annotations

- A photograph of each individual piece of equipment, including tags and labels, again, accompanied by handwritten notes and annotations

 TIP Consider creating your own forensic copy of these images and notes and storing them away in a local and a remote archive. This may mean scanning your handwritten notes and copying your videos and still photographs. Disk space is cheap, remote storage is cheap, and is much less than the cost to your investigation if this information should be lost or destroyed. Remember the old adage: The job isn't finished until the (digital) paperwork's done. Make sure that your materials are encrypted using strong encryption (AES-256 is a good choice), whether stored locally or remotely, and ensure that you take appropriate steps to physically secure the information.

Sample Consent Form
for Computer Search

CONSENT TO SEARCH COMPUTER/ELECTRONIC EQUIPMENT

I, _____, have been asked to give my consent to the search of my computer/electronic equipment. I have also been informed of my right to refuse to consent to such a search.

I hereby authorize _____ and any other person(s) designated by [insert Agency/Department] to conduct at any time a complete search of:

◻ All computer/electronic equipment located at _____ _____. These persons are authorized by me to take from the above location: any computer hardware and storage media, including internal hard disk drive(s), floppy diskettes, compact disks, scanners, printers, other computer/electronic hardware or software and related manuals; any other electronic storage devices, including but not limited to, personal digital assistants, cellular telephones, and electronic pagers; and any other media or materials necessary to assist in accessing the stored electronic data.

◻ The following electronic devices:

[Description of computers, data storage devices, cellular telephone, or other devices (makes, models, and serial numbers, if available)]

I certify that I own, possess, control, and/or have a right of access to these devices and all information found in them. I understand that any contraband or evidence on these devices may be used against me in a court of law.

I relinquish any constitutional right to privacy in these electronic devices and any information stored on them. I authorize [insert Agency/Department] to make and keep a copy of any information stored on these devices. I understand that any copy made by [insert Agency/Department] will become the property

Figure 5-2 Sample consent form (Source: Searching and Seizing Computers and Obtaining Evidence in Computer Investigations (Washington, DC: DOJ, 2008), p 253.)

Collecting and Transporting the Evidence

The next step is actually collecting the evidence. If we're lucky, all the electronic devices are powered off so you can just put them in evidence bags, label the bags appropriately, attach the appropriate chain-of-evidence forms, and head out for an early lunch. Unfortunately, things often don't turn out that way.

As we've said a number of times, a best practice is to leave the device in the state that it was in when you initially discovered it. If it's off, leave it off, and prepare the device to be collected as evidence. If the device is running, leave it running. Photograph the screen to record what was visible when you entered the crime scene.

If the machine is running, you'll need to determine if a live acquisition is necessary. It's probably safe to assume that in most cases a live acquisition will be necessary. The first principle to apply here is to collect the most significant volatile data first, in the order of difficulty. Table 5-2 compares volatility and the ease of retrieving the data, and assumes that this information is critical to your investigation.

This is low-hanging fruit: Get the most critical volatile data first that is easiest to collect. If it's of low value and difficult to collect, leave it until last.

Volatile information in a computer looks like this, from most volatile to least volatile:[9]

- Registers and cache
- Routing tables, process tables, kernel statistics, and memory
- Temporary file systems
- Disks or other storage systems
- Remote logging and monitoring data related to the system we're investigating
- Physical configuration and network topology
- Archival media

Temporary file systems also can be a source of valuable information. In some cases, all files on the temporary file system may be deleted automatically at system startup; in other cases, temporary files may only be deleted by an explicit user command. If you're doing a live collection, make sure you capture the contents of the temporary file system before initiating shutdown.

Networked computers (almost everything these days) pose their own special problems. We'll discuss this later on in this chapter.

Portable computers (everything from netbooks, laptops, smart phones, and tablets) require that you pay attention to battery life. If you need to capture live data from a portable device that is currently running on battery power, you will need to plug the

Volatility	Difficulty to Collect	Order of Collection
High	Low	1
Medium	Medium	2
Low	High	3

Table 5-2 Volatility and Difficulty Collecting Information

machine in to an appropriate recharging device, which is why you have several different kinds of charging devices in your forensics toolkit. If the device is powered off, however, just remove the battery—this will prevent the device from being powered on later, when the loss of data from startup processing is possible.

If the device is on, then we treat the portable computer as we would a desktop system. If the machine is in sleep mode and then wakes up, record when this actually occurred. Pull the battery from the device, and then pull the power cord (if you do it in reverse order, the machine may fall back to battery power). If you can't pull the power cord, holding down the power switch for five seconds or longer will usually power off the device.

CAUTION   We are trying to prevent automated processes from running that may delete important information, which is why literally pulling the plug is appropriate. The same conditions don't apply when working with virtualized machines, however. A normal shutdown or kill command may result in the machine automatically rebooting if configured as such (the machine requires high availability). In this case, the virtualization vendor usually provides commands that will simulate a "pull the plug/power off" scenario.

Shutdown procedures vary depending on whether you have access to the console (allowing you to possibly log on as an administrator) and the machine's operating system. For Windows machines, the best shutdown procedure is literally pulling the plug at the wall socket. For Linux/UNIX machines, issuing the command

```
sync; sync ; halt
```

will flush all unwritten data to associated storage devices or communication channels and then halt the machine. Failing access to the console with root (administrator) access, pull the plug. For Mac OS, accessing the shutdown option from the Special menu will perform a graceful shutdown; otherwise, pull the plug.

Collecting and Preserving Electronic Evidence

At this point, all our digital devices are shut down except for those that we wish to keep running, and we need to start bagging the evidence. Each evidence bag should have a contents list attached. We saw an example of that in a previous chapter in our sample chain-of-evidence form. One of the important elements on this list is the exhibit number. The EC-Council lists one method of creating this exhibit number[10] as *aaa/ddmmyy/ nnnn/zz*, where

- *aaa* are the initials of the investigator.
- *ddmmyy* is the date when the evidence was acquired.
- *nnnn* is a sequence number of exhibits seized by the investigator, starting at 0001.
- *zz* is the sequence number for different parts of the same exhibit. A1 might be the computer, B1 might be the keyboards, C1 the monitor, D1 an attached universal serial bus (USB) drive, and so on.

Therefore, for example, an evidence bag with the exhibit number clb/21082013/0001/A1 might be the first exhibit seized by the investigator with the initials "clb" on August 21, 2013. This bag contains the first element of one part of the associated exhibit.

Once the evidence is "bagged and tagged," it's time to actually transfer that evidence to the forensics laboratory (or to an evidence locker or storage room). The key to successful transport and storage of evidence is anticipating and understanding the varying conditions that will be encountered between the original location of the evidence and its final location.

Let's reflect for a moment about what we'd consider to be a suitable storage area for digital evidence. The space would be climate controlled: neither too hot, too cold, too dry, or too damp. Evidence would be stored away from magnetic fields, in a place where it wouldn't be bumped, jostled, kicked, or dropped. If the equipment is meant to function in a particular position, we would store it in that position (we probably wouldn't store a printer face down, for example). We wouldn't want a place that was very dusty (clogging ventilation hose), nor a place where the digital evidence and the containers would be exposed to direct sunlight (sunlight can do a number on plastic—think about that CD you left on your dashboard last summer).

We'll assume that the digital equipment and its evidence was okay where we found it. Our challenge, then, is to maintain these kinds of conditions when we transport the evidence. We will need to pay attention to heat and humidity to prevent overheating or condensation. We'll need to pack the equipment so that it will remain relatively stationary when moved (I always like to use the original packaging if it's available). Foam peanuts, bubble wrap, or crushed newspaper can all act as padding. If possible, follow a route that minimizes potholes and speed bumps; if that isn't possible, then drive as slowly as you can. Don't stow the equipment in the trunk if you have equipment back there that generates electromagnetic radiation. Rendering your digital data useless in transport isn't going to win you any friends. Treat it like you did Aunt Bluebelle's precious tea set that she brought back from England in '59.

The Crime Scene Report

The crime scene report should document the work you did when you appeared at the crime scene. The report should describe the location of the electronic devices, whether on or off, what was on the screen, who had access to the device, and so forth. The report should illustrate the crime scene using the photographs that you took as part of your initial examination.

Remember that this is a factual description of what you observed. Don't record your questions or observations that you may have written down as notes to yourself. Stick to the facts.

A Checklist for First Responders

Prepare a checklist in advance for first responders. Any forensics lab staff that are expected to appear at a crime scene representing the lab should have been trained on the actions and needs associated with each item on that checklist. The checklist has two functions and answers two questions: what do I do, and did I do it?

Things can go wrong even with the best of intentions. Remember that familiar statement: "Mistakes were made." Mistakes can be made by not doing something that was required (sins of omission) or by doing something that wasn't required (sins of commission). Consider all the steps that we've covered in this section, and consider the opposite. Evidence wasn't identified, evidence wasn't properly tagged, evidence wasn't labeled regarding cabling, evidence wasn't collected properly, evidence wasn't protected properly for transport.

Don't forget the two great laws of digital forensics: Leave the device in the same state as when you discovered it, and document everything. Common mistakes that first responders make include violating one of these cardinal rules. Volatile data were lost because a machine was either shut down or rebooted. A particular step or a particular piece of evidence wasn't documented or was documented improperly. Potential evidence was overlooked because the individual wasn't familiar with that particular machine. The evidence wasn't packaged securely for transport. And so forth.

Data Acquisition and Duplication

At this point in the investigation, you've legally obtained the digital devices that contain the electronic information that you wish to analyze. The next question is how do you actually get access to this information in such a way that you don't render the material useless as evidence (the legal term for this is *spoliation*)? How can you be sure that the material you're working with is the same as the original electronic information?

Data Acquisition: A Definition

Data acquisition is the process whereby we collect data and add that to our evidence. Data duplication is simply creating a true copy of digital evidence obtained from a particular digital container. What makes this interesting is variation in the source and destination of the data. There are three options:[11]

- **Disk-to-disk**   In this instance, this is a straight disk-to-disk copy. The source and destination are two separate hard disks. Obvious restrictions are that the destination drive must be at least as large as the source drive. An example of a disk-to-disk copy when using the Linux operating system (OS) would be

  ```
  dd if=/dev/sda of=/dev/sdb blocksize=1024
  ```

  We'll talk about other options in Chapter 7 when we talk about conducting a forensic investigation.

- **Disk-to-image**   In this case, a drive is copied from one computer system to an image file on another disk. This image file can be used as input to one of our digital forensics tools, or it can be mounted so that it appears as a disk drive on the local machine. One technique for doing this when using Linux OS is

  ```
  dd if=/dev/usb of=/var/evidence/case123/usb1.img
  ```

- **Create a sparse data copy**   In this instance, only a portion of the associated data that are directly associated with an investigation is copied. This can be the case when the source storage is much larger than the relevant material. One such example is acquiring data from a redundant array of independent disks (RAID) array. The actual size of the disk associated with the storage array may be on the order of terabytes or petabytes. In this case, simply making a copy of specific directories will speed up the process and ensure that the pertinent evidence is manageable.

CAUTION A copy of files from one file system to another is not a forensic copy. A forensic copy is a bit-for-bit duplicate or clone of the original storage device. A file system–level copy won't copy deleted files, for instance, nor will it copy files used solely by the file system.

Which acquisition method is the best? All other things being equal, data should be acquired at the physical level of the disk drive—that is, a block-by-block, bit-by-bit copy of the source drive. This ensures that we see everything on the disk. A file system copy, as in the case of a sparse data copy, requires that we use the file system as an intermediary, and the file system only sees what it is meant to see. A file system copy, for example, will not copy slack space within the drive; it will only copy the number of bytes that are recorded as the file length. If the file block size is 1,024 bytes and the file length is 457, only 457 bytes will be copied to the new file.

TIP You can save yourself some pain and heartache if you ask your client as part of your initial interview what kind of computer equipment you can expect to encounter at the scene and whether or not the data need to be collected on site, or if the drives can be taken back to the lab.

Some data acquisition systems do not require the assistance of a full forensics workstation, but instead can simply copy one disk to another, often at high speed. Remember, too, that once you've acquired the data, you'll want to make a copy of that copy, so now you have the original, the master copy of the original, and your working copy. This is especially important in the case where the original needs to be returned to its owner in a short time period. Making a copy of the original is a contingency plan in case the original should become corrupted. Likewise, using two different data acquisition tools to access the digital device serves as validation that all the data were collected.

Common Data Acquisition Mistakes

Some common data acquisition mistakes are simply to forget to collect some particular evidence, or to neglect to make a copy of the copy, or to create a copy of the original that doesn't contain all the information you need for your investigation (for example, you create a file copy that doesn't reflect files deleted on the original). Other mistakes are[12]

- Shutting down before you've completed evidence collection. Evidence can be lost and the attacker may have altered the startup/shutdown scripts/services to destroy evidence.

- Trusting the programs on the system. Run your evidence-gathering programs from appropriately protected media.

- Running programs that modify the access time of all files on the system (e.g., *tar* or *xcopy*).

- Disconnecting or filtering from the network. As tempting as it is, this may trigger "deadman switches" that will detect that the machine is off the network and will wipe evidence.

Required features for a disk-imaging tool are best taken from the National Institute of Standards (NIST) *Digital Data Acquisition Tool Test Assertions and Test Plan*. This test plan is part of NIST's Computer Forensic Tool Testing Program (CFTT), found at www .cftt.nist.gov. The test plan lists the following requirements for a disk imaging tool:

- The tool uses the specified access interface to access the digital source.

- The tool acquires the specified digital source.

- The tool executes in the specified execution environment.

- The tool creates a clone of the digital source if clone creation is specified.

- If image file creation is specified, the tool creates an image file on the specified file system type.

- The tool acquires all visible sectors from the digital source.

- The tool acquires all hidden sectors from the digital source.

- The tool accurately acquires all sectors acquired from the digital source.

- If unresolved errors occur while reading from the selected digital source, the tool notifies the user of the error type and location within the digital source.

- If unresolved errors occur while reading from the selected digital source, the tool uses a benign fill in the destination object in place of the inaccessible data.

There are multiple optional features listed for tools. In the case of data acquisition tools, 24 optional features are listed, broken out by image file, clone creation, log file creation, and acquisition of data without a write-blocker. This optional feature states, "If the tool executes in a forensically safe execution environment, the digital source is unchanged by the acquisition process."[13] This is especially important if you will need to restore the digital device and its content to the owner.

Static vs. Live Acquisition

Static acquisition (sometimes called "dead" acquisition) is the process whereby the investigator creates an image of persistent storage. This could be from a disk drive taken from a particular machine, a Secure Digital (SD) card, a USB drive, a USB pen drive, or any other kind of persistent storage.

You can acquire static data by several different methods. One method is to boot the computer using a different operating system. The disks from the evidence machine will be discovered and mounted (read-only) on the acquiring machine. The acquiring OS will run entirely from memory, or from memory and a storage device (a CD-ROM or a USB storage device). Either the data copied from the disks from the evidence machine can be copied to an acquisition drive mounted on the evidence machine, or they can be transferred over a network to an acquisition machine that then writes the data to an evidence disk. We'll see examples of this later on in this chapter.

Live data acquisition, in contrast, is gathering information from a running system. We will extract information from persistent storage, but we will also capture volatile information; that is, information that will disappear when the computer is shut down, such as the contents of memory, the state of network connections, who is logged in to the machine, and other information.

Volatile Information

Which information should you collect first? A couple of rules of thumb come into play here. First, which information is most critical to your investigation. Second, which of these data is most volatile, that is, is most likely to change the soonest. When we combine these heuristics, we see that we need to capture the most volatile and the most critical information first, while the least volatile and least critical will have to be put off until later. The following list contains items ranked in order from most volatile to least volatile:[14]

- CPU, cache, and register content
- Routing table, Address Resolution Protocol (ARP) cache, process table, and kernel statistics
- Memory
- Temporary file system/swap space
- Data on hard disk
- Remotely logged data
- Data contained on archival media

Let's consider the following example. We are investigating a running machine connected to a network. Should we collect a list of running processes first or the list of network connections? The answer is that we should consider which information has the most bearing on our case. If we believe that network information is most critical, we can collect that first. If, on the other hand, we think that the set of programs running on the computer is most critical, then we would go ahead and collect that data first.

You can use many of the standard programs on any particular OS to gather information about the state of that particular computer. Using these tools will leave their mark: Every exchange leaves a trace. Make sure that you record what you ran on the suspect machine and when, and know what changes this software will make to the underlying file system or in memory.

Don't neglect the actual capture of the contents of memory from the suspect machine. Some machines will allow you to collect data directly, while other machines require you to use a special program (which is part of your forensics toolkit). Other software can read and interpret the contents of memory to reveal what programs were running and what connections were open, both internally and externally. Having a disk containing system tools for either Linux or Windows as part of your investigation toolkit can help you perform these collections, and running from a read-only medium can ensure that these tools aren't infected if malware is on the suspect machine.

Validating the Acquisition

Disk imaging tools have one job to do: create an exact duplicate of the source device to the target. Regardless of how much we trust our tools, an abundance of caution requires us to validate our acquisition. We do that by taking advantage of algorithms that are sensitive to a one-bit difference in a particular file. As we saw in Chapter 4, several cryptographic hash functions are in use today. They include MD5 (still used, but deprecated), SHA-1 (produces a 160-bit hash values), and SHA-2, a set of functions (SHA-224, -256, -385, and -512) introduced in 2001 after a mathematical flaw was discovered in SHA-1.

Acquisition Validation for Windows and Linux

Linux and Windows validation methods are very similar. In both cases, the goal is to demonstrate that the two data copies are identical. Either you can validate the data after acquisition, or you can validate as the data are actually copied. This enhancement saves a second pass through the original and the copy. Linux and Windows systems both can utilize the *md5sum, sha1sum, sha256sum,* and *md5deep* utilities, although you will need to download these files or utilize a forensics software distribution. *md5deep* will recursively descend a directory structure, generating a digest for each file found. Although the package is named *md5deep*, multiple algorithms are supported, including SHA-1 and SHA-256. In comparison mode, *md5deep* can accept a list of known hashes, compare them against a set of input files, and list ones that either match or do not match, depending on the nature of the set of known hashes.[15] *hashdeep* can compute, match, and audit hash sets, and can report on matched files, missing files, moved files, or new files not found in a particular set.

Acquisition Issues: SSDs, RAID, and Cloud

The old model for acquiring data was based on a model of how disk drives worked at that time. Suffice it to say here that this model has been supplemented (and in some cases replaced) by different storage technologies. We'll take a quick look at three of them here: RAID, solid-state devices (SSDs), and the cloud.

RAID

RAID originally was an acronym for "redundant array of inexpensive disks," although this is usually translated nowadays as "redundant array of independent disks." RAID structures can be created on a single workstation with multiple drives, or as an external storage system.

Acquiring RAID devices can pose problems for the investigator. If the RAID is contained within the local machine, then the problem is slightly easier, in that it's just a matter of seizing the local machine. Even if the array is external to a particular machine, it may still be portable, in that it makes sense to actually seize the entire device.

One problem is that the larger the array and the more people are using it, the greater disruption to the enterprise. In some cases, losing the storage array may shut down the entire business. A second problem is that if you are bringing the disks back for investigation, you need to ensure that you have the appropriate software to actually reconstruct the RAID from the disks, and this may be difficult to do, especially if the RAID format is proprietary.

Solid-State Devices

Solid-state devices appear to the file system like regular disk drives, but they're not. In fact, they are more like computer memory (hence the term "flash drives"). At the physical level, they are very different. An SSD disk block can only be written to so many times before it becomes unreadable. To avoid this, the driver software will write a modified block to a new physical address, thereby spreading use across the disk surface. This freed block may be immediately zeroed out by the driver so it can be reused.

The Cloud

The cloud presents just two problems for digital forensics, but they are significant. One is simply finding the data. The other is retrieving it from the cloud provider. Assuming that the data are stored on a remote machine, many of the problems resolve to those associated with any remote machine. Getting network data and log data from that particular machine may be difficult, and is even more difficult if the original remote machine image has been deleted.

 NOTE Information that is stored as part of the remote machine image (for example, C:\ on Windows) will be deleted once the machine image is deleted. Externally defined data can persist after the machine image has been deleted and can be reattached to a new instance of that virtual machine.

Recall the discussions required when attempting to get data from a remote provider, and consider the difficulty arising when the storage, computer, and memory resources have been returned to a common pool of reusable resources. The question of jurisdiction is further complicated because cloud providers may not actually store data on the same physical machine. The data can move from one physical machine to another in the same data center, and may even move to a second data center that is geographically removed from the first data center (even in another state or another country).

Concepts in Practice: Data Acquisition Software and Tools

As we've already mentioned, the big three of digital forensics frameworks are

- Forensic Toolkit (FTK) from AccessData
- EnCase from Guardian Software
- The Sleuth Kit and Autopsy from www.sleuthkit.org (Brian Carrier's web site)

Many other software packages are available for Windows, Linux, and Mac OS. The best software to use, however, is the software that has been validated by the NIST CFTT program.

Acquiring Data on Windows

Acquiring data on a Windows machine is a little more complicated than acquiring data from a Linux computer. If you simply need to copy a file from one disk to another, *xcopy, robocopy,* or *Windows Explorer* will suffice. If you need to create a forensic image of a disk, however, you will usually need to use a third-party software program. One such program is FTK Imager. Figure 5-3 shows the interface to the software.

Notice the menu in the upper-left corner. The three options allow you to mount an existing image, add an image to an evidence file (more on this in a later chapter), and create a disk image. FTK Imager is a Windows program, so it could be run from a suspect's computer using protected media (a write-protected USB driver, for example) or from a Windows forensics workstation with the suspect drive attached.

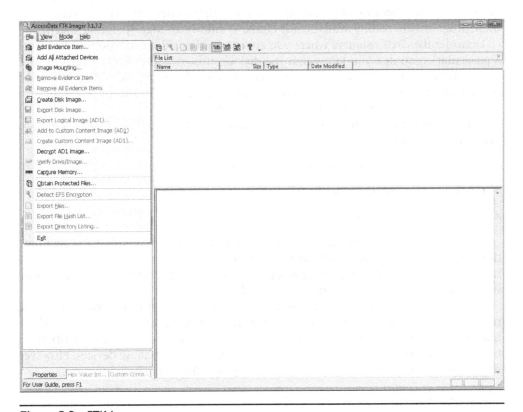

Figure 5-3 FTK Imager

Acquiring Data on Linux

The Linux *dd* command has many capabilities. It takes its name from the old IBM mainframe job control "dd" card, short for data definition. When used in forensic data acquisition, *dd* can create disk-to-disk copies, disk-to-image file, or disk-to-network copies. The *dcfldd* command is an enhanced version of the *dd* command created by the Defense Computer Forensics Laboratory (DCFL). In addition to the capabilities of *dd*, *dcfldd* provides the ability to perform hashing on the fly, output data to multiple files or disks, and pipe output and log files to commands as well as files.

Capturing the contents of the master boot record (MBR) from a particular drive is relatively straightforward. Our old friend *dd* comes to our rescue. Let's say we wish to capture the MBR from the raw disk on /dev/sda. The *dd* command to do this is

```
dd if=/dev/sda1 of=/tmp/mbr-sda1-20130728.bin bs=512 count=1
```

The *netcat* command has been around for a long time, as measured in Internet years. You may find it named *netcat, nc,* or more recently *ncat,* which I'll use going forward. Although sometimes mischaracterized as a hacker tool, *ncat* is a useful part of any DFI's toolkit, primarily because of its ability to act as either a client or a server. Versions of these programs are readily available for Linux, Windows, or Mac operating systems.

Consider the circumstances where you are conducting a live extraction of data from a particular computer. You know that the disk on this computer is encrypted in such a way that if the machine is shut down, the disk can't be decrypted unless you know the appropriate user name and password, which you don't. You want to capture the decrypted contents of the attached disk. What to do?

ncat to the rescue. On your forensics workstation (192.168.11.3), start *ncat* as a server listening on a free port:

```
forensic> ncat -l -p 24773 | dd of=/dev/sdb bs=1024
```

On the suspect machine, do the following:

```
suspect> dd if=/dev/sda bs=1024 | ncat -p 24773 192.168.11.3
```

The *dd* command will cheerfully read 1,024 bytes at a time from /dev/sda1 and send that data via a Linux pipe to a local *ncat* that is sending its output to the *ncat* process running on 192.168.11.3 and listening on port 24773. That *ncat* process is in turn writing the data to a hard disk identified as */dev/sdb*.

ncat isn't limited to just capturing data from persistent storage. The contents of memory can be collected by having *dd* read from */dev/mem* or */dev/kmem* on a Linux machine. (Please note, this may not be possible in more modern Linux distributions because of permission problems associated with reading from these devices. However, new tools exist to perform this function, such as *volatility* and *memoryze*.)

Data Acquisition Software Tools

A number of data acquisition software tools are available for Windows, Linux, and Mac OS. We've already mentioned EnCase, FTK, *dd*, and *dcfldd*. Other software includes X-Way's *WinHex* suite of tools. The majority of tools are hosted on machines running either the Windows OS or Linux. In some cases, you will find tools for Linux are available for the Mac. The problem that arises is that if the Mac tools haven't been blessed either by NIST or by digital forensics practitioners, the results produced by running these tools may not be accepted in court.

Data Acquisition Hardware Tools

As expected, there is a multitude of hardware tools for data acquisition. Some notable tools are the MASSter series of products from Intelligent Computer Solutions, Inc. Their products range from handheld devices to portable investigation stations to forensics lab stations that support capture of up to 10 suspect drives to 10 evidence drives.

 TIP Consider where and how you will use a particular tool. Will you keep it in an office, or will you be using it in the field? If the latter, spending more money on a sturdier or ruggedized device will cost less in the long run. Consider running the "Charlie Test" while the device is still under warranty: Sweep the device off a three-foot-high desktop onto a concrete floor. If it "takes a lickin' and keeps on tickin'," you have a tool worth keeping.

Chapter Review

The Fourth Amendment to the Constitution secures a citizen from unreasonable search and seizures, and requires a warrant to specify what things can be seized. Even if you don't have a warrant, you may still be able to seize digital equipment due to exceptions to the law, or if you receive the consent of an authority.

Obtaining a warrant means demonstrating probable cause for searching a person or property. If you have a warrant, then you are limited to the items mentioned in the warrant unless other rules apply, such as "plain view." Obtaining electronic communication is a different problem. The Electronic Communications Privacy Act sets limits on what information can be obtained and restricts the process for obtaining that information. The pen/trap statute and Title III cover what kind of information can be obtained. Addressing information (communication metadata) is covered under the pen/trap statute, and is usually easier to obtain than a warrant for the content (communication) itself, which is covered under Title III.

A first responder's role is to preserve and protect evidence at the crime scene, and this is the first order of business once you arrive on the scene. Preliminary interviews should be conducted as soon as you have properly secured the evidence. Next, document the crime scene using video, still photographs, handwritten sketches, and written notes (audio notes as well). Take 360-degree video first, then tag the equipment, then take still photographs that show the tags associated with that equipment (it may help to know that device A was connected to device B using network port N).

If machines are still running, you should determine if you need a live acquisition. If not, turn them off by literally pulling the power plug from the back of the machine (initiating a shutdown or pressing the power switch may trigger modifications to stored data). Make sure that any device capable of receiving radio signals is shielded. Make sure that any operating device that requires live acquisition or analysis remains powered on (usually via an external charger).

TIP Given how prevalent encrypted drives are, performing a live analysis may be the only way to access relevant information.

Make sure that you transport any electronic evidence such that it's immune from changes in temperature, humidity, or vibration, and make sure that the storage area for evidence is free from dust, heat, humidity, and electromagnetic interference.

A checklist for first responders should contain steps to guide the initial preservation of the crime scene prior to the arrival of the DFI. A checklist for first responders can alleviate many common mistakes, such as shutting down a machine prematurely, using local tools that destroy evidence, improperly documenting the data collection process, or not collecting relevant information because they're unfamiliar with that particular digital device.

Data acquisition is the process whereby data are extracted from a digital device for the purpose of examination and analysis. Extracting this data from regular disks is a known quantity: Special considerations apply when acquiring data from SSD drives, RAID arrays, or the cloud. Data acquisition may be either static (from persistent storage) or dynamic (from a running system). In dynamic data collections, collect data from the most volatile to the least volatile. Once you acquire the data, you need to validate them against the original data. You can do this by using a hash algorithm to generate a digest value from the original and the copy. If the values are identical, you know that the two files contain the same content.

There are many different hardware and software tools for data acquisition. FTK and EnCase are two of the most recognized and most used. Hardware tools can speed up the process of data duplication in the case of static acquisition. Always use a write-blocker when extracting data from a disk. Even though you may mount a disk read-only, there is a chance that data or metadata may be changed (one such case is NTFS under Windows).

Questions

1. Which of these conditions would permit seizing a computer without a warrant? (Choose all that apply.)

   A. Plain view

   B. Exigent circumstances

   C. Serendipity

   D. Hunches based on experience

2. Which of these defines when a search occurs?

   A. When the expectation of privacy that society would consider reasonable is infringed

   B. When a law enforcement office enters the crime scene

C. When a particular digital device specified in a warrant is seized

D. When computer software is used to scan a disk for particular keywords.

3. True or false: If a suspect gives you permission to search their computer, it means you can search for any evidence whatsoever.

A. True

B. False

4. Which of these actions is not part of seizing and searching a computer when you have a warrant?

A. Identification of a specific item

B. Data acquisition

C. Exigent circumstances

D. Documentation of the steps used to seize the item

5. Which of the following must be covered in a search warrant? (Choose all that apply.)

A. The person or person to be searched

B. The place to search

C. The property to be seized

D. The time during which the search can be carried out

6. Which activities are part of the role of the first responder? (Choose all that apply.)

A. Separate and identify witnesses who were actually at the crime scene.

B. Prevent anyone from touching the digital devices.

C. Ensure that crime scene tape is used to establish a perimeter.

D. Collect all digital devices in one place.

7. What is the purpose of asking about automated applications in the preliminary interview? (Choose all that apply.)

A. Determine when the next backup will occur in order to get a forensic image.

B. Determine if data can be changed on a running computer.

C. Determine other login accounts.

D. Determine the possible use of external devices.

8. The last step in a witness interview is:

A. Notify them of their Miranda rights.

B. Obtain their contact information.

C. Obtain their signature on their description of the crime scene.

D. Caution them against revealing any information to non-law enforcement people.

9. What is the benefit of removing the battery from a portable device?

   A. Wipes any transient information that can obscure significant data

   B. Forces the investigator to use external power

   C. Prevents accidently starting the device and possibly overwriting critical evidence

   D. Fingerprints may help identify the owner of the device

10. Which of these are common mistakes made by first responders? (Choose all that apply.)

    A. Shutting down a running device

    B. Using native tools that may destroy evidence

    C. Prematurely restricting access to the computer

    D. Asking detailed questions during a preliminary interview

11. Which of the following are types of data acquisition? (Choose all that apply.)

    A. Disk-to-disk

    B. Disk-to-image

    C. Sparse data collection

    D. Disk-to-compressed archive

12. How do we determine which data acquisition method is best?

    A. One that produces a forensically sound image

    B. One that copies the data most quickly

    C. One that minimizes the amount of data copied

    D. One that uses the least amount of resources on the suspect machine

13. Which action is part of contingency planning for data acquisition?

    A. Making a copy of the data using two different tools

    B. Taking multiple data acquisition hardware tools to the crime scene

    C. Reading the CFTT test plan results for each data acquisition tool

    D. Having two different DFIs acquire the same data

14. What is the difference between static and live data acquisition?

    A. Static data acquisition collects data from persistent storage only.

    B. Live data acquisition only looks at volatile data.

    C. Static data acquisition collects more data than a live acquisition.

    D. Live data acquisition can only be performed on a remote device.

15. Which of these is the most volatile?

    A. Memory

    B. Registers

C. Paging file

D. USB drive

Answers

1. **A, B.** Exigent circumstances and plain view would support seizing a digital device without a warrant.

2. **A.** A search occurs when the societal expectation of what constitutes a reasonable degree of privacy is infringed.

3. **B** False. Searches of a computer are still constrained by the nature of the original warrant.

4. **C.** Exigent circumstances come into play when you don't have a search warrant.

5. **A, B, C, D.** A search warrant will specify who, what, when, and where the search can be carried out.

6. **A, B.** Protecting the evidence and conducting preliminary interviews are part of the duties of a first responder.

7. **B, C, D.** Determining changes made to data by automated applications, as well as login accounts and external devices, can help you identify other digital devices that should be seized.

8. **C.** The last thing to do during a witness interview is to get their signature.

9. **C.** Removing the battery from a portable device avoids accidental startup that may lose information.

10. **A, B.** Shutting down a running machine and using native tools that modify critical data are both common mistakes of a first responder.

11. **A, B, C.** Disk-to-disk, disk-to-image, and sparse file copy are all methods of data acquisition.

12. **A.** The method that provides a forensically sound copy.

13. **A.** Creating copies of evidence using two different tools is an example of contingency planning for data acquisition.

14. **A.** Static data collection only collects data from persistent storage.

15. **B.** CPU registers contain the most volatile data.

References

1. *Jacobsen*, 466 U.S. at 113.

2. *Jacobsen*, 466 U.S. at 113.

3. *United States v. Matlock*, 415 U.S. 164 (1974).

4. *Searching and Seizing Computers and Obtaining Evidence in Computer Investigations*, (Washington, DC: DOJ, 2009).

5. *Searching and Seizing*, p. 42.

6. Tsukayama, H. "Judge Allows Lawsuit Against Google's Gmail Scans to Move Forward." Retrieved from http://articles.washingtonpost.com/2013-09-26/business/42421388_1_gmail-users-google-s-marc-rotenberg.

7. *Electronic Crime Scene Investigation, A Guide for First Responders*, Second Edition (Washington, DC: DOJ, 2008), p. 18.

8. Shinder, D. L. *Attack Response Checklist and Flowchart* (NY: CBS Interactive, Inc., 2011). Retrieved from http://www.techproresearch.com/downloads/attack-response-checklist-and-flowchart.

9. Brezinski, D., and Killalea, T., Guidelines for Evidence Collection and Monitoring, RFC3227 (CA: IETF, 2002). Retrieved from http://www.ietf.org/rfc/rfc3227.txt, p. 4.

10. EC-Council. "First Responder Procedures," *Computer Forensics Investigation Procedures and Response* (NY: Cengage Learning, 2010), pp. 4–14.

11. EC-Council. "Data Acquisition and Duplication," *Computer Forensics: Investigating Data and Image Files* (NY: Cengage Learning, 2009), p. 2-2.

12. Brezinski, D., and Killalea, T., Guidelines for Evidence Collection and Monitoring, RFC3227 (CA: IETF, 2002). Retrieved from http://www.ietf.org/rfc/rfc3227.txt, p. 3.

13. Digital Data Acquisition Tool Test Assertions and Test Plan (Washington, DC: NIST, 2005). Retrieved from http://www.cftt.nist.gov/DA-ATP-pc-01.pdf, p. 4.

14. Henry, P. "Best Practices in Digital Evidence," Computer Forensics and Incident Response Blog. Retrieved from http://computer-forensics.sans.org/blog/2009/09/12/best-practices-in-digital-evidence-collection.

15. md5deep and hashdeep, latest version 4.3. Retrieved from http://md5deep.sourceforge.net.

Spinning Rust

After completing this chapter, you should be able to

- Define a hard disk drive, describe the various types of hard disk interfaces, and list the components of a hard disk
- Explain solid-state drives, CD-ROM/DVD file systems, RAID storage systems, and RAID levels
- Describe disk partitions and provide an overview of the physical and logical structures of a hard disk
- Describe file systems; explain the various types of file systems; provide an overview of Windows, Linux, Mac OS X, and Solaris 10 file systems; and explain file system analysis using the Sleuth Kit
- Explain how to recover deleted partitions and deleted files in Windows, Mac, and Linux, as well as how to identify the creation date, last accessed date of a file, and deleted subdirectories
- List partition recovery tools and file recovery tools for Windows, Mac OS X, and Linux
- Summarize steganography and its types, list the various applications of steganography, and discuss various digital steganography techniques
- Define steganalysis and explain how to detect steganography
- List various steganography detection tools and picture viewer and graphics file forensic tools, describe how to compress data, and describe how to process forensic images using MATLAB
- Explain Windows and Mac OS X boot processes

Now that we have created a forensically sound copy of a device's persistent storage, it's time to begin our forensic analysis of that data. We are still in the extraction phase, however, in that we are still in the process of extracting evidence from the raw materials we've collected. We won't start our actual analysis until we've extracted all the binary objects that will provide information that help us determine which of these digital objects has evidentiary value.

Brian Carrier, in his book *File System Forensic Analysis* details a path from the physical medium all the way through application analysis, as detailed in Figure 6-1.[1] Our

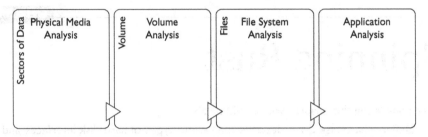

Figure 6-1 Levels of abstraction in disk analysis (Adapted from Carrier, B. *File System Forensic Analysis* (NJ: Pearson, 2005), p. 10.)

discussion of persistent storage parallels this model and helps make sense out of the seemingly random stream of bits that we have in our forensic copy.

Disk Drives and File Systems

As a digital forensics investigator (DFI), you need to understand how persistent storage is organized. While it would be convenient to focus just on files and file systems, you need to understand the physical layout of the disk drive in order to understand how data can be hidden on the disk so that it's not accessible via a file system interface.

NOTE Since I'm sure you're wondering, "spinning rust" is a nickname for disk drives, based on the color of the individual disk platters.

Everything You Wanted to Know About Disk Drives

At this time, there are two kinds of disk drives available: the regular kind of hard disk drives (HDD) and the new solid-state drives (SSDs). You may still find the plastic-covered 3¼" drives (diskettes) shown in Figure 6-2, and you need to have a drive capable of reading those disks.

Reading these disks may require an external driver (mine has a universal serial bus [USB] interface), since most computers manufactured in the last five years or so haven't included a so-called floppy drive (it's been replaced by an optical drive, or in some cases, an optical drive and a floppy drive that can be switched in and out). The original 8" floppy disks (and they were floppy—you could bend them in half), as well as the 5.5" floppies, are even rarer birds.

TIP You may not need to own an 8.5" floppy drive or a 3.5" drive, but it's prudent to do enough research to know where to find one in a hurry.

When we think of nonvolatile storage, our first thought is hard disk drives (HDDs). These hard disk drives are usually complex compared to floppy disks. These days, the most common sizes of hard disks are the 2.5-inch form factor for notebooks and

Figure 6-2 3.5", 2/5", 3¼" floppy drive, and USB stick

laptops, and a 3.5-inch form factor for larger PCs. Inside a PC, if there are two disks and the interface is integrated drive electronics (IDE) or parallel advanced technology attachment (PATA), then one of the disks is designated as the primary and one is secondary, although you may hear them referred to as master and slave. (As an aside, the original spec never mentions master and slave. The devices are referred to as device0 and device1.) The terms device0 and device1 aren't used with current serial advanced technology attachment (SATA) drives.

What Is a Hard Disk Drive?

A hard disk drive is a form of nonvolatile storage that uses magnetic media and can maintain data even in the absence of electricity. Another term for this is persistent storage. While the original definition of a hard disk was useful to compare and distinguish it from other forms of digital media (magnetic tape, floppy disks), nowadays, defining a hard disk is based on a particular interface specification and the protocols to which the storage medium responds. We'll learn later in this chapter that a solid-state drive (SSD) supports a standard interface and can be treated as if it was a hard disk drive, even though the technology used is vastly different from the earlier technologies.

Hard Disk Interfaces and the Components of a Hard Disk

First, a hard disk consists of a *spindle,* upon which are stacked *disk platters.* Data are stored on those platters in concentric circles called *tracks,* and each track consists of some number of disk *sectors* (usually 512 bytes per sector). Read/write heads, driven by an actuator motor, can move across the surfaces of the platters to read from each track.

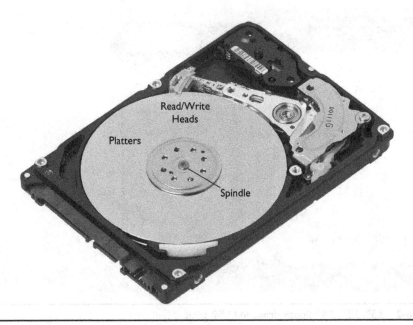

Figure 6-3 Disk drive internals

Each prescribed stopping place for the read/write heads is called a *cylinder.* Figure 6-3 shows the different parts of an HDD.[2]

There are 1,024 tracks per platter, numbered from 0 (the outermost track on the platter) to 1,023 (the innermost track on the platter), and a given number of sectors per track. Computing the total capacity of a drive is a function of the number of tracks, sectors per track, bytes per sector, and the number of read/write heads supported by the device. The resulting formula looks like this:

$$Total\ disk\ capacity = (bytes/sector) * (sectors/track) * (tracks/surface) * \#\ of\ surfaces$$

We can simplify that formula to be

$$Total\ disk\ capacity = (bytes/sector) * (sectors/track) * (total\ tracks)$$

One 2.5″ drive I have lists the following specifications: 13,424 cylinders, 15 heads, 63 sectors/track. Calculating the capacity is 512 * 63 * 13424 * 15 = 6.49 gigabytes (GB), which fortunately corresponds to the amount stated on the drive.

The computer identifies the location of the desired sector by using a sector address. The earliest form of addressing was CHS (cylinder, head, and sector). The address of the first sector on the disk would be (0, 0, 1). The first sector on the second header would be (0, 1, 1). CHS turned out to be unwieldy to use, as well as limiting the size of the disk that could be addressed, and was replaced by Logical Block Addressing (LBA). Here, the first sector of the disk is numbered 0, which is the same as CHS (0, 0, 1). LBA 2 is CHS (0, 0, 2).

One more thing: Although the size of a disk sector is usually fixed by the manufacturer, formatting the disk will allow you to specify the file system block size. The file system block size is a multiple of the sector size: 1,024, 4,028, and higher are common sizes. These file system blocks are also referred to as *clusters* (another overused word). The key point here is that the cluster size determines how much disk space is allocated to a single file. If the cluster size is 1,024 and the file size is 24, there are 1,000 bytes unused; this unused space is referred to as *slack space*. Slack space isn't the same as *unallocated space*, which refers to clusters that aren't assigned to any file (sometimes referred to as being on the "free list"). Unallocated space also isn't the same as clusters that are marked as associated with a file but no such file exists. These clusters are called *orphans* or *lost clusters* because they are unavailable to the operating system (OS) for allocation to another file... indeed, a waste of space.

The OS uses a particular protocol to send commands to the disk controller that manages read/write activity as well as using seek() commands to position the read/write heads. Communicating from the OS to the disk controller, as well as transferring data, depends on the physical interface of the device. Common interface types are

- ATA (PATA), SATA
- IDE, EIDE
- Fibre Channel (F-C)
- SCSI (small computer system interface)

Hard disks attach to the computer using a particular kind of interface. ATA stood for advanced technology attachment, and came to be called PATA (parallel ATA). SATA (serial ATA) cut down the number of pins needed in the attachment cable, as well as increasing the speed of the interface. SATA appeared in the ATA-7 specification that was released in 2003: The latest version is ATAPI-8, draft 2, released in 2006.

IDE is an acronym for integrated drive electronics, and EIDE is an acronym for enhanced IDE. Both of these interfaces actually use the ATA specification, but IDE indicated that the device controller was actually built into the drive's logic board. IDE corresponded to ATA-1, while EIDE contained some capabilities that were defined in the soon-to-be-published ATA-2 standard.

USB is short for Universal Serial Bus. It supports many different peripherals, including keyboards, mice, digital cameras, and digital audio devices. With the help of a USB hub, up to 227 devices can be connected to a single computer at one time. USB also provides an interface for hard disks that can be mounted in cases that provide a USB connection and that plugs into a USB port on the computer. The current standard for USB is 2.0, but it is backward compatible with the earlier 1.0 and 1.1 standards. USB 3.0 has appeared recently and promises to become the new standard for USB drives.

SCSI stands for small computer system interface, and provides faster transfer than IDE/EIDE. You can add a SCSI disk by adding a SCSI controller card and an expansion slot onto a computer. SCSI daisy-chains the disks together and allows for 16 disks (numbered 0 through 15).

Last, Fibre Channel is yet another American National Standards Institute (ANSI) standard that uses optical fiber to connect a device to storage devices. You won't usually encounter Fibre Channel interfaces outside of a data center. Fibre Channel technology once was the workhorse of storage area networks (SANs), although these days you may find SANs using iSCSI interfaces (SCSI over IP) as well as Fibre Channel over IP (FCIP). Gigabit Ethernet has come to challenge Fibre Channel as the medium of choice within data centers, primarily because of cost.

 NOTE It's the SCSI protocol that actually provides the commands to the disk controller; Fibre Channel and IP are the network protocols that send it on its way.

The Physical and Logical Structure of a Hard Disk

The physical structure of an HDD consists of sectors, tracks, and cylinders. Although a DFI needs to understand these structures and may find it necessary to work at that level using appropriate tools, higher-level abstractions make the problem of working with disk drives more tractable.

The Host-Protected Area and the Device Configuration Overlay

Before we leave the subject of the physical structure of a hard disk, there are two areas on an HDD that aren't usually accessible by ordinary user commands. These are the host-protected area (HPA), introduced in ATA-4, and the device configuration overlay (DCO), introduced in ATA-6. The intent of the HPA was to create a space on the disk where a vendor could locate information that wouldn't be overwritten if the device were physically formatted. The intent of the DCO was to allow configuration changes that would limit the capabilities of the disk in some ways, such as showing a smaller size or indicating that certain features were unimplemented. The DCO can hide sectors allocated to itself and to the HPA, if one exists. On a 40GB hard disk with a 1-GB DCO and a 1-GB HPA, the DCO would show the size of the disk to be 38GB. The reason a DFI needs to know this is that these areas can contain hidden data, executable files, or both. However, this requires that the suspect has access to tools that can actually access these areas on the disk and that the suspect has appropriate permissions to do so.

Partitions A partition is logical structure overlaid on a physical HDD, and is represented as a series of entries in a table that indicate a starting block and a length. Following Brian Carrier,[3] I'm going to make the distinction between partitions and volumes. A partition has all its sectors on one physical disk, whereas a volume may have sectors on multiple physical disks. Unless it's necessary, I'll follow the convention of using the word "partition" to indicate a volume on a single physical disk and the word "volume" to indicate a volume defined across multiple physical drives.

 EXAM TIP A partition will refer to a single volume unless specified otherwise.

Figure 6-4 shows the format of an MS-DOS partition table that is contained in the master boot record (MBR) of a disk specified as a boot disk. The first two entries are primary partitions(as opposed to extended), one labeled as a recovery partition and one labeled as the primary partition that contains the OS. Partition 0 is an extended partition that covers the rest of the disk and contains two logical partitions.

Figure 6-5 shows the same information but in a much friendlier format. Right-clicking the icon in the topmost window brings up a menu that, among other things, will allow you to delete that particular volume.

Notice that the graphic in the lower portion of the screen doesn't indicate the extended partition; rather, we only see the two logical partitions, both marked as primary.

SSD, USB, and Flash Memory Drives

We've mentioned USB drives previously based on their hardware connection to a digital device. Both USB drives and SSDs differ markedly from the technologies that we're used to in the HDD world. Both of these device types use flash memory chips instead of magnetic surfaces to record data. Both require memory chips that don't lose data when disconnected from a power supply.

Flash Memory Cards The cards, or "sticks," come in form factors, such as SD and microSD, with storage from 2GB all the way up to 64GB and more. All of these devices require a card reader of the appropriate type to actually read the contents of the card. Common uses of these cards include removable storage for cameras or handheld devices (old-school personal digital assistants [PDAs] and now smart phones, tablet computers, and netbooks).

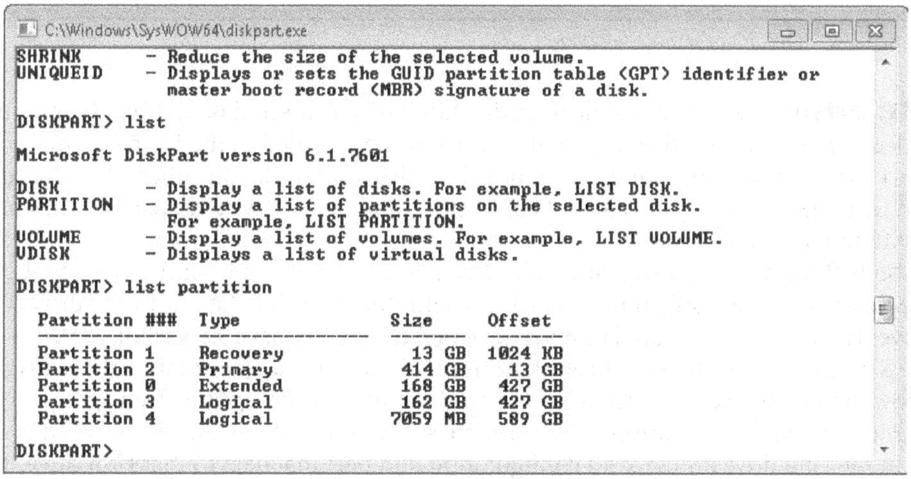

Figure 6-4 Diskpart display of partitions on disk 0

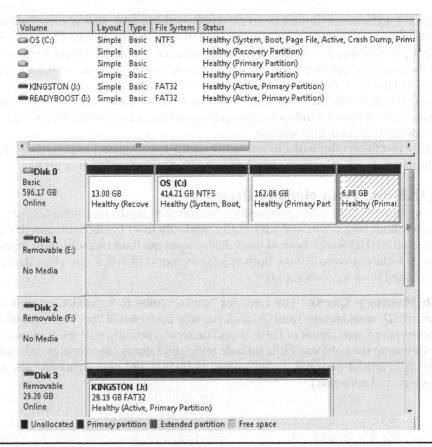

Volume	Layout	Type	File System	Status
OS (C:)	Simple	Basic	NTFS	Healthy (System, Boot, Page File, Active, Crash Dump, Prima
	Simple	Basic		Healthy (Recovery Partition)
	Simple	Basic		Healthy (Primary Partition)
	Simple	Basic		Healthy (Primary Partition)
KINGSTON (J:)	Simple	Basic	FAT32	Healthy (Active, Primary Partition)
READYBOOST (I:)	Simple	Basic	FAT32	Healthy (Active, Primary Partition)

Disk 0
Basic
596.17 GB
Online

13.00 GB	OS (C:)	162.06 GB	6.89 GB
Healthy (Recove	414.21 GB NTFS	Healthy (Primary Part	Healthy (Primar
	Healthy (System, Boot,		

Disk 1
Removable (E:)

No Media

Disk 2
Removable (F:)

No Media

Disk 3
Removable
29.20 GB
Online

| KINGSTON (J:) |
| 29.19 GB FAT32 |
| Healthy (Active, Primary Partition) |

■ Unallocated ■ Primary partition ■ Extended partition □ Free space

Figure 6-5   Disk Management window

USB Drives   Like flash memory cards, USB (Universal Serial Bus) drives (sometimes called pen drives since they are small enough to be installed in the head of a ballpoint pen) use flash memory for storage, but they also contain a controller such that they can be plugged directly into a USB connector on a digital device. Capacity varies from 64MB to 64GB and more.

Both flash memory cards and USB drives usually have a physical switch that puts the device into read-only mode, which is useful for acquiring data from the drive. USB drives can also be configured as boot devices; I personally have an 8GB drive that loads the Samurai Web Testing Framework from InGuardians. Larger bootable drives (4GB+) allow the OS to save configuration information on local storage between uses.

Another use for USB drives is for portable software—software that is packaged to run from the USB drive and save all configuration and personal data to that USB drive. This differs from the previously mentioned use of a USB drive because the drive requires an OS to actually run the files (the software from www.portableapps.com requires a Windows OS). If a suspect has been using this kind of device, certain log and history files may be stored on the USB drive and not on the HDD of the desktop or laptop computer.

SSD Drives The advent of solid-state drives (SSDs) has caused some consternation within the forensics community due to the way that data are managed on the SSD drive. Because of issues of wear (NAND memory can only be written to approximately 100,000 times), the drive controller will move a logical disk block from memory block to memory block as a way of wear-leveling access to each memory block. The sequential nature of block allocation on HDD doesn't apply to SSD drives.

Two issues further complicate retrieving data. Many manufacturers provide a SECURE ERASE function that will either automatically erase the entire drive or, in the case of encrypted driver, delete the encryption key. A second issue is how memory blocks are freed (marked as reusable). In order to inform the controller that a block marked as "Not In Use" is ready to be reused, applications can ask the controller to TRIM these blocks, with the result that these blocks are placed on a queue for the garbage collection (GC) process to erase (overwritten with all 1's) and marked as free.

All of this depends on whether the OS in question actually supports the TRIM command. Some older SSDs do not support this command, and the TRIM command is only fully supported for NT File System (NTFS) partitions and not for File Allocation Table (FAT) partitions.[4]

CD-ROM/DVD File Systems

CD-ROM (Compact Disc Read-Only Memory) (usually abbreviated to CD) and DVD (Digital Video Disc) are different specifications for optical drives. CDs are capable of storing about 700MB, while a DVD can store up to 4GBs (8GBs if recorded double-sided). CD/DVD media are usually formatted according to the ISO 9660 standard. Common extensions to that standard are Rock Ridge, which supports long filenames (128 characters) for Unix; Joliet extensions, which support 64-character filenames for Windows; and the El Torito extensions, which allow a CD/DVD to be used as a boot device.

We mentioned earlier that one of the things to avoid when transporting or storing digital devices was electromagnetic radiation (such as speakers). Fortunately, we don't have to be concerned with that for CD or DVDS, since they are electro-optical media and aren't affected by electromagnetic radiation. But since they are not encased when in use, they can be altered by scratches, especially scratches that follow the single data track that begins at the center of the platter and grows outward to the outside edge of the disk.

Blu-ray is a more recent recording technique for optical media that utilizes a blue laser instead of a red laser. Blue lasers can be focused more precisely, which allows for increased packing density. Blu-ray discs can store anywhere from 25GB (single layer) to 50GB (dual layer). In order to support the increased density, Blu-ray relies on newer hard-coating technologies to prevent scratches. Combined with improved error-correction algorithms, this means that Blu-ray disks are increasingly resistant to damage from scratches.

RAID Storage Systems

RAID originally stood for "redundant array of inexpensive disks," although the acronym is usually expanded nowadays as "redundant array of independent disks," perhaps because of the expense of several commercial RAID systems. The idea behind it is strikingly simple:

Instead of buying ever-increasing capacity on single drives, spread the storage load across multiple drives, which appear to the host OS as a single volume. RAID uses three strategies to achieve its goal:

- **Mirroring**, in which a write to a disk block on one drive is copied (mirrored) to a disk block on a second drive.
- **Striping**, where a byte or a block is written across multiple drives in stripes.
- **Parity**, where parity blocks are replicated across multiple drives. Parity is defined as a value that is computed such that the value of one of the elements that make up the calculations can be lost, but it's possible to recompute that value based on the parity settings.

Here's an example of how parity works. Imagine we have three values: A is 1, B is 0, and C is 0. We use the binary operation XOR (exclusive OR) to compute the parity. A *xor* B is 1 and 1 *xor* C is 1, so the parity calculation for these values is 1. If we lost C, we still have A and B. A *xor* B is 1, and parity is 1. Given how the *xor* function works, we know that C must have the value 0 if the parity is set to 1.

 NOTE *xor* is defined as 1 if A is 1 or B is 1, but not both, and as 0 if A and B are both 0 or both 1. Another fun fact is that A *xor* B *xor* B = A, which makes cryptographers very happy.

All RAID types are based on these three strategies: mirroring with striping, striping with mirroring, and interspersed parity (either single-disk parity or multiple-disk parity). RAID technologies are characterized by multiple levels:

- **RAID-0** Data is striped across multiple drives. There is no parity checking and no mirroring. If you lose one disk of many, you lose the entire volume. You trade off improved performance and additional storage space for fault tolerance.
- **RAID-1** Data is mirrored from one drive to another, without parity or striping. Reads are served from the fastest device, and writes are acknowledged only after both disks have been updated (which means that your writes are gated by your slowest device). The RAID array will function as long as one drive is operating.

 NOTE I'm a fan of RAID-1 after I lost a disk containing years of historical data (pictures, e-mail, papers, and so forth). With RAID-1, it was a simple matter of purchasing a new drive, slotting it into the chassis, and restarting the device. Data from the surviving disk was copied to the new disk, and I was ready to go.

- **RAID-2** Bit-level striping with parity. In this design, each bit is written to a different drive, and parity is computed for each byte and stored on a single drive that is part of the RAID set. I've never encountered one of these in the wild.

- **RAID-3**   Byte-level striping with dedicated parity. Bytes are striped across all drives, and parity is stored on a dedicated drive.

- **RAID-4**   Block striping with dedicated parity, but the parity is stored on a single drive instead of distributed across multiple drives. Each drive operates independently, and input/output (I/O) requests can be performed in parallel.

- **RAID-5**   Block-level striping with dedicated parity. In this case, however, parity is distributed along with the data. All drives but one must be present for the array to work, and there must be at least three drives (for the mathematically inclined, $N > 3$, $N - 1$ drives available). If one drive is unavailable, a read can be satisfied by using the remaining drive and the distributed parity.

- **RAID-6**   Block-level striping with distributed parity. This arrangement provides fault tolerance for up to two failed drives ($N - 2$), although failure of a single drive will affect performance until the failed drive is replaced and its data rebuilt from the parity blocks and the rest of the drives in the array.

Now comes the good part. RAID arrays can be nested, thereby creating hybrid arrays. Nested RAID types are again based on the three strategies mentioned earlier: mirroring with striping, striping with mirroring, and interspersed parity (single-disk parity or multiple-disk parity). Different RAID technologies are characterized by combining the levels described earlier:

- **RAID 0+1**   A mirror of stripes (data are striped, stripes are mirrored).

- **RAID 1+0 (aka RAID 10)**   A stripe of mirrors. Data are mirrored; each mirror is striped across multiple drives.

- **RAID 100 (RAID 1+0+0)**   A stripe of RAID 10s.

- **RAID 0+3**   Provides a dedicated parity array across striped disks.

- **RAID 30**   Supports striping of dedicated parity arrays (a combination of RAID level 3 and RAID level 0).

- **RAID 50**   This strategy combines level 0 striping with the RAID-5 distributed parity. RAID-5 requires at least six drives (four data drives and two parity drives).

Encountering a RAID system can be a "flusterating" experience (both frustrating and flustering) for a DFI. Logical volumes created on RAID arrays are measured in gigabytes, terabytes, or larger, and the larger the volume, the longer it takes to acquire, and the larger the space needed to store that data. In these cases, creating a sparse copy may be the best strategy for acquiring data. RAID is an example of an instance where we need to refer to a volume instead of a partition, since a RAID volume can involve multiple physical drives in bewildering arrangements.

 EXAM TIP   Know your RAID levels and combinations.

In RAID, you are at least one level removed from the actual physical drive. You no longer have access to the individual disk as you would on a laptop or desktop system: Instead, you are writing data that are intercepted by at least the disk controller for the RAID array, if not intervening hardware and software systems as well. Writing to hidden areas of the drives that make up the array is less likely, and the same situation arises when accessing network file systems using CIFS (Common Internet File System) or NFS (Network File System). A user simply doesn't have access to the tools or the permissions to make these kinds of modifications (and it's not clear that a storage administrator has that capability either).

In all cases, though, remember that these logical volumes will be configured with a particular file system, and any rules regarding file systems construction will apply to a logical volume as well.

File Systems

Our next level of abstraction concerning persistent storage is the file system. A file system is an abstraction overlaid on disk partitions, consisting of a set of data structures describing the various kinds of objects that a file system can contain, as well as a set of algorithms that determine where and how information is stored on that disk drive.

The usual procedure for creating a file system is relatively simple. On Linux systems, the command would be

```
mkfs.ext3 /dev/sda2      # creates an ext3 file system
```

that simply asks the OS to create an ext3 (extended file system 3) on the partition identified as /dev/sda2. The same command on Windows would be

```
format D: /FS:ntfs
```

What Are File Systems?

Most modern file systems treat everything as a file, although some files are more special than others. Most file systems provide a hierarchical view of the world where there are regular files and special files called directories that contain files and other (sub) directories. There are two general kinds of file systems: journaled and nonjournaled. Journaled file systems maintain a separate data structure to which all modifications to the disk are appended. After this journal is successfully updated, the actual data are written to disk. If the write fails, the disk can be constructed using the information provided in the journal file. Journaled file systems are faster to restore after a crash, since the entire file system doesn't have to be checked for consistency.

File Systems for Windows, Mac, Linux, and Sun Solaris

Many, many different kinds of files systems are in use, not to mention those that have fallen by the wayside and are seen infrequently, if at all. We'll cover the most likely ones that a DFI would encounter on Windows, Mac, Linux, and Sun Solaris machines.

The Windows FAT File System Windows provides two different types of file systems: variations of the FAT file system, and NTFS that originally debuted with Windows NT. FAT file systems come in different flavors: FAT, FAT16, VFAT, and FAT32. FAT32 is the most commonly used today, and many optical drives such as USB drives or SD Cards are formatted using FAT32 (most operating systems can read a FAT32 file system). Table 6-1 lists pertinent information about the various flavors of FAT file systems.

 EXAM TIP Because of the inefficient use of space, some claim that FAT16 can only handle volumes up to 2GB.

NTFS NTFS (once "New Technology File System," but now just plain ol' NTFS) is fully supported only by Windows, although there are tools on Linux and Max OS X that will read from and write to NTFS file systems. NTFS supports 64-bit cluster numbers, and when combined with a 64-KB cluster allows volumes up to 16 exabytes (16 billion gigabytes), although practical implementations are effectively limited to 32-bit cluster numbers. The default cluster size for NTFS is 4KB when the volume size is over 2GB.

The heart of NTFS is the Master File Table (MFT). An MFT is constructed for each volume configured with an NTFS file system. Among its other capabilities, NTFS can compress files and encrypt single files or entire directory hierarchies.

Table 6-2 lists the elements of the MFT.[5]

Mac File Systems Mac OS X uses the Hierarchical File System (HFS) and HFS+. HFS+ was a modification to HFS that supported larger volumes sizes. HFS itself uses seven different data structures on disk to manage its file systems:

- The Volume Header starts after the first 1,024 bytes of the volume. It contains information about the date and time the volume was created and the number of files on the volume.

- The Allocation File indicates whether a particular block is allocated or free.

- The Extents Overflow File contains file extents (allocated file blocks) if a file is larger than eight extents, which are stored in the volume's catalog file. A list of bad blocks is also kept in this file.

File System	Bits Used to Identify Clusters	Other Characteristics
FAT12	12 bits (4,096 clusters)	Limits volume size to 32MB. Mostly used for diskettes.
FAT16	16 bits (65,535 clusters)	Wasted space for disks of 2GB or more; can handle volumes up to 4GB. VFAT was an extension to FAT16 to support long filenames.
FAT32	32 bits (first 4 bits are reserved), resulting in 268,435,456 clusters	Theoretical upper limit is 8TB, with 32-KB sectors. New FAT32 volumes are limited to 32GB and file sizes are limited to 4GB because the file length is stored as a 32-bit number.

Table 6-1 FAT File System Characteristics (Source: FAT File System. Retrieved from http://technet.microsoft.com/en-us/library/cc938438.aspx.)

MFT Record	System File	Filename	Description
0	Master File Table	$Mft	Information on files and folders on an NTFS volume
1	Master File Table 2	$MftMirr	Mirror of the first four records of the MFT
2	Log File	$LogFile	Transaction log for file recovery
3	Volume	$Volume	Information about the volume, including label and version information
4	Attribute Definitions	$AttrDef	Names, numbers, and descriptions of attributes used in NTFS
5	Root Filename Index	$	Root folder
6	Cluster Bitmap	$Bitmap	Which clusters are used on the volume
7	Boot Cluster File	$Boot	Information needed to mount the volume; bootstrap loader code is stored here if the volume is bootable
8	Bad Cluster File	$BadClus	Information about bad clusters on the volume
9	Security File	$Secure	Unique security descriptors for files
10	Upcase Table	$Upcase	Information on converting Unicode characters from uppercase to lowercase
11	NTFS Extension File	$Extend	Optional extensions, including quota and object identifiers
12–15	Unused: Reserved For Future Use		

Table 6-2 NTFS Master File Table

- The Catalog File describes the folder and file hierarchy. It is stored as a B-tree to allow speedy searches. It stores the file and folder names (up to 255 characters).
- The Attributes File stores additional file attributes.
- The Startup File is used to boot non–Mac OS machines from an HFS+ volume.

The end of the volume contains a second volume header that precedes the last 512 bytes of the volume—those bytes are reserved.

One thing to remember about Mac file systems is that files are composed of two "forks": a data fork and a resource fork. The data fork stores what we normally think of as the contents of the file, while the resource fork stores such things as font files, language translation files, icons, and so forth. This file format has been superseded on other systems by a file type that appears as a single file, but is in fact an archive of files, each containing some aspect of the complete files. An example of this is the Microsoft Word .docx file. This file actually consists of several other files containing the text of the document and other information.

The Windows NTFS file system provides the capability for a user to create an alternate data stream (ADS). This capability allows you to attach one file to another, but the file that is attached is essentially invisible to normal directory listing tools. The file size of the original is the same as it was before the other file was appended.

Earlier versions of Windows (starting with Windows NT and later) would not show these files using normal directory listing tools (Windows Explorer and the *dir* command). In Windows 7, the *dir* command has a parameter (/R) that will list alternate data streams. We'll have more to say about ADS in Chapter 7 when we discuss Windows forensics.

Linux File Systems   File systems currently used in the Linux world include ext2, ext3, ext4, ReiserFS, Reiser4, and ZFS. Ext2 was the standard following the .ext file system, and ext3 and ext4 have extended its capabilities. Ext3 added journaling, and ext4 added the ability to address storage up to 1EB (exabyte) of data.

In Linux, a directory entry (*dentry*) consists of a filename and an inode (many files can refer to a single inode). Other objects in a Linux file system are superblocks, files, and inodes (the original reason for this name has been lost in the mists of time). The superblock is the first block on the disk (inode 1) and contains metadata about the file system. This block is important enough that a copy of it is stored at multiple locations on the partition. The inode holds the file's metadata as well as a list of data block addresses. Depending on the file size, the inode can point to an indirect block where each entry is the address of a disk block that contains file data. This setup is called an indirect block, and it's possible to have double- and triple-indirect blocks as well.

> **NOTE**   For the curious, the double-indirect block would have pointers to another indirect block that would itself have pointers to the actual data blocks. Triple-indirect blocks would add yet another set of pointers. Whew!

The ZFS File System   The ZFS file system had its origins with Sun Microsystems and has recently appeared as an option for Linux computers. ZFS is short for Zettabyte File System, and as you may have guessed, it was created to handle large files. ZFS utilizes *zpools* that are in turn composed of *vdevs* that map to one or more physical devices, including RAID devices. Block sizes can range as high as 128KB, with 128 bits to number clusters: For the curious, $2**128$ is $3.4028237e + 38$, or more more specifically

340,282,366,920,938,463,463,374,607,431,768,211,456

Multiplied by the block size, of course.

Example: File System Analysis Using the Sleuth Kit

The Sleuth Kit (TSK) is a set of open-source digital forensic tools overseen by Brian Carrier at www.sleuthkit.org. As described on their web site:

> The Sleuth Kit™ (TSK) is a library and collection of command line tools that allow you to investigate disk images. The core functionality of TSK allows you to analyze volume and file system data. The plug-in framework allows you to incorporate additional modules to analyze file contents and build automated

systems. The library can be incorporated into larger digital forensics tools and the command line tools can be directly used to find evidence.[6]

If you are approaching a file system analysis for the first time, three tools from the TSK stand out. *fsstat* displays details of a particular file system, including the range of metadata values (*inode* numbers) and content units (blocks or clusters). The layout for each group is listed, providing the underlying file system supports this notion (FFS and EXTFS). Figure 6-6 shows the output of *fsstat* when run on an image (istick.img) of a USB drive captured using the *dd* command.

The *fls* tool lists allocated and deleted files in a directory. Figure 6-7 shows the (abbreviated) output of the *fls* command. Deleted files are highlighted in the listing.

Once you've determined the deleted file that you're interested in, you can retrieve that file using the *icat* command, which writes the file to the standard output device

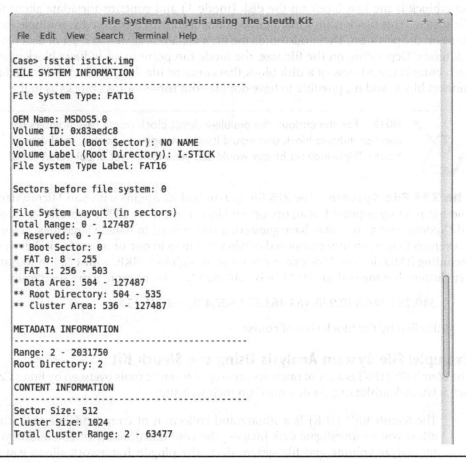

Figure 6-6 *fsstat* output

```
                 File System Analysis using The Sleuth Kit            —  +  x
 File  Edit  View  Search  Terminal  Help
Case> cat istick.lst
r/r 3:  I-STICK      (Volume Label Entry)
d/d 5:  DropBox
d/d 7:  GSAP-Assess
d/d 9:  Security Lab
d/d 10: MSIA
r/r * 11:       _~1.TRA
d/d 14: CycleOfImprovement
d/d 17: IT_Security_Program
r/r * 19:          cpu-z-141.zip
r/r 20: bcp72.pdf
d/d 21: X.80x
d/d 23: PowerPoint
[...]
r/r * 84:       note (copy).txt
r/r 86: msls31.dll
r/r * 88:       note.txt
r/r 91: ScrumMaster.gif
d/d 93: .Trash-1000
d/d 95: Licenses
v/v 2031747:    $MBR
v/v 2031748:    $FAT1
v/v 2031749:    $FAT2
d/d 2031750:    $OrphanFiles
Case>
```

Figure 6-7 *fls* command output showing deleted files

(usually the terminal) or a file. Figure 6-8 shows the results of the *icat* command and the first few lines of the recovered file.

How do I know what kind of file it is? Files can be identified by their file extension, by a "magic number" found at the beginning of a file, or by an identifiable pattern in the file structure. Microsoft Windows uses the file extension, whereas Linux looks for a "magic number" within the first file block of the file, or for a particular pattern. The Linux *file* command utilizes a database of specifications that can identify particular kinds of files.

```
                 Using The Sleuth Kit for File System Analysis
 File  Edit  View  Search  Terminal  Help
Case> icat istick.img 88 >rnote.txt
Case> cat rnote.txt
for now is the time
for all good men
to come to the aid
of the party hearty
Case>
```

Figure 6-8 *icat* command output and file listing

Getting the Boot

All operating systems go through a similar process once the power is switched on. "It's the same thing, only different" was never truer than in this case, and so it's worth looking at each of the mainstream operating systems to detail the variations in each. "Booting" the system comes from the old adage of "pulling oneself up by your own bootstraps," and this is exactly what the OS does. The general idea is to execute a small piece of code that exists in read-only memory (ROM) that loads the "bootloader "software. That software, in turn, does a little more and then hands the process off to yet more powerful and capable software, which may be the operating system itself or another bootloader.

The generic version of the boot process goes something like this. After power-on, the central processing unit (CPU) executes code from ROM that performs two steps: validate that all elements of the computer are working normally via a power-on self-test (POST), and load the OS into memory. These goals can be achieved by either a single program or multiple smaller programs (a multistage bootloader). Usually, the user is offered an option to choose a particular boot device or to use the default. Options include a hard disk, a CD-ROM drive, a USB device, or the network, where the local hard disk is the default. Choosing a CD-ROM drive or a USB device enables you to boot a computer using a different OS than what is installed on the machine's installed drive (HDD or SSD). That drive is still discovered by the booted OS, but is not modified and can be mounted as read-only.

 TIP Booting from a nonwriteable media such as a CD makes sense if you suspect that the machine may have some kind of malware installed that could affect the operation of the OS.

The MBR is the first 512 bytes on the chosen boot device and ends with two bytes 0X55AA (a boot sector signature). The MBR contains a master partition table that contains a complete description of the partitions that are contained on the storage device and the master boot code that acts as an OS-independent chained bootloader. Figure 6-9 shows the contents of an MBR on a Linux machine. You can retrieve this information via this command:

```
dd if=/dev/sda of=mbr.bin bs=512 count=1
```

The basic input/output system (BIOS) reads the master boot code from the MBR and executes that code. That code indicates which volume bootloader to use in case the computer is configured to dual- or triple-boot into a different OS. It's at this point that things start to get interesting.

Microsoft Windows

As a DFI, you will encounter many different operating systems in the field, and many of them will be running some version of Windows. As of this writing, the newest version of Microsoft Windows is 8.1, but you may encounter 7, Vista, and XP Service Pack 3. Windows XP and earlier had one type of boot process; Vista and later versions have another.

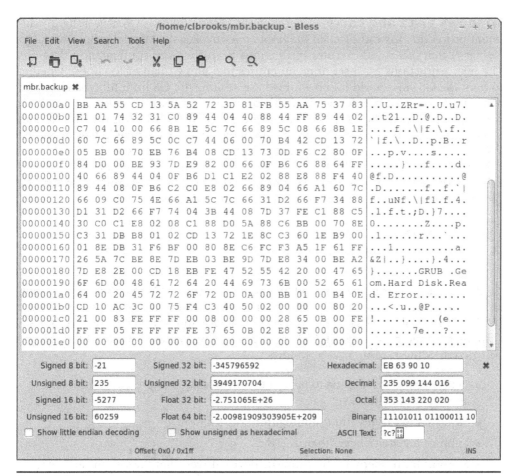

Figure 6-9 Contents of a master boot record

Windows XP Service Pack 3 The first stage of the process for booting Windows XP is starting the *ntldr* program that loads system device drivers so that it can load files from any supported file system type. If a boot.ini file exists, *ntldr* will read that file and display a menu of options. If the chosen OS is Windows XP, *ntldr* will load the ntdect. exe file to choose a hardware profile. The second stage is the *ntoskrnl*, which proceeds as follows:

- Starts all executive subsystems.
- Loads and starts the I/O manager and then starts loading all the system driver files as well as the *smss* (Session Manager Subsystem).
- The *smss* loads the win32k.sys device driver. At this point, the screen is switched into graphics mode. The winlogon.exe program starts the login process, and the local security authority (lsass.exe) processes the logon dialog box.

Windows Vista and Later Later versions of the Windows OS have a slightly different procedure. Instead of *ntldr*, the boot code invokes the Windows Boot Manager (*bootmgr*) that reads and executes instructions from the boot configuration data file. The first instructions are a set of menu entries that allow the user to choose whether to boot the OS via our old friend winload.exe, resume the OS from hibernation, boot an earlier version of Windows (via *ntldr*), or execute a volume bootloader. The boot configuration file can be edited by various programs, one of which is bcdedit.exe, and can boot third-party software. This is one point where the suspect could have modified Windows startup to invoke software that would obliterate evidence.

Winload.exe then starts by loading the OS kernel (ntoskrnl.exe) and other device drivers required at this point in the boot process. Once the OS kernel is loaded, the process is much like what happens in Windows XP and earlier.

 EXAM TIP The stages of the Windows XP boot process are *ntldr*, *ntoskrnl*, *smss*, WinLogin.exe, and *lsass*.

MBRs have been around for a good long time, as has the BIOS that provides the bootstrap code. Since 2010, a newer specification, the Unified Extensible Firmware Interface (UEFI), is gradually advancing, driven by Microsoft's announcement that Windows 8 computers would need to use it. UEFI has several improvements over the BIOS. Microsoft[7] describes these advantages as follows:

- Better security by helping to protect the pre-startup—or pre-boot—process against bootkit attacks

- Faster startup times and resuming from hibernation

- Support for drives larger than 2.2TB

- Support for modern, 64-bit firmware device drivers that the system can use to address more than 17.2 billion GB of memory during startup

- Capability to use BIOS with UEFI hardware

The key to understanding the UEFI specification as it relates to persistent storage is the notion of a GUID partition table (GPT). The GPT replaces the MBR for disk partitioning. Some OS tools already understand the structure of the GPT and are able to both recognize and create a partition of this type.

For the DFI, the GPT represents an opportunity for the technically adept suspect to hide data in yet more places, as well as providing more places for malware to hide. Fortunately, it appears that creating a forensic duplicate of a drive using the GPT format will contain all the necessary data as a drive that uses an MBR.

 TIP In order to support legacy systems, a drive that uses the GPT format will create an MBR sector that indicates that the drive is full. The experienced DFI will know to check for the presence of the GPT.

Linux

Compared to Windows, Linux is simplicity itself. The BIOS reads the master boot record and loads either LILO (Linux Loader) or GRUB (Grand Unified Bootloader), although GRUB 2 is now increasingly common. Either of these will ask the user to choose a particular OS. Once chosen, the boot loader will start the operating system and hand off control. The OS will look for the *init* program and start it (*init* is the parent of all processes that start up automatically). *init* then reads the file */etc/inittab* and executes commands listed within that file for a particular OS state called the *run level*. Successful execution of programs at a particular run level allows the system to transition to a higher run level.

Mac OS X

Mac OS X is closer to Linux than to Windows given that at the command line, at least, Mac OS X is based on a Berkeley Systems Division (BSD) version of UNIX.

 NOTE   Strictly speaking, Mac OS X runs a BSD "personality" on top of the Mach microkernel.

The boot process for Mac OS X is less readily understood because it uses Open Firmware. Open Firmware is the first program executed when the machine is powered on, and is a good place to stop and examine the configuration of the computer (provided you're familiar with the Open Firmware command set). The firmware loads the BootX loader, which goes through a number of hardware configuration steps, the last of which is to determine if the OS kernel is compressed, whether it is a "fat binary" (contains code for Intel and PowerPC processors), and whether it is Mach binary or an executable and linking format (ELF) binary. If all goes well, BootX will load the OS kernel. The kernel, in turn, starts its *init* that performs some Mach-specific tasks and then starts the */sbin/init* process. The rest of the startup process that follows is virtually identical to the Linux boot rprocess. The last step in this process is to start /sbin/Systemstarter, which starts up configured startup items (/System/Library/StartupItems and /Library/StartupItems). The login application, *loginwindow.app*, starts, and the user can log in to the running system.

What Runs When?

The primary issue with the boot process of any device is determining which programs run during initial system startup. A suspect may include code as part of this sequence that will destroy evidence related to their activities. The *autoruns* program from the SysInternals folks at Microsoft will list all the programs that are scheduled to run when the system is started. In Linux, it's easy enough to check the entries in the /etc/rcN.d directories (which in turn should be symbolic links back to programs in the /etc/init.d directory). In Mac OS X, inspecting the files in /Library/StartupItems and /System/Library/StartupItems can provide a hint as to whether additional software has been installed.

Booting from a Live CD

Since you can configure a computer to choose a different boot device (a CD-ROM, USB drive, first hard disk, or the network), you can easily boot a device from a CD-ROM or a USB key that can run an alternative operating system. Several forensic distributions are distributed as a "live" distribution that can be run directly from a CD-ROM, with the OS entirely in memory, or from a USB device that offers the ability to save data to that drive. Once the forensic software is operating, the disk of the suspect's computer could be mounted read-only.

Another technique is to use a forensics distribution provided as a virtual machine image. These images can be executed by VMware Workstation, VMware Player, or VirtualBox. External devices can be attached to these VMs and examined by the forensics software.

Recovering Deleted Files and Partitions

We've just spent the preceding section talking about the physical and logical layout of a disk drive. We have to take into account what happens when certain elements are removed or deleted from a file system. What happens when someone deletes a partition? What happens when someone deletes a file? Both of these actions can take place intentionally or unintentionally. If a file or partition is deleted accidentally, we're in the realm of data recovery. If it's done deliberately, then we're in the realm of forensic data recovery.

 NOTE I recall when a colleague of mine wrote over the partition table of a disk containing another colleague's Ph.D. thesis research—raw data, results, software developed as part of this research—everything. Although the situation turned out okay (files could be recovered), there were some extremely anxious moments and two very distraught people.

One difference between data recovery and forensic data recovery is that in forensic data recovery, we are much more interested in the modified/accessed/created (MAC) times of the deleted file. Establishing the time at which the file or partition was deleted becomes part of our forensic timeline analysis. For data recovery, we may be interested in a larger block of time ("I deleted that file last Tuesday late in the afternoon—between 4:00 and 6:00 P.M.").

Recovering Disk Partitions

As we saw earlier, disk partitions are laid out in a partition table that occupies the first 512 bytes at offset 0 of the disk. When a partition is deleted, it means that the space is reallocated to another partition, or effectively becomes unavailable because it is no longer recognized by the host OS. That doesn't mean that the data on that partition are gone forever; rather, it means that those clusters are now unavailable to the disk as a whole until the partitions are reconfigured.

If a partition is hidden, that partition is no longer visible to the end user. The OS is aware of this partition, but it won't list it on any of the standard desktop tools. Unhiding a partition is relatively easy using the system tools provided with your OS. For instance, you can unhide a partition by unsetting the "hidden" flag that is set in the partition header on some systems. On Windows, you can hide a partition by using the diskpart program to remove the drive letter assigned to the partition. Select the appropriate drive and issue the command "remove drive e:". You can also manipulate a registry key, HKEY_CURRENT_USER\Software\Microsoft\Windows\CurrentVersion\Policies\Explore, to indicate which partitions are logically hidden to Windows Explorer and other software. Create a new DWORD value named *NoDrives* for that key, and enter a value that represents a bit mask to indicate which drive letters should be ignored (drive A is 1, drive B is 2, drive C is 4, drive D is 8, and so on up to drive Z). And yes, you can combine the values: A value of 3 would ignore drives A and B.[8]

Various programs can manipulate partition tables. One of my favorites is gparted (Gnome Partition Editor), a graphical version of the Linux commands *parted* and *fdisk*. Windows offers Partition Magic, a third-party solution, as well as diskpart and disk-mgmt.msc (both native Windows software). Figure 6-10 shows the user interface to the *gparted* command.

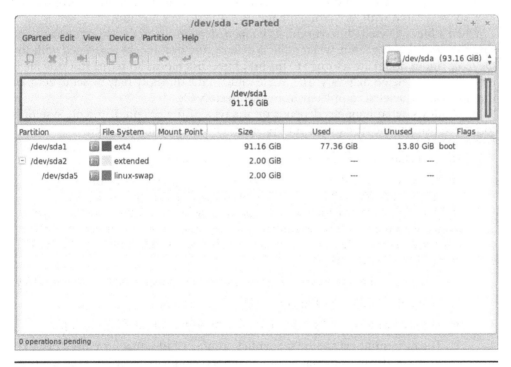

Figure 6-10 gparted user interface

Recovering Disk Partitions

Recovering deleted disk partitions is always one of my favorite jobs. Fortunately, there are multiple software tools to help you in that task. The testdisk software is multiplatform, and runs on Windows, Mac, and Linux. It searches for deleted partitions by looking at each physical sector on the disk and determining if it contains a file system. The gpart software is Linux only, but it's included on several bootable Linux distributions such that it can be applied to an ailing HDD. You can use the Mac's Disk Utility software to create and delete disk partitions.

Recovering File Systems and Files

Once we have a usable partition, we can anticipate recovering deleted files on that partition. This assumes that we can't use the simple way: retrieve the file from backup.

 TIP Asking about automatic backups of employees' drives can make file recovery a lot easier. Likewise, check TimeMachine on a Mac and Restore Points or Volume Shadow copies or Volume Shadow copies on a Windows machine.

However, if we're talking about an individual, it's a rare bird that actually systematically backs up data to a remote drive or location such as Mozy, Carbonite, Dropbox, or Box, so we're faced with recovering the file from the storage medium.

When a file is deleted, different things happen, depending on the OS running on the suspect's computer. In Linux when a file is deleted, the disk blocks associated with the file *inode* (index node) are returned to the list of free disk blocks for reuse. How the file is represented as deleted may vary: The inode value in the directory may be set to zero, or the entry can be deleted completely from the directory file.

In Windows, what happens depends on the type of file system. If the file system is formatted using some type of FAT file system, then several things happen.[9]

1. The first character of the filename is changed to 0xEH.

2. The file is moved to the Recovery Bin directory (C:\RECYCLED for FAT file systems, C:\RECYCLER\S-... in NTFS, or $RECYCLE.BIN in Windows 7). For NTFS, each user is provided with a subdirectory in the C:\RECYCLER directory named with the Windows security identifier (SID). On my computer, my SID is S-1-5-21-1145031325...-1005, and I can observe a subdirectory C:\$RECYCLE .BIN\S-1-5-21-114...-1005.

3. The file is moved to the recycle directory and renamed using the following strategy:

   a. First letter of the new filename is D.

   b. The second letter is the drive letter for the source of the file (say, E:).

   c. The next numbers are the sequential number of files that have been deleted from the drive. DE01.pdf would be the second file deleted from the E: drive.

4. Information about the file is written to the file INFO2. The INFO2 file contains the details of the original file, say, E:\documents\Guidance.pdf.

At that point, the file can be deleted from the Recycle Bin, in which case the associated disk blocks are returned to the system for reuse, or the file can be restored to its original location that has been previously saved in the INFO2 file. Mac OS X, via the Finder, operates in a similar manner, with Trash taking the place of the Recycle Bin.

 EXAM TIP Understand how files are renamed in the Recycle Bin and what information is stored in the INFO2 file.

So how do we recover a file? The simple answer is that we find the clusters that were allocated to the original file and relink them to a file that we create in a specified location. Moreover, we'd like to do this without changing any of the original file's metadata in order to preserve our timeline.

Some of the metadata that we're interested in regarding files are the times when the file was modified, created, or accessed (the MAC times). These times depend on the OS you're running and the action that you performed. You might think that accessed time would be straightforward: It's the time I last "read" the file. But does that include the last time you listed the contents of the directory?

Directories (and subdirectories) are also files, although a different kind of file. If I delete a subdirectory, all regular files contained in that directory must be deleted prior to deleting that subdirectory, and all subdirectories must be deleted as well. The user must explicitly request deleting a directory hierarchy, due to the damage that can result (consider the effects of inadvertently typing del Documents in your home directory on a Windows computer).

Theory into Practice: File and Partition Recovery Tools

As expected, there are different tools for different OSs, some that are cross-platform, dozens to choose from, and more developed every day. How to choose? Michael Graves lists four criteria for choosing third-party tools:[10]

- Accuracy
- Verifiable output
- Consistency
- Usability

Assuming that a tool meets these four criteria, the next consideration is whether the tool meets the tests established by the Daubert[11] process. Michael Graves summarizes these tests thusly:[12]

- Can the evidence presented be, or has it been, tested empirically, and can it be verified?
- Has the approach or technique been the subject of peer review and publication?
- Is the technique generally accepted within the scientific or professional community?
- Does the technique or procedure contain a high known or potential rate of error?

The choice comes down to personal preference and the ease of accessing features you use most often. Frankly, some software tools just seem to "fit" better than others do. I've listed my personal favorites next for each of the major operating systems, but they may not be yours.

Microsoft Windows

I've used gparted on a live CD to repartition and fix a balky Windows system that mysteriously lost its boot drive. I've also used diskmanagement.msc to delete and expand partitions, and I've used the Undelete software to manage file deletions on my work computer.

Mac OS X

DiskWarrior saved my Mac Mini when I powered off the machine before it had completed shutting down. None of the available Mac recovery tools would work, but Disk-Warrior was able to fix the problem, as well as cleaning up other small inconsistencies in the file system.

Linux

I've used gpart, gparted, and testdisk to recover my HDD when I typed /dev/sdb instead of /dev/sdc, and instead of overwriting the MBR on a USB disk, I overwrote the MBR on the boot disk. Testdisk ultimately came to my rescue.

 TIP On Linux, you can create a makeshift Undelete facility by aliasing the *rm* command to instead *mv* or *cp* the selected files to a new directory named Recovery Bin or something similar. If "deleter's remorse" sets in, it's easy enough to go to the Recovery Bin and retrieve the mistakenly deleted file.

Steganography and Graphics File Formats

Regardless of whether we have undeleted or recovered a graphics file, that file can be used to hide information that could be evidence in our investigation. We previously defined a graphics files as a file that can be rendered as a graphic image using appropriate software. Given that "image" is another overloaded word in the computing industry, I'm going to refer to these files as graphics files from now on.

Graphics Files

There are multiple graphics file formats from which to choose. A single photographic image can be represented by multiple graphics file formats, although they don't all offer the same features or quality.

There are two major types of graphics: raster and vector. Raster graphics represent each pixel as a bit-string, organized in rows. Displaying these files requires reading each of the values and reflecting them onto the monitor screen. Vector graphics represent an image as a series of equations, which allows the file to be expanded without losing detail.

Table 6-3 summarizes the most common file formats.

Graphics Files

A bitmapped graphics file is composed of a sequence of bits that represent a single *pixel* (picture element) on the screen. Since most displays are now color, the number of bits per pixel will depend on the color settings desired. Values are usually 8, 256, 512, 24 (millions), and 32 (billions) of colors. If we were to specify millions of colors, then each pixel would be represented by 24 bits in the graphics file. My screen is 1920 × 1080, and that's relatively small these days (for the curious, this works out to 49,766,400 bits or 6,220,800 bytes). Transferring bitmapped files of this size and larger can take time over a slow network connection or a disk-to-disk copy. Moreover, that doesn't include metadata.

Metafile graphics files contain both raster and vector images. Enlarging this file will cause the image displayed to lose detail in the raster portion, but the vector images will display at full detail.

All graphics file formats contain metadata. Figure 6-11 shows the metadata associated with a photograph.

Graphics File Compression

This is a good time to take a small detour to talk about graphics file compression. Graphics files can be large. The greater the number of pixels, the larger the file (one pixel is represented by up to 32 bits of data, allowing over 4 billion colors). Compressing these files can save storage space and decrease the time needed to send these files

File Extension	Name	Description
BMP	Bitmap	Raster image. Each pixel is represented by an N-bit value ranging from 3 bits to 32 bits. Provides the most detail as well as the largest file size.
GIF	Graphics Interchange Format	An 8-bit color palette. Uses LZW (Limpel-Zev-Welch) lossless compression. Dithering allows a portion of the file to be displayed before the entire file is downloaded, making the format good for web applications. Raster image.
JPEG	Joint Photographic Experts Group	Uses lossy compression to shrink the size of an image. Raster image.
PNG	Portable Network Graphics	Developed in part in reaction to the proprietary nature of the GIF format. Uses lossless compression.
TIF	Tagged Image File Format	Raster format file capable of containing multiple image representations. Tags indicate how the final image should be displayed.

Table 6-3 Graphics File Formats

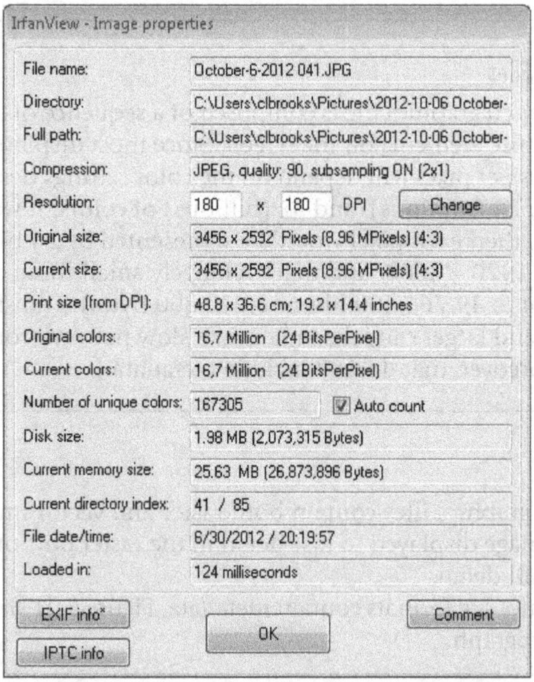

Figure 6-11

Photograph metadata

over a communications network. Unfortunately, compression algorithms are not created equal. Lossless compression means that a compressed file can be restored to an exact representation of the original. Lossy compression means that the file cannot be restored to its original, but can provide a "good enough" representation.

Some graphics file formats already compress the image, using either LZW or Huffman encoding. Huffman encoding is a fixed- to variable-length encoding scheme that provides lossless compression, and does so by assigning short codes to characters that appear frequently and longer codes to characters that appear less frequently. Consider the letter e 0 × 45 which is the most used letter in the English alphabet. Huffman encoding might assign that letter a code of 0b0, while the letter z might be assigned the value of 0b1001011. Compression is thus achieved by replacing common bit strings with shorter ones that shorten the length of the file. LZW is a variable- to fixed-length encoding scheme that also provides lossless compression. It creates a dictionary of non-overlapping bit strings and then replaces these strings in the file with code that represents the bit strings.

The JPEG format provides lossy compression, in that a file stored as a JPEG image is compressed by ignoring less critical elements of the original image. *Vector quantization* is a technique whereby certain strings of bits are represented by their average value, analogous to replacing the string of values "123123" with the value 5. Lossy compression is never used on text, since replacing a string of characters with an approximate value results in gibberish, at best, and horrible miscommunication, at worst (consider the effects of changing the "2" to a "5" in the message: "We attack at 2pm tomorrow").

File Compression

Image file compression is distinct from file compression. File compression software must be nonloss; examples of file compression software include Zip, 7-Zip, RAR, GZIP, and BZIP. From a privacy perspective, a compressed file is almost as good as an encrypted file, since the compressed data are unintelligible if simply viewed from a binary editor and would be unreadable by a program unless the data are decompressed.

Some file compression software supports encrypting the file as well. This requires that the file be compressed prior to encrypting, since compressing an encrypted file shouldn't find any repeated character sequences that can be expressed as a value and a length.

As we mentioned earlier when discussing the encrypting file system (EFS) on Windows, if you are running live on the host OS, a compressed file created via that OS will be uncompressed for you when read (and decrypted as well). Running on an image capture of a disk is another matter, since neither the decompression algorithm nor the encryption key may be known to your forensics OS. This is equally true if the file has been encrypted when the file system itself (or portions of it) have been automatically encrypted by the OS.

Locating and Recovering Graphics Files

Recall that we can determine the type of a file via either the file extension or a "magic number" that is embedded into a particular file type. Renaming the file with a different file extension will probably mean that the software that created the file won't think that it can read the file and various search programs may overlook it, especially when searching for graphics files. We can use this technique to "carve" or "salvage" graphics files from a damaged disk or from unallocated space if the graphics files have been deliberately deleted or corrupted. If the file header has been corrupted, it can be fixed by using a disk/binary file editor by either changing its contents or adding any missing information.

Identifying Unknown File Types

Imagine you're performing a file system analysis and you retrieve a file with no extension. No software on your computer recognizes the format. How might we go about identifying that file?

The answer is similar to how we locate and recover graphics files. First, we look for file signatures using, say, the Linux `file` command. The `file` command uses a set of heuristics to determine what kind of file it might be, and these heuristics are based on fixed patterns in particular kinds of files. The `strings` command from the Sysinternals suite would let us examine any ASCII or Unicode sequence of characters that might help us identify the file type.

Conversely, if you have a file extension but you have no idea what program created this particular file or how it's formatted, using a resource like www.filext.com to identify the extension and its creators can save you valuable time. Other software, such as IrfanView and ACDSee, will attempt to determine the actual file format when opening a file. Using a multipurpose viewer like Quick View Plus can also save time and the expense of obtaining the actual software used to create that file.

Steganography

Steganography is the general practice of "hiding" data within a cover medium, sometimes called a "host file." This file can be any kind of file, really, although usually it's a graphics file. While there are different methods of steganography, what they all share is an abstract view of a stegosystem. A stegosystem is composed of a message embedded in the cover medium along with a stegokey. Taken together, these three items create a stegomedium. The recipient of this medium will use the stegokey and the stegomedium to derive the (embedded) message.

 NOTE This description sounds very much like encrypting a digital object, and the message sounds a lot like a watermark. We'll compare all three later on in this chapter.

EC-Council lists two examples of steganography that aren't malicious.[13] Medical records can have a patient ID inserted within them to make sure that the information applies to a particular patient, even if other identifiers were lost or modified. Steganography can be used in the workplace to keep communications private that concern intellectual property: For example, details of a secret project could be communicated among project members without leaving a "paper" trail. Steganography is useful in any circumstance when we wish to incorporate extra information in a particular digital object such that a casual observer wouldn't know that information is being exchanged.

The EC-Council lists three major methods of steganography: technical, linguistic, and digital.[13] Technical steganography uses an outside medium, such as chemicals or liquids, to reveal the hidden message. One example of this kind of steganography is the time-honored technique of writing a message using lemon juice and milk, and then exposing the paper to low heat to reveal the message.

Linguistic steganography consists of two types: semagrams and open codes. Semagrams either can be visual, such as arranging objects to communicate the message, or can use variations in font, spelling, and punctuation to embed the message in a plain text file.

The Case of the Wondrous Window Shade

One particularly interesting story involved a federal employee who worked for the department responsible for issuing economic forecasts. Law enforcement believed that he was colluding with an investment firm to provide advance notification of the forecasts such that the firm could buy or sell before the forecast came out. There were no obvious means of communications between the firm and their accomplice: There weren't any phone calls, text messages, or hand signals. What they discovered was simplicity itself. Prior to the economic forecast, the accomplice would raise or lower his window blinds to a position either above or below the top of the lower window. Above meant a positive forecast; below meant a negative forecast. There are many ways to represent a 0 and a 1. If you string enough of them together, you can end up saying quite a bit!

Open codes modify plain text files to send the message. One technique uses *argot* codes, where information is communicated via a language that only the participants can understand. Another is *covered ciphers*, where the message is embedded within plain text, but only the receiver knows how to extract the message. The *null cipher* embeds the text of the message in the host file according to some pattern, such as the first word of each sentence, the first letter of every third word, vertically, horizontally, and so forth. *Grille ciphers* require a special form or template to be placed over the text that reveals the letters or characters of the message. No grille, no message.

Digital steganography hides messages in a digital medium, which is to say graphics files, audio, video, and so forth. The EC-Council lists the following techniques used in digital steganography:[14]

- Injection
- Least significant bit (LSB)
- Transform-domain techniques
- Spread-spectrum encoding
- Perceptual masking
- File generation
- Statistical methods
- Distortion technique

We can categorize these techniques as belonging to one of two strategies: insertion, where we include that message with the host file, and substitution, where we replace bits of the host file with bits from the message.

Steganography Methods in Text Files   As we might expect, we can apply several steganographic techniques to hide a message within a text file.[13]

- *Open space steganography* uses the presence of white space within the text (either blanks or tabs), whether as intersentence spacing, end-of-line spacing, or interword spacing.
- *Syntactic steganography* uses the presence or absence of punctuation characters to represent one and zero. A comma could represent a one; the absence of a comma could be interpreted as a zero. The sequence "a,b,c a b c" could be decoded as "11000." In this instance, letters don't matter, only the punctuation, so we're left with comma, comma, and three spaces.
- *Semantic steganography* uses two synonyms, one of which is declared primary and one secondary. The appearance of the primary synonym is read as a 1; the secondary synonym is read as a 0. For example I might use the phrase "party" as the primary synonym and the phrase "event" as the secondary.

As with any steganographic technique, the receiver must know how the secret message is included in the text in order to retrieve it.

Steganography Techniques in Graphics Files   Messages can be hidden in graphics files by using LSB insertion, masking and filtering, and algorithmic transformation. The LSB technique is used for other media as well as graphics. In this technique, the LSB of, say, a 24-bit quantity would be replaced with bits from the secret message. In the case of graphic files that utilize 24- or 32-bit color, the resulting changes would not be discernible to the viewer. In contrast to techniques like open space steganography, LSB encoding, algorithmic techniques, masking, and filtering all represent a substitution approach.

Steganography Techniques in Audio Files   A suspect can hide messages in audio files using variations on the LSB technique or by manipulating various frequencies. Techniques include phase coding, spread spectrum, and echo data hiding. Phase coding separates the sound into discrete segments and then introduces a reference phase that contains the information. Spread spectrum techniques encode the information across the entire frequency spectrum using direct-sequence spread spectrum (DSSS). Echo data hiding means introducing an echo into the original medium, and properties of the echo are used to represent information.

Steganography Techniques in Video Files   Messages can be hidden in video files using any technique that applies to audio or graphic files (a video is an audio stream overlaid on a series of images). One such technique is modifying the coefficients used in the discrete cosine transform (DCT) computation, a technique used to compress JPEG files, so as to hide parts of the messages in areas of the file that will survive expansion and recompression.

Steganographic File Systems   Steganographic file systems encrypt and hide files inside of random blocks allocated to that file system, but keep just enough information available to re-create these files when presented with a filename and a password. To an outside observer, the disk seems to be a collection of random bits that appears to be nonsensical when read. One implementation is the StegFS file system for Linux. StegFS is described as

> [...] a steganographic file system that [... offers] plausible deniability to owners of protected files. StegFS securely hides user-selected files in a file system so that, without the corresponding access keys, an attacker would not be able to deduce their existence, even if the attacker is thoroughly familiar with the implementation of the file system and has gained full access to it.[15]

Steganography, Cryptography, and Watermarking

Steganography, watermarking, and cryptography are ways of concealing the content of a message or a file such that only someone who knows the secret can retrieve that information. Nevertheless, there are significant differences among these techniques. Cryptography modifies the file in such a way that the contents are unintelligible to the software that is used to display that file. Steganography, however, inserts the secret contents into a file such that the contents can be extracted or viewed or read by the appropriate software, and the original file can still be read or displayed.

Here's an example. I want to send to a message to my friend Sam that says, "You and Barbara should meet us at the restaurant at 8:00 P.M. tonight. It's a surprise party for Helyn." I don't want anyone else to view that message (I want to keep the party small), so I encrypt it and send it to Sam. I've made the encryption key available to Sam via some other means, so Sam can use the encryption key to decrypt the file and view the message.

However, if I have reason to believe that sending an encrypted file might cause suspicion (or might be specifically forbidden by company policy), I could use steganography to embed that message in the photograph and then send the modified photograph to Sam. Anyone viewing the photograph might see a travel snapshot, but Sam, who has the stegokey, can extract the message from the photograph and hopefully join us in the festivities.

Watermarking and steganography differ in that watermarks can be either visible or invisible. Visible watermarks are meant to be clearly seen and to require a good deal of work to remove. The goal of invisible watermarks is to remain hidden from the receiver, but be visible using software in the possession of the creator, who can make the watermark visible by knowing the watermark password. This technique is used to track illegal copies of documents and to ensure that copyright laws are followed. An example of this technique is to release a set of the same document that contains different watermarks. If the document shows up in the wrong hands, the sender can retrieve the watermark to learn the source of the leak.

The major differences between watermarking and steganography in that watermarking is ultimately meant to be seen, whereas in steganography, the secret message is meant to remain hidden such that only specific individuals will be able to retrieve it from the carrier file. Cryptography is similar to steganography in this regard, but using cryptography means that everyone can tell that the content of the message is hidden, whereas in steganography, the carrier file appears to be normal.

Steganalysis

Steganalysis is the practice of analyzing a file to determine if it contains information encoded as part of the data portion of the file. It is the process by which we attempt to determine if steganography is present and, if so, to determine the stegokey and the method used to embed the message in the host file.

Kerckhoff's principle in cryptography states that the only thing that must be secret is the key itself: The encryption algorithm can be safely published. Steganography, however, needs to keep the stegokey secret, and requires that the sender and recipient must have the same software tool. The presence of steganography software on a suspect's computer is a good indicator that communications sent or received by the suspect may use steganography. Tools are available that can make an educated guess at whether a particular file contains steganography, but they can't actually extract the embedded message.

Detecting Steganography

How can we detect steganography? That part is not so easy. In many cases, the naked eye just can't distinguish between the original graphic and the modified graphic. The simplest way is to obtain a copy of the original image and compare the two files using

Entropy, Steganography, Cryptography, and Malware

In information theory, entropy is a measure of variability or unpredictability in a particular message. Seeing the opposite of what we expect (high versus low or vice versa) leads us to believe that the original material has been transformed in some way. In the case of cryptography, there should be no recognizable patterns in the cryptotext, and it would be considered to have high entropy. Malware that has been packed in order to obfuscate the code also shows high entropy, and thus appears distinct from normal executable code.

a simple file comparison utility such as comp on Windows. Differences between the two may indicate the presence of steganography (determining which is the original, however, may be more of a problem), or it can mean a change in file metadata similar to what we saw in the metadata associated with a photograph. Change the location setting in the photograph metadata, and we've changed the file signature.

Two general approaches for detecting steganography are the statistical and empirical methods. In statistical analysis, we can use a tool that measures the entropy (variability) of a particular document. Files that contain a hidden message should have more entropy than the original. Empirical approaches involve examining files directly. If we are looking at images, we can look for changes in file size, modified date, or the color palette used. If we are examining text files, we can look for such things as abnormally large payloads (data portions of a message), as well as a lot of extraneous white space.

Theory into Practice: Graphics File Tools and Steganography Detection Tools

As a DFI, you're more interested in viewing the contents of a graphics file than in changing the background to a different color. If that's all you need, acquiring software like Adobe Photoshop or the GIMP (GNU Image Manipulation Program) would be overkill. There are many software tools that you can use to view images, some free of charge and some commercial. Viewing images is not the same as modifying (editing) those images. Two things that I look for in software is the ability to display different kinds of graphics files as well as displaying file metadata.

IrfanView is a free-as-in-beer software (but the author would appreciate your buying him a virtual beer now and again). Figure 6-12 shows the user interface for the software. Notice that the software is able to extract metadata from the file.

QuickView Plus handles multiple image formats as well as popular office documents (the Professional version will even open Microsoft Project files). Although versatile and expansive in terms of the number of file formats it can interpret, QuickView Plus doesn't provide the capability to inspect file metadata. Get the picture?

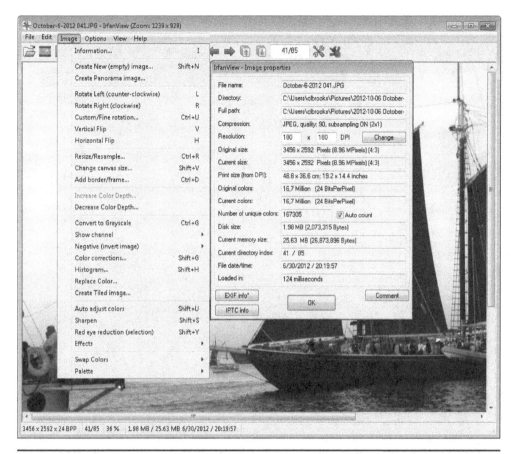

Figure 6-12   IrfanView user interface

Graphics File Forensic Tools

Likewise, there are many sources for graphics file forensic tools. Examples include Hex Workshop and Ilook. Figure 6-13 shows Hex Workshop after it's opened the same file we previously opened with IrfanView. As it happens, IrfanView can be configured to use Hex Workshop (or any other editing tool) to examine the raw bytes comprising that file. The ability to hook individual software programs together or to extend a tool via scripting language is a feature well worth having.

Steganography Detection Tools

Steganography is difficult to detect, and even harder to extract when discovered. Several tools will look for files that have hidden messages, and while they can tell you that a given file may contain hidden content, they usually can't help you in determining what that content is. Some tools will scan for known steganography software: The very presence of such software may provide a clue for conducting a deeper analysis of files on the

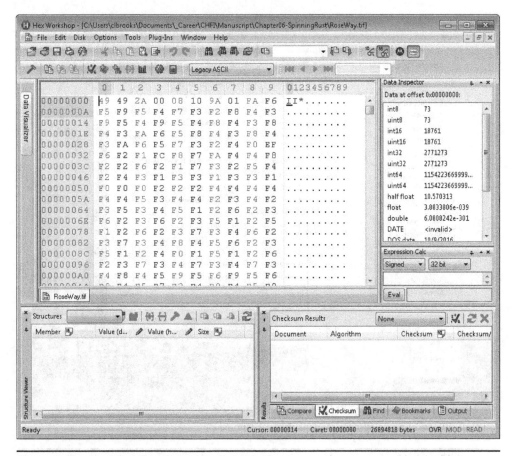

Figure 6-13 Hex Workshop view of the graphics file

suspect's computer or for files that may have been sent via other means (file transfer, e-mail, text, instant message, and so on).

There is a world of choice for steganographic tools: One web site lists over 100.[16] Some of the more noticeable tools are stegdetect and the S-Tools suite. stegdetect can discover several different steganographic techniques, and stegbreak implements a dictionary attack against three of them (Steg-Shell, JPHide, and OutGuess 0.13b). S-Tool is a single program that allows files to be embedded into a .gif, .bmp, or a .wav file. Although the program is getting a bit long in the tooth (the help file talks about running the software in Windows 95!), the software happily inserted a text file into a .gif and restored the text from the modified image.

Processing Forensics Images with MATLAB

MATLAB is a "high-level language and interactive environment for numerical computation, visualization, and programming,"[17] and has been used for multiple applications, including processing video and images. Over time, the MATLAB software package became used to analyze forensic images. The general case is to utilize specific algorithms that can detect certain kinds of transformation that indicate that the digital image has been modified in some way, either to hide a message (steganograph) or to include or exclude data from the original. One example is using MATLAB to analyze the position of light sources in a photograph to determine if certain elements of the photograph have been added (often referred to as having been PhotoShopped, in recognition of the popular image manipulation software sold by Adobe, Inc). The author of the blog post "MATLAB in Forensic Image Processing"[18] makes the claim that MATLAB is a good tool for forensic image processing because you can record every step of your analysis as well as examine the source code for the various algorithms used. This information can then support your analysis if challenged in court.

Chapter Review

Hard disk drives consist of a spindle with rotating platters and read/write heads. Each disk has a number of tracks (concentric circles on the disk platter), and each track is divided into sectors. Each sector (block) can be addressed by an LBA; a file system block or cluster is a group of disk sectors that are allocated together for a file. Disks are usually formatted into multiple partitions that provide a logical volume name for a collection of disk blocks. RAID technology supports assigning multiple physical devices to a single logical volume. RAID uses striping, mirroring, and parity to provide availability and response time.

File systems are data structures that present a hierarchical view of storage to the end user. Files are stored in directories that can contain subdirectories. Different file systems support different disk sizes and provide different file metadata, although all provide timestamps that indicate when a file was created, modified, or accessed. File systems include FAT32, NTFS, ext3, ext4, HFS+, and ISO9660 for CD/DVDs.

All computer systems go through a process of "booting" when they are powered on. Although the steps vary, most systems will run a POST test to ensure that configured hardware is present and working, and then load a bootstrap loader that loads and starts various device drivers. The bootstrap loader then reads a second-stage loader into memory, which in turn loads and starts the operating system, which ultimately results in a login prompt or the server becoming operational.

Deleted files and partitions can be recovered by multiple means. In the case of files, disk resources formerly allocated to that file are still available from the unallocated space list. Deleted partitions can be recovered by modifying existing partition tables to reflect the presence of the deleted partition.

Image (graphics) files come in multiple formats, but a graphics file can use vector graphics, bitmapped graphics, or both. Bitmapped graphics are usually lossless, while some vector graphics formats can lose detail (JPEG files).

Steganography is the practice of hiding a message with a cover file by using steganographic software along with a stegokey. The recipient can use the software and the stegokey to retrieve the message from the carrier file. Steganography can be used to embed a message in a text file, a graphics file, a video file, or an audio file. Steganography is difficult to detect and even more difficult to extract the message from the carrier file. Tools exist to analyze files for the presence of steganography, but without the software that was originally used to create the carrier file and the stegokey, it may be too time consuming to continue.

Questions

1. Tracks at the same position on each platter create what kind of structure?

   A. Clusters

   B. File blocks

   C. Cylinders

   D. Logical volumes

2. What strategy does RAID 10 use?

   A. Volume data are striped, and each stripe is mirrored.

   B. Logical volumes are mirrored and each mirror is striped.

   C. Logical volumes are mirrored, and parity is stored within each disk.

   D. Logical volume data are striped with a single parity disk.

3. A file system block or cluster is composed of a number of:

   A. Tracks

   B. Sectors

   C. Cylinders

   D. Platters

4. Which FAT version can only support disks up to 2GB in size?

   A. FAT12

   B. FAT16

   C. VFAT

   D. FAT32

5. Which of these elements make up the MAC time of a file? (Choose all that apply.)

   A. Modified

   B. Accessed

   C. Created

   D. Copied

6. What strategy does the testdisk software use to discover deleted partitions?

   A. Compares MBR partition table entries to logical disk blocks

   B. Looks for the last cluster in a cluster chain

   C. Looks for file systems

   D. Looks for partition table signatures

7. Which record in the MTF would have been damaged if I couldn't tell which file blocks were in use?

   A. Volume

   B. Cluster bitmap

   C. Boot cluster file

   D. Root filename index

8. Which of these are methods to detect steganography? (Choose all that apply.)

   A. Statistical

   B. Empirical

   C. Detective

   D. Authentication

9. Two techniques used to compress graphics files are Huffman encoding and _____.

   A. ZIP encoding

   B. LZW encoding

   C. 7bit

   D. Radix64

10. Which one of these definitions best describes steganalysis?

    A. Examining digital objects to discover embedded information

    B. Comparing and contrasting the capabilities of steganography software

    C. Building personality profiles of criminals who might use steganography

    D. Deriving the stegokey from an analysis of the cover file

11. What are legitimate uses of steganography? (Choose all that apply.)

    A. Record information in patient records

    B. Intraoffice communication

    C. Encoding manufacturing formulas for transmission

    D. Sending URLs for contraband material

12. In Windows XP, the _____ is responsible for loading the operating system into memory.

    A. ntldr

    B. Winlogin

    C. smss

    D. lsass

13. File _____ is the process where we reclaim a graphics file from a raw disk.

    A. Analysis

    B. Resuscitation

    C. Carving

    D. Extraction

14. In order to extract the message from the stegomedium, the receiver must have the _____.

    A. Symmetric key

    B. Stegokey

    C. Private key

    D. Stegomask

15. The process of detecting the use of steganography is known as _____.

    A. Steganalysis

    B. Cryptanalysis

    C. Stegodetection

    D. Cryptography

Answers

1. C. Cylinders

2. B. Volume data are mirrored, and each mirror is striped across multiple disks.

3. B. Sectors

4. A. FAT12

5. A, B, C. Modified, accessed, and created

6. C. Looks for file system information

7. B. Cluster bitmap

8. A, B. Statistical and empirical methods

9. B. LZW encoding

10. A. Examining digital objects to discover embedded information

11. A, B. Recording information in patient records and intraoffice communication are both legitimate uses of steganography

12. A. ntldr

13. C. Carving

14. B. Stegokey

15. A. Steganalysis

References

1. Carrier, B. *File System Forensic Analysis* (NJ: Pearson, 2005), p. 10.

2. Evan-Amos, http://en.wikipedia.org/wiki/File:Laptop-hard-drive-exposed.jpg, licensed under the Creative-Commons Attribution-Share Alike 3.Unported, http://creativecommons.org/licenses/by-sa/3.0/deed.en.

3. Carrier, p. 70.

4. Afonin, Y. G. *Why SSD Drives Destroy Court Evidence, and What Can be Done about It: Part 2*. Retrieved from www.dfinews.com/articles/2012/10/why-ssd-drives-destroy-court-evidence-and-what-can-be-done-about-it-part-2.

5. Microsoft, 2010. *The NTFS File System*. Retrieved from www.technet.microsoft.com/en-us/library/cc976808.aspx.

6. "Overview." Retrieved from www.sleuthkit.org/overview.

7. *What is UEFI*. Retrieved from http://windows.microsoft.com/en-us/windows-8/what-uefi.

8. NoDrives. Retrieved from http://technet.microsoft.com/en-us/library/cc938267.aspx.

9. "How the Recycle Bin Stores Files." Retrieved from https://support.microsoft.com/kb/136517, retrieved June 23, 2014.

10. Graves, M. *Digital Archaeology* (NJ: Pearson, 2013), p. 399.

11. *Daubert v. Merrell Dow Pharmaceuticals, Inc.*, 509 U.S. 579, 593 (1993).

12. Graves, *Digital Archaeology*, p. 401.

13. EC-Council. *Computer Forensics: Investigating Data and Image Files* (MA: Cengage, 2010), p. 1:9.

14. EC-Council. *Computer Forensics: Investigating Data and Image Files* (NJ: EC-Council, 2010), pp. 1–5.

15. HweeHwa Pang, Kian-Lee Tan, and Xuan Zhou, "StegFS: A Steganographic File System," 19th International Conference on Data Engineering (ICDE '03), Bangalore: IEEE Computer Society, 2003, p. 657. Abstract retrieved from www.computer.org/csdl/proceedings/icde/2003/2071/00/20710657-abs.html.

16. Johnson, N. "Steganography Software." Retrieved from www.jjic.com/Steganography/Tools.htm.

17. Home page. Retrieved from www.matlab.com.

18. Unknown author. *MATLAB in Forensic Image Processing*. Retrieved from http://draftingschool.org/matlab-in-forensic-image-processing.

Windows Forensics

After completing this chapter, you should be able to
- Define volatile and nonvolatile information and describe techniques for collecting nonvolatile information, including cache, cookie, and history analysis
- Discuss various forensic tools and how to search with the Microsoft Event Viewer
- Explain various processes involved in forensic investigation of a Windows system, such as memory and registry analysis, Internet Explorer cache analysis, cookie analysis, MD5 calculation, Windows file analysis, and metadata investigation
- Explain how to parse process memory and a memory dump, and how to analyze restore point registry settings
- Discuss Windows password security issues, including password cracking
- Describe logfile analysis, including IIS, FTP and system file logs, event logs, static and dynamic event log analysis, and account management events
- Define a password cracker and the terminologies used in password cracking, summarize the various kinds of passwords, and recall default passwords
- Describe how a password cracker works, various password-cracking techniques, and various types of password attacks
- List various system and application software password-cracking strategies and attacks, and discuss various password-cracking tools

When you have the largest market share of any other operating system, it means (among other things) that you present a bigger target. Think for a minute about the effect of finding a zero-day vulnerability in Microsoft Windows 7. The number of machines that can be exploited by this flaw is enormous.

A forensic analysis can be static ("dead"), dynamic ("live"), or both. Static analysis occurs when we have brought the digital equipment to our lab, created a forensic image of persistent storage, and then begun our analysis using that image (or, better yet, a copy of the original forensic image—remember?). Dynamic analysis occurs when we encounter a running machine at the scene and we believe that there is evidence that would be lost or destroyed if the machine were shut down. Any evidence that would exist after a shutdown would be classified as persistent (nonvolatile) data, while any information lost during a shutdown would be classified as volatile information.

Zero-Day Vulnerabilities

N-day vulnerabilities are a way of classifying vulnerabilities (security bugs) based on the number of days between when a vulnerability is announced and when an exploit for the vulnerability is published or code exploiting that vulnerability is seen "in the wild" (running on machines connected to the Internet). The longer it takes for an exploit to be developed, the greater the opportunity afforded to an organization to repair that vulnerability or to develop a work-around to avoid that particular exploit.

Zero-day vulnerabilities exist when an exploit is present the same day that the vulnerability is announced. This leaves an organization with no chance to patch affected systems or to develop a work-around for that particular flaw, except for those defensive security measures that are already in place.

According to EC-Council, a digital forensics investigator (DFI) can examine three general areas as part of their analysis. These are the event logs, memory dumps, and Windows registry.[1] In the case of static analysis, we can examine event logs and the Windows registry: They're both part of persistent storage. The contents of memory, however, reflect dynamic information. Turn off the device, and essentially, the information is lost. The DFI has two choices here: collect the information that is stored in memory and reflects the dynamic state of the device, or capture all the memory and perform this analysis later without the same constraints of time and place.

The challenge is how to maximize our chances of retaining information that would help us in our investigation. Table 7-1 lists some alternatives.

If we need to collect volatile information, we can either perform a live analysis or dump the contents of random access memory (RAM) from the device to analyze later. In dynamic analysis, we can perform a live analysis immediately (both for memory and file system information), as well as a live capture of file system information.

 CAUTION Factor time into your decisions. It takes time to perform a live analysis or capture, time that may be better spent elsewhere.

Table 7-1		Volatile	Nonvolatile
Methods of Collecting Volatile and Nonvolatile Information	**Static**	Memory dump	Disk image
	Dynamic	Live analysis	Live analysis/live capture

Windows Forensics Analysis

My personal perspective on Windows operating systems is that you can divide the history into three segments: before Windows NT, up to Windows XP, and Vista and beyond. That is to say, certain features appeared in Windows XP as an add-on facility, but then became part of the standard distributions in Vista and then Windows 7 (the PowerShell software is a good example). Microsoft Vista and later versions packaged two different command-line programs: *cmd.exe* and *powershell.exe.* Cmd.exe has been around since the Windows NT days (1992) and remains an efficient way to access various utilities to gather information with a minimal amount of muss and fuss (but you do need to know your command-shell features, such as I/O redirection). Figure 7-1 shows an example of the Windows command shell running the *tasklist* command.

Powershell.exe has shipped with Windows since Windows 7 and Windows Server 2003 (it was available as a separate download for Windows XP). The advantage to the DFI is that its command set is more regular, and the ability to pipeline command output displays information more efficiently. Figure 7-2 shows the *powershell* command that produces output similar to the *tasklist* command (don't worry, though, those same ol' command-line programs are still there should you need them).

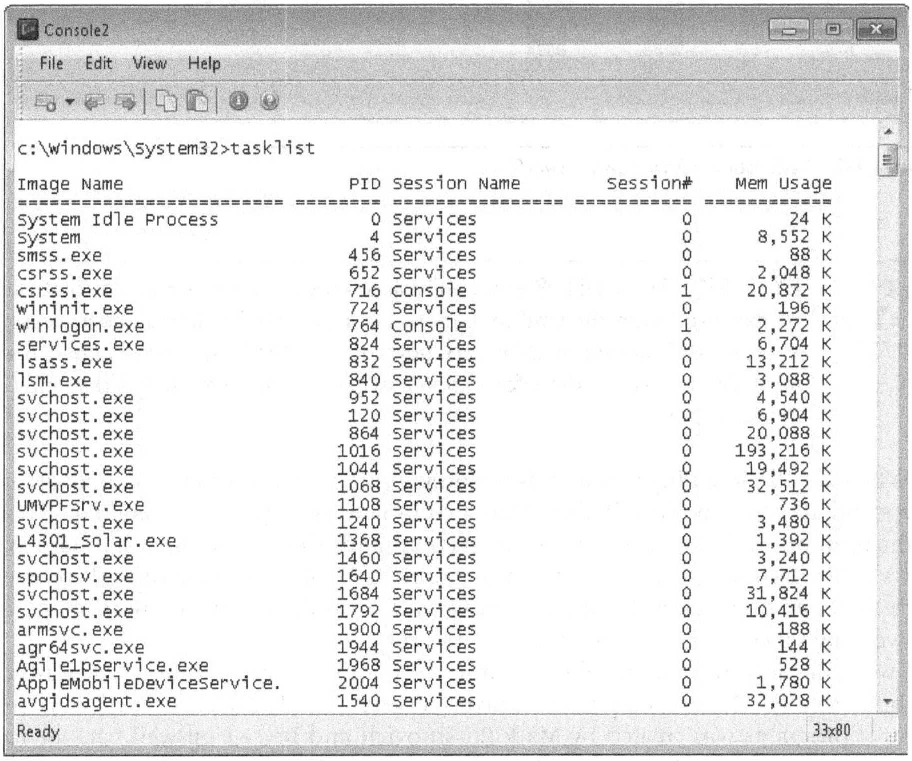

Figure 7-1 Output of the *tasklist* command

```
Windows PowerShell                                                  ☐ ⬜ ✕

 File  Edit  View  Help

 🔲 ▾ 🖫 🖫 | 🗅 🗅 | ❶ ⓦ

c:\windows\system32>powershell                                           ▲
windows PowerShell                                                       ▤
Copyright (C) 2012 Microsoft Corporation. All rights reserved.

PS c:\windows\system32> gps

Handles  NPM(K)    PM(K)    WS(K) VM(M)   CPU(s)      Id ProcessName
-------  ------    -----    ----- -----   ------      -- -----------
    332      32    22440     3904   186     8.53    4444 1Password
    327      27     5420    11336   103     0.36   11664 ACDSeeFreeInTouch2
    277      28    12136     7400   117    86.41    4628 Agile1pAgent
    119      23     3268      528    47             1968 Agile1pService
     41       5     1156      144    17             1944 agr64svc
    416      33     4984     5136   185     1.72    3920 Amazon Music Helper
    207      24     3392     1780    91             2004 AppleMobileDevices...
    209      22    12448    10800   134     0.51    7104 ApplePhotoStreams
     75       8     1232      188    42             1900 armsvc
    131      10    15888    15700    51            12636 audiodg
    195      13    24280    99928   205             5020 avgcsrva
    106       8     2412     1436    43             3712 avgemca
    570      32    30548    32140   278             1540 avgidsagent
    219      13    11220     9240    89             3508 avgnsa
    925      26    59844    62532   246             4244 avgrsa
    809      64    28812    22240   276   239.01    5584 avgui
    913      39    12144    10208   140             1612 avgwdsvc
    210      20    19816     1836   178     0.36    3468 Box Edit
    473      46    45532     6876   278    11.15    3760 Boxcryptor
    751      65    98384    56000   700    71.34    4236 BoxSync
    188      34    32156     2504   553     0.55    2584 BoxSyncHelper
    381      29    11316     9252   141     8.27    3928 chrome
    148      12     6208     8524    78     0.37    8336 cmd
     31       5     1172      468    29             5364 conhost
                                                                         ▼
Ready                                                              33x80
```

Figure 7-2 Task listing in Windows PowerShell

 EXAM TIP The CHFI v8 exam will ask questions about commands that can be executed from the cmd shell. However, PowerShell will become increasingly available as Windows machines are upgraded to Windows 7 or Windows 8 and it's easier to extract the information that you need. Powershell is the wave of the future.

Where do all these nifty command-line programs come from? Many of them are part of a standard Windows installation. Start a command shell (cmd.exe) and type "help" at the prompt. Table 7-2 lists several useful commands that are part of a standard Windows 7 distribution. Other native tools are part of a set of administrator tools provided with the operating system (OS) (such as *nbtstat*) or tools meant to report on various networking aspects (*arp, netstat, tracert,* and so on).

Two collections of tools are absolute musts for your forensic toolkit. These tools can be burned to a CD or loaded onto a universal serial bus (USB) stick. The Sysinternals suite of programs was created by Mark Russinovich and Bryce Cogswell back in 1996 (www.sysinternals.com). Sysinternals.com was eventually purchased by Microsoft, but

Program	Description
ATTRIB	Displays or changes file attributes
BCDEDIT	Sets properties in boot database to control boot loading
BREAK	Sets or clears extended CTRL-C checking
CACLS	Displays or modifies access control lists (ACLs) of files
CHKDSK	Checks a disk and displays a status report
CHKNTFS	Displays or modifies the checking of disk at boot time
DISKPART	Displays or configures disk partition properties
DOSKEY	Edits command lines, recalls Windows commands, and creates macros
DRIVERQUERY	Displays current device driver status and properties
FC	Compares two files or sets of files and displays the differences between them
FIND	Searches for a text string in a file or files
FINDSTR	Searches for strings in files
FOR	Runs a specified command for each file in a set of files
FSUTIL	Displays or configures the file system properties
ICACLS	Displays, modifies, backs up, or restores ACLs for files and directories
OPENFILES	Displays files opened by remote users for a file share
PATH	Displays or sets a search path for executable files
RECOVER	Recovers readable information from a bad or defective disk
REPLACE	Replaces files
ROBOCOPY	Advanced utility that copies files and directory trees
SC	Displays or configures services (background processes)
SCHTASKS	Schedules commands and programs to run on a computer
SHUTDOWN	Allows proper local or remote shutdown of machine
SYSTEMINFO	Displays machine-specific properties and configuration
TASKLIST	Displays all currently running tasks, including services
TASKKILL	Kills or stops a running process or application
VER	Displays the Windows version
VERIFY	Tells Windows whether to verify that your files are written correctly to a disk
VOL	Displays a disk volume label and serial number
WMIC	Displays WMI information inside an interactive command shell
XCOPY	Copies files and directory trees

Table 7-2 Windows Native Commands

the tools are still available and are steadily being improved upon even as new tools are added. A second collection of tools is the NirSoft Utilities collection by Nir Sofer (www .nirsoft.com) A third program, Windows System Control Center (WSCC)(www.kls-soft .com/wscc), bundles both of these collections and provides a front-end graphical user

Figure 7-3 Windows System Control Center choices

interface (GUI) for managing these programs. Figure 7-3 shows the user interface (UI) for this program.

WSCC offers the advantage of updating and gathering new tools as they become available. Each tool is assigned a category; categories are listed in Table 7-3.

We'll be referring to several of these tools as we talk about static and dynamic forensic activities. We'll use the convention that the program name will be suffixed by an "(s)," an "(n)," or an "(m)," indicating that the software is provided by Sysinternals, NirSoft, or Microsoft, respectively, as a separate download. The absence of a suffix indicates that the program is part of a standard Windows OS distribution (XP, Vista, or 7).

Live Investigations: Volatile Information

The prevailing wisdom these days is that capturing volatile information is as important, if not more important, as the static acquisition of persistent storage. In order to capture volatile information, you need to know which tools are needed to capture specific

Program Category	Sysinternals	NirSoft	Windows	System
File and disk	Yes	Yes	Yes	--
Network	Yes	Yes	Yes	--
Process	Yes	Yes	Yes	--
Security	Yes	Yes	--	--
System information	Yes	Yes	Yes	--
Miscellaneous	Yes	Yes	Yes	--
Desktop	--	Yes	--	--
Video/audio	--	Yes	--	--
Web browser	--	Yes	--	--
Password recovery	--	Yes	--	--
Administrative tasks	--	--	Yes	--
Services	--	--	--	Yes

Table 7-3   Tool Categories in the WSCC Software

information. Second is your plan of action. You can collect this information manually or by running a script that you've written previously. You can run a command-line tool to capture all of the information specified as volatile.

Volatile and Nonvolatile Information

In his paper, "Live Response Using PowerShell 2," Sajeev Nair lists these elements of volatile and nonvolatile data.[2] Volatile data includes such data as

- Machine and operating system information
- User accounts and current login information
- Network configuration and connectivity information
- Antivirus application status and related logs
- Startup applications
- Running process-related information
- Running services-related information
- Drivers installed and running
- Dynamic link libraries (DLLs) created
- Open files
- Open shares
- Mapped drives
- Scheduled jobs
- Active network connections and related process

Nonvolatile data includes data such as

- Hotfixes applied
- Installed applications
- Link files created
- Packed files
- USB related
- Shadow copies created
- Prefetch files and timestamps
- Domain Name System (DNS) cache
- List of available logs and last write times

- Firewall configuration
- Audit policy
- Temporary Internet files and cookies
- Typed uniform resource locators (URLs)
- Important registry keys
- File timeline
- Important event logs

Intimidating?! Nah.

As it turns out, some of the volatile information may actually persist. For example, a list of installed drivers can be obtained via a static analysis, but which ones were actually running at that particular time would depend on a dynamic analysis. Certain data will be available from your forensic disk image, regardless of the analysis you're doing: Anything written to the file system (and this includes the Windows registry) should persist after the device is shut down, assuming there are no specific shutdown procedures that would remove that data. Essentially, volatile information will disappear upon shutdown.

Understanding Network and Process Information

In order better to understand volatile information, let's do a quick review of some operating system details. A process is a computer entity that consumes system resources (memory, storage) and is runnable (that is, the computer will execute instructions associated with that entity). At rest, it's a program; while running, it's a process. Each process has at least one (many have more than one) "thread of control" (abbreviated as "thread") that is defined as a set of instructions and an indication of which instruction should execute next (the "program counter"). Some computer architectures schedule threads; other architectures schedule processes. Generally, since resource usage is associated with processes, we'll focus on those. Each process is identified by its process ID (PID). Processes can create new processes that either can run independently of the parent process or can run as a child of that process.

Much of this information is associated with running processes and their use of system resources. One set of resources shared among processes is network connections—that is, data structures that associate a port assigned to a particular process with an external device. The OS kernel is responsible for sending information via the network to these destination devices and making sure that the response is delivered to the correct process. In the TCP/IP protocol, these end points are described by a protocol/port number pair, so the kernel might send data addressed to the pair (TCP, 23) to a process that is awaiting for data ("listening") on that port.

Capturing Volatile Information

The first thing to do is determine the system date and time. The command line to do this is:

```
date /t & time /t >G:\VolatileData.txt
```

This will output the current date and time to a file that will store the results of our volatile information capture. Running software to capture volatile information will "leave a mark," so it's a good idea to reflect the date and time when we started our analysis. The DFI will create some of the activity that occurs on the device after this time, but not all.

Any data collection after this should be appended to the output file. For example, if we wanted to get a list of running tasks, we could do so by issuing the following command:

```
tasklist >>G:\VolatileData.txt
```

Logged-in Users and Open Files   We need to determine who is logged in to the device, what files are open, what programs are running, and what external connections exist. The *psloggedon*(s) command will list the users logged on to the device, either locally or remotely, as will the *net session* command. We are most concerned with open files that are the result of an external user connected to a file share. Here again our faithful friend the *net* command will serve us well. The *net view* command will list local resources that are available as shares, and *net file* will show files that are open remotely.

Who's Running What?   The next information we want to collect is what programs are running on the device. The Sysinternals suite provides a number of tools that will list various information about all running processes. The *tasklist*(s) command has several options for listing running programs, as you can see in Figure 7-4. The command can be run on a remote device, the command output can be filtered, and you can specify the output format (table [default], list, or CSV [comma-separated values, suitable for importing into a database or a spreadsheet]). For example, the command

```
tasklist /M bcrypt.dll /FO CSV
```

would list all the processes on the local machine that incorporated the bcrypt.dll library and output the results in CSV format.

Network Connections   *Nbtstat.exe* indicates the status of the Windows NetBIOS connections. Figure 7-5 lists the various options for this command.

Capturing the state of the non-NetBIOS network connections (TCP/IP) is another critical step in live forensics. We'll cover networking details in Chapter 9, but it's worth mentioning the *netstat.exe* command. This command provides a wealth of information about the device's network connections. Figure 7-6 lists the various options supported.

Netstat can be found on Windows, Mac OS X, and Linux systems. Each system has its own variations on the command-line arguments, but the standard options chosen are list all connections, just display host IP addresses, and list the process ID of the process

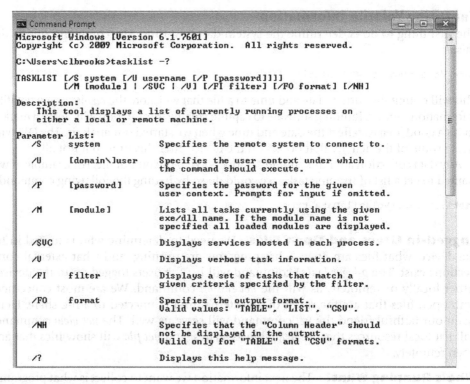

Figure 7-4 *Tasklist* options

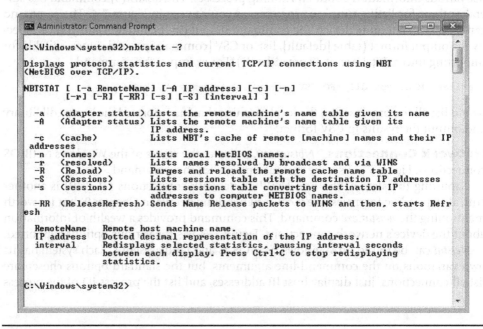

Figure 7-5 *Nbtstat.exe* options

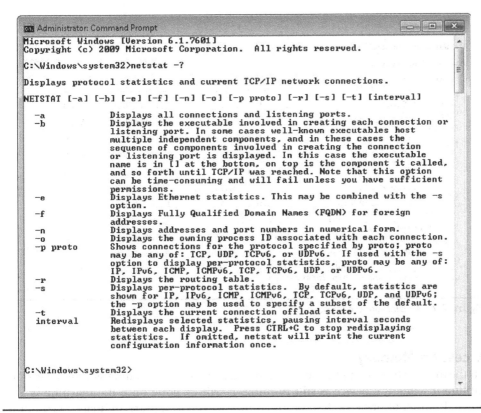

Figure 7-6 *Netstat.exe* options

that owns that connection. On Windows, these arguments are -**a** (all connections), -**n** (addresses and port numbers only), and -**o** (display the owning process ID), abbreviated as -**ano**. The -**b** option will list all the executables involved in creating that connection. As the help options mention, you may need special permission to use the -**b** option. Figure 7-7 shows the output of that command when run on my desktop computer. In addition to the process ID, the name of the executable file is listed.

> **TIP** I've frequently encountered the "access denied" problem when invoking a command from a *cmd.exe* window when running on a 64-bit system, even with administrator privileges. The solution is to create a command-line window by using a Start | All Programs | Accessories menu entry and executing *cmd.exe* as an administrator. The problem has to do with running 32-bit Windows commands from a 64-bit context: Executing *cmd.exe* from the Start menu as an administrator and then running the offending command from that window will often prove successful.

```
Administrator: Command Prompt                                        _  □  x

C:\Windows\system32>netstat -nob

Active Connections

  Proto  Local Address          Foreign Address        State          PID
  TCP    127.0.0.1:1063         127.0.0.1:19872        ESTABLISHED    4752
 [Dropbox.exe]
  TCP    127.0.0.1:1068         127.0.0.1:7112         ESTABLISHED    4560
 [vprot.exe]
  TCP    127.0.0.1:2248         127.0.0.1:2249         ESTABLISHED    8816
 [thunderbird.exe]
  TCP    127.0.0.1:2249         127.0.0.1:2248         ESTABLISHED    8816
 [thunderbird.exe]
  TCP    127.0.0.1:2357         127.0.0.1:27015        ESTABLISHED    12276
 [iTunesHelper.exe]
  TCP    127.0.0.1:7112         127.0.0.1:1068         ESTABLISHED    5852
 [loggingserver.exe]
  TCP    127.0.0.1:19872        127.0.0.1:1063         ESTABLISHED    4752
 [Dropbox.exe]
  TCP    127.0.0.1:27015        127.0.0.1:2357         ESTABLISHED    2004
 [AppleMobileDeviceService.exe]
  TCP    192.168.1.20:3951      173.194.68.16:993      ESTABLISHED    8816
 [thunderbird.exe]
  TCP    192.168.1.20:3952      17.172.34.85:993       ESTABLISHED    8816
 [thunderbird.exe]
  TCP    192.168.1.20:3955      192.168.1.15:445       ESTABLISHED    4
 Can not obtain ownership information
  TCP    192.168.1.20:3956      192.168.1.1:445        ESTABLISHED    4
 Can not obtain ownership information
```

Figure 7-7 *Netstat -anob* command

Accessing Memory

All the information we discussed is stored and used by the operating system. If we don't capture it while the device is still running, it will be gone once the machine is shut down. In order to preserve that information, we need to capture an image of computer memory (RAM). Software exists that will allow us to retrieve our volatile information from a memory dump like we could from the memory of a running machine.

A memory dump simply creates a copy of memory from a running computer. How we get access to memory will vary from OS to OS and from version to version of that OS. Assuming that all memory was utilized, we could be storing anywhere from 2 to 8GB of data or more. This calls for intelligent parsing of memory to determine which memory "pages" are in use. One particularly useful combination of software tools is the DumpIt utility (www.moonsols.com/resources) paired with the Volatility framework (code.google.com/p/volatility). The DumpIt utility is the essence of simplicity: It creates a dump file in the connected directory and asks one question: Are you feeling lucky? (Okay, it actually asks, "Do you want to continue?") Answer yes, and the dump file is created after a suitable pause.

 NOTE Think first and then press ENTER. The file that will be generated will be a number of gigabytes of storage, not something that you want to continually copy from place to place. But that was part of your forensic analysis plan, wasn't it?

Once the file has been created, you can provide that as input to the Volatility framework. Basic Volatility commands take the form of

```
python vol.py --profile <machine profile name> <plug-in> <arguments> -f
<dumpfile>
```

In my case, the name of my dump file is CLB-WIN7-20131125-205740.raw (let's call it CLB.raw for short) and my machine profile is WIN7SP1x64 (Windows 7, Service Pack 1, 64-bit OS). The command to run the *pslist* command on that image would be

```
python vol.py --profile WIN7SP1x64 pslist -f CLB.raw
```

Volatility will accept a wide range of input formats. As stated on the software's Web page:

> Volatility supports memory dumps from all major 32- and 64-bit Windows versions and service packs, including XP, 2003 Server, Vista, Server 2008, Server 2008 R2, and 7. Whether your memory dump is in raw format, a Microsoft crash dump, hibernation file, or virtual machine snapshot, Volatility is able to work with it. It also now supports Linux memory dumps in raw or Linux Memory Extractor (LiME) format and includes 35+ plug-ins for analyzing 32- and 64-bit Linux kernels from 2.6.11 to 3.5.x and distributions such as Debian, Ubuntu, OpenSuSE, Fedora, CentOS, and Mandrake. It supports 38 versions of Mac OS X memory dumps, from 10.5 to 10.8.3 Mountain Lion, both 32- and 64-bit. Android phones with Advanced RISC machines (ARM) processors are also supported.[3]

That should be enough to get you going.

Live Investigations: Nonvolatile Information

Nonvolatile data are data that remain (persist) after the device is powered off. Some of the volatile data that we've talked about can still be recovered from persistent storage if certain conditions are met. Microsoft has documented that one condition is whether the pagefile.sys file on Windows is wiped clean when the machine shuts down (this can be controlled by the HKEY_LOCAL_MACHINE\System\CurrentControlSet\Control\Session Manager\Memory Management\ClearPageFileAtShutdown registry key).

What kind of information must persist? Logically, the OS needs to keep enough information available to be able to boot up in essentially the same state it was in when the machine was powered off.

 NOTE One difference would be if there were pending updates, deletions, or other tasks scheduled to run at system shutdown or system startup.

Likewise, information must be kept for any individual user that would allow the user to return to their previous state (for example, restoring the open tabs present when you shut down your web browser).

TIP   Current thinking is that the DFI should perform some live investigation prior to shutting down the computer in order to capture the most valuable information from a running system.

The challenge for a DFI is remembering what all those places are, what tool to use to display the information, and what information will be the most important to either confirm or deny the initial hypothesis. As an experienced DFI, you will learn not to depend on your own memory, but rather create a script file that you can run from an attached portable drive that will retrieve all relevant information.

Earlier we said that there are three general sources of information for forensics analysis. The Windows registry is a treasure trove of information about the state of the device, past and present. History files kept by various applications such as web browsers or Windows 7 jump lists track which web sites have been visited or which files have been accessed. Finally, event log files are either generated by the OS or created by various applications. Combining these sources of information can help the DFI create a timeline of activities on the device where these activities can be corroborated by information stored in other locations. This chapter focuses on information stored on the device itself. In Chapter 9, we'll examine information that is collected external to the device.

Forensic Investigation of a Windows System

Recall that our main purpose in performing this analysis is to prove or disprove our hypothesis concerning the 5WH (who, what, when, where, why and how) for that particular device. One aspect of this analysis is looking at the history of activities: web sites visited, files uploaded, files deleted or modified. A second aspect of our analysis is to ensure that we can prove "individuation"—that is, that the suspect and only the suspect could have performed those activities.

Registry Analysis

Registry analysis is a huge topic, and you literally could write a book on the subject. (And someone did—Harlan Carvey in his book *Windows Registry Forensics: Advanced Digital Forensic Analysis of the Windows Registry*.) The Windows registry is actually composed of multiple files that live in the %Systemroot\system32\Config directory (you will probably need administrative privileges to access this directory if you're running live). The files are named SYSTEM, SECURITY SOFTWARE, and SAM. SAM is the security hive, and isn't accessed via the standard registry tools regedit.exe and reg.exe.

The registry is organized in a hierarchy. At the root of the hierarchy are five major keys, also known as "hives" or root keys. The five root keys are special: You can't modify them, nor can you delete them. In addition, two of them (HKEY_CURRENT_USER and HKEY_CURRENT_CONFIG) are created at runtime and point back to the other keys.

- HKEY_CLASSES_ROOT
- HKEY_CURRENT_USER (subkey of HKEY_USERS)
- HKEY_LOCAL_MACHINE
- HKEY_USERS
- HKEY_CURRENT_CONFIG (subkey of HKEY_LOCAL_MACHINE)

Each cell in the registry is one of the following types:

- **Key cell**   Contains a named key.
- **Value cell**   Contains data. Several registry data types are listed in Table 7-4.
- **Subkey list cell**   List of subkeys for a given key.
- **Value list cell**   List of values for a given subkey.
- **Security descriptor cell**   Security identifier for a particular cell.

Figure 7-8 shows the registry as it appears when using the Regedit program. The root keys are listed in the left pane, and the HKEY_CURRENT_CONFIG has been opened to view the Software\Quicken PDF Printer subkey. The right pane lists values associated with that key. The TC value is stored as REG_BINARY, meaning that only the Quicken PDF Printer software can derive its meaning.

Malware often tries to hide information within the registry. Although ultimately limited, values of type REG_BINARY or REG_EXPAND_SZ can store arbitrary data. Malware can also set itself up to run automatically when the device is powered on. The *Autoruns*(s) tool shows all of the registry keys and their values that pertain to software that is automatically run. For example, the HKLM\SOFTWARE\Microsoft\Windows\CurrentVersion\Run lists all programs that are automatically started. The reg.exe utility allows the DFI to query registry values from the command line. The equivalent *reg* command to list the contents of the HKLM\...\CurrentVersion\Run is

```
reg query HKLM\SOFTWARE\Microsoft\Windows\CurrentVersion\Run
```

Although the output of that command is less visually pleasing, all of the information is there. Harlan Carvery's RegRipper toolset (regripper.wordpress.com) provides yet another means of selectively accessing information based on a profile. Standard profiles exist for the system, software, and security hives.

Windows File Analysis   Several registry keys provide information about user activity in the file system. Table 7-5 lists several registry keys and their description.

Table 7-4 Windows Regis- try Data Types (Source: Russino- vich, M., Solomon, D. *Microsoft* *System Internals*, 4th ed. (WA: Russinovich and Solomon, 2005) p. 185.)	Registry Data Type	Description
	REG_NONE	Key has no value
	REG_SZ	A Unicode string of fixed size
	REG_EXPAND_SZ	Unicode string, varying length
	REG_BINARY	Byte string of variable length
	REG_DWORD	Two 16-bit words, 32 bits
	REG_LINK	Symbolic link
	REG_QWORD	4 16-bit words, 64 bits

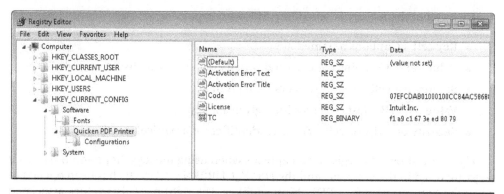

Figure 7-8 Windows registry showing hive, keys, values, and data

Now that you've seen what information is available from registry keys and you know how to access these keys (*regedit, reg,* RegRipper), a better strategy is to obtain a toolset such as the NirSoft utilities or the OSForensics software (www.osforensics.com). These tools provide a canned list of programs that will retrieve the same information and format it to make it more readable. The OSForensics software provides the ability to save this information as a part of a case.

As a DFI, you should also learn at least one scripting language (Perl, Python, PowerShell) so that you can create your own tools if necessary. Perl and Python both offer modules that let you access the Win32 application programming interfaces (APIs) and various system objects like the registry (the RegRipper main program, rr.exe, is written in Perl and has been compiled into a stand-alone .exe file). You won't need to program a solution for every investigation, but you'll be a better investigator if you know how to look under the hood.

Registry Key	Description of Information
HKLM\System\MountedDevices	Various devices mounted on an NT File System (NTFS) file system
HKLM\System\CurrentControlSet\Enum\USBSTOR	USB devices that have been connected to the system
HKCU\Software\Microsoft\Windows\CurrentVersion\Explorer\RecentDocs	Most recently used documents
HKCU\Software\Microsoft\Windows\CurrentVersion\Explorer\RunMRU	Commands executed by the Start | Run options from the Start menu
HKCU\Software\Microsoft\InternetExplorer\TypedURLs	URLs that the user has typed into the address bar
HKCU\\Software\Microsoft\Windows\CurrentVersion\Explorer\ComDLg32\OpenSavePidlMRU	Files accessed by the Open or Save dialog boxes

Table 7-5 Information Stored in Registry Keys (Adapted from: EC-Council, "Windows Forensics I", Computer Forensics: Investigating Hard Disks, File and Operating Systems, (MA: Cengage Learning, 2010), pp. 4:30-4:31.)

Metadata Investigations   All files contain metadata. Some of it may be brief, consisting of the filename, its extension, and its Modified/Accessed/Changed (MAC) times. Other file types contain more extensive metadata. Microsoft Office files often contain information about the author, organization, department, recipients, and so on, as do Portable Document Format (PDF) files. We've already seen that graphics files contain extra metadata that can indicate where and when a particular photograph was taken.

As with any information retrieved from a suspect machine, you need to cross-check information retrieved with other information from that same investigation. Phil Harvey's exiftool software (www.sno.phy.queensu.ca/~phil/exiftool/) allows a user to modify image file metadata such as the date and time the photo was taken. Any discrepancies between the file metadata and the file system metadata will need to be understood and explained.

Analyzing Restore Point Registry Settings

Restore points were introduced in Windows XP, and are an attempt by the OS to capture a snapshot of the state of the OS prior to installing new software. This facility has been updated in Vista and Windows 7 under the name volume shadow copy. Regardless of the name, both techniques will create a copy of files that may be changed during an update so that the update can be rolled back if necessary (such as when a new device driver is uploaded that causes the machine to not boot successfully). Other examples include backing up the Windows registry prior to removing incorrect or outdated information. A DFI can view the earlier version of a file that has been modified since the creation of the last restore point.

Malware Analysis

On occasion, a DFI may be asked to evaluate a claim that a particular system was infected by malware (Trojans, worms, viruses, adware, spyware, and so on). You will need to determine if there is any truth to that claim, and in order to make that determination, you will need to evaluate where there is any evidence of malware on that particular machine. This analysis may require that you make a copy of a running process to disk. The *procdump*(s) utility will do exactly that. The copy of the running program may not be exactly as the file would appear on disk since the malefactor often will use "packer" software—software that compresses ("packs") the file. This is done in order to avoid antivirus or malware scanners that attempt to recognize malware based on its file signature (which, as you may have guessed already, is a hash of the file). True evildoers will use a known packer to pack a program that includes packed code that is password protected.

Static File Analysis   A file on disk can be examined with all the tools we've mentioned previously as applicable to other file types. The *strings*(s) program or Bin-Text (http://www.mcafee.com/us/downloads/free-tools/bintext.aspx) can search for sequences of printable characters, the *grep*(w) program can search for patterns, or the file can be opened using a universal hex editor such as Win-Hex (www.winhex.com). More specialized tools such as PEview or Dependency Walker (www.dependencywalker.com) can list the contents of the header for the portable executables (PE) file, while Dependency Walker will show relationships between various .dll files. These last two programs and other similar programs are meant for the malware analyst. As a rule, a forensic analyst should consider running the file through an antivirus program or sending the file to the www.virustotal.com web site for analysis.

Dynamic File Analysis   Dynamic file analysis requires that the suspicious code be run within a test environment so the DFI can observe its behavior. Two things to watch for are the network connections that are made and the access to files and the registry.

The Wireshark network protocol analyzer (www.Wireshark.org) is your best bet for capturing network traffic. The *procmon*(s) utility from the Sysinternals software suite is an excellent tool for observing runtime behavior on Windows: It captures all calls to the registry as well as opening and closing files. Lastly, running the program under the control of a debugger such as Ollydbg (www.ollydbg.de) or Immunity Debugger (www.immunityinc.com) or a disassembler like Ida Pro (www.hex-rays.com) provides an instruction-by-instruction look at exactly what the software is doing.

You should only run malware on systems that will wiped after the analysis, or on virtual machines. Virtual machine (VM) software such as Parallels, VMware, Microsoft Virtual PC, VirtualBox, or QEMU has excellent candidates for installing versions of various operating systems. Be aware, though, that some malware will behave differently when run in a virtual environment rather than on actual hardware. Once you've finished the analysis, forensically delete the files containing the VMs.

 CAUTION   Don't run malware on your forensic production systems. Malware has been known to "escape from the lab," and cleaning up the mess is neither fun nor quick.

An Overview of Cache, Cookie, and History Analysis

One thing you can count on in a forensic investigation is human laziness. Given a choice, we'd rather have our computers take care of things rather than have to remember what to do. The other aspect of this is that most people won't take the time to read the instructions. While there are ways to delete all of the data saved by a browser, most people won't set it up that way. The same is probably true for "private browsing" that states any file retrieved or any history of the sites you visit won't be recorded.

All browsers, unless instructed otherwise, will keep information around that will allow a user to return to a previous site, quickly, and without having to enter information again. This information includes the following:

- **Cache**   The cache is used to store files downloaded as part of visiting a particular web page, usually graphic images displayed as part of the web page, or ancillary files that may be downloaded, such as video or audio. These data are cached to improve display performance—your browser doesn't have to go back to the web server to retrieve these resources.

- **Cookies** Cookies are collections of name/value pairs that are stored for a particular web site. They can contain information that you've entered for a particular site (such as your login name, e-mail address, and so forth). When you access a web page, the server can request that these cookies be stored on your computer such that if you access the page again, the data stored by the server will be returned in that request.

- **History** Most browsers will gladly keep a history of web sites you've visited in the recent past. Since this history information is labeled with the time and date of access, the history list provides a time-ordered map of where the suspect has been on the Internet. This kind of history will be merged with other time-based events to create a timeline for analysis.

Windows Log Analysis

Logs, log, logs. Sometimes it feels that there are just too many log files to analyze. Windows (and many other operating systems) have system logs, generated by OS services and the OS itself, and application-specific log files. These logs may be stored in a single location (in Linux, it's usually /var/log), by a centralized service (in Linux, it's syslog or syslog-ng), or by individual applications.

Event Logs

The third primary source of information about Windows is the event logs. Event logs are generated either by the OS or by individual applications. If you have created a forensic image of the device's persistent storage and you mount this as a particular file system, your software should be able to access these files directly, assuming that the disk hasn't been encrypted, which presents a different problem. You can view system event logs under the registry key HKLM\System\CurrentControlSet\Services\Eventlog.

The location of the three Windows OS event logs varies depending on the version of the OS in use. In Windows XP, event logs can be found in the %SystemRoot%\System32\Config directory, and are named sysevt.evt, secevent.evt, and appevent.evt. Internally, the files consist of a header record, a floating trailer record, and a set of event records. In Windows 7, they are in %Systemroot%System32\winevt\Logs, and have an .evtx extension, since log file entries in Windows 7 are written in Extensible Markup Language (XML).

The content of these files will vary, depending on the version of Windows you're running. In XP, the files are binary and consist of a header and a series of event records. The event records are treated as a circular buffer, which means that over time, older records are overwritten with newer records. The header record itself consists of 48 bytes that we can represent using the following C programming language structure. The label "uint32" means a 4-byte (32-bit) unsigned integer value that can store values from 0 through 4,294,967,295 inclusive.

```
structure event_header {
        uint32 record_size,      # always 48 (0x30) bytes
        uint32 magic_number,     # always "eLfL" (0x 654c664c)
        unit32 offset_oldest,    # offset of oldest event record
```

```
        unit32 next_event_id,    # ID of the next event record
        uint32 oldest_event_ID,  # ID of the oldest event record
        uint32 max_file_size,    # max file size (from registry)
        uint32 retention_time,   # retention time(from registry)
        unit32 dup_records_size,     # same as record_size above)
}
```

In Vista and Windows 7, the event file is stored in XML format. In Windows 7, the log file extension is .evtx and the files are stored in %Systemroot%\system32\winevt\ logs. You can examine the system event log using standard Windows system administration tools such as eventvwr.exe. Microsoft also provides software called *logparser.exe*(m), and if you're an SQL wizard, this might be your tool of choice. If you're not, then the Log Parser Lizard software provides a GUI interface for searching the event logs.

The three standard event logs are

- Application
- System
- Security

OS event log files can be found in the %Systemroot%\System32\Config directory, and are named sysevt.evt, secevent.evt, and appevent.evt. Internally, the files consist of a header record, a floating trailer record, and a set of event records.

Application Events

Individual application logs can provide more detailed information about application behavior than is recorded in the Windows systems logs. Applications are free to create their own event logs. One location is under the %SystemRoot%\users\<username>\ AppData file system hierarchy. Other applications, especially those that run as services, may store their log files under %SystemRoot%\ProgramData\<progname>. Among the many applications running on a Windows computer, three stand out for forensic investigations: the IIS server (Internet Information Server [web server]), the FTP server, and the system firewall logs. IIS and FTP are two services that allow data from the machine to be read (and written) remotely without a console login. In addition, the firewall log can provide information about traffic in and out of the computer: what was blocked and what was accepted. This information helps to build the case for local information that has been accessed by devices, or data that have been accessed or stored external to the device we're analyzing.

If the firewall log indicates that the user directly connected to the Dropbox file storage service, then we can ask ourselves about what other information we should be seeing. Where's the companion Dropbox folder on the machine? What are the MAC times of files contained within that folder? Do they match? If not, why not? And so forth.

IIS and FTP Server   The IIS stores its log files in the %WinDir%\System32\Log-files directory as a text file, although the location can be reconfigured. Files are stored using a naming convention of *exyymmdd*.log. The default options for storing this log are to have logging enabled and to use the W3C (World Wide Web Consortium) extended log file format. Each field in this record format is named such that you can determine whether the information pertains to the client, the server, or a communication between them. Names beginning with a "c" pertain to the client, "s" to the server, "cs" to client to server, and "sc" to server to client. Table 7-6 lists the fields in the IIS log and their descriptions.

Other fields in the log include bytes sent and received, duration of the action, protocol version (HTTP or FTP), the host name used, the user agent (browser) used to issue the request, the cookie sent or received, the referrer URL, and the protocol substatus error code.

The FTP server stores its logfile in %WinDir%\MSFTPSVC as ex<*yymmdd*>.log. The FTP server uses the same field names as the IIS server, with the exception of fields that don't apply to the FTP service, such as cs-uri-query and the cookie sent or received.

DHCP Server and the Windows Firewall The DHCP (Dynamic Host Configuration Protocol) stores logs in the %SystemRoot%\System32\DHCP directory. If the Windows Firewall is running, logs for that service are stored in %SystemRoot%\System32\pfirewall.log and %SystemRoot%\System32\Wbem\Repository\FS\objects.data.

Figure 7-9 shows the beginning of a Windows Firewall log. Thanks to the helpful headers, we can determine that the time stamps in the file are based on machine local time. The first line of the file is that at 9:58:23 AM on November 26, 2013, TCP traffic from 192.168.1.147 on port 53645 was allowed to 192.168.1.20 port 445. Remaining fields are either zero or not set or available, and the PATH (the module processing the incoming packets) was RECEIVE.

EXAM TIP Know your log file format, since these logs can tell you a great deal about who, what, when, and where information was accessed.

Field Name	Description
Date	Date for this event
Time	Time in UTC
c-IP	Client IP address
cs-Username	Authenticated user name who initiated the request, '-' if anonymous
s-ip	Server IP address
s-port	Server port
cs-method	HTTP method requested (GET, POST, HEAD, and so forth)
cs-uri-stem	The local target of the action, for example, index.html
cs-uri-query	The query requested by the user, only necessary if dynamic pages are in use
sc-status	The HTTP status code
sc-win32-status	The Windows status code

Table 7-6 IIS Log Fields and Descriptions. (Source: W3C Extended Log File Format (IIS 6.0), http://www.microsoft.com/technet/prodtechnol/WindowsServer2003/Library/IIS/676400bc-8969-4aa7-851a-9319490a9bbb.mspx?mfr=true.)

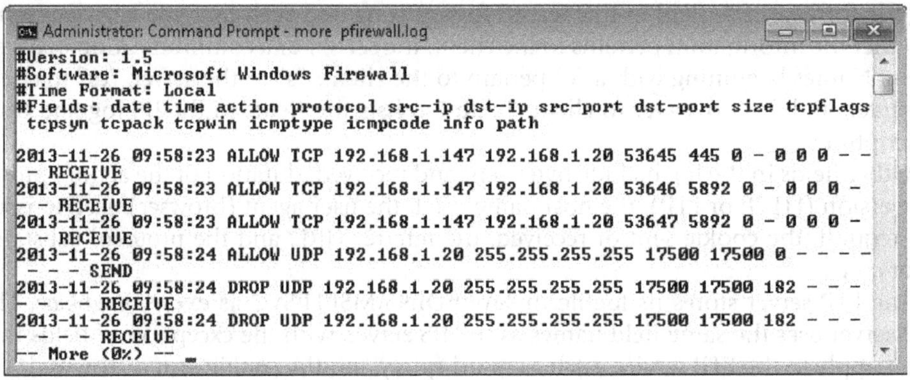

Administrator: Command Prompt - more pfirewall.log

```
#Version: 1.5
#Software: Microsoft Windows Firewall
#Time Format: Local
#Fields: date time action protocol src-ip dst-ip src-port dst-port size tcpflags
 tcpsyn tcpack tcpwin icmptype icmpcode info path

2013-11-26 09:58:23 ALLOW TCP 192.168.1.147 192.168.1.20 53645 445 0 - 0 0 0 - -
- RECEIVE
2013-11-26 09:58:23 ALLOW TCP 192.168.1.147 192.168.1.20 53646 5892 0 - 0 0 0 -
- - RECEIVE
2013-11-26 09:58:23 ALLOW TCP 192.168.1.147 192.168.1.20 53647 5892 0 - 0 0 0 -
- - RECEIVE
2013-11-26 09:58:24 ALLOW UDP 192.168.1.20 255.255.255.255 17500 17500 0 - - - -
- - - SEND
2013-11-26 09:58:24 DROP UDP 192.168.1.20 255.255.255.255 17500 17500 182 - - -
- - - RECEIVE
2013-11-26 09:58:24 DROP UDP 192.168.1.20 255.255.255.255 17500 17500 182 - - -
- - - RECEIVE
-- More (0%) --
```

Figure 7-9 List of the Windows Firewall log

The Importance of Event Logs

Events stored in the OS event logs are one of three types: error, warning, or information. Events are stored with an event ID, and several event records signify information about the state of the machine that helps the DFI determine the timeline of events that occurred on that particular device. Consider the various programs that run as services on Windows (Linux users will recognize that as system daemons). Two significant events are[4]

- Event ID 7035 (a service has been requested to stop)
- Event ID 7036 (the service has stopped)

Account management events include

- Event ID 624 (an account has been created)
- Event ID 642 (an account has been modified)
- Event ID 612 (modifications were made to the audit policy)

Event IDs 560 (an object has been opened), 567 (object access attempted), and 562 (handle closed) indicate access to a particular object if auditing is enabled.

Another critical aspect for the forensic analyst is identifying who and when someone was logged onto the system. Several events provide data concerning logins:

- Event ID 4624 (successful logon)
- Event ID 4647 (user-initiated logoff; both logon and logoff events are correlated by logon ID)
- Event ID 4625 (logon failure)

The logon failure codes provide additional information for the forensic analyst. Table 4-7 presents the failure codes that are most interesting for the analyst since they indicate an abnormal condition.

Failure Code	Description
0xC0000064	User name does not exist.
0xC000006A	User name is correct but the password is wrong.
0xC00000234	User is currently locked out.
0xC000006F	User tried to log on outside of restricted times.
0xC000015b	The user hasn't been granted the requested logon type.

Table 7-7   Interesting Login Failure Codes and Descriptions

Windows Password Storage

Windows password storage is provided in the Security Account Manager (SAM) hive file in the %SystemRoot%\System32\Config directory. Passwords are not stored as cleartext; instead, various algorithms are used to create a hash code from the entered password. Algorithms for creating the password hash include the Lanman (LM) hash function (still in use, primarily for backward compatibility) and the NT Lanman (NTLM) hash that repairs several security flaws with the LM password. Systems that are members of a domain will use Kerberos authentication. The RegRipper tool provides a specific profile for accessing SAM information.

Theory into Practice: Forensics Tools for Windows

We've already talked about a number of tools that are provided either as part of a standard Windows OS distribution or as a suite of third-party tools. We'll look further at several integrated forensic tools suites in Chapter 8. The OSForensics software straddles the line between a tool suite and a more full-featured forensic suite.

Frequently, alternatives exist for performing a particular type of analysis. As an example, consider the different tools available for searching the event logs. If we don't have anything else available, the standard Windows event viewer supports searching for particular events. The DFI will turn to the Windows system event logs for more general analysis. You can access these logs via the command C:\Windows\System\eventvwr.exe, or click the Event Viewer entry under the Administrator menu. Where this entry is located will vary based on your OS; on my Windows 7 machine, it's in the Start menu under All Programs | Administrator Tools.

As is the case with other kinds of treasure, just because you know where it is, this doesn't mean that you won't have to work to get it.

Figure 7-10 shows the dialog box for searching the system event log for all error events.

The Windows LogParser.exe software is a command-line tool that enables the user to search multiple log formats using an SQL-like syntax. The command

```
LogParser "Select * from System where EventTypeName = 'Error Event'"
```

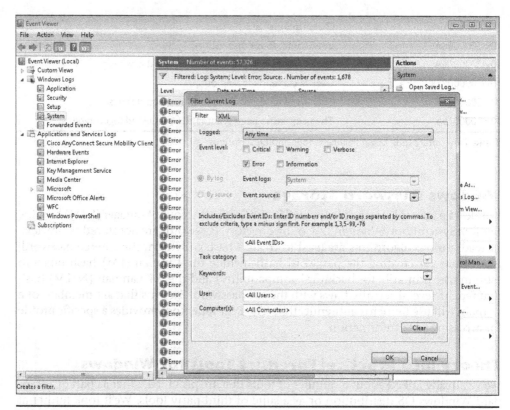

Figure 7-10 Searching with Windows Event Viewer

would list all error events from the System event log. The Log Parser Lizard software (www.lizard-labs.net) provides a powerful GUI front end to this program. Figure 7-11 shows the results for the aforementioned command when using this tool.

Cracking Passwords

In this section, we will examine the various techniques and tools used when cracking passwords. A "password cracker" (usually abbreviated to "cracker" versus "hacker") is someone who specializes in extracting and decoding passwords from applications or operating systems. A software program used to extract and decode these passwords can be called a "password cracker" as well, although context should distinguish between the two. The goal of this software is to retrieve the plain text password ("plain") from its encrypted form by effectively "guessing" the password or by using all possible combinations of characters entered from a computer keyboard (called "brute forcing" the password).

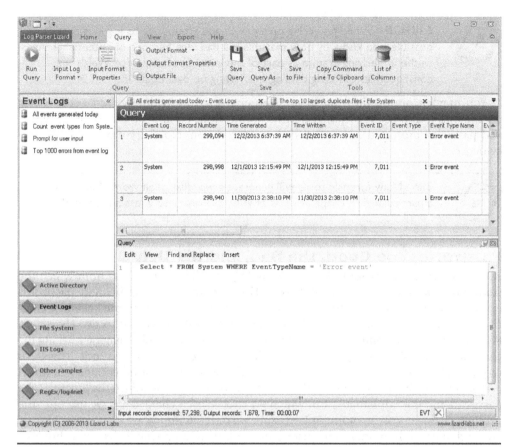

Figure 7-11   Log Parser Lizard GUI for the Windows event logs

A DFI becomes a password cracker at certain stages in an investigation. One stage could be booting up a machine where the BIOS has been password protected, or attempting to log in as an administrator or other privileged user. The BIOS password can be defeated by removing the battery that provides power to the system when the device itself is powered off. About half an hour later, you should be able to replace the battery and power up the device such that you can access the BIOS, and the password should be blank. If you're attempting to log on to a device as an administrator, you can use a special boot disk called a rescue disk to modify passwords on the subject disk in order to log in. On such disk is the "ntpasswd" disk that can change the administrator password on a Windows OS. This disk boots up a live Linux distribution that contains a program that will search out the password file on the subject disk and set the administrator password to blank (meaning no password). Restart the subject machine and log in as an administrator with no password. Done and dusted.

CAUTION While powering on a device and attempting to log in is certainly possible, you know by now that this is a bad idea because of potential changes to the underlying system as part of the initial boot sequence. Weigh the consequences of losing data against having no data at all.

You may encounter files that have been encrypted individually (Microsoft Office documents, .pdf files, .zip files, and other applications all allow a file to be encrypted and password protected). No password, no decryption. No decryption, no probative evidence.

 TIP Many forensic tools will generate a wordlist of all words found on a particular disk image. Try this as your dictionary to guess a password.

Passwords: The Good, the Bad, and the Ugly

Before we begin, let's establish some terminology. The set of characters from which the password is created is called the "alphabet." The larger the alphabet, the more passwords we can generate of length N (the "keyspace"). For example, if we have the lowercase characters "abcde" in our alphabet and I limit the length of the password to two characters, then we have 25 possibilities (5 * 5)—so few, in fact, that you could imagine cracking the password by simply entering all the possibilities until you find the right one. This technique is called "brute forcing," and is guaranteed to work, given world enough and time.

The time needed to examine all the possible candidates depends on the length of the password and the "alphabet" from which we choose each character. If we use only the printing characters on a computer keyboard, we have 26 uppercase characters, 26 lowercase characters, 10 numeric characters, and 33 punctuation characters, for a choice of 26 + 26 + 10 + 32 = 95 possible characters. If we allow control characters (CTRL key + an alphabetic characters), we add another 26 characters to the mix (CTRL -A through CTRL -Z). Assuming that each character is equally probable, all two-character printing sequences are 95 * 95 = 95^2 = 9,025 possibilities. Three-character strings result in 857,375 possibilities, and six-character strings result in 735,091,890,625 possibilities. If you could guess 1 million passwords per second, it would take 735,091 seconds, or roughly 8.5 days, to brute force this password; 1,000 guesses per second would require 23+ years.

Standard Password Advice

Standard password advice is a combination of do's and don'ts.[5] When creating a password, *don't*

- Use words from a dictionary. *Any* dictionary.
- Use personal information (family members, birthdays, favorite sports teams, and so on).
- Use a small alphabet (for example, all lowercase letters and numbers).
- Use passwords shorter than 8 characters.

Conversely, when you create a password, *do* make sure that you

- Change the password frequently.
- Use one password in one place only.
- Use a phrase that you can remember, and then use a system of replacing letters with numbers and symbols. As an example: "Mary had a little lamb / its fleece was white as snow" might become "Mh@ll/1fw**@5"—13 characters long, upper-/lowercase alphabetic, numbers, and printable symbols. Looks promising, doesn't it? Read on.

NOTE Remember that your password has to be chosen randomly. The problem with "Mary had a little lamb..." is that it follows an algorithm for replacing characters as well as dictionary words and is a phrase from a well-known nursery rhyme in North America and the United Kingdom.

Longer is better—the more characters in your password, the more time it would take to crack. The best way to choose a password is to use a generator. Figure 7-12 shows the generation dialog box from the 1Password program. In addition to specifying the

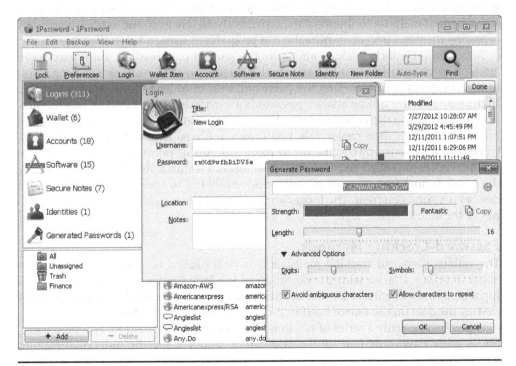

Figure 7-12 Password generation dialog from 1Password

length of the password and the alphabet, you can specify whether to duplicate characters and not to use characters that can be mistaken one for another. My personal favorites are "0" and "O" and "l" and "1": In many cases, the font chosen will represent these characters such that they aren't distinguishable to the human eye—at least not to this human's eye.

Classifications of Password-Cracking Software

Password-cracking software can be designated as either system software or application software. The examples we've shown so far have been system software, as it's aimed at deriving the passwords for system applications (such as the logon applications). Application software is meant for particular applications. The major components of Microsoft Office (Word, Excel, and PowerPoint) all have individual programs aimed at retrieving the password from files created by those applications. Other tools are available to look up passwords for web browsers: the NirSoft utilities include *ChromePass*(n), *IE Passview*(n), and *PasswordFox*(n).

Password-Cracking Types

Password-cracking types generally are considered either online or offline and active or passive. Passive online attacks include extracting passwords from network communications (aka "sniffing the wire") or by initiating a "man in the middle" (MiTM) attack, grabbing a hash, and then initiating a replay attack. Passive offline attacks include using some form of malware to intercept the separate characters from the user's password by capturing the password, or starting the real program, or using a keystroke logger.

Active online attacks include attempting to guess a password via automated login attempts, such as to a web site. Hash injection attacks involve an attacker gaining access to a user's device and extracting the password hash in order to impersonate the user. In the case of active online attacks, passwords are extracted from network communication or by directing the victim to a site that is impersonating a real web site in order for the victim to enter their credentials. In all cases, our goal is to obtain either the password itself or an encrypted value of the password. At this point, most direct attacks at online services are foiled because of account lockout features. As a defender, increasing the "work factor" (the amount of time an adversary has to spend compromising your device) is a good deterrent. The longer it takes, the greater the chance that someone will notice the attack.

Password-Cracking Methods

The various password-cracking methods that we'll discuss here are all methods that apply to offline attacks, with the exception of the "educated guess." Given that, most login accounts will enforce a timeout after a certain number of bad entries, or possibly destroy the data on the device itself in the case of certain smart phones.

A *guess* isn't usually a series of random words or characters. Instead, educated guessing is using passwords that utilize information about a specific individual (family, friends, hobbies, religious affiliation, favorite movies or books, and so on). In addition, these words will be transformed in regular ways based on research indicating that many people modify their passwords in particular ways, including capitalizing the first letter and ending the passphrase with a punctuation symbol.

A *dictionary* attack will try a set of words from a dictionary or wordlist. Dictionaries are available for multiple languages, and you can obtain lists of passwords of users who have been part of a logged-in community. There are multiple variations on a dictionary attack. These include a hybrid attack where the attackers use dictionary words with other characters either appended or prepended (passwords that consist of a word plus a "!" character are quite popular). Similar to this is the syllable attack that combines brute force and dictionary attacks. Instead of the whole word, the attacker combines syllables to create nondictionary words (think "psydood").

 TIP Many forensic tools will generate a wordlist of all words found on a particular disk image. Try this as your dictionary to guess a password.

The most basic attack is the *brute force* attack. Here, the attacker tries to derive a password by creating strings of all possible characters. Given world enough and time, brute force will always find a password (on the average, this will take 50 percent of the time required to guess all the passwords).

As Bruce Schneier once said, attacks against cryptography just keep getting better, never worse. So it is with password cracking. Ars Technica (www.arstechnica.com) ran a series of articles during 2013 that clearly demonstrated recent advances in password cracking. Using GPUs (graphics processing units—like CPUs but part of the graphics hardware) markedly increases the number of tries per second. "A PC running a single AMD Radeon HD7970 GPU, for instance, can try on average an astounding 8.2 billion password combinations each second, depending on the algorithm used to scramble them."[6] A major source of new information is a security breach where user names and password hashes are downloaded. Aside from impersonating a legitimate user, these password lists provide a treasure trove of actual password usage "in the wild." A professional cracker will add these passwords to their dictionaries to use in future password-cracking attempts. Astute password crackers are now entering phrases from Wikipedia and the Bible: One researcher was able to crack the password "Ph'nglui mglw'nafh Cthulhu R'lyeh wgah'nagl fhtagn1" because it had appeared in a Wikipedia article.[7]

Rule-based attacks are used when a particular set of constraints is known. For example, some systems provide rules for passwords that look like this: The password must be at least eight characters long; have at least one uppercase character, one number, and one special character (what we've listed as "printable" previously); and cannot be a word found in the dictionary. Given this information, a cracker can program these into a rule that will only select strings that match these criteria.

Finally, *rainbow tables* are special files that contain starting and ending values of a chain (sequence) of a particular length. The chain is produced by alternating a particular hash function (say, MD5) with a reduction function that can generate a new (plain text) password given a hash value. If we want to derive the plain text password given its hash value, we apply the reduction function and see if the result is in one of our end points. If so, we start at the beginning of the chain and alternate applying hash and

An Example of Brute Force Searching

Many years ago, in a country far, far away, I worked for an organization that had a secure room—a sensitive compartmented information facility (SCIF, pronounced "skiff") in military parlance. There were two doors: The external door was protected by a four-digit button lock, and, as I recall, the second was secured by a lock requiring two-factor authentication (you needed a particular badge as well as a passcode). One of my colleagues decided to brute force the lock on the exterior door, so every time he passed by that door (it was on the way to the bathrooms, the cafeteria, and the building exit), he would key in a different four-digit number. It took him two or three weeks, but he finally obtained the combination. He never opened that exterior door or went any farther into the secure room, and policies would have dictated changing that combination in short order, regardless.

reduction functions until we find the plain text that creates our initial hash. This technique allows us to store and recompute hash chains that can reflect all possible passwords given a particular alphabet (such as all lowercase letters). By precomputing our hash chains and by saving only the starting and ending plain text values, we trade off storage space for computation time. This doesn't mean that rainbow tables are small: Collections of rainbow table files can easily exceed 1TB of storage.

Social Engineering Passwords

Social engineering occurs when a victim somehow is convinced to reveal their password. Good social engineers understand what motivates people to reveal information (such as helping someone in trouble, or baser instincts like the love of chocolate), and are experts at working their confidence games. After all, why waste time trying to brute force an eight-character password when a well-chosen tale of hard luck and desperation might extract the password much more quickly?

The online version of this game is the "phishing" e-mail that announces a bank account has been blocked and you should really log in to the bank's web site using the URL provided. If you do access that site, it will look remarkably like the real bank's web site (it should—most of the data have been downloaded from the actual site), including the dialog box where you're asked for your login information (user name and password). Enter your credentials here, and you will find yourself redirected to the actual web site. It will ask you to re-enter your credentials, which is a little surprising, but you assume that you mistyped something, and all goes smoothly after that, until the day you discover that your account balance is now $0. "Spear phishing" is when a high-value executive is made a target—often, high-level executives have a great deal of privilege regarding what information they can access.

Default Passwords

Many vendors ship products with a default password. The Internet is littered with lists of particular vendors and the default passwords for their products. For many reasons (most including human laziness and ease of use), the default passwords are never changed, although some vendors require that you change the default password when installing their software products.

 TIP When encountering a new device that is password protected, look to see if that make and model is contained in a default password list. Try that one first. You may be pleasantly surprised.

Theory into Practice: Password-Cracking Tools

Some of the classic password-cracking tools are still available. Among them are Cain and Abel (www.oxid.it/cain.html) and Ettercap (www.ettercap.github.io/ettercap) that are used for capturing passwords from the network. John the Ripper (www.openwall.com/john) and L0phtcrack6 (www.l0phtcrack.com) are offline tools. Figure 7-13 illustrates the Cain UI. In this case, we see the password listed between a Dropbox client and the Dropbox server.

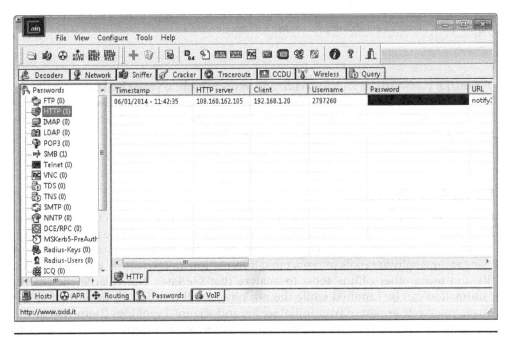

Figure 7-13 Cain UI displaying captured password

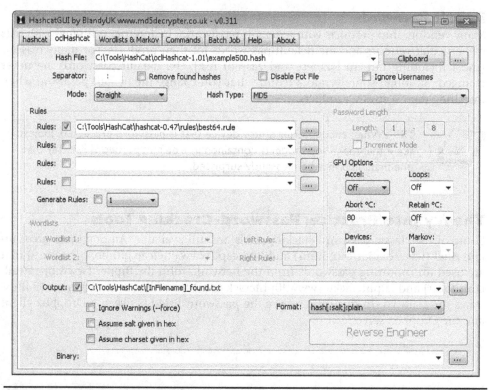

Figure 7-14   Hashcat-gui showing parameter settings

A major password-cracking tool currently in use is hashcat (www.hashcat.net/hashcat). This software supports over 80 different hashing algorithms and five attack modes (straight, combination, toggle case, brute force, permutation, and table lookup), the first two of which can support external rules. Figure 7-14 illustrates the hashcat-gui front end to the tool.[8]

Chapter Review

Conducting a forensic analysis on a computer running a Windows OS is a matter of knowing where to look for the information you need to place the suspect at the key-board. Volatile information can only be captured if the machine is already running by using various software tools to extract that information, or by creating a memory dump file and using other offline tools to analyze that file later. Nonvolatile (persistent) information can be captured while the machine is still running, or from the forensic image you create as part of your initial search and seizure. Event logs (both system and application) and the Windows registry provide nonvolatile information that can help you identify a suspect's actions prior to the seizure of the device.

Password hashes are stored in the SAM hive in the %systemroot%\system32\config directory. Passwords can be computed using the obsolete LM function, NTLMv1 or NTLMv2, or via MD4. Passwords for web sites are stored either in a Windows-protected area or in database files maintained by individual browsers.

Password cracking is the attempt to determine the password used by a particular application or to log on to a device. Online attacks against passwords may involve repeated login attempts or using software tools to extract the hashed password from the network traffic. Offline attacks attempt to crack the password when provided with the hashed version of the password. It's becoming much easier to crack a password given the increases in computing power (using GPUs in parallel to increase the number of candidate searches). Also, crackers have become more proficient in generating dictionaries. Combine the two, and even the seemingly best passwords may fail in time.

Questions

1. Dumping a copy of memory saves what kind of information?

   A. Volatile

   B. Nonvolatile

   C. Historical

   D. Snapshot

2. Where would a forensic analyst look for web sites that were previously accessed? Choose all that apply.

   A. Registry

   B. Shared cookie

   C. Page cache

   D. Browsing history

3. Where are Internet Explorer saved passwords stored?

   A. The Windows protected area

   B. IEPasswd.dat

   C. NTuser.dat

   D. The HKEY_CURRENT_USER registry key

4. Microsoft's log parser software uses which language to query the registry?

   A. Perl

   B. Python

   C. SQL

   D. PowerShell

5. Which of the following tools can be used to dump memory for a particular process?

    A. DumpIt

    B. Procdump

    C. Procmon

    D. MemDump

6. Which files contain metadata beyond file size, filename, modified times, and so forth? Choose all that apply.

    A. EXE files

    B. JPEG files

    C. Microsoft Office files

    D. PDF files

7. What can an analyst use to view previous versions of a file? Choose all that apply.

    A. Windows restore points

    B. Recycle Bin

    C. The HKEY_CURRENT_USER\...\FileVersions registry key

    D. Windows backup volumes

8. True or false: The MD5 algorithm is used to compress file data.

    A. True

    B. False

9. Which tool allows the analyst to view all registry and file system access?

    A. Procexp

    B. Procmon

    C. ListDLLs

    D. ProcViewer

10. What is the purpose of establishing a timeline of activity?

    A. Correlate suspect's activities with external activities

    B. Identify possible network activity

    C. Track failed logins

    D. Identify gaps in use of the device

11. What is the term for targeted e-mail or social engineering attacks against a high-value target?

    A. Whaling

    B. Tagging

    C. Spear phishing

    D. Frack attack

12. Given a hash value, a password cracker tries to derive the _____ password.

    A. Cryptotext

    B. MD4

    C. NTLMv2

    D. Plain text

13. Hash injection attacks occur when _____.

    A. Hashed passwords are replaced in network traffic

    B. Hashed passwords are modified, thereby denying service

    C. Hashed passwords from previous logins are used to impersonate another user

    D. Hashed passwords are passed in carrier files

14. This form of password cracking uses precomputed tables with hash chains to derive all possible passwords for a given alphabet.

    A. Rainbow tables

    B. Dictionaries

    C. Brute force

    D. Intelligent guessing

15. Using _____ allows a password cracker to look up the hash of a password in a list of passwords and their associated hashes.

    A. Rainbow tables

    B. Dictionaries

    C. Brute force

    D. Intelligent guessing

Answers

1. A. Volatile.

2. A, D. Registry and browsing history.

3. A. Windows protected area.

4. C. SQL.

5. **A.** DumpIt.

6. **A, B, C, D.** All these file types contain extra metadata.

7. **A.** Windows restore points.

8. **B.** False.

9. **B.** Procmon.

10. **A.** Correlate suspect's activities with external activities.

11. **C.** Spear phishing.

12. **D.** Plain text passwords.

13. **C.** Hashed passwords from prior logins are used to impersonate that user.

14. **A.** Rainbow tables.

15. **B.** Dictionaries.

References

1. EC-Council. "Windows Forensics I", *Computer Forensics: Investigating Hard Disks, File and Operating Systems*, (MA: Cengage Learning, 2009), pp. 4:2.

2. Nair, S. *Live Response Using PowerShell 2* (MA: SANS, 2011), pp. 10–11.

3. "The Volatility Framework." Retrieved from www.google.com/p/volatility.

4. EC-Council. "Windows Forensics II," *Computer Forensics: Investigating Hard Disks, File and Operating System* (MA: Cengage Learning, 2009) pp. 5:8-5:9.

5. EC-Council. *Computer Forensics: Investigating Hard Disks, File and Operating Systems* (MA: Course Technology, 2010), pp. 7–28.

6. Goodin, D. "Why Passwords Have Never Been Weaker—and Crackers Have Never Been Stronger" (Ars Technica, 8/20/2012). Retrieved from http://arstechnica.com/security/2012/08/passwords-under-assault/.

7. Goodin, D. "How the Bible and YouTube Are Fueling the Next Frontier of Password Cracking" (Ars Technica, 10/8/2013). Retrieved from http://arstechnica.com/security/2013/10/how-the-bible-and-youtube-are-fueling-the-next-frontier-of-password-cracking/.

8. Retrieved from Hashcat.org/hashcat-gui.

Forensic Investigations

In this chapter, you will learn how to
- Install and configure Forensic Toolkit and EnCase
- Create a case and add the data
- Analyze the data
- Generate the report

We've talked about individual analysis tools in a previous chapter. An alternative to creating your own forensic software toolkit is to use a software distribution specifically configured for forensic investigations, or to use a particular forensic software program.

A forensic software distribution combines a collection of programs with a host operating system. Many of these distributions are Linux based, and can be either installed to a hard disk or run "live" from a bootable medium such as a CD-ROM or a universal serial bus (USB) drive. Multiple distributions exist, and some are available to everyone, while others are restricted to law enforcement. The following three distributions are freely available for everyone:

- The SANS (Systems Administration, Networking and Security) SIFT (SANS Investigative Forensic Toolkit) workstation is packaged either as an .iso file or a VMware image. The current version as of this writing (winter 2013) is 2.14. The distribution is Linux based.

- The Digital Evidence & Forensics Toolkit (DEFT) distribution (www.deftlinux.net) is packaged as an .iso file, and is Linux based. The distribution also includes the Digital Advanced Response Toolkit (DART) program suite that can be run either under a Windows operating system (OS) (in the case of live capture), or by using the Wine package (a Windows environment) that is part of the Linux distribution. The current version as of winter 2013 is DEFT 8 with DART 2.

- The Appliance for Digital Analysis and Investigation (ADIA) distribution (www .cert.org/forensics/tools) is packaged as either a VMware or VirtualBox virtual machine (VM), or as an .iso file. It is based on either Fedora or CentOS Linux. The current release is hosted on Fedora 17 for i386 and x86-64 versions.

Each of these distributions contains several frameworks for digital forensic investigation. These frameworks include Autopsy/The Sleuth Kit (TSK), Ptk (another GUI front end for TSK), and PyFlag. In each case, the framework organizes material in such a way as to make it easier for the digital forensics investigator (DFI) to discover and categorize evidence.

We will use several different instances of forensic investigation software to illustrate applying the process. Our primary software will be the Forensic Toolkit (FTK) from Accessdata (www.accessdata.com) and EnCase Forensics from Guardian Software (www .encase.com). We'll also include examples from ProDiscover (www.techpathways.com), Forensic Explorer (www.getdata.com), and Autopsy/TSK from Brian Carrier (www .sleuthkit.org/autopsy). We'll use a common case as the source of our analysis. The case is called "Hacking" and is available at www.cfreds.nist.gov. The case consists of either a set of raw files (in .dd format) or two EnCase evidence files, EO1 and EO2. We've chosen to use the EnCase Evidence files in our example.

 EXAM TIP Without going into excruciating details, you will need to know on which screen information will appear for EnCase and FTK.

Forensic Investigations

At this point, we've usually acquired the source of our digital evidence, either in the form of raw files (captured with dd, for example), or in a particular specialized format, the most notable of which is the Evidence Witness Format (EWF) used by EnCase. As a rule, any forensic distribution will be able to read and use raw files and EWF files, or convert them to their own proprietary format.

There is ongoing debate regarding which OS should be used to investigate disk images produced by another OS. An advantage in using the same OS as was used by the device that was captured is that you can use native tools to interrogate and examine the data extracted from the digital device. Table 8-1 shows the breakdown of the analysis OS versus the OS running on the suspect machine.

Clearly, the issue is whether the analysis distribution or workstation is able to interpret the file systems most commonly associated with a particular OS, as well as with any historical information or configuration information. Linux, for example, has nothing that compares with the Windows Registry or the Windows Event Log files.

In our examples, we'll be using Windows versions of our investigative software, since only Autopsy provides a Linux version, which presently lags behind the Windows version.

Distribution OS	Device OS	Example
Linux	Linux, Mac OS	Autopsy
Linux	Windows	Autopsy
Windows	Linux, Mac OS	FTK, EnCase, ProDiscover, Autopsy
Windows	Windows	FTK, EnCase, ProDiscover. Autopsy

Table 8-1 Host OS and Supported OS

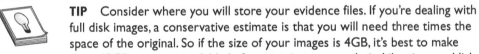 **TIP** Familiarize yourself with the options, capabilities, and performance characteristics of your chosen software prior to installation. Pay close attention to the machine specifications recommended by the vendor, and assume that these are the *minimum* criteria needed to have the software stagger to its feet. Running like the wind will require a beefier machine.

This chapter discusses disk-based forensics. We previously said that a DFI needs to avail herself of information from all relevant sources, and these include network activity on the seized device, network logs from other devices on the network, and logs from applications that have network connections. Chapters 9 and 11 discuss network forensics and application forensics, both web and e-mail applications.

Installation and Configuration

Installation for all of these software suites will be familiar to anyone who has used the Microsoft Windows OS. Installation files are provided as an .msi (Microsoft Installer file), .exe file, or .zip archives, and executable files are stored in the usual places (C:\ Program Files or C:\Program Files (x86)). Configuration varies for each software package, although common elements include where to install case files, naming conventions for case containers, where to store evidence files, where to store backups, and so forth.

TIP Consider where you will store your evidence files. If you're dealing with full disk images, a conservative estimate is that you will need three times the space of the original. So if the size of your images is 4GB, it's best to make sure that you have 12GB or more available before starting your analysis. Likewise, establish a naming convention for your cases and for your directory structures if your software doesn't enforce it.

Creating the Case and Adding Data

So what's the next step in our investigation? If you had said, "Fire up the software and get to analyzing," you would have been a bit premature. The first thing a DFI needs to do is review the information they have about the case and develop a hypothesis. Sure, you could go ahead and fire up the software, import your forensic image, and start clicking around like a drunken monkey. (I've heard the phrase "click monkeys" used to describe such individuals. No disrespect meant to any monkeys that might be reading this book.)

Let's look at the description of our sample case. We've been provided the following information:

On 09/20/04, a Dell CPi notebook computer, serial # VLQLW, was found abandoned along with a wireless PCMCIA card and an external homemade 802.11b antenna. It is suspected that this computer was used for hacking purposes, although it cannot be tied to our hacking suspect, Greg Schardt. Schardt also goes by the online nickname of "Mr. Evil," and some of his associates have said that he would park his vehicle within range of wireless access points like Starbucks and other T-Mobile hotspots, where he would then intercept Internet traffic, attempting to get credit card numbers, user names, and passwords.

Find any hacking software, evidence of their use, and any data that might have been generated. Attempt to tie the computer to the suspect, Greg Schardt.

A DD image (in seven parts) and an EnCase image of the abandoned computer have already been made.[1]

Our challenge (should we choose to accept it) has two parts:

1. Find any hacking software. Determine when it was used and any data generated from those tools. Questions: Do I, as the investigator, know what constitutes "hacking software"? Do I know what kind of output these programs generate and where it might be stored?

2. Tie the computer to Greg Schardt. This is a good example of individuation, better known as "placing the suspect behind the keyboard." (The title of a great book by Brett Shavers.) Questions: How might I map ownership of this computer to a particular individual? Where would I find the data to prove or disprove this?

Armed with this strategy, I can now start my forensics analysis software. Figure 8-1 illustrates the opening screen for the Autopsy graphical user interface (GUI).

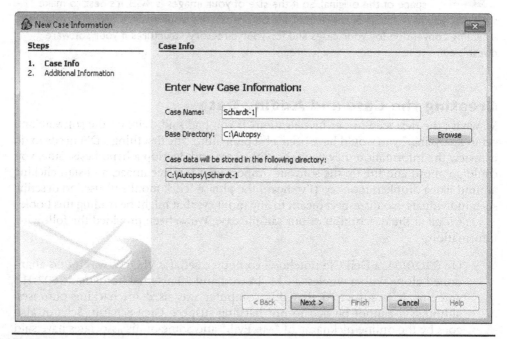

Figure 8-1 Autopsy GUI

Regardless of what software you're using, the first thing that you will be asked to do is generate a case structure. A case structure combines metadata about a particular case with a defined storage area that will contain the evidence that you collect to support your assertions. In most instances, this disk area may well be protected by operating systems capabilities such that only the investigator who opened the case can access the data stored within it.

At a minimum, the software will ask you to create a case name and a case identifier. In our example case, I chose to create a case name of GSchardt-1 and a case identifier of 20131213-GSchardt-1. You may be asked to provide a description, as well as to enter the evidence identifier that was generated when the digital device was actually seized. Figure 8-2 shows the interface for entering that data.

In the Linux version of Autopsy, a case is structured as a set of hosts (physical or virtual devices) and a set of images taken from that host. In Windows, Autopsy simply requests a single disk image or a live disk. Figure 8-3 shows the interface for entering this information. In this instance, I simply pointed Autopsy at the evidence file provided as part of the hacking case.

TIP You cannot be detailed enough in this kind of recordkeeping. Our goal is to identify a particular device and a particular set of images obtained from it. The closer you tie the results of your investigation to the physical devices seized, the easier time you will have when writing your reports and testifying in court. Including make, model, and serial number of the device as part of your case file definitely is called for. Even though you're using an automated tool, manual recordkeeping still has its place. It's a habit worth developing.

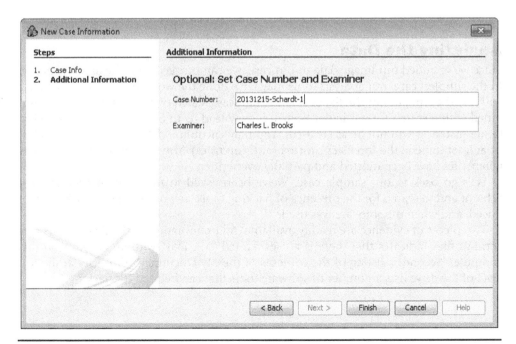

Figure 8-2 Autopsy GUI for creating a case

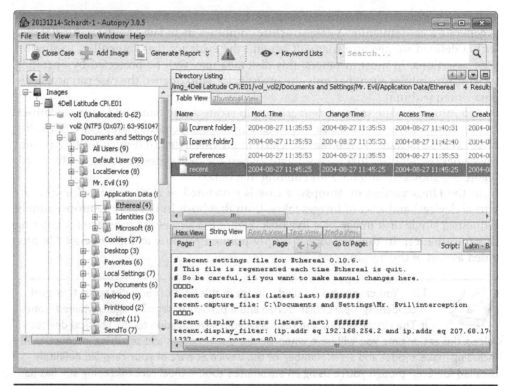

Figure 8-3 Autopsy GUI for adding a disk image file

Analyzing the Data

Once we've added our image data to our case, we can proceed with the analysis phase. In the simplest case, our analysis tools may have done the work for us. If we're dealing with child pornography, the list of images that was created by the software when combined with a search for particular keywords may lead us to our evidence very quickly. Other instances will not be as clear-cut. You may encounter deliberate attempts to foil or at least impede the forensics process (anti-forensics). You may encounter instances where files have been deleted and partially overwritten.

Let's go back to our sample case. We've been asked to tie the computer to Greg Schardt and to search for the presence of hacking tools, any output they may have produced, and when the software was used.

Two pieces of evidence are readily available. An examination of the Documents and Settings files indicates that there is a user named "Mr. Evil" with an account on this computer. Second, a listing of the contents of the My Documents directory at the top level of the drive lists a number of software tools that can be used for hacking.

NOTE The presence of certain software programs isn't necessarily an indication of hacking activity. Tools such as nmap, Wireshark, nc, and others are used for systems administration and infrastructure debugging. One story tells us of an investigator who spent days discovering what appeared to be hacking tools on an employee's workstation only to discover that the device was assigned to a network/system administrator who used these tools as part of their normal duties.

What isn't usual is a set of tools that enable someone to monitor Wi-Fi networks to steal user credentials and account numbers. The Cain and Abel software, for example, supports retrieving and cracking passwords from network traffic. Other software tools include ethereal (a network packet capture program and the precursor to Wireshark), netstumbler (an 802.11 network discovery tool), and l0pht301 (a password-cracking tool).

 NOTE How did I know what these tools do? An experienced digital forensics/incident response (DFIR) professional will recognize certain software tools that are common to white hats and black hats alike. Looking through the list of software provided on the Kali Linux distribution (a distribution aimed at supporting penetration testers) will give you a good idea of what these tools are.

Generating the Report

Once we've collected the evidence that fulfills the work that we've been assigned to do or that supports our working hypothesis, it's time to generate a report on the results of our examination. Figure 8-4 shows a portion of the report generated by Autopsy about the work that we've done. In the case of Autopsy, we've used the Bookmark and Tags features to list important files along with their significance.

Bookmark		
Comment	File Name	File Path
Ethereal run on final day	ethereal-setup-0.10.6[1].exe	/img_4Dell Latitude CPi.E01/vol_vol2/Documents and Settings/Mr. Evil/Local Settings/Temporary Internet Files/Content.IE5/PN0J7OQM/ethereal-setup-0.10.6[1].exe
agent.exe is a newsreader	agent.exe	/img_4Dell Latitude CPi.E01/vol_vol2/Program Files/Agent/agent.exe
My_Documents in C:\ directory	My Documents	/img_4Dell Latitude CPi.E01/vol_vol2/My Documents
Mr. Evil is only registered user	Mr. Evil	/img_4Dell Latitude CPi.E01/vol_vol2/Documents and Settings/Mr. Evil

Figure 8-4 Bookmark section of an Autopsy report

Choosing the Proper Forensic Software

A DFI has several different forensics distributions and software suites available for performing examinations. FTK, Win-Hex Forensics, and EnCase have been verified by the National Institute of Standards (NIST) Computer Forensics Tool Testing (CFTT) program. Others either have not been verified or may be in process of being verified. Several companies (AccessData, Guardian Software, X-Ways, and Technology Pathways) provide training on using their software; all offer formal certifications of expertise as well. Usually, these commercial tools are purchased by enterprise-sized businesses that can afford the upfront costs and the annual maintenance fees.

You probably have guessed by now that these commercial software suites are expensive, and one consideration for choosing your software for your own use will depend on your commitment to your career as a DFI and how much time it will take to recoup your investment. Also, avail yourself of the community editions, demo versions, or free tools available from each vendor. Encase provides EnCase Forensic Imager; FTK provides FTK Imager. In both instances, the software reflects a subset of capabilities included in the commercial version, namely the ability to acquire data and to save it in an abbreviated format. Analysis of the data is not included.

 NOTE If you are just starting out as a DFI, or if you want to see if you enjoy the work, I would strongly recommend that you experiment with forensic software distributions such as SIFT that include the Autopsy/TSK GUI and other free or open-source tools.

Forensic Investigations Using FTK

AccessData's FTK is one of the "big two" forensic software programs.[2] Now at version 5.1, FTK has been available for well over a decade. I was first exposed to the software in a Computer Hacking Forensic Investigator (C|HFI) course in 2005, when FTK was at version 1.8. Things have changed for the better in the last few years! One of the most significant changes is FTK Imager, an independent, stand-alone acquisition tool that can be installed on a USB drive and run on a target device to capture the digital evidence. FTK also provides other tools that are integrated with the main FTK Examiner software. The Password Recovery Toolkit (PRTK) does exactly what its name suggests, and RegViewer helps in listing, searching, and analyzing the Windows Registry.

AccessData also offers Mobile Phone Examiner Plus (MPE+), a software tool for acquisition and analysis of mobile phone data, and AD Triage, a software tool for previewing and acquiring live or static data for users who are inexperienced in acquiring data in the field. AccessData's Live Response tool is a USB drive that contains software that can collect volatile data and store it on the USB drive itself.

Installation and Configuration

Installing the FTK software requires downloading an .iso file. Once downloaded, the file either can be burned to a CD/ROM or can be mounted locally using software like

VirtualCloneDrive or ImFile. In either case, the FTK software is then installed from an .exe file. Installing the analysis software requires a license dongle (a dongle is a small USB device, resembling a USB memory stick or widget, that is plugged into a port on the computer). Older dongles may also plug into a FireWire or serial port on a computer.

 NOTE Use of a dongle varies. In some instances, it's required to install the software; in other instances, it may be required to run the software. Regardless, a dongle is used to enforce license agreements. No dongle, no usable software.

FTK requires that a suitable database be installed on the target computer. The PostgresSQL database is provided as part of the distribution, and Oracle and MS SQL Server are supported as well. FTK also provides additional software tools. FTK Imager is a tool that provides a similar function to the data acquisition and investigation of the FTK software itself—what's missing are the analysis capabilities. Figure 8-5 shows the user interface for the FTK Imager software after loading our image from the Hacking scenario. The PRTK can be used to crack passwords that were used to encrypt an NT File

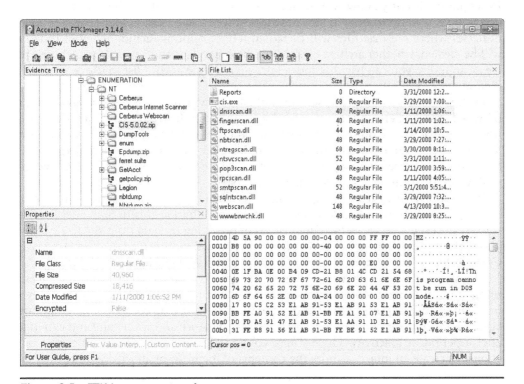

Figure 8-5   FTK Imager user interface

System (NTFS) drive using Windows Encrypting File System (EFS). The Registry Viewer tool can list and search the contents of a Windows Registry hive, either from an image or from a running system.

FTK divides the forensic analysis functions across multiple programs. FTK Imager supports creating forensic images of digital data, performing a quick review of the data, and creating a logical evidence file (.ad1) for further analysis. The FTK Examiner software also provides for raw data acquisition or using a logical evidence file and integrating that data into a case container.

Creating the Case and Adding Data

The FTK Case Manager is that part of FTK that supports the definition, creation, and population of cases. Case Manager provides the interface whereby an administrator can manipulate the case database to create users, roles, and access rights. For the rest of this chapter, we'll assume that you, the DFI, have been assigned the role of case administrator that gives you permission to actually create case structures (the role of case reviewer doesn't permit case creation).

Creating a case in FTK starts with selecting the New item from the Case menu on the Case Manager interface. The case is given a name (remember those naming conventions!) and, optionally, reference information for the case, as well as a description. The Description File entry allows you to attach a specific file, whether it be a more detailed description, a warrant, or evidence description form. The Case Folder Directory field indicates where the case files will be stored. Other options include whether indexes will be created, whether archive files should be expanded, and so on. If you choose to create an index, you can use that index later on to create a word list to use as a custom dictionary with PRTK.

Once we've defined our case, we can start adding evidence. How we do this depends on whether we're performing a static or live acquisition. If we're doing a static acquisition, we already have our forensic images, either as raw data or in Evidence Witness format or some other forensic container. On the other hand, if we're doing live acquisition, how we proceed will depend on whether we are running on the local live system or if we are performing a remote data collection.

If we're doing a live acquisition, we can collect data from the local target device, or we can acquire data from a remote system. In the case of local acquisition, the best choice is to create a static image of the data instead of operating on data from the live system. This is because accessing the data on the live system will modify the Modified/Accessed/Created (MAC) times on the file, and possibly create event entries in the Event Log.

FTK also can acquire data from a remote system, by using either a temporary agent or an enterprise agent. An enterprise agent is permanently installed on the computer in question and supports both memory and file acquisition. In comparison, temporary agents are loaded on demand to acquire specific evidence and will expire and expunge after a period of inactivity. Once you're connected to the remote machine, you can choose to create an image, acquire the contents of memory, or attach a remote drive so that it appears to be mounted on your local machine. If we are working with the enterprise agent, we also can request collection of volatile information, including process and Dynamic Link Library (DLL) information, open network connections, network interfaces, and so forth.

Once we've incorporated a drive into our case, we need to verify that the hash values of the import match those of our original. During normal incorporation of files into a case, the file is hashed as well as indexed. If the Known File Filter (KFF) data is installed, the file can be categorized as Alert, Ignore, or Unknown, depending on whether the file is known to be bad, known to be good (a standard system library, for example), or is simply known. Usually, a DFI will be interested in either the "known bad" or the "unknown" files. In addition to labeling the file, the hash value can be used to verify that a file that is extracted to external storage is the same as the file that was incorporated into the case. We also need to verify the integrity of the drive image, which we can do by selecting the Verify Image Integrity menu item of the Examiner Tools menu.

In addition to mapping our images into a case file, we may need to mount that image on an external drive so it can be accessed by other tools if need be. FTK allows us to do that by selecting Tools | Mount Image To Drive. The image is mounted read-only and can be accessed from the workstation running FTK via a drive letter, allowing the use of third-party tools external to FTK. If you need to restore an image to a physical disk, in Case Manager, select Tools | Restore Image To Disk. If you're collecting data remotely, whether it's optical media, a USB drive, or a disk partition, you can do so by selecting Evidence | Remote Data and then choosing the Install Temporary Agent item. In the resulting Add Remote Data dialog box, choose the Mount Device option.

 CAUTION If you are saving an image to a new disk, ensure that you have forensically wiped the target drive prior to restoring the image, and check twice to ensure that the target drive is large enough to hold the image.

Analyzing the Data

Now that we've completed our initial walkthrough of our digital crime scene, we can begin further analysis. The FTK Examiner system offers several options from which to choose. Figure 8-6 shows the various options available from the Examiner window.

The Explore tab provides a Windows Explorer–like view of the evidence by way of three panes: the File List pane, the file content Viewer pane, and the Explorer Tree

AccessData Forensic Toolkit							
File	Edit	View	Evidence	Filter	Tools	Manage	Help

| Explore | Overview | Email | Graphics | Bookmarks | Live Search | Index Search | Volatile |

Figure 8-6 Tabbed options in the Examiner window

pane. The Explorer Tree pane provides a hierarchical tree structure that shows each evidence item, which in FTK is "a physical drive, a logical drive or partition, or drive space not included in any partitioned drive, as well as any file, folder, or image of a drive, or mounted image."[2] The File List pane provides more information about an individual case file, such as pathname, filename, file type, and so forth. Last, the File View pane displays the contents of a selected file. How this is displayed depends on the file content: The Natural tab will display the file in its original format; additional choices include text, hexadecimal, and so on.

As described in the AccessData Forensic Toolkit Users Guide, the Overview tab provides an overview of the entire case, organized into eight category trees:[2]

- **Evidence Groups** Each evidence item can be assigned to an evidence group. This expandable category shows which groups are active and which items are assigned to each group.

- **File Items** This lists files that have been checked as part of the ongoing analysis and lists all evidence files.

- **File Extension** Files listed here are categorized by file extension.

- **File Category** This categorizes files based on use, such as a folder, a document, or an executable program. File categories include archives, e-mail, executables, folders, and graphics, among others.

- **File Status** This category is further subdivided into categories that may be of interest to the DFI. Categories include Bad Extensions (an executable file labeled as a .jpg), Data Carved Files, Decrypted Files, and Deleted Files, among others. One important category is labeled "Flagged Ignored," indicating that these files are probably not of interest to the case in question.

- **Email Status** This category identifies files as attachments, replies, forwarded e-mail, and from e-mail, indicating anything derived from an e-mail message.

- **Labels** Lists all labels created as part of this analysis and each evidence item assigned to each label.

- **Bookmarks** This container lists all bookmarks as they have been created.

The Email tab, surprisingly enough, displays e-mail files discovered on that particular device, as well as their attachments. The Email Status tree includes such items as sender, receiver, if the e-mail has attachments, and so on. The Email Archive tree lists all e-mail files that are considered containers, such as PST files, Saved Mail, and the Trash. The Email Tree lists counts of various types of e-mail, such as PST and MBOX.

Similarly, the Graphics tab displays all the images in an investigation in a "slide-sorter" view of thumbnails. Each thumbnail can be checked to include that graphic as part of the investigation report. The thumbnail pane can be detached and moved to a second monitor in order to free up space on the first monitor for ongoing analysis.

Bookmarks are a quick way to document and comment on particular pieces of evidence for later retrieval, and can even support attaching external files to the bookmark. Bookmarks are enhanced by allowing user-specified tags that allow a piece of evidence to be entered into multiple "categories." Using our Hacking example, we can find mentions of "Schardt" in both the Event Log files and within the Windows Registry. Using tags, we could categorize these bits of evidence under "Logs" as well as "Owner Identification."

The next two tabs are for two kinds of searches: live search and index search. A live search searches the entire evidence collection for a fixed string of text or a combination of alphanumeric and nonalphanumeric characters. You can also search for patterns either as hex values or as a regular expression. Regular expressions are a way of specifying a pattern that can match multiple sequences of characters. For example, the regular expression "^[Pp]eter?" would match the text "Peter," "peter," "Pete," or "pete." The "^" character means that the string must occur at the beginning of a line of text, and the brackets indicate which characters will be searched for.

You can choose to generate an index file when you are initially incorporating data into your case. This option will create an index file containing words or numeric strings found in allocated and unallocated space. This index provides for quick lookup of fixed strings, but requires that the word you're searching for be an exact match to one in the index ("Peter" won't match "peter"). The results of a live or an index search can be bookmarked as part of your investigation.

Creating an index file serves another purpose. You may find that a particular file or directory on an NTFS file system has been encrypted using Windows EFS capabilities. You can save this list of words gathered from the digital evidence and repurpose it as a dictionary for the PRTK that will attempt to discover the password by using this word list. FTK offers automatic decryption (AD) of files as well. Life is easier if you have the password for the encrypted object; otherwise, you will need to depend on PRTK or AccessData's Distributed Network Access (DNA) product that uses a client-server model where the server allocates a certain portion of the key space to multiple clients that can be local or running remotely.

Generating the Report

Generating a report in FTK is as simple as selecting the Report Wizard menu entry. FTK can create a report as a Hypertext Markup Language (HTML) file or as a Portable Document Format (PDF) file, and this file can contain any bookmarks you created. These bookmarked files can be exported so they are available along with the report, and are viewable by means of hyperlinks in the HTML or PDF file. You can also save customized graphic references and file listings.

Forensic Investigations Using EnCase

EnCase Forensics from Guardian Software is their premiere digital forensics product.[3] Guardian Software also sells EnCase Portable, a suite of tools delivered on a USB stick that "is designed to address the challenge of completing forensic triage and data collection in the field for both forensic professionals and non-technical personnel."[4] The EnCase E-Discovery and EnCase CyberSecurity products are specialized software for e-discovery and incident response. EnCase also provided the stand-alone EnCase Forensic Imager software that can be operated from a USB drive for initial data acquisition.

EnCase provides multiple capabilities that support a variety of uses. It can import data from mobile phones and tablets, as well as various kinds of removable media and hard disk drives. Once the data are imported into EnCase, the investigator can apply various forensic analytic functions using EnCase's forensic modules.

Installation and Configuration

Installing the EnCase software tools is very similar to FTK and other forensic analysis software. You will be asked where to install the executable files (either in C:\Program Files or C:\Program Files (x86)), and then you'll be asked to enter your dongle serial number and then to install a certification key into the installation directory. Once you have done that and have registered your software, the EnCase user interface (UI) will open to the home screen where you'll be presented with three major options: Open Or Create A New Case, Set Various Global Options, or Ask For Help.

Configuring EnCase begins during the installation process when you specify the installation directory. In EnCase v7, EnCase-related files are stored in the C:\Users\<name>\My Documents\EnCase folder, while per-user application data are stored in C:\Users\<name>\AppData\Roaming\Encase. Global settings are saved in C:\Users\Default\Appdata\Roaming\Encase1, and shared files are stored in a directory that is specified on a per-user basis. This is a change from earlier versions of EnCase and prevents overwriting user-specified data when a new version of EnCase is installed.

Creating the Case and Adding Data

Case management for EnCase consists of creating a case file. In EnCase version 7, the case file is stored as a folder that contains multiple components, including the evidence file, searches, hashes, and so forth. A case file must be created before you actually start your analysis. One constraint is that only one examiner at a time can work on that particular case.

You can set options for cases either from the Case menu or from the case selections on the case home page. Among the options you can select are to create a package file for portability, save the existing case as a template, or actually edit the case options for an active case.

The Case Options dialog box presents several different elements for modification. Case options are expressed as a series of name/value pairs that include such names as case number, date, examiner name, examiner ID, agency, and description. You may also choose the location for the primary evidence cache and a secondary evidence cache. Last, you can specify backup settings by specifying the frequency, a maximum size for the case backup file, and the location of that backup file.

 TIP Best practices indicate saving your backups and your evidence caches on separate storage devices. This has something to do with not risking everything on one endeavor.

You can acquire a device or add a device to a case through the EnCase UI, or you can use a stand-alone tool: EnCase Forensic Imager (EFI). You can incorporate an image into EFI by choosing the Add Evidence File link from the home screen. Figure 8-7 shows the EFI user interface. In this instance, we are acquiring the same evidence files as we have done in our previous examples.

Once the device is incorporated into a case, you should verify that the hash values are identical between the image and the original capture from the device. EnCase does this for you in the background when you add an evidence file by computing a hash value. The EnCase Forensic Imager User Guide does mention that the Imager should not be run on the suspect machine, since it does modify the host machine file system by creating temporary files.

Since this is an EnCase evidence file, we have more information about the contents than we might have otherwise. Figure 8-8 shows the Report tab from the File Content pane. Notice how our previous examiner, Mr. Shane Robinson, has thoughtfully provided

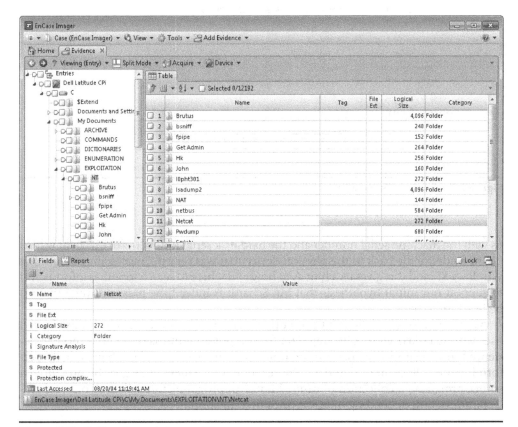

Figure 8-7   EnCase Forensic Imager UI

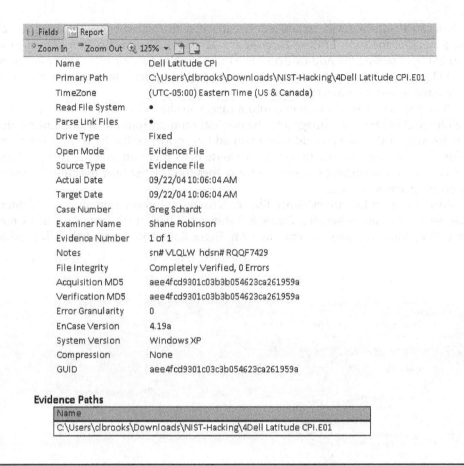

Name	Dell Latitude CPi
Primary Path	C:\Users\clbrooks\Downloads\NIST-Hacking\4Dell Latitude CPi.E01
TimeZone	(UTC-05:00) Eastern Time (US & Canada)
Read File System	•
Parse Link Files	•
Drive Type	Fixed
Open Mode	Evidence File
Source Type	Evidence File
Actual Date	09/22/04 10:06:04 AM
Target Date	09/22/04 10:06:04 AM
Case Number	Greg Schardt
Examiner Name	Shane Robinson
Evidence Number	1 of 1
Notes	sn# VLQLW hdsn# RQQF7429
File Integrity	Completely Verified, 0 Errors
Acquisition MD5	aee4fcd9301c03b3b054623ca261959a
Verification MD5	aee4fcd9301c03b3b054623ca261959a
Error Granularity	0
EnCase Version	4.19a
System Version	Windows XP
Compression	None
GUID	aee4fcd9301c03c3b054623ca261959a

Evidence Paths

Name
C:\Users\clbrooks\Downloads\NIST-Hacking\4Dell Latitude CPi.E01

Figure 8-8 Evidence file metadata

us with the machine serial number and the hard disk serial number—an excellent way to tie the evidence file back to the physical device that was seized. The machine is running Windows XP, and this gives us a hint as to how and where to search for other information to support our initial hypothesis that Mr. Schardt is indeed the password thief that we believe him to be.

As we mentioned earlier, EnCase Portable software is aimed at the inexperienced user who is tasked with collecting data from a possible intrusion so that more experienced investigators can spend more time analyzing captured data than actually performing the collection of that data. EnCase Portable achieves this goal by providing a source processor, a collection of canned EnScript programs that will seek out and collect information depending on the type of investigation.

Analyzing the Data

Once we have incorporated our raw data into our case container, we can begin our analysis. We start by invoking the EnCase Evidence Processor. In Evidence Processor, there are two phases: preparation and processing. In the preparation phase, the examiner ensures that all evidence has been incorporated into the case and that the time zone selected is the same as when the evidence was first acquired. The actual searching and categorizing of data occur in the processing phase.

The actual processing phase specifies which functions should be performed on the acquired evidence. The Encase Forensic v7 Essentials paper lists these functions:[3]

- **Recover Folders** Will recover deleted or corrupted folders from File Allocation Table (FAT) or NTFS file systems.

- **File Signature Analysis** Validates file content against the file extension.

- **Protected File Analysis** Selects files that are either password-protected or encrypted.

- **Thumbnail Creation** Creates thumbnails for each graphic image found.

- **Hash Analysis** Generates MD5 or SHA1 hashes for each file.

- **Expand Compound Files** Expands compound or compressed files, such as ZIP, RAR, GZ, or Windows Registry files, into their component parts.

- **Find E-mail** Breaks apart e-mail containers into the individual e-mail messages.

- **Find Internet Artifacts** Identifies browsing histories, cached files, and so forth.

- **Search For Keywords** Searches raw text for specified keywords.

- **Index Text And Metadata** Creates an index for compound documents such as .docx and .xlsx files generated by Microsoft Office. Also useful if indexing a large amount of data. The DFI can specify whether to use a noise file that contains lists of words that should be ignored. Indexing can also look for credit card data, phone numbers, e-mail addresses, and Social Security numbers.

- **Modules** This provides access to several other actions, including gathering system information with the System Info Parser, the Windows Event Log Parser, the Windows Artifact Parser, and others.

Once the processing phase has completed (and this can take hours, depending on the actions chosen), we can start our actual analysis. In many instances, analysis is simply viewing the results of the processing phase. Once we've identified interesting files based on our keyword search, we can view their contents in the View pane displayed as text, hexadecimal, or a graphics image. Files that have been identified via our file signature analysis need to be investigated, especially when an executable file has been renamed to appear as an image file. If we've chosen Windows artifact parsing, we can look at link files, Recycle Bin files, and transactions against the NTFS Master File Table (MFT).

Bookmarks also are an important analysis aid in EnCase Forensics, as are user-defined tags. Bookmarks allow the analyst to record items of interest—in particular, these items will be mentioned in the final report, and may, in fact, be presented verbatim as part of that report.

Generating the Report

You can access the reporting functions from the case home screen in the report section. The report section has three buttons: Reports, Bookmarks, and Report Templates. EnCase Forensics provides a set of default case templates categorized by the type of investigation. Each case template contains a report template, all of which are customizable by adding new metadata fields and new records. A report template consists of two parts: one part that holds the formatting layout and style report, and a second part that contains bookmark folders that refer to specific items and notes stored for that case. Formatting layout and styles can be modified to have a new font type, font size, alignment, and so on. A report template links to these bookmark folders to populate content into that report. All evidence fields are available, and these field values can be displayed in the report. All entry record and item bookmark fields can be added to the report template as well.

You can view a report in two different ways. If you are in the report template view, you can simply select the View Report item from the toolbar. You can also select the Reports tab from the case home page or from the View menu. When you choose to generate a report, you can simply choose an output format from text, RTF, HTML, XML, or PDF.

So Did We Get the Evidence We Need?

To be honest, we did not get all the evidence we need. What we did observe was that the laptop has various programs that can be used for monitoring and capturing Wi-Fi traffic. We observed that there is indeed a logon account named Mr. Evil, and we have identified instances in the Windows Registry where Greg Schardt is identified as the registered owner of installed software and of the machine itself. Figure 8-9, from the Forensics Explorer software, shows the instances of where the name Greg Schardt was found

At this point, we haven't discussed looking at log file data or network data to establish a timeline. Never fear, dear reader, all will be revealed in Chapter 9 (well, most of it anyway).

Which One to Choose?

After all this, which forensic analysis framework should you choose? Let's assume that budget isn't a concern, your organization hasn't standardized on one particular framework, the software has been approved by NIST, and it has been used and evaluated within the forensic community. Given this set of assumptions, you should choose whichever software provides the most direct mapping to your forensic analysis methods. In other

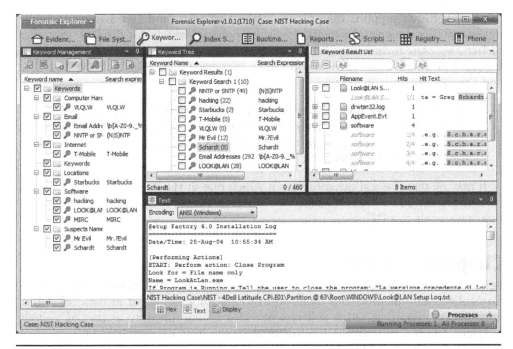

Figure 8-9 Search results for Greg Schardt

words, the software shouldn't get in your way. Software should be there to support you if you need it via help scripts, info tags, and so on, and get out of your way if you don't. You need to spend your time analyzing the evidence rather than trying to remember which command performs the particular action that you need. Another concern is your need to extend the software, which usually means learning a scripting language that is supplied along with the software. EnCase uses EnScript; FTK doesn't appear to support a scripting language internal to the software; ProDiscover uses Perl. Depending on your background and on other resources you have available—knowledge of a programming language (SQL counts) or other in-house programming support—one of these languages may be a better fit.

In a blog entry entitled "What 'Tier 3' and 'Tier 2' Tools Do You Load on Your Forensics Workstation(s)?"[5] Lance Mueller divides software tools into one of three tiers. Tier 1 is primary forensic analysis software, under which he lists EnCase, X-Ways Forensics, FTK, and others.

NOTE In a response to this blog post, Harlen Carvey mentions that without access to the listed Tier 1 tools, Tier 2 software becomes Tier 1 software by default.

Tier 2 software supports the primary analysis software, and Tier 3 software, while not specifically designed for digital forensics, provides benefit for the DFI. Examples of Tier 2 software include the SIFT workstation, RegViewer (a registry viewer), and FTK Imager. Tier 3 tools include Microsoft Office, Notepad++, Wireshark, ActiveState Perl, and VMware. He goes on to say:

> This post is really about the often-unmentioned supporting tools that make my life easier as an examiner. They are the tools that I rely upon during almost every examination to help process or view the data from whatever primary analysis tool (FTK, EnCase X-Ways, etc.) that I may be using.

It may be that the real question is not which one of the primary forensic analysis tools to choose, but what Tier 2 and Tier 3 tools to choose to make you more productive in your role as a DFI.

Chapter Review

Several software distributions focus exclusively on forensic investigations. The distribution collects various tools and frameworks to aid the investigator in data collection, analysis, and reporting. Other software provides similar functions as part of a single program, and typically approaches the investigation from a higher level rather than as a collection of individual tools.

Software programs are installed via the usual installation mechanisms: .msi files, .exe files, or even .zip files on Windows; .zip, .tar, or a package file depending on the OS software (Debian distributions use .pkg or .deb files, while Fedora distributions will use .rpm files). Installation consists of running the install program and answering installation questions, such as where to install the software (Linux will store the files in preconfigured locations unless specifically overridden). Individual programs may request further information when first run after installation, such as where to store evidence files and so forth.

The software can be used to both acquire data and analyze it. FTK Imager and EnCase Forensic Imager are stand-alone tools that can provide a case management structure and populate the case with associated evidence. FTK Examiner and EnCase Forensics are the primary analysis tools offering ways to search files for content, identify deleted files and mismatched files (content differs from the file extension), and examine various configuration and historical information stored in the Windows Registry.

Once the analysis is complete, both software suites enable automatic generation of a report. The report can utilize several different presentation formats, but both tools allow items of interest (evidence) to be recorded in the report and incorporated into the report body as desired, or to be included as separate files along with the report itself.

Questions

1. Which Forensic Toolkit component supports recovering passwords?

   A. Examiner

   B. PRTK

   C. Registry Viewer

   D. Imager

2. Which of these is *not* an evidence item in FTK?

   A. File folder

   B. File

   C. Disk image

   D. Registry key

3. Which software captures network traffic and attempts to crack or display passwords?

   A. Netstumbler

   B. Ethereal

   C. l0phtcrack

   D. Cain and Abel

4. ____ allow the examiner to include items under more than one category.

   A. Bookmarks

   B. Tags

   C. Keywords

   D. File types

5. What is the purpose of a logical evidence file?

   A. Trace the progress of the examiner's analysis

   B. Present all evidence in the same format

   C. Only provide data that have evidentiary value

   D. Serve as an attachment to the final investigative report

6. Which tool would a nontechnical person use to collect static and dynamic data from a suspect device?

   A. EnCase Password Recovery Toolkit

   B. EnCase Forensics

   C. Forensic Imager

   D. EnCase Portable

7. In which phase of the Evidence Processor would you determine the appropriate time zone?

   A. Preparation

   B. File signature analysis

   C. Processing

   D. Indexing and searching

8. File signature analysis is a process where:

   A. File hash values are matched against a file of known malware

   B. Executable file contents are searched for .dll usage

   C. File contents are matched against the file extension

   D. Files are sent to www.virustotal.com to compute a unique signature

9. What elements of EnCase are most likely to be included in a report?

   A. File signature analysis

   B. Entries

   C. Records

   D. Bookmarks

10. Which language would you use to extend the EnCase Forensics software?

   A. Lua

   B. EnScript

   C. ProScript

   D. Python

Answers

1. **B.** The Password Recovery Toolkit (PRTK) is used to recover passwords—for example, those used to encrypt a file.

2. **D.** A registry key is not an evidence item in FTK.

3. **D.** Cain and Abel.

4. **B.** Tags allow the examiner to include a bookmark in more than one category.

5. **C.** Logical evidence files contain only that data that have evidentiary value.

6. **D.** EnCase Portable is used by nontechnical personnel.

7. **A.** The preparation phase.

8. **C.** File contents are matched against the file extension.

9. **D.** Bookmarks are the elements of EnCase that are included in a report.

10. **B.** EnScript is EnCase's scripting language.

References

1. "Hacking Case." Retrieved from www.cfreds.nist.gov/Hacking_Case.html.

2. AccessData. AccessData Forensic Toolkit Users Guide (UT: AccessData, 2013). Retrieved from www.AccessData.com.

3. Guardian Software. EnCase Forensics V7 Essentials (CA: Guardian Software, 2011). Retrieved from www.encase.com.

4. "EnCase Portable," EnCase_Protocol_Brochure_9-11-13-webready.pdf. Retrieved from www.encase.com/resources/Pages/doclib/Document-Library/EnCase-Portable-v4.aspx, p. 1.

5. Mueller, L. "What 'Tier 2' and 'Tier 3' Tools Do You Load on Your Forensic Workstation(s)?" Retrieved from www.forensickb.com/2013_10_01_archive.html.

## CHAPTER 9

Network Forensics

In this chapter, you will learn how to

- Explain why we investigate network traffic; summarize network forensics concepts; and define the terms firewall, honeypot, and IDS
- List various kinds of network vulnerabilities and network attacks, and where to look for and gather evidence for wired and wireless networks
- Analyze the data: how to handle logs as evidence, and how to condense a log file
- Explain the function of log management, the legality of using logs, and combining event and log management to correlate local and remote events

I've been involved with IP networking and data communications for a long, long time, as both a software developer and a software and application security architect. Of all the areas of digital forensics, network forensics is my passion. Give me a .pcap file and the latest version of Wireshark, and I'm one happy person.

One thing we should note here is that we are changing our perspective on digital forensics. In the preceding chapters, we've been focusing on the computer or digital device as a tool used to commit the crime or policy violation. This will still be true in our chapter on mobile device forensics, but in this chapter and the chapter on web and e-mail forensics, we will be focusing on the computer as the target, where obtaining control over the computer is the goal of a particular activity.

Of course, once the attacker has achieved their goal, the compromised machine may be used as a tool to further the attack. One thing to learn in network forensics is that a compromise is usually a series of smaller compromises, each one furthering the attacker's ultimate objective. Although the end goal of the Rivest, Shamir, and Adleman (RSA) breach in 2012 was to obtain information that would weaken the protection provided by RSA SecurID tokens, the initial attack focused on gaining a foothold on an employee's machine. This was accomplished by convincing the person to open an Excel spreadsheet that contained an Adobe Flash file which leveraged a flaw in the software that gave the attacker a cmd shell on the user's machine.

 NOTE Did you know that you could embed a Flash file in an Excel spreadsheet? Until this happened, I hadn't really thought about it. But somebody had.

Once we enter the realm of the computer as a target, we are dealing with unauthorized access to a computing device. This is addressed by the Computer Fraud and Abuse Act, passed in 1986, and is incorporated into Section 1030 of Title 18 of the U.S. Code, and amended by the Patriot Act of 2001 and by the Identity Theft and Restitution Act of 2008. Section 1030(a) is the significant portion of this statue for the DFI engaged in network forensics. Section 1030(a)(5) lists three circumstances that define computer abuse. Abuse occurs when a person knowingly sends a program, information, code, or command, and as a result intentionally causes damage without authorization to a protected computer; intentionally accessing a protected computer without authorization, and as a result recklessly causes damage; or causes damage and loss[1]. These circumstances could cover malware, Web site defacement, DNS hijacking, DDoS, and so forth.

Network Forensics: A Definition

Simpson Garfinkle credits Marcus Ranum with defining network forensics as "the capture, recording, and analysis of network events in order to discover the source of security attacks or other problem incidents."[2] Garfinkle lists two techniques that are commonly used to collect network data: a brute-force "catch it as you can" method and a more intelligent "stop, look, listen" method. Between these is "capture the flow," where header information is collected but the payload isn't (similar to when we capture HTTPS traffic: The payload is encrypted, but we are able to read the headers).

Data communication networks can utilize either physical wires or cables (Ethernet via coaxial cable or twisted-pair) or wirelessly via cellular networks or via 802.11 wireless networks (Wi-Fi). Regardless of the transmission medium, network forensics exploits certain commonalities in data networking. Attacks differ, however, when we look at the actual physical means of transmitting and receiving the data.

Network Forensics and Wired Networks

The International Systems Organization (ISO) defined a set of standards called the Open System Interconnection (OSI) model. At the same time, other data networking standards and protocols were defined by the U.S. government under the sponsorship of the (Defense) Advanced Research Projects Agency (once ARPA, now DARPA). Both groups created general networking models. I need to stress that these are indeed models and were meant to be prescriptive rather than proscriptive. Essential to both models is that traffic would flow from the source end point (end system, or ES) through one or more intermediate systems (IS) to the destination ES. A critical insight into the nature of networking is that the means and methods of communicating between the source ES and the first IS don't need to be the same as those used by the IS to another IS, nor between the destination IS and the destination ES. Figure 9-1 shows the different layers defined by the OSI model and the ARPANET model and lists some common protocols that appear at each layer. The description of the message passed between layer N and layer N-1 is based on the terminology used by Cisco systems.

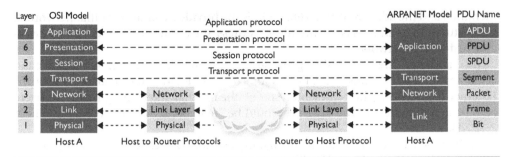

Figure 9-1 The OSI and ARPA network protocol stacks (Adapted from: Tanenbaum, A., Computer Networks (4th), (NJ: Prentice-Hall, 2002), p. 39.)

 NOTE If you're familiar with the OSI and Internet protocols, feel free to skip ahead to the section "Investigating Network Traffic."

The lowest layers of the network stacks are the physical (the actual physical medium) and the link (frame) layer, and this is where the differences exist between wired and wireless networks. Once we reach the (inter)networking layer with the IP packet, there is no difference between the two, which is why a computer attached to an Ethernet network can happily communicate with another computer connected via a wireless access point (WAP).

The network layer and the link layer each has its own address. Each computer connected to an Ethernet network has an Ethernet address that consists of six bytes (or 48 bits), usually represented as a 12-digit string of hexadecimal characters separated by a dash (c0-c1-c0-0a-a8-11 is the address of the default router on my home network). The first three bytes denote the manufacturer of the physical interface, and the last three bytes are a unique identifier assigned by the manufacturer to this particular network card. In theory, this should uniquely identify each attached device; in fact, it is trivially easy to reassign a Media Access Control (MAC) address.

The Internet Protocol (IP) generally is used as the network protocol. An IPv4 Internet address is four bytes long (32 bits), usually represented as a "dotted quad" in the form 192.168.1.1. Each IPv4 address is divided into a network identifier and a host identifier. Originally, there were three different network classifications: class A network (1 byte: 254 networks, 16,777,214 hosts), class B networks (2 bytes: 65,534 networks, 65,534 hosts) and class C networks (16,777,214 networks, 254 hosts). Eventually, network identifiers were no longer considered to be fixed length. The classless interdomain routing (CIDR) represented each address as a dotted quad followed by the number of bits comprising the network identifier. The address 192.168.1.0/28 indicates that the network ID is the leftmost 28 bits in the IP address, leaving 4 bits for 14 different hosts (in case you're wondering, the values of 0 and $2**N - 1$, where N is the number of bits in the identifier, are reserved for the network identifier and the broadcast address for that network). For my local network, the address of 192.168.1.0 would be the network identifier, and the address of 192.168.1.255 is the broadcast address for that network. If the destination IP address is the broadcast address, the packet is delivered to all devices attached to that network.

IPv6 addresses are 16 bytes long and are represented as a set of hexadecimal characters separated by colons: fe80::bdf2:60d5:c0c2:792d%10 is the IPv6 address of my Ethernet connection (the representation "::" means that intervening bytes are set to zero—the full address of the interface would be "fe80:0000:0000:0000:bdf2:60d5:c0c 2:792d%10").

Each packet (also called an IP datagram) contains a header portion and a data portion, called the payload. The IP header provides source and destination Internet addresses, a checksum of the data to assure that there have been no errors in transmission, and a protocol value indicating which higher protocol should receive the payload. IP is a connectionless (stateless) protocol that offers "best effort" delivery with no other guarantees concerning data transmission. Packets may arrive out of sequence or may be dropped without warning anywhere along the network path.

The most significant protocol layers on top of IP are the Transmission Control Protocol (TCP) and the User Datagram Protocol (UDP). UDP is the simplest: It allocates port numbers and computes a checksum over the UDP header and the data portion of the segment, and depends on a higher-level protocol to provide reliable delivery.

TCP does offer guarantees. Data will arrive in the order sent when delivered to the application layer, and each TCP segment will be acknowledged as to success or failure. The IP packets containing the TCP segments may arrive out of sequence, but the sequence number allows TCP to reconstruct the segment in the proper order. TCP is a connection-oriented protocol, in that a connection between the local and remote host must be established prior to sending data, and this connection should be terminated in an orderly fashion. Like UDP, TCP adds a source and destination port identifier and a checksum, but it also specifies a sequence number and a set of control bits that supply metadata about the connection itself (for example, FIN means that the sender won't send any more data, while RST means that the sender has reset the connection).

Laura Chappel, author and advocate for Wireshark software, coined the phrase "packets don't lie."[3] The header information within the packet must be correct in order for that packet to be delivered to the destination (this is similar to Brian Carrier's notion of essential data that we discussed in Chapter 3). That is, the protocol fields must be correct; otherwise, the packet would have been dropped along the way.

 NOTE My corollary to Chappel's axiom is "packet's don't lie, but payloads do."

An IP packet contains a protocol field indicating the higher-level protocol. TCP is assigned protocol number 6; UDP is assigned protocol number 17. Internet Control Message Protocol (ICMP) is protocol 1, and Internet Group Management Protocol (IGMP) is assigned protocol number 2.

Both TCP and UDP utilize port numbers ranging from 1 to 65,535. Port numbers from 0 to 1,023 are considered well-known and reserved port numbers (system ports) that are administered by a central authority called the Internet Assigned Numbers Authority (IANA). Ports numbered from 1024 through 491,151 are called registered ports and are considered reserved for local services or for "lesser known" services. Ports numbered above 491,152 are temporary (also called dynamic, private or ephemeral) ports that can be assigned to client applications attempting to connect to a service port. Table 9-1 lists several well-known ports and their service mapping.

 EXAM TIP Know the well-known port numbers for various Internet services.

A construct called a "5-tuple" consists of the source IP address, source port, protocol, destination port, and destination IP address. This construct represents an established connection between two end systems, often called a "socket." A server listening on a well-known port will have a source address and a destination port of 0 (0.0.0.0, 0, TCP, 80, 192.168.1.20), while a live connection would have a 5-tuple of (192.168.1.20, 49152, TCP, xfinity.com, 80).

Figure 9-2 is an abbreviated listing from the netstat command run on Windows. We've chosen only to show the IP addresses and port numbers in this listing for established connections and for services listening on a given port.

Attackers will use these conventions as a way of hiding traffic. The NetWitness Investigator software reports on two different fields—the IP protocol number (ICMP) and the higher-layer protocol (say, HTTP). If you observe an ICMP protocol message carrying

Table 9-1	Port #	Service	Description
Well-Known Service Ports	23	Telnet	Terminal Emulation
	20	FTP data	FTP Data Transfer
	21	FTP	File Transfer Protocol
	22	SSH	Secure Shell
	25	SMTP	Simple Mail Transfer Protocol
	53	DNS	Domain Name System
	80	HTTP	Hypertext Transfer Protocol
	110	POP3	Mail (Post Office Protocol)
	137	Netbios-ns	NetBIOS Name Server
	138	Netbios-dgm	NetBIOS Datagram Service
	139	Netbios-ss	NetBIOS Session Service
	143	IMAP	Mail protocol
	443	HTTPS	HTTP over SSS
	445	Microsoft-DS	Microsoft-DS

```
Active Connections

  Proto  Local Address            Foreign Address      State            PID
  TCP    192.168.1.20:17126       17.172.34.81:993     ESTABLISHED      5720
  TCP    192.168.1.20:20001       192.168.1.14:445     CLOSE_WAIT       4
  TCP    192.168.1.20:28215       192.168.1.1:445      ESTABLISHED      4
  TCP    192.168.1.20:48545       173.194.68.109:993   ESTABLISHED      5720
  TCP    127.0.0.1:1171           127.0.0.1:7112       ESTABLISHED      6000
  TCP    192.168.1.20:14403       192.168.1.14:445     ESTABLISHED      4
  TCP    192.168.1.20:17126       17.172.34.81:993     ESTABLISHED      5720
  TCP    192.168.1.20:20001       192.168.1.14:445     CLOSE_WAIT       4
  TCP    192.168.1.20:28215       192.168.1.1:445      ESTABLISHED      4
  UDP    0.0.0.0:7                *:*                                   3756
  UDP    0.0.0.0:9                *:*                                   3756
  UDP    0.0.0.0:13               *:*                                   3756
  UDP    0.0.0.0:17               *:*                                   3756
  UDP    169.254.199.181:137      *:*                                   4
  UDP    169.254.199.181:138      *:*                                   4
  UDP    169.254.199.181:1900     *:*                                   2352
  UDP    169.254.199.181:54874    *:*                                   2352
  UDP    192.168.1.20:137         *:*                                   4
  UDP    192.168.1.20:138         *:*                                   4
```

Figure 9-2 Netstat listing showing process ID numbers

HTTP data or a DNS protocol message carrying HTTP traffic, you know that something is not right. (Congratulations! You've just found a needle in the haystack!)

Along with the network infrastructure components (routers and switches and cables), two other devices provide information about possible network malfeasance. A firewall is a network component that is programmed to accept or reject network traffic based on certain conditions. These conditions can be as simple as a destination IP address, or as complicated as looking for an HTTP header within a web browser session. Initially, firewalls operated at the network and transport layers of the Internet Protocol stack. Today, many enterprise-class firewalls operate at the application layer as well, and this enables deep application and content inspection. A special case of this is the Web Application Firewall (WAF), a device that "front-ends" a web server and is deeply familiar with the format of HTTP, as well as the content that can be delivered via this protocol (which is pretty much anything and everything).

An intrusion detection system (IDS) will drop or modify network traffic based on known or presumed anomalies within the packet itself; that is, an IDS works at the TCP/IP layer and doesn't necessarily understand the exact structure or format of the application layer protocol. An intrusion prevention system (IPS) acts to deny or terminate a particular network session by dynamically creating new rules (such as firewall rules) that will deny the accompanying network flow. Combined systems for detection and prevention are known as intrusion detection and prevention systems (IDPSs).

Where Does SSL Fit in the OSI Model?

The Secure Socket Layer (SSL) protocol and its Internet Engineering Task Force (IETF)–sponsored counterpart, Transport Layer Security (TLS), don't fit nicely into the OSI reference model. SSL has elements of a presentation protocol (it negotiates an encryption protocol suite), a session layer protocol (the protocol negotiation, again), and a record definition protocol (defining the different kinds of data messages that can be transmitted between end points). Some folks classify it as a transport layer protocol. I consider it a session layer protocol, but reasonable people can (and often do) disagree.

One way to track the behavior of an attacker is by using a honeypot. A honeypot is a machine with multiple vulnerabilities that appears to have valuable information (such as source code or industrial plans), or it may seem to be a good machine to use to mount further attacks. The intent is to use this machine as a way to observe attacker behavior and the tools that they use. A second use is as a decoy for an attacker: an attack could be routed to a honeypot to observe how the attacker uses their attack software.

Investigating Network Traffic

Investigating and recording network traffic provide several benefits. The first is to identify "known bad" traffic (perhaps from a host known to distribute malware). A second benefit is to determine the source and destination of malicious traffic in order to generate a complete picture of what has happened during this incident, especially when the attack occurs in phases. In addition, investigating network traffic allows an organization to build up a profile of "normal" network activity. Anything that is outside the range of activities is considered suspect until proven otherwise.

A network may be vulnerable to attack for several reasons. Vulnerabilities may exist in infrastructure software that can be exploited to gain entry. Security patches may not have been applied to systems. Access permissions may be too broad with respect to accessing network resources. For example, a service may allow access from any source address when the IP addresses should be restricted. Permissions for outbound traffic may be too broad as well. Encrypted outbound traffic may be allowed without considering the reputation of the destination device (a known attacker) or an external network service. Accessing this service may violate the company's security policy concerning how and where confidential and sensitive information can be stored (think of an employee uploading trade secrets to a Dropbox account).

Network attacks fall into one of two categories: attacks that utilize the network as a communications channel to deliver a malicious payload, or attacks that exploit a vulnerability in the network communications channel itself. Consider the following "classic" network attacks.

Attack	Description	Focus of the Attack
Ping of death	Malformed ICMP echo request (Ping)	Protocol
Teardrop	Fragmented packets cause buffer overflow when reassembled	Protocol
SYN flooding	Multiple TCP connection requests freeze the computer	Protocol
LAND	IP packet has the same address and port for source and destination address	Protocol
Smurf	Send broadcast ICMP echo requests to all hosts on a subnetwork, who then all respond to the spoofed IP address	Protocol
Fraggle	Multiple UDP packets overwhelm the network	Protocol
OOB attack	Exploited a bug in the Microsoft IP stack when giving out-of-band requests	Software
Buffer overflow	Sends more data than the program has allocated storage to receive	Software
Nuke attack	Multiple fragmented or invalid ICMP echo requests	Protocol
Reflected attack	Multiple destination hosts respond to a SYN packet from a forged IP address	Protocol

As you can see, almost all of these are attacks against errors in the implementation of the network protocols. Two attacks (OOB and buffer overflow) are the result of careless programming.

Multiple attacks can be mounted against an enterprise via its data communications networks.[4] These include

- IP spoofing (affects confidentiality, integrity, and availability)
- Router attacks (affect confidentiality, integrity, and availability)
- Eavesdropping (affects confidentiality)
- Denial of service (DoS and DDoS—distributed DoS—affects availability)
- Man-in-the-middle attack (MITM—affects confidentiality and integrity)
- Sniffing (affects confidentiality)
- Data modification (affects integrity)

Attacks can be active or passive. A passive attack occurs when the attacker simply eavesdrops on passing traffic to gain information about various devices, applications, and protocols running in a particular environment. An active attack occurs when the attacker actually initiates an action against a particular device in order to compromise the security of data stored on that device (or the device itself). Of the attacks listed in the table, eavesdropping, sniffing, and IP spoofing are passive attacks, while DoS, MITM, and data modification are active attacks.

Intruders can use several methods to enter a system, although these all follow a common pattern. The first step is to collect information about the enterprise that could include the topology of the network, a list of live hosts; the network architecture; kinds of application traffic; vulnerabilities in host systems; or the names, login identifiers, or e-mail addresses of key personnel.

Once a target has been identified (a person or a computer), vulnerabilities in hardware or software can be used by an attacker to attack a particular end-user system, a network infrastructure component (firewall, router, antivirus server), or a particular service (DNS, e-mail, web, and so forth). Once the vulnerability has been exploited, the compromised system becomes a target for malware. Malware is a catchall term for unwanted software that could be adware, spyware, remote administration tools (RATs), robot (bot) software (software that periodically connects back to a command and control [C2] system for instructions), data mining tools, and so on. Malware can either be downloaded from an infected website or via an e-mail message specifically addressed to a user ("phishing") or a specific high-value target ("spear phishing" or "whaling") to entice them to execute a particular program and thereby infect their local system. The malware can then gather information or use the devices as a launching pad for further attacks inside the enterprise.

The most dominant form of network intrusion at present is the "invite me in" strategy whereby an unsuspecting victim is tricked into downloading the malicious software. The methods used can be "drive-by attacks," where visiting a compromised site can cause the transfer of the malware, or via a "watering hole" attack whereby a machine that is connected to a popular site is infected. This is particularly insidious, since the original site is considered safe by its user community.

DoS attacks affect the availability and integrity of the network infrastructure. DDoS attacks are the same, except multiple hosts participate in the attack. One example of a DDoS attack is using a network stress testing tool called the "low orbit ion cannon" (LOIC) to flood the target with traffic, a favorite technique used by the hacktivist collective Anonymous.

Some attacks attempt to hide the true source of the attack by using systems like The Onion Router (TOR). The TOR network consists of a set of cooperating servers that encrypt network traffic between one system and its peer. The encryption used differs from machine to machine. The only time that a source address appears in the clear is when the traffic exits the last TOR router and is sent on to the destination. A wise digital forensics investigator (DFI) will have a list of known TOR routers available in order to avoid attempting to trace traffic back to the computer, or risk triumphantly announcing that they have found the source of the attack.

IP routers also can be a target for an infrastructure attack. Routers can be breached in typical ways: default or no credentials, exploitable bugs in the router's OS, or easy to guess passwords. Once an attacker has control of the device, they can reroute traffic to sites they control, drop traffic entirely, or inject or delete packets to cause errors that result in increased host traffic (a DoS) or misinform other routers about destinations, thereby decreasing network throughput. One very old example of what can happen during this kind of attack occurred when a misbehaving router announced that it had infinite bandwidth and minimal delay to every other organization attached to the network. All the other nodes were overjoyed to hear this and started to route all their traffic to the misbehaving node. Needless to say, the network eventually ground to a halt until the error was corrected. Although this episode was the result of a software flaw, an actual attack could result in similar behavior.

Network forensics gathers evidence from several sources. The first source is the attack computer itself (assuming it's accessible to the investigator), intermediate computers and firewalls, and networking infrastructure devices (routers and switches). Information resources gathered from each device include logs, configuration files, and transitory information that is stored in device memory, such as active network connections and actual running configurations. The last source is from the victim's computer itself. Live analysis or offline analysis of a memory dump can list the details of what network connections were live at the time of capture, what network services were in use (DNS, NTP, default gateway), which interfaces were in use, and so forth. Internal lists such as Address Routing Protocol (ARP) tables and routing tables also reveal useful information concerning the actual configuration of the device at the time of the incident or following the initial compromise.

Discovering the ultimate source and destination of the network data is a major goal of network forensics. This fits very nicely into 5WH (who, what, when, where, why, and how). Recall the VERIS A4 taxonomy from Chapter 4: asset (what), attacker (who), action (how), and attribute (which one of CIA was attacked). Capturing this information provides historical data you can use to recognize future attacks. Recording all the intermediate devices between the source and destination provides other sources for corroborating evidence in addition to the source host and the destination host that provide information about the attacker and the victim.

Network evidence is, by its very nature, volatile and thus transitory. Log files can be overwritten if not acquired quickly, and information stored in memory will vanish if the machine is shut down and restarted. Given the nature of the Internet, permission may be required from one or more Internet service providers (ISPs) in order to access log files from devices in their infrastructure. For these reasons, critical information may not be available in a timely manner, and records may be incomplete or at least suspect if the device has been compromised. Network forensics by itself isn't sufficient to solve a case, and network activity by itself is not conclusive proof that a particular individual was seated at the keyboard. An IP address, a login account, and a MAC address don't equate to a person.[5]

Once we collected all our information and correlated events from multiple devices, we can then begin our analysis to understand the complete end-to-end view of the network-based attack.

CAUTION This incident may be a single step in a chain of incidents preceding or subsequent to an intrusion. The investigator must be conscious of whether this intrusion represents the initial compromise, a step in a series of compromises, or the end goal of an attack.

> ## Who Had Access to a Device?
> With our goal of placing devices in the hands of the suspect, the more devices we have to examine, the more likely we will be able to accomplish this task using all available information. By obtaining the likely physical location of an electronic device through forensic analysis and obtaining the physical locations of a suspect through means other than a forensic analysis, inferences can be made as to the likelihood the suspect controlled the device. Not a certainty, but definitely a piece of circumstantial evidence to build upon.[6]

Network Forensics: Attack and Defend

There are several places to look for network forensics evidence. `Netstat` will provide a listing of open connections and the state of the connection, as well as which ports have active listeners. The `arp` command shows a listing of MAC addresses and associated IP addresses. The `ipconfig` utility on Windows (ifconfig on Linux) will show you a list of interfaces, assigned IP addresses for each, and the state of the interface. The command `ipconfig /displaydns` will show the contents of the local DNS cache

The `arp /a` command lists the mapping of MAC address to IP address for each network interface on the computer. Each address is listed as static or dynamic. Static indicates that the IP address to MAC address has been configured, while dynamic indicates that the address has been resolved using the ARP protocol itself. Static addresses are permanent. Dynamic addresses can be modified by an ARP broadcast address, and will eventually time out and be deleted from the cache.

An attacker can manipulate the ARP cache in several ways. One is to enter a static MAC address for an IP address that should be resolved dynamically. Another is to issue an ARP broadcast that announces that the attacker's machine now has the IP address of a significant network resource. One such attack claims that the attacker machine is now the default gateway to the rest of the Internet. All outbound traffic will now be directed to that computer and is visible to the attacker. This is a type of MITM attack.

Another attack method is to inject misinformation into cached DNS records, an activity called "DNS poisoning." These DNS caches exist at several places within the network. The first is the host file on the device itself, which is usually consulted first in the attempt to resolve the fully qualified domain name (FQDN) into an IP address. Another location on a local machine is the DNS cache: `ipconfig /displaydns` will show the current entries, and `ipconfig /flushdns` will purge the resolver class. `ipconfig /registerdns` will cancel all DHCP leases and reregister the DNS resource records. The `netsh` command allows you to manage network services both locally and remotely. The command `netsh interface ipv4 show dnsservers` will list all the configured DNS servers for each interface, and the command

```
netsh interface ipv4 set dnsserver name=""interfacename"" \
source=""static"" address=""208.67.222.222""
```

will assign a DNS server to a particular interface.

Yet another attack at the local machine level is to reconfigure the machine's proxy server settings to redirect all traffic to a machine under the attacker's control. As in the case of changing the hosts file or modifying the local DNS cache, the attacker needs to be able to execute commands on a local machine and to have a presence on the enterprise network (many organizations would catch a local machine attempting to proxy to a remote computer).

Many organizations configure DNS resolution to use a DNS server that is local to a particular location and to request further information from an enterprise-level DNS server or servers. Poisoning the cache at a DNS server at the enterprise level guarantees that everyone in that enterprise sees the attacker's address. ARP poisoning and DNS poisoning all have the same goal: redirect the network traffic from the desired, legitimate site to a site controlled by the attacker. Here, the attacker can pretend to be the original site (a bank or a retail enterprise), or can simply infect the system with malware that allows the attacker to gain a foothold on the victim's machine.

Network Security Monitoring

Network security monitoring (NSM) is the "collection, analysis and escalation of indications and warnings to detect and respond to intrusions."[7] This definition summarizes the mechanisms used for network forensics analysis. Collection is the process whereby network traffic is captured and stored. Analysis can occur either in real time (as is the case with an IDS system or when capturing raw packets on a network interface) or post-capture. One challenge for packet capture is whether to place the capturing device inline (such as a network tap) or utilize a special port on a switch known generically as a switched port analysis (SPAN) port.

One advantage with a network tap is that the traffic is split and sent to the sensor without any inspection. SPAN ports require device configuration, and may lose traffic if the load on the switch is too high. A second decision is where to place the sensor. The simple answer is to place the sensor at a location in the network where the actual source and destination addresses will be visible. The Network Address Translation (NAT) device will rewrite the source IP address to be its own IP address; any traffic captured after that point will appear to originate and terminate from the NAT device. Likewise, capturing network traffic after a proxy server will record the source and destination addresses as that of the proxy server.

In order to gain the full benefit of NSM for the purposes of network forensics analysis, you need to capture full packets (not just headers) and capture all packets in order to successfully reconstruct objects that are transmitted over the network (images, executable files, scripts, documents, and so forth).

Theory into Practice: Network Forensic Tools

Dozens of network forensics tools are available. Some of these tools have achieved the status of classics, enough so that they are still covered in courses on digital forensics and incident response.

Tcpdump and friends are command-line tools that will collect packets from a specific interface or interfaces on the local device and display the data in multiple ways.

Output can be sent to a console or to a packet capture file for future analysis. The packet-capture library (libpcap) is the basis for many other tools.

Wireshark is the pre-eminent open-source network sniffer and analyzer. It supports a three-pane view of captured traffic: a listing of the packets, a pane that shows the protocol nesting within that packet, and a third pane that show a hex-dump of the raw packet. Figure 9-3 shows the Wireshark user interface. Tshark is a text-mode version that is very similar to tcpdump.

Wireshark supports adding capture and display filters. Capture filters will only collect specific traffic; display filters will only display specific traffic. For example, the display filter "tcp" will only display TCP packets.

NetWitness Investigator from NetWitness, now a part of RSA (the security division of EMC[2]), provides a system of data collection, retrieval, reporting, and analysis. The software can retrieve data from Netwitness's own collection subsystem, from a raw network interface, or from a .pcap file. Investigator can also send its output to Wireshark for more detailed packet analysis.

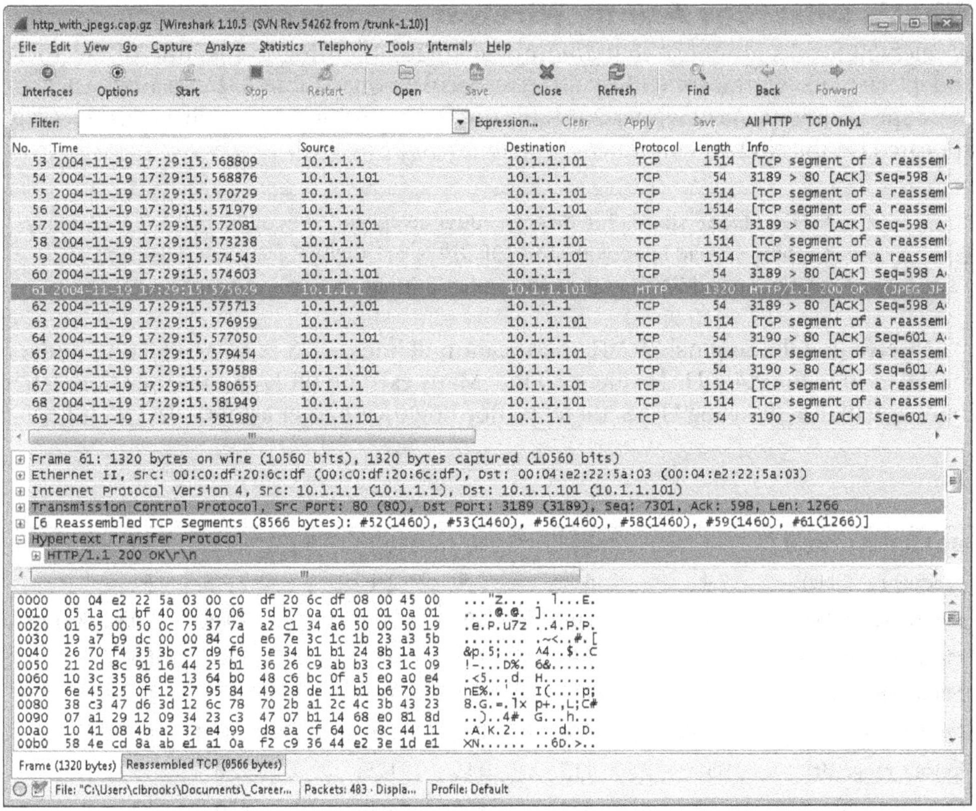

Figure 9-3 Wireshark three-pane user interface

NetworkMiner is a relatively new tool with a different view of network forensics. It, too, can listen to a live interface or ingest a packet-capture file. One major feature is that it will collect and dump all files downloaded as part of an HTTP session.

Network Forensics and Wireless Networks

At layers 3 and above (IP), network forensics is the same. Below layer 3, however, the world is very different. The structure of wireless networks is much different from the Ethernet networks (a model of simplicity compared to the mare's nest of protocols that support the various wireless transmission mechanisms). The differences are masked, in part, because most wireless interfaces create an Ethernet "pseudo-packet."

NOTE If you're familiar with the 802.11x family of protocols and the encryption methods used, please feel free to jump ahead to the section "Investigating Wireless Attacks."

What's Different About Wireless?

Wireless networks are those that are implemented according to Institute of Electrical and Electronics Engineers (IEEE) 802.11 specifications. Table 9-2 describes each of these specifications. As of winter 2014, products supporting 802.11ac have just recently appeared on the consumer market.

NOTE DSSS stands for direct-sequence spread spectrum, FHSS is frequency-hopping spread spectrum, and OFDM is orthogonal frequency-division multiplexing. MIMO stands for multiple-input, multiple-output.

Observe that the original 802.11 specification defines FHSS as an accepted frequency modulation in the 2.4-GHz frequency band. Many existing Wi-Fi sniffers may not search that particular band using FHSS, thereby affording the attacker a good place to hide.

802.11 Protocol	--	a	b	g	n	ac
Frequency (GHz)	2.4	5	2.4	2.4	2.4/5	5
Bandwidth (MHz)	20	20	20	20	20/40	20/40/80/160
Max. data rate (Mb/s)	2	54	11	54	72.2	866.7
MIMO streams	1	1	1	1	4	8
Modulation	DSSS, FHSS	OFDM	DSSS	OFDM, DSSS	OFDM	OFDM
Indoor range (ft)	65	115	115	125	250	250
Outdoor range (ft)	300	390	460	460	820	820

Table 9-2 802.11 Protocols

An enterprise wireless network consists of at least one WAP and at least two clients (nodes) that are capable of using the same Wi-Fi communication protocols. Wireless networks have the advantage in that they can be set up without requiring physical cabling or extra networking equipment. The disadvantage is that Wi-Fi networks are truly broadcast networks, since they utilize radio transmissions at various speeds and frequencies. This means that if steps aren't taken, any node can eavesdrop on the transmission of any other node. In a wired network, network access could be limited by the presence of an Ethernet connector. In the wireless world, the node need not even be on the same premises as the enterprise, but could be in a vehicle parked across the street.

Wi-Fi networks can run in one of two modes: enterprise or ad hoc. In an enterprise configuration, all nodes associate with the AP. In ad hoc mode, nodes can associate with any other node(s) if they agree on the parameters and on network addresses and so forth. Networks are identified by their service set identifier (SSID). We can think of this as the "name" of the network. For example, "xfinitywifi" is the name of my local cable provider's wireless metropolitan area network (MAN).

A Wi-Fi network could operate with only an AP and no external connection if communication was restricted to only those nodes that were associated with the access point (in this case, the network would look like an ad hoc network). The more usual configuration is that the access point connects to a router that connects to the rest of the enterprise network and to the greater Internet. Recall our original description of the OSI and ARPANET network models. In this case, the link layer protocols will differ between the wireless nodes and the AP, and the AP and the router. On the router side, frames most likely will be actual Ethernet frames.

The popular Linksys series of network appliances combine the functions of a wireless AP, a switch, and a router, as well as a firewall and a DHCP server. One way to envision this is to imagine that the AP is connected to the switch via a cable, and the switch is likewise connected to the router via a cable. A single access point may support multiple media access protocols simultaneously, but this may restrict bandwidth on a mixed network (for example, a mixed 802.11g and an 802.11n network may only operate at 11g speeds).

Other IEEE standards are necessary for the full function of an 802.11 wireless LAN (WLAN). The 802.11f standard defines how a node behaves when it moves between two access points using the same SSID. The 802.11i standard (also known as WPA-2 or the Robust Security Network (RSN)) defines a series of authentication and encryption protocols between the AP and the individual node or station (STA).

Encryption in 802.11i is link-layer (layer 2) encryption, and has nothing to do with Internet Protocol Security (IPsec) or TLS/SSL encryption, which occurs at the network (IP) layer and the application layer, respectively. 802.11i uses the 802.1X protocol to authenticate the user of the device as well as the device itself: other protocols such as WEP would only authenticate the device. Authentication is supported by various flavors of the Extensible Authentication Protocol (EAP). The EAP-TLS protocol type uses Transport Layer Security (TLS) to mutually authenticate the user to the network, while the protected EAP (PEAP) extension uses TLS, but only authenticates the server and not the client.

The Saga of Wireless Encryption

The story of wireless encryption is a prime example of why cryptography is hard, and implementing it is even harder. The first encryption algorithm provided by the 802.11b standard was the Wired Equivalent Privacy (WEP). As originally implemented, WEP required a shared key between the wireless client and the AP. The issue here was that there was one and only one key for that given SSID. Changing that key for all users of the SSID quickly became an administrative nightmare, especially for a large number of users.

The discovery that the WEP protocol was easily broken made a bad situation worse. The problem was with the poor implementation of the RC4 encryption protocol, as well as a weak 24-bit initialization vector, that was initialized as 0 and monotonically increased for each packet until it wrapped around to 0 again. Without going into detail, it was very easy to determine the WEP key simply by generating enough traffic on the network to cause the wrap-around, and, because of fixed information in the WEP header, this provided the same information effectively generated from the same key. As a result, the WEP key could be determined in as little as one minute (yes, you read that correctly) by means of what is called a "known plaintext" attack.

Investigating Wireless Attacks

Wireless attacks can be generalized into MITM attacks and impersonation attacks. In the former case, an attacker attempts to usurp the responsibilities of a particular WAP. One way to do this is to utilize the same network SSID, but generate a stronger signal. In the latter case, the attacker can eavesdrop on network traffic and then configure their device with a supported MAC address. Assuming that the first device has disconnected, the attacker is viewed as legitimate and associates with the WAP.

MAC filtering is a technique used to restrict access to the network by whitelisting certain MAC addresses. One of the best defenses in wireless networking, in addition to using Wireless Protected Access (WPA) or WPA2 to authenticate, is to limit the number of DHCP addresses, as well as whitelisting the MAC addresses allowed to associate with the WAP. This can work for a very small network, such as a small office/home office (SOHO) network, but becomes unwieldy when larger networks are considered. At this point, a more robust and extensible protocol such as Remote Authentication Dial-In User Service (RADIUS) and two-factor authentication are necessary.

Searching for WAPs with the same SSID as the known network, or for unknown or unregistered WAPs ("rogue APs"), is another technique to identify potential intruders.

Theory into Practice: Wireless Forensic Tools

If you're doing a forensic examination of network traffic at the IP layer and above, you can utilize many of the tools described for wired networks. Wireshark on Windows, for example, can capture packets from a wireless local area network (LAN) connection, but you won't see control messages. To see control packets, you would need an interface like AirPcap or Microsoft's own Network Monitor application.

TIP The words "monitor mode" and "promiscuous mode" are often used interchangeably, but there are subtle differences worth knowing. A network interface card (NIC) in monitor mode will receive all wireless frames, including control frames, without actually associating with an AP. Promiscuous mode requires an association with an AP and receives all wireless frames as well.

AirPcap (www.riverbed.com) is a Wi-Fi universal serial bus (USB) interface that can be put into promiscuous mode to capture all node traffic, and into monitoring mode to capture control messages that are part of the 802.11 specification. An interface in monitoring mode should see a request from an unknown device to learn of access points in addition to the response from your AP with its identity.

NOTE A frequent topic of conversation is whether an AP should broadcast its SSID or not as a security measure. Some argue that if an attacker is running an interface in monitor mode, then probe messages from other nodes will cause the AP to respond with its information (a passive attack). The attacker listening in monitor mode isn't required to associate with a WAP in order to capture traffic. If the attacker generates the probe message in an attempt to associate with an AP, its presence can be noticed, especially if the organization is monitoring for unknown MAC addresses (we've moved from a passive to an active attack).

NetStumbler is a Windows-based Wi-Fi scanner. Software in this category is useful for determining which WAPs are available and information about each one, such as signal strength, channel used, security software enabled, and which version of the 802.11 protocol is used. Although NetStumbler is a classic scanning tool, it's starting to show its age, and new software called Vistumbler (www.vistumbler.net) supports more recent Microsoft operating systems like Windows 7. Figure 9-4 demonstrates the initial pane of Vistumbler when run on a laptop. I'm proud to say that most of my neighbors are using WPA2 to secure their computer to AP connections, although I do notice that there is a wireless HP printer with an open port somewhere in the neighborhood. Hmmm—I wonder what operating system (OS) the device is running?

Aireplay-ng and Airodump are software tools distributed as part of the aircrack-ng software package (www.aircrack-ng.org). Aireplay-ng is used to inject Wi-Fi control packets into the WLAN (the wireless analog of tcpreplay). The command

```
aireplay-ng --deauth 5 <MAC address of the AP> wlan0
```

would send a deauthenticate control message to all nodes associated with that AP. Deauthentication can result in capturing information like the WPA/WPA2 handshake sequence (useful to gather information to attempt to break WPA keys) and can often generate ARP requests from nodes that have flushed their ARP cache when disconnecting.

The Airodump-ng software will capture packets from the wireless interface (think of it as the wireless version of tcpdump.) Remember that your success in monitoring and capturing wireless traffic is dependent on your wireless network interface: Only certain chipsets (such as Orinoco) can be set to monitor mode.

#	Active	Mac Address	SSID	Signal	High Signal	RSSI	High RSSI	Channel	Authentication	Encryption
1	Active	58:6D:8F:49:FF:60	c16419wifi	99%	99%	-46 dBm	-44 dBm	1	WPA2-Personal	CCMP
2	Active	C0:C1:C0:0A:A8:13	c16419wifi	70%	75%	-58 dBm	-55 dBm	1	WPA2-Personal	CCMP
3	Active	F8:7B:8C:05:E5:37	Deckhouse	46%	50%	-72 dBm	-70 dBm	1	WPA-Personal	CCMP
4	Active	20:AA:4B:C6:A3:64	AttackCat	35%	40%	-79 dBm	-76 dBm	11	WPA2-Personal	CCMP
5	Active	20:AA:4B:C6:A3:66	AttackCat-guest	33%	41%	-80 dBm	-75 dBm	11	Open	None
6	Dead	20:AA:4B:C2:BE:1A	Water	0%	31%	-100 dBm	-81 dBm	11	WPA2-Personal	CCMP
7	Active	C4:27:95:34:6C:CE	HOME-6CCE	36%	40%	-78 dBm	-76 dBm	11	WPA2-Personal	CCMP
8	Active	D8:9D:67:89:D1:3A	HP-Print-3A-Photosmar...	23%	28%	-86 dBm	-83 dBm	11	Open	None
9	Active	C0:C1:C0:83:7D:A2	RCN Wifi	25%	30%	-85 dBm	-82 dBm	11	WPA2-Personal	CCMP
10	Active	E8:89:2C:D5:3D:D0	med26	38%	46%	-77 dBm	-72 dBm	6	WPA2-Personal	CCMP
11	Active	E6:89:2C:D5:3D:D0	xfinitywifi	36%	45%	-78 dBm	-73 dBm	6	Open	None
12	Active	28:CF:DA:B5:20:99	Rohlicek-n	20%	23%	-88 dBm	-86 dBm	6	WPA2-Personal	CCMP
13	Active	00:1F:F3:C0:1E:EB	White	28%	35%	-83 dBm	-79 dBm	6	WPA2-Personal	CCMP
14	Active	E2:89:2C:D5:3D:D0		35%	45%	-79 dBm	-73 dBm	6	WPA2-Personal	CCMP
15	Active	C4:39:3A:A5:9B:09		31%	31%	-81 dBm	-81 dBm	1	WPA2-Personal	CCMP
16	Active	C4:39:3A:A5:9B:0A		25%	31%	-85 dBm	-81 dBm	1	WPA2-Personal	CCMP
17	Active	C4:39:3A:A5:9B:0B		26%	31%	-84 dBm	-81 dBm	1	WPA2-Personal	CCMP
18	Active	C4:39:3A:A5:9B:08	HOME-9808	26%	28%	-84 dBm	-81 dBm	1	WPA2-Personal	CCMP
19	Dead	08:86:3B:28:3F:74	Gemini	0%	35%	-100 dBm	-79 dBm	11	WPA2-Personal	CCMP
20	Dead	00:21:29:C4:68:C0	TopoftheHill	0%	25%	-100 dBm	-85 dBm	6	WPA2-Personal	CCMP
21	Dead	68:7F:74:C8:CA:22	SilverMonkey-guest	0%	25%	-100 dBm	-85 dBm	11	Open	None

Figure 9-4 Vistumbler listing of APs within range

Log Capturing and Event Correlation

Computer security logs record various events on a computer that may be related to a security breach. On some systems, security logs are separate from other logs. Microsoft Windows stores security-related events in the security event log. Syslog-based systems can create logs based on a particular facility code that reflects a security-related event. We'll have more to say about syslog facility codes later on in this chapter.

The kinds of events recorded will depend on how the system is configured. For syslog events, the kinds of events recorded are defined in the /etc/syslog.conf file. For Windows systems, the kinds of events recorded depend, in part, on which audit events have been configured.

Logs, Logs, Logs

We talked about Windows logs in a previous chapter. Unlike centralized logging schemes, Windows stores its logs in three different files: security, application, and system. Applications are free to maintain their own log files as well: On my workstation, Cisco AnyConnect keeps its own log file. Other system services (daemons in the *nix world) can contain event records that provide extra evidence. We talked about Internet Information Services (IIS) logs and DHCP logs in a previous chapter. Others logs on Windows systems include the Open Database Connectivity (ODBC) log file.

On Linux systems, the DHCP logs are found in /var/log. Strangely enough, the security log file is the place to look for security events: /var/log/auth.log and /var/log/authpriv.log.

Legal Issues and Logging

If you intend to use a log file as evidence in court, it must undergo the same precautions as are used with any other form of digital evidence. This means that you must maintain chain of custody, as well as create a forensics image of the evidence (and create a second working copy of that image). As we saw earlier, logs must be kept as part of regular business practice, and must be authenticated by a person knowledgeable of how the records are produced and stored, as well as the accuracy and reliability of the log data.

The EC-Council points out, however, that using logs as part of a court case means that the organization must make their log collection and monitoring software available to the defense for examination, and must include any exculpatory evidence that would exonerate the accused. Logs that are recorded after an intrusion are not admissible as evidence, since they are not considered part of normal business practices, and the contents of the logs are suspect if the collection occurred after the breach. Likewise, data will be considered suspect if the host collecting the logs has a record of security failures or incidents prior to the incident in question.[8]

Another consideration when presenting log files as evidence is that the contents of the files must be unchanged. Therefore, a log management solution should be capable of storing data on a write-once, read-many (WORM) device such that the original logs are preserved.

One technique used to combat the overwhelming amount of data is to condense log files. Any non-loss technique for file compression is acceptable, such as WinZip or GZip file compression. Since many logs are text files, compression can work well. For binary log files, consider extracting only the events of interest that are related to a particular incident. Since you've already stored the originals, going back to the original logs as part of analysis may be feasible.

Log management is "the process for generating, transmitting, storing, analyzing, and disposing of computer security log data."[9] Logging isn't free. It requires processing time on the local system that's writing the logs, and it requires network bandwidth and disk space to store log files (and offsite backups of log files as well). What to log? How much? How long to keep them? What's required by regulatory agencies? What level of detail? When can I delete logs? (Regulations may require that log file be kept for years.)

Centralized logging occurs when a single host or hosts are designated as official logging hosts (log-hosts). All systems will either forward their logs to that host or run an agent locally that can collect local logs and forward them to the log-host. The log-host is a significant part of the network infrastructure: Losing it effectively blinds the enterprise to any system activities. Multiple log-hosts can be distributed in the enterprise in order to support local security monitoring and control; for security purposes, however, it makes sense to roll up these logs to a centralized server so as to get a complete picture.

NOTE   One of the watchwords for event log collection is "Collect everything." There are two reasons for this: to avoid missing "dark corners" where illicit activity can occur, and to fulfill the legal requirements of collecting data as part of standard business operations.

It's extremely important to prevent modification of any logs. Daniel Grezlak describes six log-modification attacks, all of which depend on injecting data into the log record.[9] One such attack is new-line injection. New-line injection occurs when an attacker enters data into a field and includes extra new-line characters. Grezlak uses the example where the phrase "User01" becomes "User01\nFailed to 'rm -f /*' for Manager01\n" (the "\n" character sequence represents a new-line character, which can be a carriage return, a line feed, or both). The appropriate defense is simply to remove new-line characters before the input is actually written to the log. A second attack is timestamp injection, where a log record with a falsified timestamp is injected into the log file (this is more difficult than it might appear on the surface). If the log is searched in timestamp order, the new log record will appear between other records. This type of attack can be thwarted by including a potentially random sequence number for each log record.

Syslog

One classic example of log collection software is the syslog software, originally from Berkeley Systems Division (BSD) UNIX. Now syslog or a variation thereof can be found on most *nix systems and Microsoft Windows, as well in the form of the Kiwi Syslog Daemon. Multiple versions of syslog exist: standard BSD format (as defined in Request for Comments [RFC] 5424 [www.rfc-editor.org/rfc/rfc5424.txt]), syslog-ng, and rsyslog. As a friend of mine once said, "It's the same thing, only different."

A standard syslog message consists of a header followed by structured data and a message. A header is defined as the sequence of values representing "Priority Version Timestamp hostname application-name processID messageID"; the structured data is simply a sequence of name/value pairs, followed by an optional message.

The priority code in a syslog event message is a combination of the facility and the severity of the event. Table 9-3 shows the various facilities listed in the standard syslog message.

Number	Facility ID	Description
0	Kern	Messages from kernel
1	User	User-generated message
3	Daemon	Other daemon processes
4	Auth	Security/authorization messages
5	Syslog	Messages generated internally by syslog itself
6	Lpr	Line printer subsystem
7	News	Network news
8	UUCP	UNIX-to-UNIX copy
9	Cron	Clock daemon
10	Authpriv	Security/authorization messages (sensitive)
11	FTP	File Transfer Protocol daemon
12	NTP	Network Time Protocol
13	LogAudit	Log audit
14	Log Alert	Log alert
15	CRON	Clock daemon
16–23	Local0–7	Reserved for local use

Table 9-3 Syslog Facility Values (Source: RFC5242: The Syslog Protocol (CA: IETF, 2009) Retrieved from www.rfc-editor.org/rfc/rfc5254.txt. p. 9-10.)

Table 9-4	Severity #	Name	Description
Severity Values	0	Emerg	System is unusable
and Definitions	1	Alert	Take action immediately
	2	Crit	Critical condition
	3	Err	Error condition
	4	Warning	Warning
	5	Notice	Normal but significant condition
	6	Info	Informational
	7	Debug	Debug-level messages

The severity code is an indication of the seriousness of a particular event. Severity can take on one of the values listed in Table 9-4.

The priority code is a combination of the facility number multiplied by 8 (left-shifted 3 bits), with the severity code added (logical OR'ed) to the result. For example, the priority code for the daemon facility at a critical severity level would be encoded as (3 * 8) + 2, or 26.

The syslog daemon is configured via the /etc/syslog.conf file. The general format of that file is a list of entries; each entry consists of a selector and an action, which can be to write to a file, send it to a remote host, pipe the results to another program, or send a message to all logged-in users or only some of the users. Sending to a remote host is a good choice that can prevent losing data if log files are deleted on the local computer.

The following listing shows a portion of a sample syslog.conf file with examples of all the actions.[10] Each selector is in the form "facility.severity:"—an asterisk (*) indicates that all of the corresponding elements should apply. For example, the selector "*.err" means to select all message of severity err or higher for all facilities, and "kern.*" will select all messages for the kern facility. The special severity of "none" indicates that no messages from the facility should be included. An action of "*" means to send to all logged-in users.

```
# Log all kernel messages, authentication messages of
# level notice or higher, and anything of level err or
# higher to the console.
# Don't log private authentication messages!
    *.err;kern.*;auth.notice;authpriv.none;mail.crit         /dev/console

# Log anything (except mail) of level info or higher.
# Don''t log private authentication messages!
    *.info;mail.none;authpriv.none        /var/log/messages
# Everybody gets emergency messages, plus log them on another
# machine.
    *.emerg                                *
    *.emerg                                @arpa.berkeley.edu
# Root and Eric get alert and higher messages.
    *.alert                                root,eric
# Pipe all authentication messages to a filter.
    auth.*                                |exec /usr/local/sbin/authfilter
```

Synchronizing Time

Collecting log data from multiple sources helps to either support or negate various assumptions concerning how an event may have happened. Ideally, information gained from multiple sources will support a particular hypothesis: Yes, indeed, we see that the suspect accessed a particular web site, and the router logs confirm it.

Now imagine that the time-of-day clocks in the suspect's computer and the router were wildly out of synch. The router might show this access as one hour earlier or one hour later. If these two times cannot be reconciled, and given the legal necessity of testifying as to the accuracy of log file collection, then we have just lost a piece of evidence.

Network Time Protocol (NTP) version 4 is defined in RFC 5905. It is based on the notion that there is one true time on planet Earth, as measured by Coordinated Universal Time (UTC). UTC is, in turn, based on International Atomic Time (TAI), which is determined by the rotation of the Earth. Stratum 1 (primary) servers are connected to national time services by one of several methods, including radio and satellite signals. Stratum 2 (secondary) servers contact primary servers for the time and then adjust their time based on round-trip time and the clock offset. Other servers usually contact secondary servers. (If this architecture sounds much like that of DNS, you've been paying attention!)

 NOTE Don't mistake the Network Time Protocol (NTP) for the Network News Transfer Protocol (NNTP). Not the same thing at all.

The web site www.ntp.org provides a list of open-access NTP primary and secondary servers. In addition, various Linux distributions may provide their own NTP server lists—for example, Ubuntu distributions list ntp.ubuntu.com as the default time server.

The Linux `ntpdate` command will obtain a time from a designated server and update the system clock depending on how far the clock is out of synch with the server's clock. If the discrepancy is more than 0.5 seconds, ntpdate will modify the clock immediately; if less than 0.5 seconds, ntpdate will adjust the clock based on the offset between the local system clock and the server.

Windows has other means to implement time service. Usually, the Windows time service will run on the domain controller for a Windows domain. The command line

```
net time /DOMAIN[:domainname] /SET
```

will retrieve the time for the given domain and set the time on the local machine. If a machine is not a part of a domain, an external time service can be specified by setting HKLM\System\CurrentControlSet\Services\w32time\Type to "ntp" and HKLM\...\ w32time\NtpServer to "time.nist.gov."

SIM, SEM, SIEM—Everybody Wants One

One recent development in log capture and analysis is the Security Information and Event Management (SIEM) system. Products in this space are meant to collect and store enormous amounts of event data, as well as report significant events in real time and retrieve the results of ad hoc queries as a reporting function and forward important events to other management systems. Two such products are HP Arcsight and RSA's Security Analytics.

Events can be correlated based on time, source/destination IP address, severity, application used, and so forth. One simple technique is to create a timeline with a sequential representation of when each event was recorded. Another technique used in conjunction with timelines is to create a histogram of how many events happened at a particular time. Combining these two approaches creates a visual display of the number of events occurring at a particular time. This graphic presentation can help identify certain traffic patterns. For example, multiple events sent periodically can indicate malware "phoning home" to the associated C2 server. A pattern of bursts of activity followed by periods of silence or only a few events is representative of a human behind a keyboard ("type a little, think a little").

Theory into Practice: Log Capturing and Analysis Tools

You probably won't be surprised to learn that there are many log capturing and analysis tools available, including free for download, free open-source software (FOSS), and commercial. One example of a log capturing and analysis tool is the log2timeline software that is packaged with The Sleuth Kit (TSK) from Brian Carrier. log2timeline leverages TSK's ability to create a timeline of file modification, access, or creation and adds data from multiple log sources. The web site www.log2timeline .net lists over 30 different input sources, including Firefox bookmarks, generic Linux log files, the MS-SQL error log, and Windows Restore Points. Output formats for this tool include a SQLite database, a .cvs file, and an HP Arcsight's Common Event Format (CEF) file.

Splunk (www.splunk.com) is a commercial product (a free version is available) that aims to "deliver real-time operational intelligence to IT and business users."[11] Splunk claims to be able to collect and index any machine data. Combined with a powerful search engine processing language (SPL) and reporting capabilities that extend from developing charts and dashboards that support drill-down to the individual event, Splunk "scales to collect and index tens of terabytes of data per day across multi-geography, multi-datacenter, physical or virtual infrastructures."[12] Splunk's search interface is shown in Figure 9-5.

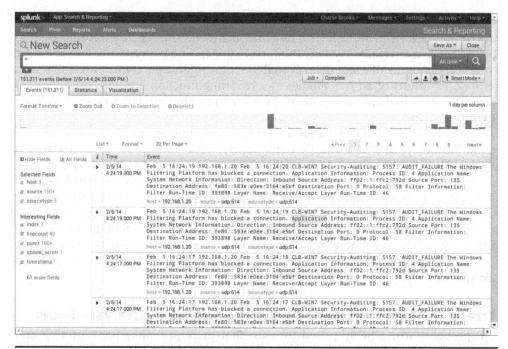

Figure 9-5 Splunk's search interface

Chapter Review

Network forensics is "the capture, recording, and analysis of network events in order to discover the source of security attacks or other problem incidents." The main source of information about network events is log files from various devices and packet captures of the original traffic. Log files relating to network traffic are under the same restrictions as other computer log files if they are going to be introduced as evidence.

At higher levels of the networking protocol stack (the network layer and above), analysis can proceed identically for both wired and wireless networks. Information varies considerably at the data link and physical layers. Types of attacks and attack methods are very different in wired and wireless networks, and thus require different kinds of security controls to monitor traffic and raise an alarm if anomalous or suspicious traffic is observed.

SIEM products go beyond standard log collection and analysis tools to provide data management and real-time reporting of events, as well as demonstrating compliance with various regulatory requirements.

Questions

1. An attacker monitors all activity on a LAN. What kind of attack is this?

   A. Active

   B. Passive

   C. Indirect

   D. Enumeration

2. Which wireless protocol supports moving a node from one AP another?

   A. 802.11fx

   B. 802.1X

   C. 802.11g

   D. 802.11ac

3. Which wireless protocol supports authenticating a node to an AP?

   A. 802.1X

   B. 802.11x

   C. 802.11g

   D. 802.11ac

4. In order to observe 802.11 control packets without associating with an AP, a wireless NIC must be put in _____ mode.

   A. Promiscuous

   B. Listening

   C. Extended

   D. Monitor

5. Which protocol is in use if you observe traffic with port 22 as a destination?

   A. FTP

   B. Telnet

   C. HTTP

   D. SSH

6. Which method would a nontechnical person use to collect static and dynamic data from a suspect device?

   A. Chain of custody

   B. Preservation of the original logs

   C. Working from a copy of the original

   D. Reformatting original log files to a standard format

7. IP is a _____ network protocol.

   A. Reliable

   B. Connection-oriented

   C. Connectionless

   D. Stop-and-wait

8. How should you interpret the syslog.conf entry "kern.*   /var/log/kernel"?

   A. All messages with a severity of "kern" should be written to the file /var/log/kernel.

   B. All messages from the "kern" facility should be written to the file /var/log/kernel.

   C. Messages with a severity "kern" should be read from the file /var/log/kernel.

   D. Messages for the kern facility should be read from the file /var/log/kernel.

9. At what protocol layers are wired and wireless networks most different?

   A. Network, link

   B. Link, physical

   C. Transport, link

   D. Network, physical

10. What happens in a new-line injection attack?

   A. New log entries are created.

   B. New timestamps for log records are recorded.

   C. Multiple entries in the log are combined.

   D. Any information following the first new-line is skipped.

Answers

1. B. Eavesdropping on network communications is a passive attack.

2. B. 802.11fX

3. A. 802.1X

4. D. Monitor mode

5. D. SSH (Secure Shell)

6. D. It's bad practice and isn't required to reformat log files.

7. C. IP is a connectionless protocol.

8. B. All messages from the kernel facility should be written to the /var/log/kernel file.

9. B. Wired and wireless networks differ the most at the data link and the physical layers.

10. A. New log entries are created.

References

1. 18 U.S. Code § 1030 - Fraud and related activity in connection with computers. Retrieved from http://www.law.cornell.edu/uscode/text/18/1030.

2. Garfinkel, S. "Network Forensics: Tapping the Net." Retrieved from http://www.oreillynet.com/pub/a/network/2002/04/26/nettap.html.

3. Chappel, L. *Wireshark Network Analysis*, 1st ed. (CA: Protocol Analysis Institute) p. xxiii.

4. EC-Council. *Computer Forensics: Investigating Network Intrusions and Cybercrime* (NY: C-Engage, 2009), pp. 2–6.

5. Shavers, B. *Putting the Suspect Behind the Keyboard* (MA: Syngress, 2014). Retrieved from http://my.safaribooksonline.com/book/-/9781597499859/chapter-4dot-technical-investigations/st015_chp004_html.

6. Shavers. Retrieved from http://my.safaribooksonline.com/book/-/9781597499859/chapter-4dot-technical-investigations/st015_chp004_html.

7. Bejtlich, R. *The Practice of Network Security Monitoring* (CA: No Starch Press, 2013), p. 3.

8. EC-Council, *Computer Forensics*, pp. 1–4.

9. Kent, K. and Souppaya, M. "NIST800-92: Guide to Computer Security Log Management (MS: U.S. DOC 2006). Retrieved from http://csrc.nist.gov/publications/PubsSPs.html. p. ES-1.

10. Syslog.conf(5). Retrieved from www.unix.com/man-pages/FreeBSD/5/syslog.conf/.

11. "Splunk Enterprise: The Platform for Operational Intelligence," Splunk Product Data Sheet.pdf. Retrieved from www.splunk.com.

12. "What is Splunk Enterprise?" Retrieved from http://www.splunk.com/view/splunk/SP-CAAAG57.

Mobile Forensics

In this chapter, you will learn how to

- Define a cellular network, list different mobile devices, and describe the hardware and software characteristics of mobile devices
- Provide an overview of a mobile operating system and discuss different types of mobile operating systems
- Articulate what a criminal can do with mobile phones
- Describe different mobile forensics challenges, including the various memory considerations in mobiles
- Explain the process involved in mobile forensics, including which precautions to take prior to the investigation
- List several hardware and software tools for mobile forensics

Some of us go back to the days of the "personal digital assistant" (PDA). Aside from acting as a geek badge of coolness, a PDA was actually occasionally useful! I myself owned a Palm Pilot, a HandSpring Visor (always looking for bigger real estate), and a Sony Clie that is still alive and ticking. When a colleague bought a Sharp Zaurus SL-5500 that had a pull-out keyboard and ran Linux, I suffered such an attack of geek envy that I ran out and bought one immediately. It, too, is still alive and mostly well. (Given that these devices are over 10 years old, I think it's testimony to how well they were made to begin with.)

Of all the areas of digital forensics, mobile devices have seen the most change over the last five years. New models appear about every year, along with new versions of handheld operating systems, new applications (apps), and new communications capabilities.

What exactly is a mobile device? Is a smart phone running Android OS with a cellular telephone connection and a Wi-Fi connection a mobile device? How about an Android 7" tablet with a Wi-Fi connection? What about a laptop computer using a wireless modem to send and receive data over the Internet? For the purposes of this chapter, we're going to restrict ourselves to digital devices that communicate via cellular telephone networks as their primary means of external communication, whether it is voice, data, or both. One distinguishing characteristic of all mobile devices, however, is that their network location will change over time as they move, and this change is transparent to the user; that is, their network address isn't static. This distinguishes a true mobile device from a moveable device where an address is assigned and remains unchanged until the machine is rebooted or manually changed by the user, or reassigned by a local server (such as a DHCP server) from its local pool.

Cellular Networks

Before we get started, let's do a little review. Cellular networks are used for sending and receiving voice traffic. In its simplest form, a cellular network consists of two radio transceivers: the mobile device and the cell tower. A set of cell towers, each arranged in some geometric configuration (circle, square, hexagon, and so on), can talk to each other, to intermediary switching and network equipment, and to other mobile devices. Figure 10-1 shows a model configuration. Cell tower ranges don't overlap much, just enough so that as the mobile device moves, it associates with a particular tower. As it moves out of range of that tower, the tower will "hand off" the call to an adjacent tower. This is transparent to the user.

There were initially three main categories of cellular networks, based on their mode of transmission. The first was based upon the older Global System for Mobile Communications (GSM) standard, used by the whole world except for the United States, which used one flavor of Time Division Multiple Access (TDMA). The other flavor of TDMA was based on IS-36, and the two protocols did not interoperate. Circuit Division Multiple Access (CDMA) was previously used in the United States by particular cellular service providers, though these days, most U.S. carriers have also migrated to GSM and its technological descendants. A device using one of those technologies couldn't communicate on a network that uses another. Your CDMA phone would have been useless on a GSM network, though some vendors previously offered a dual-mode phone that supported both GSM and CDMA, sometimes called world phones.

Life is different these days (perhaps not better, but different). With the advent of 3G technologies (Edge, UMTS, iDEN, and so on), phones increased in speed and memory capacity. Over time, these technologies have merged into today's 4G Long Term Evolution

Figure 10-1
Cellular network model, showing frequency assignments

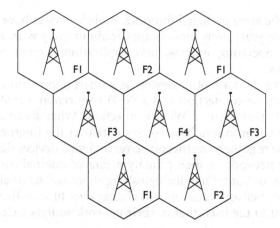

Figure 10-2
Wireless speci-
fications for my
Samsung S III

Wireless Technology	
GSM/GPRS/EDGE	850/900/1800/1900MHz
UMTS/HSPA+	850/1900/2100MHz
4G HSPA+	4G speeds delivered by HSPA+ (with enhanced backhaul)
4G-LTE	Band 4 and 17
EDGE high speed data network	✔
Bluetooth® technology	v4.0
FOTA capable - upgrade Firmware Over The Air	✔

(LTE) standards and technologies. Figure 10-2 shows the wireless specifications for my Samsung S III. For me, the most important aspect was the check box that read "World Phone" (not shown). What can I say? I'm old school.

There are three essential components of a cellular network (NIST SP-101):[1]

- The base transceiver station (BTS), more commonly described as a cell tower.

- The base station controller (BSC)—the hardware and software to manage calls. A BSC will connect to the MSC.

- The mobile switch center (MSC), which supports routing of digital packets and maintains a database that contains information on location data, account data, and other subscriber information. Obtaining data from an MSC will require a warrant or a subpoena.

The GSM standard calls the mobile device a "mobile station" (MS). Each MS consists of a subscriber identity module, the universal integrated circuit card (UICC), frequently referred to as the subscriber identity module (SIM), and the mobile equipment (ME) that comprises the rest of the phone. The SIM itself is a tiny device (about the size of a fingernail or smaller) that has a CPU, RAM (program execution), ROM (the OS), and EEPROM. Together, they comprise the mobile device execution environment: A device won't function without the UICC.

The international mobile equipment identifier (IMEI) consists of 15 digits (14 digits plus a check digit), and is illustrated in Figure 10-3. The first eight digits represent a type allocation code (TAC), while the last six identify the manufacturer and possibly the phone type as well. The TAC is further broken down in two subfields. The first two digits of the TAC represent the reporting body identifier and are always decimal. If the first two digits are 0xA0 or greater, the identifier is understood to be a mobile equip-ment identifier (MEID) used in CDMA phones.

If a GSM phone is powered on, you can retrieve the IMEI by keying in "*#06#". If the phone is turned off, you can remove the back of the phone and the battery, which should reveal the identification number. Figure 10-4 shows my late, lamented Black-berry 8510 with the back and battery removed so that the IMEI number is clearly visible. On more modern phones, such as the Samsung S III, the IMEI can be displayed in the "About Device" page that's part of the System settings.

Figure 10-3
IMEI fields

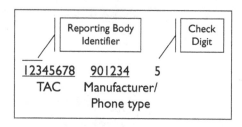

The UICC contains several identifiers. The integrated circuit chip identifier (ICCID) identifies a particular UICC to the network service provider or operator. The ICCID can be up to 20 digits long. The first portion, the issuer identification number (IIN), is a maximum of seven digits—the first two digits are the major industry identifier (MII) (these are two-digit codes; 89 is for telecommunications). The next three digits are the country code, and the last field, the issuer identifier, can be from one to four digits long. The rest of the ICCID represents an account identification number that will vary, depending on the length of the previously mentioned fields, but all account IDs from the IIN are the same length. Table 10-1 summarizes these fields.

The international mobile subscriber identity (IMSI) consists of a three-digit mobile country code, two to three digits for the mobile network code (three digits are used in the United States and Canada), followed by either nine or ten digits that represent the

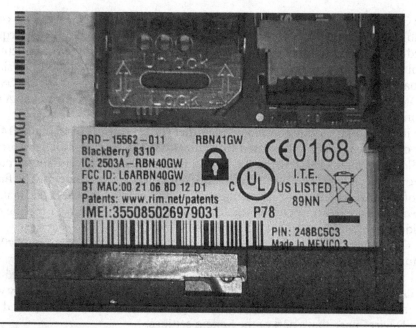

Figure 10-4   Blackberry 8310 with battery removed showing IMEI number

Table 10-1	Field	Length
ICCID Identifier Fields and Their Lengths	Issuer identification number	Maximum of seven digits. The first two digits are the MII code.
	Country code	Three digits.
	Issue identifier	One to four digits.
	Account identification number	Remaining digits, up to 20.

mobile subscriber identification number (MSIN) for that particular country and network. All of this means that, given a particular phone, we can identify the manufacturer, the device identifier, and an identifier that tells us who the subscriber is on a particular network. Table 10-2 summarizes the IMSI fields and their lengths.

The DFI may find that the device is locked and it requires a personal identification number (PIN) to unlock. The device has two passwords: the PIN and a personal unblocking code (PUK) for PIN unlocking. This code is sometimes called a personal unlock code (PUC) or PIN unlocked key (PUK). Some phones will respond with an unlock code if you key in "#*06#" from the keyboard. Other manufacturers may provide different unlock codes. If an incorrect password is entered three times in a row, the SIM card is blocked and must be unblocked using the provided code.

 EXAM TIP You should know the difference between a PIN, a PUC, and a PUK. A quick tip: C for code, K for key.

Although mobile devices share many of the same characteristics as less-mobile devices (laptops come to mind), there are differences in how these devices secure the data. Many devices support a configuration such that data will be wiped from the device if a correct password or PIN isn't entered in a certain number of tries (10 tries is common). This is in addition to wiping the device by means of a remote command. Given that the number of password attempts is limited, it's not a good idea to guess.

The file structure on a SIM card is a hierarchy based in the root directory (the master file, or MF). Beneath the root directory are directory files (DF) directories, each of which contains element files (EF). Figure 10-5 illustrates the hierarchy of the SIM file system. The MF contains an entry for all the other files in the file system. Files are either DF or regular files, called element files (EF). Note that the directory files contain information based on the type of network to which the device can connect and has connected to (some phones support dual band in that they have a GSM and a CDMA radio).

Table 10-2	Field	Length
IMSI Field Identifiers and Their Lengths	Mobile country code	First three digits
	Mobile network code	Two to three digits (three digits in United States and Canada)
	Mobile subscriber identification number	Nine to ten digits

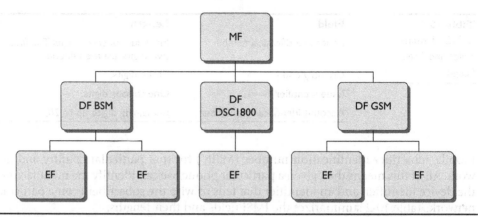

Figure 10-5 SIM card hierarchy (Source: Ayers, R., Brothers, S., Jansen, W. Guidelines on Mobile Device Forensic, NIST Special Publication 800-101, Revision 1, (dx.doi.org/10.6028/NIST.SP.800-101r1), p. 9.)

The data stored on a SIM card is a treasure trove of information for the DFI. A subscriber to a cellular phone service is charged based on usage and location (roaming charges), and if there's one thing that phone companies are good at, it's keeping detailed call records and charging you for the minutes you used. The SIM file structure can include the ICCID and the IMSI identifiers. Additional information stored on the device includes

- An abbreviated dialing number (AND) that accesses the phonebook stored on the SIM
- The last number dialed (LND)
- Short Message Service (SMS) and Enhanced Messaging Service (EMS) messages
- Location area information (LAI) for voice
- Routing area information (RAI) for data communications

The LAI indicates where the device was last located. Cross-checking this evidence with GPS data or other location data as determined by gathering Wi-Fi data can create a strong circumstantial case that the suspect's device (and, we assume, the suspect) was indeed at a particular location at a particular time.

Armed with this information, a DFI can approach a vendor and request call records, assuming a valid warrant has been issued. Pertinent fields from the call record are listed in Table 10-3. An "M" in the Key field indicates a mandatory field; a "C" means the field is conditional.

Given this information, we can identify the number dialed and the country, the manufacturer, and the brand of the calling party. Since the IMSI has local significance, the provider can be asked to deliver subscriber information that is used for billing purposes. Notice that while this identifies the person who received the call, this doesn't necessarily mean that the owner of the phone is the individual who actually answered

Field	Key	Description
Served IMSI	M	IMSI of the called party
Served IMEI	C	IMEI of the calling ME, if available
Called Number	M	The address of the called party (the number dialed by the subscriber)
Location	M	The cell identity where the call originated, including the area code
Call Duration	M	The chargeable portion of the call

Table 10-3   Call Record Fields of Forensic Interest

the call. Nor does it prove conclusively that the owner was in possession of the phone at the time of the call.

Cellular Data

Cellular phone networks also support data communications, which is unsurprising given that people have been using modems attached to phone lines for decades.

Just as with a voice connection, transmission between source and destination IP networked devices must survive a hand-off between cell towers, similar to transferring a Wi-Fi connection between access points (APs). Addressing is different—a mobile device has two Internet addresses: its "home" address and its "mobile" address (a "care of" address). Initial contact is made with the device's "home" network, and the sender is then told to access that device via its "care of" address.

At 3G transmission levels and above, data are encrypted between the mobile device and the cell tower. People who are concerned about privacy and confidentiality of their data communications will want to use a higher-level protocol such as Internet Protocol Security (IPsec), Secure Shell (SSH), or Secure Socket Layer/Transport Layer Security (SSL/TLS) to enforce end-to-end encryption.

Mobile Devices

Keeping up with the latest models, software revisions, and new applications is more than a full-time job—as you can undoubtedly see from the number of pundits and bloggers. There are shared characteristics that let us generalize across device types. In this section, we'll address these shared characteristics and then approach four different classes of devices: personal digital assistants (PDAs), music and game players (personal entertainment devices), standard cell phones, and smart phones.

All mobile devices share certain hardware and software characteristics. All devices will have, at a minimum, a transceiver for voice and data communication. All devices will have various types of memory: read-only memory (ROM) for the OS, random-access memory (RAM) for use by applications, and on-board memory for persistent SIM storage. All devices will have a connector (some use a form of USB; others use proprietary connectors) that allows the device to communicate with another device for backup and upload. Most devices will have a built-in GPS receiver and a camera.

In the case of software, mobile devices will have an operating system, supporting utilities for device management and configuration, and a set of hard-wired applications. A clock, an address book/contact list, a calendar, to-do list, and memo-pad applications—the usual personal information manager (PIM) applications—are standard. Different vendors may supply additional software that highlights their additional features, such as a camera application, an audio and video player, and an application to manage photographs and other images and so forth.

PDAs

Handheld devices that offered PIM capabilities were called personal digital assistants (PDAs). In most cases, access was restricted to synchronizing either with a desktop application provided by the manufacturer or with applications that were already installed with the desktop OS. We'll look at two such systems that are still extant (as of 2014).

PalmOS

PalmOS first appeared with the Palm Pilot PDA in 1996. This generation didn't have much in the way of untethered network connections. My Clie could communicate using infrared, using a proprietary protocol over a USB cable, or using TCP running over a USB cable. In all cases, though, it was intended to allow the device to synchronize with the desktop software. It came standard with the usual PIM suite, as well as an e-mail application that would synchronize with Palm's own desktop software or Microsoft's Outlook software. The latest release running on my Clie was 4.1.0.3. The last release of PalmOS (as WebOS from HP) was in 2011.

In Palm OS, both the OS and the standard applications were stored in ROM. RAM was divided into dynamic RAM, used by running applications, and storage RAM, used for actual file storage. Since memory protection wasn't available, applications could use each other's data and potentially modify each other's code, whether intentionally or unintentionally. Security features were minimal, although the screen could be locked when turned off and require a password to unlock.

Windows Pocket PC

Another example of a PDA was the Windows Pocket PC running the Windows CE (Compact Edition) OS. The original Pocket PC became available in 2002 and lives on under the name of Windows Phone. The OS and certain applications are stored in ROM; otherwise, applications run and store data in RAM. RAM is divided into three sections: the registry, file system, and property databases. Property databases act as data stores where data can be stored, searched, and retrieved.[2]

Plain Ol' Cell Phones

The original cell phones offered a minimal user experience: black and white screen, call logs, phonebooks (name and number), and user-assignable ringtones. Navigation was via arrow keys and possibly by a track ball. Competition between manufacturers and cellular telephone companies resulted in ever-increasing capabilities ("creeping featurism"), leading up to today's smart phones. What's the difference between a "smart

	Feature Phone	Smart Phone
Processor	Limited speed (~52 MHz)	Superior speed (~1 GHz dual core)
Memory	Limited capacity (~5MB)	Superior capacity (~128GB)
Card Slots	None	MiniSDXC
Camera	Still	Still, panoramic, and video (HD)
Cell Interface	Voice and limited data	Voice and high-speed data (4G LTE)
Positioning	None	GPS receiver
Wireless	IrDA, Bluetooth	Bluetooth, Wi-Fi, and NFC
OS	Closed	Android, Blackberry OS, iOS, Symbian, WebOS, and Windows Phone
Call	Voice	Voice, video
Chat	Instant messaging	Enhanced instant messaging
Messaging	Text	Text, enhanced text, full multimedia messaging
Email	Via text messaging	Via POP or IMAP server

Table 10-4   Feature Phones Versus Smart Phones

phone" and a "not-so-smart" phone (a feature phone[3])? Table 10-4 compares and contrasts the two.[4]

Music Players (Personal Entertainment Devices)

As more and more audio was delivered as digital content instead of vinyl records, cassette tapes, or compact discs (CDs), music players such as the Diamond Rio became more popular. The iPod is the classic example of this kind of device. The original iPod (now called the iPod Classic) used USB for file transfer and a click wheel for navigation. The iPod touch, released in 2007, ran the same OS (iOS) as the iPhone, as well as offering the same set of applications through the Apple iTunes Store. Earlier versions of the iPod offered up to 80GB of storage, accessible via a USB interface and formatted as FAT32 or Hierarchical File System (HFS)+, depending on whether the desktop was a Windows or Macintosh machine. Later releases of iOS and the iPod only allowed access to the device via the iTunes software and a proprietary protocol.

Smart Phones

At present (spring 2014), Apple's iOS-based iPhone line is battling with Samsung, a legion of Android-based phone makers, and Windows-based phones for global market share. We already talked briefly about the Windows Phone OS earlier in this chapter.

iOS (Apple)

iOS is a closed-source, proprietary OS from Apple, Inc. (www.apple.com) that was released in 2007 with the first iPhone. Applications for this platform are only available via the iTunes Store. Versions 4 and above support multitasking; iOS 7 includes the ability for foreground applications to execute updates in the background. For forensics, access to data is through backup via the iTunes desktop software or by using a driver that mimics the behavior of the iPhone software.

Android (Google)

Google released the Android OS in 2007 as well (clearly, 2007 was a good year for mobile operating systems). Now at revision 4.4, the OS is used by many device manufacturers (Samsung, Motorola, Asus, and HTC, just to name a few of the major ones). Android is a Linux-based, multitasking OS that supports many apps for examining the file system, as well as transferring data from the device to a desktop computer. If mounted as a USB device, disk images can be acquired by imaging the device using the dd command on Linux or other device-imaging software.

Android also allows applications to run in the background while the device is turned on, even if another app is running in the foreground (displaying on the screen). Some devices support MicroSD cards for permanent storage, although regular RAM is available, usually in 8-, 16- or 32-GB configurations. Apps are available at the Google Play Store (http://play.google.com/store) or from other major vendors (such as the Amazon Store for Kindle variants of Android), and from third parties such as F-Droid (www.f-droid.org). Given the nature of the open source, alternative versions of the OS exist, such as CyanogenMod.

Tablets and Phablets

The release of the Apple iPad in 2010 started a major change in mobile computing. Tablet computers (sometimes called slates), powered by operating systems originally developed for smart phones, rapidly became powerful enough to replace laptops as the computer of choice for frequent travelers. The original specs for the iPad 1, running iOS, were 9.56" × 7.47" × 0.5" thick. Smaller tablets quickly followed: The Nexus 7 2013 tablet, running the Android OS, measures 7.87" × 4.49" × 0.34".

As tablets grew smaller, smart phones grew larger. Samsung released the original Galaxy Note in 2011. The current Note 3 measures 5.95" × 3.12" × 0.33" and weighs 3 grams. It also sports a 1920 × 1080 screen—the same resolution as my current 21" monitor. Was it a large phone or a small tablet or a mixture of the two (and hence "phablet")? Moreover, should a DFI care? Patience, dear reader, patience.

What Can Criminals Do with Mobile Phones?

There's an old joke that goes like this. Question: What can an 800-pound gorilla do? Answer: Anything it wants. So it is with mobile phones and criminal activity. Communication, either by telephone or data networks, recordkeeping, audio, video, photographs... all available for storing and communicating information. Space is not an issue: A 128-GB MicroSD card was recently announced by SanDisk. You can run your business from a mobile phone. Both iOS and Android support encryption of main storage, and stolen or lost devices can be wiped remotely. Cellular phones have become enough of a commodity that purchasing a "throw-away" for transient communications is available to virtually anyone, especially for the "pay as you go" phones that provide (semi)anonymous communication. A criminal also can use the phone in the commission of a crime: sending abusive e-mail, text messages, spam, replacing the SIM card, and so on. Given enough storage, a phone could carry illegal materials, such as stolen intellectual property or child pornography.

Retrieving the Evidence

A DFI can obtain a wealth of data from a mobile device.[5] Even the earliest PDAs could provide the following capabilities:

- Phonebook
- Calendar
- To-do list
- Electronic mail
- Electronic documents
- Photos
- Videos
- Audio
- Graphics

The addition of phone capabilities to PDAs (for example, the Palm Treo added telephone capabilities), or mobile phones themselves (such as the Motorola flip-phone), provided more information sources specific to telecommunications:

- Instant messages
- Web information
- Subscriber identifiers
- Equipment identifiers
- Service provider
- Last dialed numbers
- Phone number log
- Short text messages (SMS)
- Last active location (voice and data)
- Other networks encountered

In addition, smart phones included Wi-Fi networking along with existing cellular networking. In some instances, Wi-Fi was added to music players: The Apple iPod touch looks remarkably like the iPhone series without the telephone portion (including running the same version of the OS as well as applications from the iTunes Store). Smart phones also enabled enhanced messages and multimedia messages along with text.

Is a smart phone or phablet with a cellular data connection the equivalent of a laptop with a cellular data connection? Strictly speaking, yes. These devices share similar sets of applications and similar hardware characteristics (smart phones now have up to 3GB of RAM, along with up to 32GB of flash storage). In February 2014, SanDisk announced a 128-GB MicroSD card. Cards are usually formatted as FAT32 devices. Ultimately, the DFI will use similar tools, techniques, and processes to analyze data from these devices as they would to acquire evidence from more traditional desktop or laptop computers.

Challenges in Mobile Forensics

Mobile devices come with their own set of challenges. Accessing memory is different from on a laptop computer. With mobile devices, there is memory you can get to, and memory you can't get to easily. Memory used as a file system can be acquired using logical or physical acquisition. Electrically erasable programmable read-only memory (EEPROM) is harder to acquire.

Another consideration is that each device requires a different cable—even devices in the same family from the same manufacturer. Figure 10-6 shows a set of different USB connectors.[6] Some devices require Micro USB B-type, USB 1.1 Micro, Mini USB B-type, female A-type, male A-type, or male B-type. The female A-type connector is displayed "upside down" in Figure 10-6 in order to make the pins visible. In addition to USB connectors, a DFI needs proprietary connectors such as those from Apple and Samsung (and, with Apple, it will vary depending on the generation of your device). You need a large collection of cables, or a single cable with a set of replaceable connectors.

Precautions to Take Before Investigating

Mobile devices, especially smart phones, have progressed to the point where they compete with laptops in terms of storage and software. Given the range of software available, as well as the various types of network connectivity (Wi-Fi, mobile data, Bluetooth, NFC), a criminal can effectively keep all their information on a mobile device. Data sent via Bluetooth or near-field communication (NFC) is less subject to eavesdropping or wiretapping, but it does require the owners of the equipment to be in close proximity.

Given the "always on, always connected" nature of mobile devices, a DFI must take precautions when seizing the device, since a criminal can issue commands to lock the

Figure 10-6
USB connectors

phone or to delete all data on that phone via the network. This means leaving the device connected to the network, but shielded from radio communication by means of a Faraday bag or another means of blocking the transmissions.

 CAUTION Isolating a device in this manner can cause excessive battery drain. Carry batteries or extra power supplies in your kit.

Once the device has been isolated from the network, the DFI can begin to acquire the data on that device. A DFI can acquire data from the device itself by mounting the device as a USB device, looking for data backups on a desktop machine (Macintosh or Windows), or using an external device to read memory not available via the file system. Once the DFI has acquired the data, analysis can proceed in much the same way as with data collected from any other digital device.

The Process in Mobile Forensics

The first challenge that arises when working with mobile devices is simply trying to acquire the data. Tools and techniques can be classified in various ways: one classification system (NIST) categorizes each tool into one of five classes, as shown in Figure 10-7. As we progress from level 1 to level 5, the "methodologies involved in acquisition become more technical, invasive, time consuming, and expensive."[7]

1. **Manual Extraction** This method only involves viewing and recording the information displayed on the device's screen. There's no access to deleted data, and navigating through the device's menu hierarchy may have side effects such that crucial data are obscured or deleted. Information is collected by taking photographs of the device screen.

2. **Logical Extraction** The DFI connects to the mobile device using one of a number of wired or wireless network connections (USB, RS-232, IrDA, Wi-Fi, or Bluetooth).

3. **Physical Extraction** This method varies from acquiring an image of device storage mounted as a USB device to using a particular device called a flasher box to read protected memory.

4. **Chip-Off** Here, the DFI removes the memory chip from the device and creates a binary image of the contents. This image will need to be parsed by software that understands the logical and physical composition of the device (for example, understanding how the wear-leveling algorithm of the memory functions to gather logical contiguous memory blocks).

5. **Micro Read** The DFI captures the changes to the gates on a chip, using an electron microscope.

Depending on the importance of the case, a DFI would most usually use tools and techniques classified from levels 1 to 3. Chip-off techniques are the highest level currently

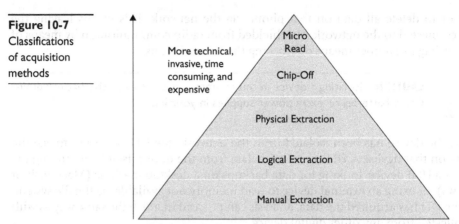

Figure 10-7 Classifications of acquisition methods

(Source: Ayers, R., Brothers, S., Jansen, W. Guidelines on Mobile Device Forensic, NIST Special Publication 800-101, Revision 1, (dx.doi.org/10.6028/NIST.SP.800-101r1), p. 17.)

available—while micro read is theoretically possible, time, expense, and training all weigh against this method.

Once the data have been obtained, tools can be used to perform a standard analysis based on the nature of the investigation. Are we looking for evidence that the owner committed a crime, such as storing illicit materials on the device? On the other hand, are we looking for evidence of connections to others who may have been involved in planning or committing the crime? Regardless, work with the data as you would any other digital evidence. Maintain the chain of custody; document all analysis work performed; and store the evidence in locations where it will not be destroyed by heat, cold, or dampness. Make sure that you consider and correlate all available information, including GPS location, cell locations, etc., in addition to messages sent and received and data stored or modified in the file system.

Theory into Practice: Mobile Forensic Tools

Many software tools are available to the DFI for analysis. Some focus on data extraction; others on data analysis. We'll focus on three of them in this section.

EnCase Forensic 7.0 incorporates mobile device acquisition into the main product. Data can be acquired directly into EnCase Forensic and stored in EnCase evidence format. EnCase will usually recognize the appropriate OS simply by plugging in the device; recognized operating systems include Apple iOS, Google Android, BlackBerry, Windows Mobile OS, iTunes, and backup files and SIM cards. The predefined smart phone report will provide information about the data stored on the device.

Paraben Corporation (www.paraben.com) offers several different products that support mobile forensic investigations. Their Mobile Field Kit[8] offers a one-stop shopping product for the DFI. Forensic hardware includes the Project-A-Phone ICD-8000 for photographing mobile device screens, a SIM reader, and a Bluetooth adapter. Acquisition hardware includes a remote charger, a multihead charging cable, AC power adapter, a DC car adapter, and a multimedia card reader. A Stronghold (Faraday) bag isolates live devices from their connected networks, and a Save-A-Phone drying bag helps preserve devices that have been submerged in water.

Device seizure cables are provided for many mobile products (iPhone, Samsung Galaxy tablets, Nokia, Samsung, Motorola, and LG phones). Software products available on a tablet computer include Device Seizure, Deployable Device Seizure, and analysis software. The link2 software is used for visualizing interactions between individuals identified by phone records, e-mails, SMS messages, and so on, and the P2 Commander Companion software is used to perform the actual analysis.

The Oxygen Forensic Suite 2014 provides an analytical tool and a stand-alone data extraction tool. The data extraction tool can retrieve and analyze data from various devices. Since each device is supported by a particular device driver, adding a new device only requires developing a driver. Figure 10-8 shows the device information screen when applied to a third-generation iPod. The panel on the left displays both common and extended device information, including the device model, serial number, and MAC addresses for both Wi-Fi and Bluetooth. The panel on the right contains information about the case (inspector, case number, and evidence number) and details about the device owner—useful when the device must be returned.

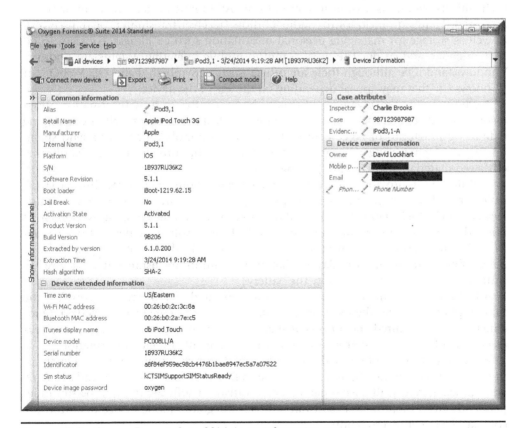

Figure 10-8 Oxygen Forensic Suite 2014 device information screen

The Standard edition supports the overall device information as well as displays for files, calendar, notes, and phonebook. A separate screen displays search results across all these data sources. The Analyst edition of the product includes timeline reporting of activities, aggregated contact information (all contacts, regardless of the method used to store them), and bookmarks for emphasizing key evidence. The tool also collects and displays web connections and location services, such as Wi-Fi hotspots, social graphs, a dictionary of a user's vocabulary, and a catalog of links and statistics based on the types of communication (voice, SMS, e-mail, and so on).

The addition of time and location data to the investigation results in a much larger context for the investigator. Given that the purpose of an investigation is to "place the suspect at the keyboard," the combination of the type of communication, duration, date and time, and results of that communication (files uploaded, downloaded, or deleted) can provide strong circumstantial evidence that the suspect was indeed the person who operated the mobile device.

Chapter Review

A cellular network is a telephone network that divides a geographic area into a set of cells, each with its own transmission/reception tower. All mobile devices share similar characteristics: Hardware includes the radio portion (receiver/transmitter, or transceiver), as well as storage for managing personal information such as address, contacts, to-do lists, calendar, and so on. The most common mobile operating systems are Android, Windows, and iOS, although there are others, such as Symbian, Palm OS, WebOS, or Windows CE, that may appear depending on the age of the device.

A criminal can take advantage of smart phone features to store information about associates and contact them via e-mail, phone, or text messages as well as exchanging data using Bluetooth or NFC. Criminals can also use mobile devices to send spam, threatening, or harassing messages. Expanded storage supports storing and distributing outlawed materials such as child pornography.

Mobile devices provide their own sets of challenges. Some memory within the UICC isn't accessible to user programs and requires special hardware and software to acquire. Devices can be locked or wiped clean of information by remote commands. Because of this, prior to beginning an investigation, the DFI must isolate the device from its networks by turning off communications, either by setting the device into "airplane" mode or encasing the device in a Faraday bag (taking precautions to ensure that the device has sufficient power so as not to empty the battery).

A DFI must take care to determine the time on the device in order to correlate the time of phone call and the location, perhaps cross-checking by using GPS data. Once data have been acquired, the process of analyzing data captured from a mobile device is essentially identical to the process used to capture any other digital information.

Forensic software for mobile devices can provide for data acquisition, data analysis, or both. Oxygen Forensic Suite 2014, Paraben's Device Seizure hardware and software, and EnCase Forensic all have separate data acquisition software that can be run independently from their analysis software. All can integrate mobile device data into the context of a larger investigation.

Questions

1. Where would an investigator find details of calls made, subscriber information, and the locations of those calls?

   A. BTS

   B. ME

   C. MCS

   D. MS

2. When did encryption of voice traffic first appear?

   A. LTE

   B. 4G

   C. 2G

   D. 3G

3. What problem can result from putting a mobile device into a Faraday bag?

   A. Moisture accumulation

   B. Excessive battery drain

   C. Overheating

   D. Notification of loss of network connectivity

4. What kind of memory is *not* found in a SIM card?

   A. ROM

   B. RAM

   C. EEPROM

   D. NDROM

5. Which communication technologies require the sender and receiver to be in close proximity? (Choose all that apply.)

   A. NFC

   B. Bluetooth

   C. Wi-Fi

   D. IrDA

6. Using a standard file copy from a mobile device to local storage is an example of _____ acquisition.

   A. Micro read

   B. Physical

   C. Manual

   D. Logical

7. In addition to cell phone records, a device's location can be determined
   by _____
   A. Web sites visited
   B. GPS
   C. E-mail server domain
   D. Default language for the device

8. The ability to delete the contents of a cell phone or tablet is known as _____.
   A. Remote wiping
   B. Secure deletion
   C. Secure wiping
   D. Remote delete

9. What would you need to support a new mobile device in Oxygen Forensic
   Suite 2014?
   A. Analysis module
   B. Device driver
   C. Content-specific module
   D. Multihead cable connector

10. What functions are usually provided by mobile forensic software? (Choose all
    that apply.)
    A. Data extraction
    B. Data analysis
    C. Data verification
    D. Data archiving

Answers

1. C. The MCS (mobile switch center) maintains the databases.
2. D. Encryption of cellular voice traffic first appeared in 3G.
3. B. Inserting a device into a Faraday bag can result in excessive battery drain.
4. D. NDROM is a distractor: SIM cards support ROM, RAM, and EEPROM.
5. A, B, D. IrDA, NFC, and Bluetooth require that the sender and receiver be
   within 50 feet or so of each other.
6. D. Logical acquisition.
7. B. GPS data can help pinpoint the location of a mobile device.
8. A. Remote wiping.

9. **B.** Oxygen Forensic Suite 2014 supports new devices by adding new device drivers.

10. **A, B.** Most mobile forensic suites will provide data extraction and analysis capabilities.

References

1. Ayers, R. et al. *Guidelines on Mobile Device Forensics* (DRAFT), NIST SP800-101 (revision 1). Retrieved from http://csrc.nist.gov/publications/PubsDrafts .html#SP-800-101-Rev.%201, p. 16.

2. EC-Council. *Computer Forensics: Investigating Wireless Networks and Devices* (NY: EC-Council, 2010), pp. 2–5.

3. Ayers, R. et al. *Guidelines on Mobile Device Forensics* (DRAFT), pp. 5–6.

4. Ibid.

5. Ayers, R. *AAFF–Mobile Device Forensics*. Retrieved from www.cftt.nist.gov/AAFS-MobileDeviceForensics.pdf.

6. Viitanen, V. *USB Conectors.jpg*. Retrieved from http://commons.wikimedia .org/wiki/File:Usb_connectors.JPG. Placed into the public domain by the creator of the work.

7. Ayers, R. et al. *Guidelines on Mobile Device Forensics* (DRAFT), p. 16.

8. *Paraben's Mobile Field Kit 2.0: Data and Specifications Sheet.* Retrieved from www.paraben.com/downloads/mfk-brochure.pdf.

Attacking Applications

In this chapter, you will learn how to

- Define web applications, explain web application architecture, and explain why web servers are compromised and web pages are defaced
- Provide an overview of web logs, describe Internet Information Services (IIS) and Apache web server logs and how to investigate them
- Discuss different types of web attacks, how to investigate web attacks, and explain the investigation process for attacks in Windows-based servers
- Articulate when web page defacement occurs and discuss various security strategies for web applications
- List several web attack detection tools, and discuss different tools for locating IP addresses
- Explain the terms e-mail system, e-mail clients, e-mail servers, and e-mail message
- Discuss different types of e-mail crimes, the different laws and acts against e-mail crimes, articulate why we investigate e-mails, and discuss the steps
- Provide examples of e-mail headers and list common headers
- List several e-mail forensics tools

Although it may sound strange to say, most organizations are relatively good at preventing network-based attacks at the transport layer and below. Intrusion detection systems/intrusion prevention systems (IDS/IPS) systems, enterprise-class firewalls, distributed-denial-of-service (DDoS) protection, and improved network analytic capabilities all contribute to thwart network-based attacks. Like water, attackers will always follow the path of least resistance, and will always look for the easiest and quickest way to gain their objectives.

The current strategy used by attackers is "invite me in." In these attacks, the attacker attempts to convince the user to visit a compromised web site or to open a file that contains malicious code (malware). The files can be executable files, such as an .exe file on Windows, or a file that contains a macro language whereby you can specify a program to run when the document is opened. As we mentioned earlier, one common trick is to rename an executable file with a different extension. The file may be displayed as being of a particular type, such as a graphics file, while the content of the file may be a Windows portable executable (PE) file.

NOTE   It's surprising how many documents have contained a macro language capable of executing code when the file is open. The RSA breach depended on executing an Adobe Flash file that was embedded within an Excel document. Portable Document Format (PDF) files can execute embedded JavaScript code.

At the start of the Internet, enabling remote login to a particular computer and transferring files from one machine to another were two of the major goals. These goals were satisfied by Telnet and the File Transfer Protocol (FTP), respectively. With the benefit of 20/20 hindsight, we can see that the meta-issue was to transfer a collection of bytes from one machine to another. One way to do so is using FTP; another is to use the Simple Mail Transfer Protocol (SMTP)[1] to send data formatted as a message, possibly with a file attachment. The Hypertext Transfer Protocol (HTTP) protocol[2] also allowed the client to request a particular resource, and usually deliver it as a "document" of some sort (I can recall hearing HTTP described as "Visual FTP"). Other applications such as AOL's Instant Messenger and Microsoft's late and lamented NetMeeting also supported file transfer as part of remote conferencing.

A number of Internet protocols consist of a series of request and response messages (usually one party is the client and one is the server, though each member may switch roles during the course of the session). Each session consists of a request, an optional set of headers, and optional data. The headers are meaningful to the application protocol itself, while the contents (data) are meaningful to the entity that has invoked that particular application (usually a person, but certainly can be an automated process).[3]

Although the usual content of a message is plain text or Hypertext Markup Language (HTML), the messages can also include encoded binary data. The Multipurpose Internet Mail Exchange (MIME) is used in both e-mail and web applications to encode the data in the message. In addition to plain text, MIME can create messages with multiple parts, incorporate nontext attachments such as images or executable files, and utilize non-ASCII character sets.

HTTP and SMTP follow this model. SMTP is a "push" design from the attacker's perspective (the attacker sends the e-mail message), while HTTP is a "pull" design (the victim requests a resource from the server). Regardless, the intent is to have the victim execute code on their machine that takes some malicious action to jeopardize their security and well-being.

Web-based Attacks

We'll begin by looking at web-based attacks—attacks that are aimed at a particular application that uses the World Wide Web (WWW) and the HTTP/HTTPS protocol to implement its interface with the client. Compromising that application is not the ultimate goal of the attack; instead, the attacker may wish to gain a foothold on a particular machine such that further network activity will be seen as originating from inside the network perimeter. As with all network-based attacks, we know that the payload delivered to the remote machine must be correct enough such that the data will be delivered and not dropped along the way.

Web Applications: A Definition

A web application, loosely defined, is any application that uses the HTTP protocol as a means of requesting a particular "resource" from a server and retrieving that data. Web applications are accessible using a web browser as a user interface and a client-side execution engine.

Web application architecture is essentially client-server architecture. The client (using a web browser, a software program that speaks the HTTP protocol) accesses a server either using HTTP or its TLS/SSL version, HTTPS. HTTP usually uses TCP port 80, and HTTPS uses TCP port 443, although ports 8080, 8080, or 8000 are sometimes used for HTTP as well. Although the path between client and server is usually end to end, proxy servers can be used at either end of the connection. Clients can use Proxy HTTP to access a proxy server, which connects to the target web server on their behalf. Likewise, an organization can "front-end" the real web server with a "reverse proxy" that can offer added services such as protocol verification and content inspection. These are often called web application firewalls (WAF).

Why compromise a web server? A web server acts as the face that an organization presents to the outside world, and creates an Internet-based presence for that business. Modifying that presence affects the perception of that organization. Modifying or redirecting traffic from the web server can prevent the server from performing its original function. Imagine if all traffic to Amazon.com were redirected to BobsDepartmentStore.com—good for Bob, not good for Amazon. Or imagine if all outgoing invoices for the company were modified to order goods and services far below the retailer's marked prices.

Web page defacement occurs when the attacker has write access to the web server's content storage. Another event that appears to be (but isn't) web page defacement happens when the attacker can modify Domain Name Service (DNS) records such that it directs the web browser to a site under the control of the attacker, although the actual web page on the valid server hasn't been modified.

Mounting the Attack

From a forensics perspective, we're interested in two aspects of web applications. The first is the HTTP protocol itself—specifically, the HTTP headers that accompany the request and response messages. The second aspect is the actual contents of the HTTP response message—specifically, the behavior of the HTML markup language that can result in a compromise.

An HTTP response can indicate to the client that the resource should be requested from a different location as specified by the Location: header. A response code of 301 (Moved permanently) instructs the browser to redirect all queries for a URL from server A to server B, which is under the control of the attacker. Response codes 302 (Found) and 303 (See other) can also result in the browser accessing another URL. Accessing server B can result in either downloading malware or mistakenly providing account information to the attacker. An example of abuse of the content is when the Content-type: header identifies the content as one type, while the actual content is another type.

A second area of concern is how the contents of the HTTP response are processed. Message content can include formatting elements and indications that the client should execute the following code within the context of the client's browser. One particular tag is the <script> tag, the contents of which can be JavaScript or another scripting language such as Windows Script Host (wsh) or VBScript. As we will soon see, using tags that contain executable content can result in several different types of attacks.

Adding yet another level of indirection, the actual contents of the script can be downloaded from another site entirely by using the "url=" attribute indicating where the script should be retrieved. Another technique is using the <img> tag, which allows the specification of the source of the image. As an example, the HTTP tag

```
<img src="http://mrevil.com/something/>
```

requests that an image be loaded from an external site and displayed in the browser window.

 NOTE It's shocking to me how many sites are needed sometimes to display a single web page. I use an extension named NoScript with the Firefox web browser that requires explicit permission to execute scripts within the browser. It's not uncommon to find that scripts are being downloaded from over a dozen external sites. Right now, my top count is 16. This brings home to me the old adage "all trust is misplaced."

The Open Web Application Security Project (OWASP) at www.owasp.org publishes a top 10 list of the most critical web application security risks. We've listed those in Table 11-1, along with a corresponding set of attacks as defined by the EC-Council.[4]

Cross-site scripting (XSS) attacks occur when the attacker can inject a script into the content returned by a server. One example is inserting a script into the comments section of a blog post; if the server and the browser aren't careful, this script will be executed in the user's browser when they read the comment.

Cross-site request forgery (CSRF) occurs when the attacker can inject a script such that an action takes place on a different server where the user has already established credentials. One example is when a user visits a corrupted site after having logged in to their banking web site. A script could then issue a request to the banking site web server that takes advantage of the user's pre-existing credentials to perform an action that they never requested, such as transferring money from one account to the attacker's account.

Injection attacks can take on multiple forms, but one of the most prevalent is SQL injection. This occurs when data are taken directly from an incoming request and passed to an external application (in this case, a database system that uses the SQL query language) with no validation or interpretation.

```
"Select * from account where name = '" + username + "'"
```

The attacker supplies the phrase "' or 1=1 '" that translates into the query

```
"Select * from account where name = '' or 1 =1 ;'"
```

In this case, all data for all accounts are returned since "1=1" evaluates to true.

	OWASP Security Risk	Web Attack
A1	Injection	SQL injection Code injection Command injection
A2	Broken Authentication and Session Management	Cookie poisoning Authentication hijacking Impersonation attack
A3	Cross-Site Scripting (XSS)	Cross-site scripting (XSS)
A4	Insecure Direct Object References	Statically coded internal resources that become visible as part of a transaction
A5	Security Misconfiguration	DMZ protocol attack
A6	Sensitive Data Exposure	
A7	Missing Function Level Access Control	
A8	Cross-Site Request Forgery (CSRF)	Cross-site request forgery (CSRF)
A9	Using Components with Known Vulnerabilities	Buffer overflow Zero-day attack
A10	Unvalidated Redirects and Forwards	Automatically following a redirect or forward without asking the user or checking if the address is known to serve malicious content
	Unvalidated input	Directory traversal URL interpretation
	"Transport" security	Cryptographic interception Cookie snooping

Table 11-1 OWASP Top 10 Security Risks and Associated Web Attacks

Directory traversal occurs when a URL is constructed so that the browser is tricked into accessing content outside the storage areas defined for the web server. A classic example on a Linux system would be

```
GET /../../etc/password
```

assuming that the web storage area was defined to be in */var/www*. Directory traversal is a specific example of the more general case of URL interpretation, which involves the use of the special encoding of meta-characters that have specialized meaning to a browser. Encoding these characters is a way of altering the URL so that it will be handed off to the web browser for interpretation and execution.

Authentication hijacking "can lead to theft of services, session hijacking, user impersonation, disclosure of sensitive information, and privilege escalation."[5] One easily avoidable instance is when someone leaves their workstation with an open session to a server after they have authenticated. An attacker can sit down at the workstation and utilize their credentials. Timing out a session at the server end, as well as a password-lockable screen saver, can prevent such attacks.

Web Applications: Attack and Defend

How can we protect and secure web applications? The answers are simple to state but difficult to achieve in practice. You need to address security in three areas: the network, the server (OS and hardware), and web application security itself.

First, provide good network defenses using routers, firewalls, and IDS/IPS. Install the web server in a demilitarized zone (DMZ) that is separate from the production networks, and control traffic into the server from the wider Internet and from the server to internal networks (we should only see a limited number of ports and protocols on the web server, both inbound and outbound). Consider using a proxy server or a full-fledged WAF to examine the form and content of HTTP transactions.

Second, harden any machine hosting web applications. Hardening includes restricting running programs and services, running web servers as a separate user (not as root or administrator), and restricting access to other portions of the file system not specifically allocated for the web server. Consider using Security Enhanced Linux (SELinux) to restrict further privileges. Patch management is critical—keep up with security vulnerabilities in all software that supports the web application: database, application server, the web server itself, and any third-party software libraries.

At the application level, ensure that all inputs to the web server and application server are validated and sanitized. Enforce access controls throughout the system: Access to one set of functionality shouldn't mean access to all functions available. Implement timeouts for all sessions—this limits your exposure to authentication hijacking. Don't hard-code resource names.

We can detect web attacks by using tools such as IDS/IPS systems to recognize malicious queries on the wire before the query ever reaches the server, or by using a WAF to provide strict checking of the query regarding structure and content. Malformed messages should always be suspect, or at least contribute to the final score determining if the query should be processed. An example of this is if the query has only an IP address and no hostname in the Host: header, there is no Content-length: header, and the content doesn't match the Content-type: header, then flag this query as suspicious.

Host-based IDS (HIDS) can look for anomalies on the server, including modified files and unauthorized processes. Standard network and performance monitoring systems can alert when there is a marked deviation from normal behavior. None of these tools is specific to web applications, however. We need tools that are specific to web applications to get the greatest amount of pertinent information.

Web Tools

The best way to avoid vulnerabilities in web applications is not to code them in the first place. But "to err is human," as the poet said, so we need tools that can help us identify vulnerabilities in our software before the bad guys do. We need tools that can monitor and filter web traffic when our applications are in production, and we need tools to help us analyze and diagnose the damage done because of an attack.

HP WebInspect is representative of tools that help find vulnerabilities in our web applications. HP describes it as "… an automated and configurable web application security and penetration testing tool that mimics real-world hacking techniques and attacks, enabling you to thoroughly analyze your complex web applications and services for security vulnerabilities …by enabling you to test web applications from development through production, efficiently manage test results, and distribute security knowledge throughout your organization …"[6]

Web application firewalls dynamically detect flaws or malicious code in web traffic. The ModSecurity project (www.modsecurity.org/projects/) was released in 2002 as a WAF module for the Apache Web server. The current release (2.7.7) runs on Apache, IIS, and Nginx web servers. ModSecurity is also available for embedding into a reverse-proxy server.

Log analyzers help us identify web activities leading up to a breach. The Deep Log Analyzer software from Deep Software (www.deep-software.com) is one example of this kind of tool. Figure 11-1 illustrates the user interface (UI) for this program.[7] Although not specifically a forensic tool, software like this can record the source of the request (the Referrer: HTTP header) and track pages that the user has accessed.

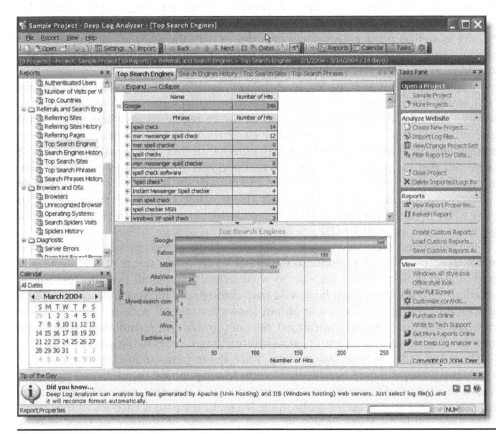

Figure 11-1   Deep Log Analyzer user interface

Mapping IP addresses to domain names is required when analyzing web attacks. Tools that support analysis of an IP address include nslookup, host, and dig. Host and dig are much easier to use than nslookup when you only have an IP address. The command

```
dig -x 75.75.75.76
```

will return information concerning the hostname that is assigned that IP address; the nslookup command is

```
nslookup 76.75.75.75.in-addr.arpa.
```

and uses DNS pointer (PTR)–type records to perform a reverse-name lookup. These are all command-line tools. If you want or need a visual experience, there are web sites that offer a web-based UI to access this functionality, and there are stand-alone programs that do so, as well.

The whois software queries the appropriate database that contains information on IP address blocks, autonomous systems, and domain names and returns information about a particular domain. Figure 11-2 shows the results querying for information for www.ec-council.org. I've deleted some of the information returned in the interests of brevity as well as privacy. This query provides us with the registration authority who registered the domain, administrative and technical contacts for the domain, and the top-level names of servers for that domain.

Although it seems as if the top-level domain, especially country domains (.us, .ru, .cn), would provide a good indication of where particular servers are physically located, it turns out to be a bad assumption. A server can be registered anywhere in the world and can be located physically somewhere else (which is why it's so difficult to determine where an attacker is actually located, especially if they are logged in remotely). It turns out that my personal domain is actually registered with a registrar in Australia; my mailbox is hosted on a Yahoo! server, and my web site is hosted on www.edublogs .com. No wonder they call it "the cloud"! This situation helps to illustrate issues that arise when trying to determine jurisdiction and whether evidence can be obtained from an Internet service provider (ISP).

The traceroute program (tracert on Windows, also pathping) will document the route taken by an HTTP response to the source of the query. Figure 11-3 is a listing of pathping output from my computer to www.sectools.org. Recall that in order for an attack to succeed, there must be a valid path through the Internet from the attacker's machine to our server. Traceroute output shows how the IP packets transit different networks—in our example, comcast.net, telia.net, and he.net. A whois lookup on these networks would provide us with contact information in order to dig deeper.

Graphical tools such as Open Visual Trace Route (www.sourceforge.net/projects/ openvisualtrace) will map intermediate points to geographical coordinates. Figure 11-4 shows the output of the program when provided with the same query. The geographic information is encoded on the globe in the left pane; the path is encoded in the upper-right pane, while the lower-right pane shows the latency introduced by DNS lookups for the hostname. This wealth of visual information is difficult to appreciate given the

```
c:\Tools\SysinternalsSuite>whois www.ec-council.org

Whois v1.11 - Domain information lookup utility
Sysinternals - www.sysinternals.com
Copyright (C) 2005-2012 Mark Russinovich

Connecting to ORG.whois-servers.net...

Domain ID: D107691738-LROR
Creation Date: 2005-10-04T04:11:54Z
Updated Date: 2013-10-04T17:29:07Z
Registry Expiry Date: 2014-10-04T04:11:54Z
Sponsoring Registrar:PDR Ltd. d/b/a PublicDomainRegistry.com (R27-LROR)
Sponsoring Registrar IANA ID: 303
WHOIS Server:
Referral URL:
Domain Status: clientTransferProhibited
Registrant ID:PP-SP-001
Registrant Name:Domain Admin
Registrant Organization:Privacy Protection Service INC d/b/a
PrivacyProtect.org
[[Lines deleted for brevity]]
Registrant Email:contact@privacyprotect.org
Admin ID:PP-SP-001
Admin Name:Domain Admin
Admin Organization:Privacy Protection Service INC d/b/a
PrivacyProtect.org
[[Lines deleted for brevity]]
Admin Email:contact@privacyprotect.org
Tech ID:PP-SP-001
Tech Name:Domain Admin
Tech Organization:Privacy Protection Service INC d/b/a
PrivacyProtect.org
[[Lines deleted for brevity]]
Tech Email:contact@privacyprotect.org
Name Server:SK.S5.ANS1.NS52.ZTOMY.COM
Name Server:SK.S5.ANS2.NS52.ZTOMY.COM
```

Figure 11-2 Whois query for www.ec-council.org

reduced size of the screen capture. Here's a shining example of where more screen real estate is better!

Follow the Logs

We mentioned log analysis in a previous chapter. All web servers generate log files. The Internet Information Services (IIS) web server stores its logs in %SystemRoot%\Logfiles, while the Apache web server stores two logs, an error log and an access log, usually in the log subdirectory of the Apache installation directory. The access log is written using the Common Log Format (CLF) and can be read by multiple third-party tools. It contains the original query, the status code returned, and the size of the content that was returned to the client. The error log is less structured, but will at least indicate the time of the error, the severity, the client that caused the error, and a general description of what happened. IIS uses the World Wide Web Consortium (W3C) extended logfile format. Default fields for IIS 6.0 are

```
Date Time Client-IP User Server-IP Server-Port Method URI-stem URI-query \
HTTP-status Protocol-Status
```

```
c:\users\clbrooks>pathping www.sectools.org

Tracing route to www.sectools.org [173.255.243.189]
over a maximum of 30 hops:

  0    CLB-Win7 [192.168.1.20]
  1    CISCO1 [192.168.1.1]
  2    *       *       *      Request timed out
  3    te-0-1-0-1-sur01.needham.ma.boston.comcast.net [68.86.237.233]
  4    69.139.221.1
  5    he-2-5-0-0-cr01.newyork.ny.ibone.comcast.net [68.86.94.201]
  6    he-0-13-0-1-pe03.111eighthave.ny.ibone.comcast.net [68.86.85.190]
  7    66.110.96.161
  8    63.243.128.121
  9    nyk-b5-link.telia.net [213.248.100.177]
 10    nyk-bb1-link.telia.net [213.155.130.246]
 11    sjo-bb1-link.telia.net [213.155.130.129]
 12    hurricane-ic-138359-sjo-bb1.c.telia.net [213.248.67.106]
 13    10ge3-2.core3.fmt2.he.net [184.105.222.13]
 14    linode-llc.10gigabitethernet7-6.core3.fmt2.he.net [65.49.10.218]
 15    nmap.org [173.255.243.189]

Trace complete.
```

Figure 11-3   Pathping out for sectools.org

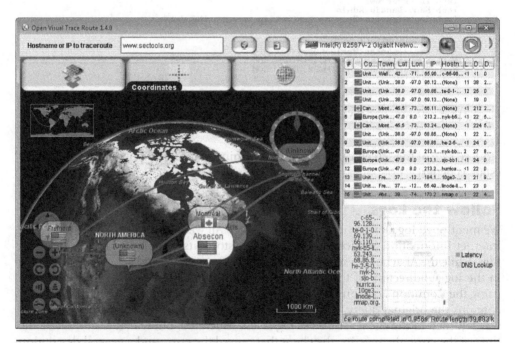

Figure 11-4   Open Visual Trace Route output for www.sectools.org

Fortunately, the log file should contain a description of which fields are used and which order they're in.

A common task when investigating an attack via a web service is to correlate information in the logs with other evidence. In the case of Apache, correlating the access log and the error log can fill in a timeline of which transactions were received by the server and in what order. Logs from firewalls and routers will also supply information about the timing of traffic. Obviously, if the query reached the web server, it passed through the rules governing acceptable traffic for both the firewall and the router. You can consult IDS/IPS logs as well for indications of known issues. Another source of information is a caching proxy server: In this case, the actual contents of the query may have been stored and can be retrieved, including any attachments associated with the message. Likewise, e-mail messages may still be stored on a Post Office Protocol (POP) server or an Internet Message Access Protocol (IMAP) server, or possibly on an Exchange server, assuming that not all recipients have downloaded the message.

Investigating the Breach

How we go about investigating a breach that involves a web server depends on whether we are participating as part of an incident response (live analysis) or conducting an investigation of a compromise after the attack has succeeded. In either case, we need to investigate two general areas: what modifications have been made to the compromised server, and where the attack might have moved after compromising this machine. The next two tables show how we might get answers to several questions when investigating a breach of a Windows server.[8]

We can address the first issue by answering the questions posed in Table 11-2.

Question	Command
Have there been any changes to users or groups?	*lusrmgr.msc* (requires admin privileges) A Windows Management Console snap-in that will bring up a screen listing local users and groups. Make sure to check if a user has received elevated privileges.
What TCP/IP connections are open, as either a client or a server, and is Windows file sharing going on (NetBIOS over TCP)?	*netstat -na* and *nbtstat -S* (works for servers) or *tcplist* Look for unusual destination addresses. Run as *netstat -a* if you wish to see the real hostnames.
Are any tasks scheduled to run in the future?	*at* or *schtasks* *at* requires a 32-bit context and provides minimal information. *schtasks* is more detailed and thus verbose.
What tasks are currently running?	*Tasklist* Lists running tasks. *tasklist /m <name>* will list all processes using a particular .dll.
What network services are running on the local machine?	*net start* or *sc query* Lists all services running. *sc query* provides more detail.
Have there been other indications of compromise (IOCs)?	*eventvwr.msc* (requires admin privileges) Another Windows Management Console snap-in for viewing events in all the defined event logs.

Table 11-2 Assessing Local Machine Activity

An attack can spread by transferring data to other connected computers via shared resources or by establishing remote connections. In all cases, we are looking for the unusual, either something present that shouldn't be there or something missing. Any activity on the local machine between the time of compromise and the time of discovery is questionable.

E-mail Attacks

In the very first chapter of the book, we made a distinction between situations where digital devices were used in the commission of a crime and those situations where the computer itself was a target of the crime. This same distinction applies to e-mail–related crime. Several crimes are identical to their nondigital manifestations: stalking, harassment, blackmail, and so forth. Other crimes are specific to electronic mail: spamming, phishing, mail bombing, acting as a transport for malware, and so on. Regardless of the crime, one thing remains fixed. A digital forensics investigator (DFI) needs to trace the message back to its source, as well as determine if the message has been altered in transit or if the information regarding the sender has been forged. In order to do this, we need to learn a bit more about the architecture of Internet-based e-mail.

E-mail Architecture

In electronic mail (e-mail), messages are sent via a user agent (MUA) to a message transfer agent (MSA) or a mail transfer agent (MTA). The set of cooperating MTAs comprise the message transfer service (MTS). An MTA can receive e-mail from another MTA, an MSA, or an MUA directly. Figure 11-5 shows how these pieces fit together.[9] Another piece of the puzzle is a mail distribution agent (MDA) that takes care of distributing e-mail to each user.

The combination of MUA (client) and MTAs (server) creates an e-mail system. Table 11-3 shows the relationships among e-mail system components, the message elements used by each component, and the type of protocol used by each component.[10]

Question	Command
Has the local machine shared resources with other computers?	*net view* /27.0.0.1
Is the local machine using external resources?	*net use* will show if the local machine has mounted other shared directories. *net view* will list which machines are available.
Are there active sessions?	*Logonsessions* from SysInternals (Windows XP and above); also *psloggedon*.
Are there indications of activity outside the network perimeter?	*netstat -na* or *tcpview* from SysInternals. *tcpview* provides more information.

Table 11-3 Assessing Local Machine Resource Sharing

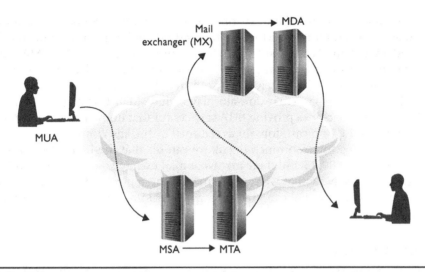

Figure 11-5 Mail system components

An MTA will use SMTP to pass messages consisting of headers and a body between itself and another MTA. The SMTP methods are quite simple: (E)HELO, MAIL, RCPT, DATA, and so on. Likewise, the POP3 protocol recognizes commands such as USER, PASS, RETR and DELE, and LIST.

An important fact to grasp here is that e-mail transfer is based on a store and forward model. A message may pass through several MTAs prior to being delivered to the MTA associated with the intended recipient. Mail transfer is third party by design—that is, systems other than the ones associated with the sender and the recipient will have access to a particular message.

The protocols used between an MUA, an MTS, and an MTA need not be the same. Two e-mail–specific submission/delivery protocols are POP3 and its SSL version, POP3S, and IMAP and its SSL version, IMAPS. In the case of POP3, the MUA will contain the POP3 server and download all mail currently waiting for delivery. Unless told otherwise, POP3 will then delete that mail from the server. IMAP, on the other hand, retrieves e-mail from the server but doesn't create a local copy. If a particular message is deleted, it's gone from the server.

Message Element	Component That Uses	Protocol Type
Envelope	MTA	Relaying protocol (SMTP)
Headers	MUA	Submission/delivery protocol (POP3)
Body	Users (people or other programs)	Messaging protocol (RFC)

Table 11-4 Protocols Used by E-mail Components

SMTP transfers e-mail between one MTA and another. Some e-mail applications (such as Microsoft Outlook, Mozilla Thunderbird, and others) combine the functions of an MUA and an MTA. Thunderbird, for example, can use POP3 or IMAP for retrieving mail from a server and can use SMTP to deliver e-mail to that remote server.

The final piece of the puzzle is our old friend the Domain Name System (DNS). A DNS record for a particular domain may include Mail Exchange (MX) records that indicate which machines provide MTA services for that domain. Figure 11-6 shows the full listing for the Comcast domain as returned by the *host* command.

Without going into too much detail, we can see that the IP address for www.comcast.net is 69.252.80.75 and there are two e-mail exchange servers, mx1 and mx2, and five DNS servers. Now that we've seen how all these pieces fit together, we can begin to address how a criminal can manipulate header information and protocols for their own purposes.

E-mail Crimes

As we mentioned earlier, certain crimes are specific to electronic mail: spamming, phishing, mail bombing, acting as a transport for malware, and so on. Spamming occurs when an individual receives unrequested commercial e-mail. Mail bombing is similar to spamming, but the purpose of this action is to perform a denial-of-service (DoS) attack against the recipient or e-mail server. Mail bombing differs from a mail storm in that a mail storm is usually the result of malformed messages or misconfigured servers where the software is generating the flood of messages automatically.

Phishing is a term applied to e-mail messages that attempt to induce the recipient into accessing a web page or opening an attached file, such as a .pdf file that contains malicious JavaScript code (yes, PDF files can contain JavaScript). In some instances, simply opening an e-mail message may send information back to another party.

```
c:\Tools\dig>host -a comcast.net
Trying "comcast.net"
;; ->>HEADER<<- opcode: QUERY, status: NOERROR, id: 1773
;; flags: qr rd ra; QUERY: 1, ANSWER: 9, AUTHORITY: 0, ADDITIONAL: 0

;; QUESTION SECTION:
;comcast.net.                   IN      ANY

;; ANSWER SECTION:
comcast.net.            25      IN      A       69.252.80.75
comcast.net.            76      IN      MX      5 mx1.comcast.net.
comcast.net.            76      IN      MX      5 mx2.comcast.net.
comcast.net.            7195    IN      NS      dns105.comcast.net.
comcast.net.            7195    IN      NS      dns102.comcast.net.
comcast.net.            7195    IN      NS      dns101.comcast.net.
comcast.net.            7195    IN      NS      dns103.comcast.net.
comcast.net.            7195    IN      NS      dns104.comcast.net.
comcast.net.            3600    IN      SOA     dns101.comcast.net.
domregtech.comcastonline.com. 2008182426 7200 3600 1209600 3600

Received 254 bytes from 208.67.222.222#53 in 16 ms
```

Figure 11-6 DNS records for the Comcast domain

That Old One-Pixel Image Trick

A favorite trick is to use a one-pixel image as a tracking device. When the recipient views the e-mail that is formatted using HTML, a one-pixel image can be retrieved from a particular web server <img src="http://ImWatchingYou.com/1pixel.gif">. Information sent as part of the HTTP request can be stored and analyzed to see who has accessed a particular document.

Laws Regarding E-mail

Two main areas of e-mail use are covered in the United States. The CAN-SPAM Act of 2003 (Controlling the Assault of Non-Solicited Pornography and Marketing Act of 2003), combined with 15 U.S.C. § 7704(a), defines limits on commercial spam (unsolicited commercial e-mail, either a single e-mail message or the result of a bulk mailing). But, as is stated by the U.S. Federal Trade Commission (FTC), following the rules doesn't have to be complicated.[11] CAN-SPAM requires that you

1. Don't use false or misleading header information. Your "From," "To," "Reply-To," and routing information—including the originating domain name and e-mail address—must be accurate and identify the person or business who initiated the message.

2. Don't use deceptive subject lines. The subject line must accurately reflect the content of the message.

3. Identify the message as an ad. The law gives you a lot of leeway in how to do this, but you must disclose clearly and conspicuously that your message is an advertisement.

4. Tell recipients where you're located. Your message must include your valid physical postal address. This can be your current street address, a post office box you've registered with the U.S. Postal Service, or a private mailbox you've registered with a commercial mail-receiving agency established under Postal Service regulations.

5. Tell recipients how to opt out of receiving future e-mail from you. Your message must include a clear and conspicuous explanation of how the recipient can opt out of getting e-mail from you in the future. Craft the notice in a way that's easy for an ordinary person to recognize, read, and understand. Creative use of type size, color, and location can improve clarity. Give a return e-mail address or another easy Internet-based way to allow people to communicate their choice to you. You may create a menu to allow a recipient to opt out of certain types of messages, but you must include the option to stop all commercial messages from you. Make sure your spam filter doesn't block these opt-out requests.

6. Honor opt-out requests promptly. Any opt-out mechanism you offer must be able to process opt-out requests for at least 30 days after you send your message. You must honor a recipient's opt-out request within 10 business days. You can't charge a fee, require the recipient to give you any personally identifying information beyond an e-mail address, or make the recipient take any step other than sending a reply e-mail or visiting a single page on an Internet web site as a condition for honoring an opt-out request. Once people have told you they don't want to receive more messages from you, you can't sell or transfer their e-mail addresses, even in the form of a mailing list. The only exception is that you may transfer the addresses to a company you've hired to help you comply with the CAN-SPAM Act.

7. Monitor what others are doing on your behalf. The law makes clear that even if you hire another company to handle your e-mail marketing, you can't contract away your legal responsibility to comply with the law. Both the company whose product is promoted in the message and the company that actually sends the message may be held legally responsible.

These guidelines describe what an organization can, can't, and must do in order to send commercial e-mail. Remember, however, that this law only applies to commercial e-mail: It doesn't address noncommercial bulk e-mail or unsolicited advertisements from an individual.

EXAM TIP   Make sure you know which laws affect commercial e-mail and which laws pertain to child pornography.

Other laws affecting e-mail are 18 U.S.C. § 2252A[12] and 2252B[13] that, respectively, apply to child pornography and using misleading domain names on the Internet. 2252A defines the knowing transmission, sharing, distributing, or viewing of child pornography as a criminal act that can result in prison sentences stretching from 10 years to life, and defines the actions that are illegal and the resulting punishment. The phrase "by any means, including by computer" is included in many of the subparagraphs.

Section 2252B defines as a crime using a misleading domain name on the Internet with the intent to deceive a person into viewing material constituting obscenity, or deceiving a minor into viewing material that is defined as harmful to minors. This can result in a prison sentence of 2 to 10 years.

E-mail Headers and Message Structure

After all the intermediate headers are added by each SMTP server on the path to the recipient's SMTP server, the complete source of an e-mail message can be much larger than the message itself. The headers for this message are listed in Figure 11-7, and the actual message contents are displayed in Figure 11-8. The real message is simple—in this case, it's some text that's formatted using HTML, as well as formatted using plain text.

```
Delivered-To: xxxxxxxxxxx@gmail.com
Received: by 10.76.169.230 with SMTP id ah6csp133670oac; Tue, 4 Mar 2014
14:07:41 -0800 (PST)
X-Received: by 10.229.241.9 with SMTP id lc9mr2707817qcb.15.1393970861716; Tue,
04 Mar 2014 14:07:41 -0800 (PST)
Return-Path: <xxxxxxxxxxx@comcast.net>
Received: from qmta15.westchester.pa.mail.comcast.net
(qmta15.westchester.pa.mail.comcast.net. [2001:558:fe14:44:76:96:59:228])
    by mx.google.com with ESMTP id 96si123293qgs.169.2014.03.04.14.07.41 for
<xxxxxxxxxxx@gmail.com>; Tue, 04 Mar 2014 14:07:41 -0800 (PST)
Received-SPF: pass (google.com: domain of xxxxxxxxxxx@comcast.net designates
2001:558:fe14:44:76:96:59:228 as permitted sender) client-ip=
2001:558:fe14:44:76:96:59:228;
Authentication-Results: mx.google.com;
    spf=pass (google.com: domain of xxxxxxxxxxx@comcast.net designates
2001:558:fe14:44:76:96:59:228 as permitted sender)
    smtp.mail=xxxxxxxxxxx@comcast.net;
    dkim=pass (test mode) header.i=@comcast.net
Received: from omta07.westchester.pa.mail.comcast.net ([76.96.62.59]) by
qmta15.westchester.pa.mail.comcast.net with comcast
    id ZWTL1n0061GhbT85Fa7hFU; Tue, 04 Mar 2014 22:07:41 +0000
Received: from [192.168.1.20] ([65.96.213.34])      by
omta07.westchester.pa.mail.comcast.net with comcast
    id Za7h1n00E0I5bsZ3Ta7h6H; Tue, 04 Mar 2014 22:07:41 +0000
Message-ID: <53164EA9.4070308@comcast.net>
```

Figure 11-7   Sample e-mail message MTA headers

The MUA uses the MIME multipart message format to include both forms in the message body. E-mail headers will be added to the message by the MUA. Once the message has been composed, it's sent to the SMTP servers specified by the recipients or recipient. In this example, I'm using smtp.comcast.net as my SMTP server, and I'm sending a message to my own e-mail address at google.com.

Given that we know how e-mail is sent through a network of MTAs, let's follow that through in our example. The initial lines at the beginning of the message are added by each MTA that was part of the network path followed by the message. The first "Received: by" line was added by the last MTA to receive the message; the last "Received: from" line represents the first MTA that received the message. Looking at this in more detail, we can see that the message traveled from my local machine (192.168.1.20) to omta07.westchester.pa.mail.comcast.net, then to omta15.westchester.pa.mail.comcast.net, then to mx.google.com, and finally to an address internal to google.com, 10.76.169.230. Notice how the SMTP ID field changes from server to server, but the Message-ID remains constant.

The first line of the message received by the first MTA starts with the line

```
Message-ID: <53164EA9.4070308@comcast.net>
```

and continues through the line

```
This is a multi-part message in MIME format.
```

```
Date: Tue, 04 Mar 2014 17:07:37 -0500
From: Charles Brooks <xxxxxxxx@comcast.net>
User-Agent: Mozilla/5.0 (Windows NT 6.1; WOW64; rv:24.0) Gecko/20100101 Thunderbird/24.3.0
MIME-Version: 1.0
To: David Lockhart <xxxxxxx@comcast.net>
Subject: Example of an e-mail message
X-Enigmail-Version: 1.6
Content-Type: multipart/alternative;
   boundary="------------030208080009040907040101"
DKIM-Signature: v=1; a=rsa-sha256; c=relaxed/relaxed; d=comcast.net; [[contents deleted]]
This is a multi-part message in MIME format.
------------030208080009040907040101
Content-Type: text/plain; charset=ISO-8859-1
Content-Transfer-Encoding: 7bit
_This _is an /example /of an e-mail *message *that contains multiple
parts. :-)
------------030208080009040907040101
Content-Type: text/html; charset=ISO-8859-1
Content-Transfer-Encoding: 7bit
<html>
  <head> <meta http-equiv="content-type" content="text/html; charset=ISO-8859-1"> </head>
  <body bgcolor="#FFFFFF" text="#000000">
   <u>This </u>is an <i>example </i>of an e-mail <b>message </b>that
   contains multiple parts. <span class="moz-smiley-s1"><span> :-) </span></span><br>
  </body>
</html>
------------030208080009040907040101--
```

Figure 11-8   Sample e-mail message contents

Following that line, we then see the multipart-MIME message itself in Figure 11-8. When writing this message, I specified the To: address, the Subject: field, and the message contents ("This is an example ..." with a smiley face). Everything else was added on by my MUA (Mozilla Thunderbird).

Why bother going through this message in such detail? A key to understanding e-mail delivery is knowing which component of an e-mail system created which headers and how SMTP servers prepend entries to that message. This information is critical when it comes time to undertake an investigation.

We've already mentioned the From: and To: headers. RFC 5322, Internet Message Format,[14] specifies how the contents of messages are structured and which headers are allowed, as well as their interpretation. Ken Lucke, in his paper on e-mail messages,[15] lists several headers that you will likely encounter; these are listed in Table 11-5. Headers that begin with "X-" are eXperimental, and usually contain more explicit information than that provided by the standard headers. An application safely can ignore these.

E-mail messages often have attachments. These attachments are encoded using MIME and are part of the message body sent to the initial MTA. The type is encoded from the file extension provided to the MUA and can be forged.

Header Name	Description
Content-Type	A MIME header indicating the contents of the message. Usually in the form <class>/<type>. A classic example is "text/html".
Content-Transfer-Encoding	How a MIME-compliant program should interpret the contents. One common value is "gzip", indicating that the contents of the messages have been compressed using the gzip software.
Date	Usually the date the message was sent, set by the sender's MUA. This is untrustworthy, as it may be set by any other machine along the path.
Message-ID	A semi-unique identifier added by the first MTA encountered along the path. Lucke indicates that any message without a message ID or a malformed message ID is probably a forgery.
Reply-To:	To whom the response should be sent, which is useful to redirect responses to a different e-mail address than the From: address. Heavily used by spammers for this reason.
Subject	Created by the sender. In some cases, this may be the only content provided (for example, Subject:"Meeting at 1pm today is OK").

Table 11-5   Standard Internet Message Headers

Understanding response codes from an SMTP or HTTP server is a benefit when investigating attacks. Transaction-oriented protocols such as HTTP and SMTP consist of a query and response. Response codes are three- or four-digit numbers of the form $<xxx><yyy><zzz>$. One of the simplest HTTP responses is simply "204 No Content" that means exactly what it says. HTTP status codes are taken from the following categories shown in Table 11-6.

SMTP status codes are more complicated, but also provide more information.[16] These codes have the form $<class><subject><specific-code>$. The document "Simple Mail Transfer Protocol (SMTP) Enhanced Status Code Register" from www.iana.org lists three classes of codes and eight subjects, as presented in Tables 11-7 and 11-8.

A fully enumerated status code combines class, subject, and specific status code. The complete status code 4.2.2 indicates a "mailbox full" condition that is classified as a "persistent transient failure," while 5.7.4 indicates that security features are not

Table 11-6	Category	Description	Examples
HTTP Status Codes	1xx	Informational	100: Continue
	2xx	Success	204: No Content
	3xx	Redirection	301: Moved Permanently
	4xx	Client Error	404: Not Found
	5xx	Server Error	500: Internal Server Error

Table 11-7	Class	Description
SMTP Response Class Codes	2.x.y	Success
	4.x.y	Persistent Transient Failure. The situation may be resolved in the future, but right now, the error condition holds.
	5.x.y	Permanent Failure. No point in retrying.

supported (a permanent condition). Status codes are reported as a whole number (for example, 422), and it's up to the receiver to determine the actual code, such as 2715 (priority level too low) by separating out relevant fields.

Interpreting status codes is one technique for investigating application attacks. When you know what responses are usual and expected and what error codes mean, you can more accurately diagnose misbehaving applications and identify applications that use nonstandard behavior or invalid or misleading responses as a way of circumventing various security controls.

Subject Code	Subject	Description
X.0.YYY	Other or Undefined Status	There is no additional subject information available.
X.1.YYY	Addressing Status	Report concerning the originator or destination address, and may include address syntax or validity. These errors can generally be corrected by the sender and retried.
X.2.YYY	Mailbox Status	Mailbox status indicates that something having to do with the mailbox has caused this DSN. Mailbox issues are assumed to be under the general control of the recipient.
X.3.YYY	Mail System Status	Represents some condition in the mail system.
X.4.YYY	Network and Routing Status	Status of the delivery system itself, including infrastructure such as directory and routing services.
X.5.YYY	Mail Delivery Protocol Status	Failures involving the message delivery protocol, possibly from implementation errors or an unreliable connection.
X.6.YYY	Message Content or Media Status	Failures involving the content of the message due to translation, transcoding, or otherwise unsupported message media.
X.7.YYY	Security or Policy Status	Failures involving policies such as per-recipient or per-host filtering and cryptographic operations. The sender and recipient must permit the exchange of messages and arrange the exchange of necessary keys and certificates for cryptographic operations.

Table 11-8 SMTP Subject Codes

Electronic Records Management

The EC-Council defines electronic records management (RM) as the "efficient and systematic control of the creation, receipt, maintenance, use, and disposition of electronic records, including the processes for capturing and maintaining evidence of and information for legal, fiscal, administrative, and other business purposes."[17] In addition to providing a vast amount of material for analysis, storing e-mail messages can support nonrepudiation so that someone cannot deny sending the message. Interestingly enough, only people can repudiate; machines or automated processes can't.

E-mail Investigation

Why investigate e-mail? Aside from the content of the message, the individuals who are named in To: and Cc: or Bcc: headers may become suspects during the course of an investigation. As an example, during the Enron investigation back in 2001–2002, investigators looked through gigabytes of stored e-mail messages. Who received this message, and when did they receive it? To whom did person X send e-mail, and from whom did person X receive e-mail?

The first step in investigating suspected criminal activity that has used e-mail is to get permission to actually perform the investigation. E-discovery is the process by which one party in a court case requests access to electronic records of another company. Aside from emphasizing the importance of electronic record keeping, e-discovery includes the retrieval of e-mail messages, a process complicated by files that may be stored locally. In other cases (such as Microsoft Exchange), e-mail messages are stored on a central server, and the process of retrieval is easier.

Forensic retrieval of e-mail only differs from the retrieving of other digital evidence in the actual processing of the messages. Otherwise, our rules of evidence gathering still apply:

- Work with a copy of the data, never the original.
- Ensure that the checksums of the original and the copy match.
- Work with a read-only copy of the evidence if possible.

How you obtain a copy of the e-mail message will depend on the type of e-mail client (MUA) used. If you're using Outlook or Outlook Express, you'll need a program that can parse the .pst file or .dbx files, respectively. Other e-mail clients, such as Mozilla Thunderbird, store the messages in plain text. Forensics suites like Forensic Toolkit (FTK) and EnCase include modules to parse e-mail discovered on the evidence files.

Once you've obtained a copy of the message, you can now begin the analysis. The most important thing to do is to trace the message on its journey from the sender to the receiver, including the intermediate systems. This journey is recorded in the "Received:" headers that begin the message. Here's a list of the envelope headers I recently received in a phishing e-mail:

```
From - Thu Mar 06 15:06:26 2014
X-Account-Key: account4
X-UIDL: 1396660.+pQg0DDvZL5MAg2xgNQXDCHxL0p6l7sUNSdoSNb9gWo=
X-Mozilla-Status: 0001
X-Mozilla-Status2: 00000000
X-Mozilla-Keys:
(1) Return-Path: kbxfns@notify.wellsfargo.com
(2) Received: from omta13.emeryville.ca.mail.comcast.net (LHLO omta13
    .emeryville.ca.mail.comcast.net) (76.96.30.52) by
    resmail-ch2-105v.sys.comcast.net with LMTP; Thu, 6 Mar 2014 02:48:50
    +0000 (UTC)
(3) Received: from User ([70.89.109.162]) by omta13.emeryville.ca.mail
    .comcast.net with
    comcast id a2od1n0033WG5MA8Z2oeGZ; Thu, 06 Mar 2014 02:48:49 +0000
X-CAA-SPAM: F00000
X-Authority-Analysis: ...
```

The From (no colon) and the Received: headers and the Return-Path: headers are all created by the intermediate MTA. Line (3) shows us that the mail originated from a computer with the IP address 70.89.109.162 and was originally sent to the computer omta13.emeryville.ca.mail.comcast.net. Line (2) indicates that the message was then forwarded to resmail-ch-105v.sys.comcast.net. Line (1) indicates the return path as kbxfns@notify.wellsfargo.com.

The "Message-ID" header marks the beginning of the content that was transferred from the MUA via the "local" MTA or MDS (I use "local" here in the sense that this is the first MTA that is accessed by the MUA). Following that header are the headers added by the MUA and the contents of the message:

```
Reply-To: kbxfns@notify.wellsfargo.com
From: Wells Fargo<kbxfns@notify.wellsfargo.com>
Subject: Important Notice Regarding Your Account
Date: Wed, 5 Mar 2014 18:48:48 -0800
MIME-Version: 1.0
Content-Type: text/html; charset="Windows-1250"
Content-Transfer-Encoding: 7bit
X-Priority: 3
X-MSMail-Priority: Normal
X-Mailer: Microsoft Outlook Express 6.00.2600.0000
X-MimeOLE: Produced By Microsoft MimeOLE V6.00.2600.0000
```

The Reply-To: header is identical to the Return-Path header—not surprising since the Return-Path: header is generated from it. The From: header seemingly indicates that the sender is "Wells Fargo," with the e-mail address of kbxfns@notify.wellsfargo.com. The Date: header indicates that the message was sent from a machine configured as Pacific Time, and the e-mail client used was Microsoft Outlook Express. Interestingly enough, there's no "To:" header—meaning that all recipients were listed as part of the Bcc: header, and yet the e-mail was obviously addressed to me or to someone with a similar name.

The actual message body truly marks this e-mail as a phishing attempt. I've reformatted some of the HTML to conserve space.

<strong>Dear Wells Fargo Customer,</strong>
<p>We recently have determined that different computers have tried to log in to your account. Multiple password failures automatically places your account on hold. We now need you to re-confirm your account information to us.
To remove limitations from your account click on the following link
<p><font size="4">[<b>
<span class="Object" id="OBJ_PREFIX_DWT24644_com_zimbra_url">
<a tabindex="0" target="_blank" href="http://server.358server.net/~via3inte/cache/">
Login to Customer Central</a></span></b>]</font>

Hmmm. Why is a message ostensibly from Wells Fargo directing me to a user's (~via3inte) directory on a computer named server.358server.net? A few minutes' work using dig and whois tells us that this machine (358server.net) is actually administered by someone from Sao Paulo, Brazil, and the user's IP address (70.89.109.162) resolves to 70-89-109-162-Busname-pittsburgh.hfc.comcastbusiness.net. So we have a server in Brazil that is directing us to a user's directory, and the computer where the message originated is not, in fact, within the wellsfargo domain. I tried accessing the site using a text-based web browser, and that access resulted in a redirection to yet another web server. Following that URL resulted in a 505 (server error). Looks like the phishers have moved on to another part of the ocean.

Outsourcing? I don't think so.

Looks like this phish slipped the hook.

While the message can, in theory, be modified anywhere along the network path, the most common modifications will occur at the sender. Common modifications include the From:, From and To: message headers that are trivially easy to modify, and the resulting envelope fields are set from the To: and the From: fields. Return-Path headers are also very easy to modify or falsify.

Concepts in Practice: E-mail Forensic Tools

As you might expect, there are many e-mail forensic tools. Many of them are restricted to Windows e-mail (Outlook, Outlook Express, or Windows mail) or other proprietary formats such as Lotus Notes and Novell GroupWise.

FTK from AccessData and EnCase from Guardian Software both contain facilities that will parse and display the contents of e-mail stores, and Paraben (makers of write blockers and other forensics tools) supplies the E-Mail Examiner and Network-Examiner software. E-Mail Examiner will extract e-mail from Outlook, Outlook Express, and Windows Mail, as well as Thunderbird and Eudora. Paraben claims that the software supports 750 different kinds of e-mail formats and that the output has been upheld in court. Using tools that are recognized within the digital forensics community and that have been used to present evidence in court will decrease the chances that your results will be challenged based on unproven technology.

Chapter Review

Some Internet protocols consist of a series of queries and responses from a client to a server. SMTP, POP3 (e-mail), and HTTP (Web) protocols all use this design. These protocols include application-layer headers that qualify the request, and an optional body that is formatted based on the MIME specifications.

Web applications use the HTTP protocol to communicate between a client and a server. Usually, web applications are web browser based and use HTML as their content encoding, although using HTML isn't a necessity. The web architecture assumes a direct path between client and server, although proxy servers can be used by clients, and reverse proxies can act as web application firewalls (WAFs) and load balancers for web traffic to the server.

Web servers are attacked because they can provide a way to gain a foothold inside an organization, either to work deeper into the infrastructure or to extract or alter incoming or outgoing web traffic. Web page defacement occurs when the attacker is provided with excessive write privileges, either through the server itself or after the attacker has gained a presence on the server (usually called a shell). Web page defacement can affect the reputation of an organization, as well as acute embarrassment.

Web access logs, as well as error logs, are the first source of information for the investigator. Both the IIS web server and the Apache web server store information in their logs, including the time of the request, the identity of the requestor, the request itself, the status code, and the size of the request. The Apache error log records details concerning server errors: Combining the access logs and the error logs can point to the request that caused the failure. A DFI can find more details by examining firewall, router, and IDS/IPS logs. Tools like Deep Log Analyzer provide an automated way to view these logs. Tools like dig and nslookup can map hostnames to IP addresses and vice versa. The whois program will retrieve contact information about a particular domain, while traceroute (tracert or pingpath) will report the path followed through the network from source to destination. This path can help identify which domains host the attacker's computers and suggest who needs to be involved in further examination. If you're investigating a live attack on a Windows server, an investigator can determine who might be logged in to the machine, what extra processes are running, and whether the server mounts external shares or whether other machines have mounted shares on the server.

There are four primary reasons for successful web attacks. This first is injection of malicious code into the output returned from the server that is then executed in the victim's browser. Such attacks include cross-site scripting (XSS), cross-site request forgery, (CXRF), and SQL injection.

The second is weak security: The application doesn't check that the client is authenticated for all functions or information that they request, or the server doesn't time out existing session credentials and prompt for the credentials to be re-entered. Third, input is not validated to inspect for meta-characters or path-traversal requests, or is simply passed on to another portion of the application where unexpected consequences occur (SQL injection is a prime example of this). Last, a failure to provide proper operating security can result in leaking sensitive data or modification of input parameters if intercepted by an attacker.

Software tools that will investigate web application vulnerabilities include HP WebInspect, Nikto, and Nessus. These can determine web vulnerabilities based on sets of rules and a deep knowledge of the structure and purpose of HTTP, HTML, and database languages such as SQL, along with web application programming languages such as PHP.

E-mail systems consist of e-mail clients (an MUA) and e-mail servers (MTAs). SMTP is used between MTAs and by MUAs to connect directly to the assigned mail server. Clients use either POP or IMAP to retrieve e-mail. The major difference is that the POP3 protocol deletes the original message from the server by default, while IMAP leaves the mail on the server unless explicitly asked to delete it. If you're using web-based e-mail in the United States, such as Yahoo!, Gmail, or Outlook, you are using a web application that acts as an MUA.

E-mail can either be used in the commission of a crime (such as harassment, blackmail, or stalking), or can be a crime in and of itself (sending a forged e-mail message, such as a phishing attempt, sending unsolicited commercial e-mail [spamming], or sending a quantity of e-mail messages with the intent of overloading the server or a user's account). Laws affecting e-mail in the United States include 15 U.S.C. § 7704(a) that underpins The CAN-SPAM Act of 2003. This law defines limits on the sending of unsolicited commercial e-mail. Other laws affecting e-mail are 18 U.S.C. § 2252A and 2252B. 2252A defines the penalties for sending, receiving, sharing, or distributing child pornography, and 2252B makes it a crime to use a misleading domain name to persuade someone to view obscene materials or, if the person is a minor, to view material that is designated as harmful to minors.

We investigate e-mail for two reasons. The first is to identify the individual or organization that committed the crime. The second is to use e-mail messages as a way of tracking communications networks: who communicated with whom, when, why, and where. Identifying these patterns can identify ringleaders and co-conspirators. Investigating e-mail crime is initially similar to gathering other forms of electronic evidence: The DFI must seize and acquire the evidence in a forensically sound matter and preserve that evidence to enforce the chain of custody. Once acquired, and working from a read-only copy of that evidence, the investigator can begin analyzing the messages for content and senders and recipients. Common e-mail headers are From:, To:, Cc:,

Subject:, Reply-To:, and Date:. Criminals most often forge the From:, Return-Path:, and Reply-To: headers. The Date: header is also untrustworthy, since it can be added or changed along the delivery path. Investigators can use the Received: headers in the full message to determine the path from the sender through the network to the recipient's e-mail server.

There are multiple software programs to analyze and extract e-mail. Both FTK and EnCase include e-mail analysis as part of their standard evidence analysis. Utilizing the same software used to send and receive e-mail can produce good results. For example, if the suspect was using Outlook Express, analyzing the mail databases using Outlook Express provides a "suspect's-eye view" of the evidence. Paraben (www.paraben.com) provides the E-Mail Examiner and Network E-Mail Examiner that enable the investigator to search nonlocal e-mail stores, such as those provided by Microsoft Exchange and Lotus Notes.

Questions

1. An HTTP server response that indicates the client should look elsewhere for a particular resource is known as a(n) _____.

    A. Permanent transitory failure

    B. Redirect

    C. Resource rejection

    D. HTTP indirection

2. When does web page defacement occur?

    A. The attacker redirects the client to a site under their control

    B. Attackers modify the web page in transit

    C. The attacker has write permission to the web content directories

    D. An attacker injects a script into a web page that downloads malware

3. Which field is not recorded in the Apache request log?

    A. Date

    B. Client

    C. HTTP response code

    D. URI-query

4. Which command might an investigator use to determine if there were changes to accounts on the local machine? (Choose all that apply.)

    A. eventmgr.msc

    B. net sessions

    C. lusrmgr.msc

    D. net use

5. What command could you use to discover the administrative contact for a domain?

   A. whois

   B. nslookup

   C. netstat

   D. host -R

6. What area is addressed by 15 U.S.C. § 7704(a)?

   A. Using e-mail for extortion

   B. Misleading domain names

   C. Penalties for handling child pornography

   D. Limits on commercial e-mail

7. What role does Microsoft Outlook play in an e-mail system?

   A. MTS

   B. MUA

   C. MTA

   D. MDS

8. A spammer will usually forge the _____ header in order to hide the true source of the message.

   A. From:

   B. Received: From

   C. Reply-To:

   D. Return-Path:

9. The _____ protocol is used to transfer e-mail between two MTAs.

   A. NNTP

   B. HTTP

   C. POP3

   D. SMTP

10. An intermediate server located between the client and the destination web server is called a(n) _____ server.

    A. Filtering

    B. Gateway

    C. Proxy

    D. Front-end

Answers

1. **B.** This action is called a redirect.

2. **C.** The attacker has write permission to the web content directories.

3. **D.** The URI-query field isn't present in the Apache access log.

4. **B, C.** Both of these commands could indicate if changes had been made to local accounts.

5. **C.** whois can provide the administrative contact information.

6. **D.** 15 U.S.C. § 7704(a) lists the limits on commercial e-mail.

7. **B.** All e-mail clients act as an MUA, although they may contain elements of an MTA as well.

8. **A.** The From: header. Recall that the From: header is generated by the MUA, while the From (no colon) envelope header is generated by the MTA.

9. **D.** The SMTP protocol is used between two machines in the role of MTA.

10. **C.** Proxy server.

References

1. Klensin, J. *RFC 5321: Simple Mail Transfer Protocol* (CA: IETF, 2008). Retrieved from http://tools.ietf.org/html/rfc5321.

2. Fielding, R. et al. *RFC 2126 The HyperText Transfer Protocol – Version 1-1* (CA: Internet Society, 1999). Retrieved from http://tools.ietf.org/html/rfc2616.

3. Marshall, R. *The Internet Message: Closing the Book with Electronic Mail* (NJ: Prentice-Hall, 1993), p. 2.

4. EC-Council. *Computer Forensics: Investigating Network Instructions and Cybercrime* (NY: EC-Council, 2009), p. 2:3.

5. EC-Council. p. 3:7.

6. WebInspect. Retrieved from www8.hp.com/us/en/software-solutions/software .html?compURI=1341991#.UyB2D_ldWtM.

7. *Deep Log Analyzer Screenshots*. Retrieved from www.deep-software.com/ screenshots.asp.

8. EC-Council, p. 3–13.

9. Ale2006-from-en. File:SMTP-transfer-model.svg. Retrieved from https:// en.wikipedia.org/wiki/File:SMTP-transfer-model.svg March 10, 2014. This file is licensed under the Creative Commons Attribution-Share Alike 3.0 Unported license.

10. Rose, p. 2.

11. "CAN-SPAM Act: A Compliance Guide for Business." Retrieved from http://business.ftc.gov/documents/bus61-can-spam-act-compliance-guide-business.

12. "Certain Activities Relating to Material Constituting or Containing Child Pornography." Retrieved from www.law.cornell.edu/uscode/text/18/, 2252A.

13. "Misleading Domain Names on the Internet." Retrieved from www.law.cornell.edu/uscode/text/18/2252B.

14. Resnick, P. *RFC 5322: Internet Message Format* (CA: IETF, 2008). Retrieved from https://datatracker.ietf.org/doc/rfc5322/.

15. Lucke, Ken. *Reading E-mail Headers: All About E-Mail Headers* (2004). Retrieved from www.owlriver.com/spam/stop-spam.html.

16. *Simple Mail Transfer Protocol (SMTP) Enhanced Status-Code Registry.* Retrieved from www.iana.org/assignments/smtp-enhanced-status-codes/smtp-enhanced-status-codes.xhtml.

17. EC-Council, p. 4:7

## CHAPTER 12

The Whole Truth, and Nothing But the Truth

In this chapter, you will learn how to

- Explain the need for and the importance of an investigative report, describe how a report is classified, discuss the salient features of a good report, and describe best practices for investigators
- Summarize the guidelines for writing a report, provide an overview of the investigative report format, and provide a layout for an investigative report
- Provide a computer forensic report template, show how to document a case report, and demonstrate how to write a report using FTK and ProDiscover
- Define an expert witness, explain the role of an expert witness, and describe various types of expert witnesses, as well as how to find a computer forensic expert
- Explain the differences between a technical witness and an expert witness, articulate the scope of expert witness testimony, and recall the rules pertaining to an expert witness's qualifications
- Recall the steps involved in processing evidence and preparing a report
- Testify in court during direct and cross-examination and explain the general ethics applicable when testifying

There's an old saying that "the job ain't finished until the paperwork's done." This certainly is the case with digital investigations. As a digital forensics investigator (DFI), you've been assigned to investigate a particular situation and report your conclusions, regardless of whether you've been hired as an independent consultant, you're a member of law enforcement, or you're part of an investigative team for an organization. In some cases, your report may initially be a verbal response to a decision-maker, followed by a written report or presentation to upper-level management or to your peers. If you've been hired as part of legal proceedings, you may be asked to appear in court as a witness.

We've already discussed the format of a preliminary summary of findings, sometimes called a threshold assessment.[1] Since these are preliminary reports, they may contain various avenues for further investigation, depending on evidence yet to be discovered. A formal investigative report will contain more details regarding the evidence, as well

Threshold Assessment

1. Abstract - summary of conclusions
2. Summary of examinations performed
    2.1. Examination of log files, computers, digital devices, etc.
    2.2. Employee interviews, victim's statements, etc.
3. Detailed case background
4. Victimology/Target assessment
5. Equivocal analysis of other's work
    5.1. Missed information or incorrect conclusions
6. Crime scene characteristics
7. Investigative suggestions

Figure 12-1 Threshold report format (Adapted from Casey, E. et. al., *Digital Evidence and Computer Crime*, 3rd ed. (MA: Elsevier, 2011).)

as firmer conclusions based on that. The key difference between a threshold assessment and an investigative report is that an investigative report will confine itself to the evidence discovered, while a threshold assessment will focus on other areas of investigation based on the evidence gathered to date. Figure 12-1 shows a common format for a threshold assessment.[2]

An interesting aspect of this report is the section on victimology, the "investigation and study of victim characteristics."[3] Understanding the characteristics of the victim may provide a clue to the perpetrator's methods and predilections; the time just prior to the incident may reveal other activities of the suspect that may put them in contact with the victim. Another characteristic of a threshold report is that the investigation may be halted at that point. Enough evidence may have been found to support the case, or further investigation may be unwarranted because of cost or difficulty in obtaining more evidence.

Can I Get a Witness?

Depending on the organization where you are employed as a DFI, you can reasonably expect to be called as a witness in a court case. Your role as a witness may be to act as a technical or evidentiary witness, or as an expert/scientific witness. Regardless of how and when you are testifying, presenting, or writing a report, always remember who your audience is. Your presentation and style can and should vary depending on whether you are presenting a paper at a technical conference, reporting information to an attorney, or testifying under oath. Are you attempting to communicate information, or are you attempting to persuade someone to adopt your point of view? Are you talking to your peers or to senior management?

TIP   Tailor your presentation to your audience and its purpose.

Technical vs. Expert Witnesses

As a technical/scientific witness, you are called to support the facts of the case. You will be asked to speak to the nature of the evidence, as well as how that evidence was obtained. You will not be asked to express an opinion or conclusions. ("Just the facts, ma'am," as Jack Webb of TV's *Dragnet* used to say.)

An expert witness has a very different role to play in legal proceedings. The phrase "expert witness" has a specific meaning within the legal profession. An expert witness is called specifically to offer an opinion of the evidence, as well as to draw conclusions based on that evidence. Although expert witnesses come in all shapes, sizes, and areas of expertise, the scope of the testimony of an expert witness should be solely within the bounds of his or her expertise. As a DFI, it's not your job to explain the law or to detail the minutiae of why SHA-256 is different from MD5. In some engagements, appearing in court may not be necessary, in that you may be hired as a consultant who works with the attorney, and thereby act as a consulting witness. Regardless, you will need to generate a report, and you may be required to provide testimony in the form of a deposition during the discovery phase of the legal process or a testimony preservation deposition.

Two significant cases have defined the rules for expert witness testimony. The first case was *Frye v. United States*, 293 F. 1013 (D.C. Cir. 1923). In this case, the court ruled that testimony is inadmissible unless it is "testimony deduced from a well-recognized scientific principle or discovery; the thing from which the deduction is made must be sufficiently established to have gained general acceptance in the particular field in which it belongs."[4] The second case was *Daubert v. Merrell Down Pharmaceuticals, Inc.*, 509 U.S. 579 (1933). *Daubert* was significant in that it established a set of principles to use to determine if expert witness testimony was reliable.

> *Daubert* set forth a nonexclusive checklist for trial courts to use in assessing the reliability of scientific expert testimony. The specific factors explicated by the *Daubert* Court are
>
> 1. whether the expert's technique or theory can be or has been tested—that is, whether the expert's theory can be challenged in some objective sense, or whether it is instead simply a subjective, conclusory approach that cannot reasonably be assessed for reliability;
> 2. whether the technique or theory has been subject to peer review and publication;
> 3. the known or potential rate of error of the technique or theory when applied;
> 4. the existence and maintenance of standards and controls; and
> 5. whether the technique or theory has been generally accepted in the scientific community.

The Court in *Kumho* (526 U.S. 137, 119 S.Ct 1167) held that these factors might also be applicable in assessing the reliability of nonscientific expert testimony, depending upon "the particular circumstances of the particular case at issue."[5]

Depending on the state in which you practice, courts may use either Daubert or Frye as a standard for determining expert witness testimony.

 EXAM TIP You will need to know the difference between *Frye* and *Daubert.* In essence, *Daubert* provides a set of criteria for determining whether scientific testimony is admissible; *Frye* is more general.

If you are going to testify as an expert witness, you will need to meet those standards set forth for expert witness testimony. These standards are outlined in the Federal Rules of Civil Procedure (FRCP) 26(a)(2) and the Federal Rules of Evidence (FRE) 702, 703, and 705. FRCP 26(a)(2) simply states that an attorney must specify the identity of someone they intend to call as a witness, as well as the evidence that the witness has available to them.

FRE articles 702, 703, and 705 address the qualifications of an expert witness and the basis of how the witness came to arrive at a particular conclusion. Rule 702 addresses the qualifications and the conditions under which a witness can testify:

A witness who is qualified as an expert by knowledge, skill, experience, training, or education may testify in the form of an opinion or otherwise if:

    a. the expert's scientific, technical, or other specialized knowledge will help the trier of fact to understand the evidence or to determine a fact in issue;

    b. the testimony is based on sufficient facts or data;

    c. the testimony is the product of reliable principles and methods; and

    d. the expert has reliably applied the principles and methods to the facts of the case.

FRE 702 effectively summarizes the principles laid out in *Daubert*. FRE 703 lays out the basis for an expert witness's opinion and testimony. I myself find it interesting that the opinion can be admitted as evidence even though facts or data are not!

An expert may base an opinion on facts or data in the case that the expert has been made aware of or personally observed. If experts in the particular field would reasonably rely on those kinds of facts or data in forming an opinion on the subject, they need not be admissible for the opinion to be admitted. Nevertheless, if the facts or data would otherwise be inadmissible, the proponent of the opinion may disclose them to the jury only if their probative value in helping the jury evaluate the opinion substantially outweighs their prejudicial effect.

Last, FRE 705 speaks to disclosing the facts or data underlying the expert opinion and clarifies FRE 203. "Unless the court orders otherwise, an expert may state an opinion—and give the reasons for it—without first testifying to the underlying facts or data. But the expert may be required to disclose those facts or data on cross-examination."[6]

An expert witness is more than a subject matter expert (SME). FRCP 26(2)(b) defines who has to supply a written report and the contents of that report. We'll address the content of the report later on this chapter. For now, we'll focus on the applicable history and experience required for an expert witness. Items 4, 5, and 6 of 26(2)(b) indicate that the witness must provide a list of other cases in which they've testified/been deposed in the preceding four years and ten years of published writing, as well as any previous compensation they have received for testifying.

This means that an expert witness needs to have an up-to-date *curriculum vitae* (CV). The CV should demonstrate how the witness has enhanced their skills via "training, teaching, and experience."[7] The CV describes tasks that the witness has performed that demonstrate particular accomplishments, and it should contain a list of basic and advanced skills and how they were obtained. The CV also should include general and professional education, such as courses sponsored by people who train government agencies, courses offered or sponsored by professional organizations, and training to which the witness has either contributed or provided. A CV is similar to a resume, but doesn't focus on a particular trial. Rather, the CV is more like a skills-focused resume that attests to skills, abilities, and knowledge rather than justifying one's suitability for particular employment.

Pre-trial Report Preparation

For civil cases, U.S. district courts require an expert witness to submit reports. Federal courts require that all scientific, technical, or expert witnesses must provide a report *prior* to trial in civil cases, as indicated in FRCP 26(2)(b). FRCP 26(2)(b) also states that a report must contain

- All opinions
- The basis for the opinions
- Information considered in forming those opinions

Appendices should include

- Related exhibits, such as photos or diagrams
- Expert witness's CV

Actually preparing the report usually involves organizing your supporting evidence to write that report. Ensure that your CV is up to date. Organize the related exhibits into appendices that reflect the evidence used to support your opinions. For each stated opinion, make sure that you have the evidence available on which you based your opinion and any references to outside studies or techniques that you used to reach those opinions. Make sure as well that your outside sources or techniques meet the criteria laid out in *Daubert* for accuracy and acceptance by your peers.

I Just Want to Testify

The majority of work in preparing evidence for testimony should have been completed before you started writing the report and preparing your testimony. Two things need to be accomplished: preparing an examination plan and organizing the presentation materials for your testimony.

An examination plan is a guideline regarding the questions that you can expect your attorney to ask you in the process of testifying.[8] One important aspect of this plan is that it allows you to make changes to the questions that the attorney may ask, and it allows your attorney to gain familiarity with digital forensics if they have no prior knowledge. Look at the examination plan as a way to improve communication between you and your attorney.

Depending on the results of the examination plan, you may decide to prepare some "visual aids" as part of your testimony. Diagrams, maps, photographs, and so on can support your verbal testimony by making it noteworthy.

Remember to use good presentation style: no more than 3 bullet points per slide, a font large enough to be seen anywhere in the room and no extraneous decorations. If permitted, provide handouts for judge, jury, and both attorneys. Make eye contact, and always face your audience.

Ethics and Testimony

Ethics are codes of professional conduct or responsibility. Ethics help you, as a professional, to control your bias. Everyone has a bias in one form or another; the key to managing those biases is to become aware of them and learn how to present evidence calmly and objectively.

Nelson lists three sources of ethics.[9] Foremost are your internal values, derived from your upbringing, personal independent experience, religion, morals, culture, and so forth. Many professional certifying bodies also list a code of conduct or ethics, and many professional associations do as well. EC-Council has its own code of ethics for those who achieve their certifications, and these are listed here:

EC-Council Code of Ethics[10]

1. **Privacy**. Keep private any confidential information gained in [your] professional work (in particular as it pertains to client lists and client personal information). [Do not] collect, give, sell, or transfer any personal information (such as name, e-mail address, Social Security number, or other unique identifier) to a third party without client's prior consent.

2. **Intellectual Property**. Protect the intellectual property of others by relying on [your] own innovation and efforts, thus ensuring that all benefits vest with its originator.

3. **Disclosure**. Disclose to appropriate persons or authorities potential dangers to any e-commerce clients, the Internet community, or the public that [you] reasonably believe to be associated with a particular set or type of electronic transactions or related software or hardware.

4. **Areas of Expertise**. Provide service in [your] areas of competence, being honest and forthright about any limitations of [your] experience and education. Ensure that [you] are qualified for any project on which [you] work or propose to work by an appropriate combination of education, training, and experience.

5. **Unauthorized Usage**. Never knowingly use software or a process that is obtained or retained either illegally or unethically.

6. **Illegal Activities**. [Do not] engage in deceptive financial practices such as bribery, double billing, or other improper financial practices.

7. **Authorization**. Use the property of a client or employer only in ways properly authorized, and with the owner's knowledge and consent.

8. **Disclosure**. Disclose to all concerned parties those conflicts of interest that cannot reasonably be avoided or escaped.

9. **Management**. Ensure good management for any project [you] lead, including effective procedures for promotion of quality and full disclosure of risk.

10. **Knowledge Sharing**. Add to the knowledge of the e-commerce profession by constant study, share the lessons of [your] experience with fellow EC-Council members, and promote public awareness of [the] benefits of electronic commerce.

11. **Confidence**. Conduct [yourself] in the most ethical and competent manner when soliciting professional service or seeking employment, thus meriting confidence in [your] knowledge and integrity.

12. **Extreme Care**. Ensure ethical conduct and professional care at all times on all professional assignments without prejudice.

13. **Malicious Activities**. [Do not] associate with malicious hackers [or] engage in any malicious activities.

14. **No Compromise**. [Do not] purposefully compromise or cause to be compromised the client organization's systems in the course of your professional dealings.

15. **Legal Limits**. Ensure all penetration-testing activities are authorized and within legal limits.

16. **Involvement**. [Do not] partake in any black hat activity or be associated with any black hat community that serves to endanger networks.

17. **Underground Communities**. [Do not] be part of any underground hacking community for purposes of preaching and expanding black hat activities.

Three certifying organizations stand out for a DFI:

- The EC-Council offers the Computer Hacking Forensic Investigator (C|HFI) certification. The EC-Council Code of Ethics applies to anyone who earns one of their certifications, including the Certified Ethical Hacker (C|EH).

- The International Society of Forensic Computer Examiners (ISFCE) at www.isfce.com provides a Code of Ethics and Professional Responsibility. ISFCE offers the Certified Computer Examiner (CCE) examination both for individuals in law enforcement and for others.

- The International Association of Computer Investigative Specialist (IACIS) at www.iacis.com offers the Certified Forensic Computer Examiner (CFCE) certification and the Certified Advanced Windows Forensic Examiner (CAWFE) certification. Both of these exams include a written examination and a practical examination or assessment.

Other professional associations may be important to your career as a DFI, depending on your area of specialization. These associations include the American Bar Association (ABA), the American Medical Association (AMA), and American Psychological Association (APA). All of these associations have codes of conduct and ethical behavior, and it's a good idea to know what these ethical standards mean for each of these professions since, as an expert witness, you may be working with other individuals from these professions.

In sum, a DFI has a duty to appear impartial and to present (or at least not ignore) any exculpatory evidence found during the investigation and analysis.

How to Testify

As an expert or technical witness, you can expect to participate in multiple phases of a court case. These phases are prior to the trial, during the trial, and after the trial has concluded (although the case may be appealed further). Although circumstances differ among these three phases, one aspect is clear: Don't discuss the case with others except for your client (usually an attorney). These next two sections address concerns that are specific to the first two phases. We'll look at after the trial a bit later on in this chapter.

Prior to Trial   There are several things that you should observe in the preliminary events leading up to the actual trial. First, keep your own counsel (no pun intended): remember, your client is the attorney who hired you the case at which you will testify). Don't discuss the case with other people or express your opinions. Practice saying "no comment" to members of the media. Avoid conflicts of interest: these could arise if you develop a personal relationship with the opposing attorney, or you become involved in activities where the outcome of the case could benefit you. Finally, get paid before you testify. If you don't, the opposing attorney can suggest that you're being paid based on the outcome of the case, and not for the work that you had done in preparation for testifying.

When actually testifying, your effect will be determined by both what you say and how you say it. Consider the following suggestions as best practices:

- Always remain professional in both dress and demeanor. That is, dress professionally based on the standards of the community in which you're appearing. Cowboy boots may be acceptable attire in Austin, Texas; they would appear eccentric at best in Boston, Massachusetts. All night partying will demonstrate a lack of seriousness on your part, and a hung-over witness won't appear credible.

- Practice beforehand. Prepare answers to standard questions based on your expertise and in consultation with your attorney.

- Address the audience directly, regardless of who it is (judge, jury, opposing counsel). Prepare for, and adjust your presentation to, your audience based on their educational and vocational background.

- Be prepared to stay within the scope of your expertise; if the question is outside that scope, say so. In addition, indicate if you weren't asked to investigate a particular aspect of the case. If in doubt about the direction or intent or meaning of a question, simply ask that the question be repeated.

During the Trial   Court testimony includes both direct examination and cross-examination. During direct examination, you can expect to present information, testify, or attest to facts based on three things[11]:

- Independent recollection (what you know about this case and others without prompting)

- Customary practice (procedures that are traditionally followed in similar cases)

- The documentation of the case (written records you've maintained)

As an expert witness, you don't need to have been involved in the case from the beginning. Rather, you are basing your opinion on the evidence gathered as part of the investigation rather than direct participation in that investigation.

During cross-examination, don't appear to be too friendly or too hostile with the opposing attorney. Maintain your composure. During the course of the trial, maintain a professional distance and a professional decorum. Don't talk to anyone during a court recess; if you need to have a conversation with your attorney, do so in private so that your conversation doesn't become an issue during cross-examination. If you should find exculpatory evidence during the trial, report it immediately to your attorney. Hopefully, any exculpatory evidence will be found well before the case goes to trial, but you have an ethical responsibility to report this evidence whenever it is discovered.

Other Proceedings   You can participate in legal proceedings in other ways than appearing at a trial as a witness. You may be called to testify at a hearing, whether an administrative hearing or a judicial hearing. An administrative hearing takes place in front of an administrative agency, either state or federal. Judicial hearings usually occur prior to the case going to trial, and focus on whether evidence will be found to be admissible. These kinds of hearings are very much like testifying at a trial, and it's particularly important that you have your methods of evidence collection and preservation down pat.

Depositions are yet another form of testifying. There are discovery depositions and testimony preservation depositions. As you might expect, the discovery deposition is part of the overall discovery process for a particular trial. Usually, both attorneys are present. Be aware that in the U.S. adversarial justice system, the opposing attorney may use several means to discredit your testimony. This can include peppering you with questions, asking complex hypothetical questions, or acting aggressively and combative. Keep in mind as well that an attorney will have access to testimony that you have provided in previous cases through services that provide access to libraries of testimony called deposition banks. Make sure that you haven't refuted your own testimony! If your opinions have changed, be prepared to state why.

A testimony preservation deposition is a way of preserving testimony in case you would not be able to testify later. In some instances, the testimony may be videotaped; in other instances, the testimony preservation may take the form of a demonstration of techniques used to produce that evidence.

Regardless of when and where you provide testimony, follow these simple rules:

- Be professional and polite.
- Just the facts.
- Keep cool; don't become flustered or rattled.

Writing a Good Report

In addition, what is good, Phaedrus, and what is not good?
Need we ask anyone to tell us these things?[12]

Whether you have been hired simply to undertake an investigation or you are asked to appear as a witness, you will need to produce a report of your findings. The exact format of this report will vary depending on your audience and the method of delivery. Regardless of these conditions, a report must be *effective*. An effective report is one that provides the necessary supporting information to persuade a particular audience of the accuracy of the report's conclusions. FRCP 26(2)(b) indicates that a report must include[13]

- A complete statement of all opinions the witness will express and the basis and reasons for them
- The facts or data considered by the witness in forming them
- Any exhibits that will be used to summarize or support them

Therefore, an effective report provides details that document and illustrate the investigation. Usually, the client (an attorney or another investigator) defines the goal of the investigation. An effective report ultimately supports that goal. A good report is thus an effective report, and a report is good when it covers the essential elements of the investigation.

Goal of the Investigation	Conclusion	Evidence	How Collected
Find any hacking software, evidence of its use, and any data that might have been generated	Hacking software was found, as was evidence of its use	Item 1 Item 2 Item 3	Analysis of disk image using ProDiscover and Forensic Explorer
Tie the computer to the suspect, Greg Schardt	This computer can be tied to Greg Schardt	Item 1 Item 2 Item 3	Analysis of disk image using ProDiscover and Forensic Explorer

Table 12-1 Evidence Traceability Matrix

What Makes an Effective Report?

Remember that the primary goal of a technical report is to communicate information. You can improve communication by using a simple format, avoiding slang or technical jargon, and taking care to expand a TLA when used (TLA stands for a three-letter acronym such as NSA, FBI, or DOJ). Avoid hypothetical questions, but do use theoretical questions as a way to structure your narrative and as a way to demonstrate how the evidence supports and answers this question.

Although you may use a particular template for all your reports, each report must be specific to a particular incident and uniquely identify that incident. Here's where your documentation of the crime scene, the tagging and bagging of evidence, and your chain-of-custody documentation all come into play. These materials will help you provide a consistent and well-organized description of how the evidence was collected, preserved, and analyzed.

One effective technique for determining the consistency of reports is to match the goals of the investigation with the evidence that you've produced. Let's return to the case of Greg Schardt, aka Mr. Evil. Our goals for that investigation were twofold: demonstrate that Greg Schardt and Mr. Evil were one and the same (putting the person, Greg Schardt, in front of the keyboard when logged in as Mr. Evil), and demonstrate that Mr. Schardt had been cracking wireless network traffic in order to gain login credentials and passwords.

We can express our results in Table 12-1, which is loosely based on the notion of a requirements traceability matrix from the software engineering discipline. A technique like this can provide you with assurance that you have addressed the goals of the investigation and your conclusions are supported by the evidence collected.

Documenting the Case

The EC-Council offers the following as an example of an investigative report template.[14] I've taken the liberty of rearranging and editing the different topics to clarify the organization of the report.

I. Summary

   1. Case number

   2. Names and Social Security numbers of authors, investigators, and examiners

   3. Purpose of investigation

    4. Significant findings

    5. Signature analysis

  II. Objectives of the investigation

 III. Incident description and collecting evidence

    1. Date and time the incident allegedly occurred

    2. Date and time the incident was reported to the agency's personnel

    3. Name of the person or persons working the investigation

    4. Date and time investigation was assigned

    5. Nature of claim and information provided to the investigators

    6. Location of the evidence

    7. List of the collected evidence

    8. Collection of the evidence

    9. Preservation of the evidence

    10. Initial evaluation of the evidence

  IV. Investigative techniques

   V. Analysis of the computer evidence

  VI. Relevant findings

 VII. Supporting expert opinion

VIII. Other supporting details:

    1. Attacker's methodology

    2. Users' applications

    3. Internet activity

  IX. Recommendations

How you intend to deliver the report will affect the preparation. We can classify reports as formal or informal, verbal or written. Table 12-2 describes each type of report.

Formal reports are more structured and are more likely to follow a set format. If you are delivering a formal verbal report, make sure that it follows your examination plan.

	Formal	Informal
Verbal	Delivered to senior management or board of directors	Preliminary report.
Written	A report sworn under oath, such as an affidavit or a declaration	Usually preceding the actual trial. This report may be subject to discovery by opposing counsel.

Table 12-2 Forensics Report Types

If you're delivering a formal written report, such as what is required for submission to a court, make sure you follow the outline or format that is required for these documents. Once again, consistency is critical here.

 TIP Choose a report format that you like and use it for all your reports. It's better to label as section as "not applicable" (NA) and the reasons why you believe it's inapplicable rather than skip the section entirely.

An example of an informal verbal report is a status report provided to someone in the attorney's office. A written informal report could be a more detailed description of the entire case (an investigative report would fall under this heading). This kind of report is subject to discovery by an opposing attorney. Destroying the report might be considered destruction of or the concealment of evidence, also known as *spoliation*, defined as "the destruction or alteration of a document that destroys its value as evidence in a legal proceeding."[15]

A well-written report tells a story that answers the 5WH (who, what, when, where, why, how) questions.[16] Your narrative is supported by including figures, tables, data, and equations. All of these can and should be referenced in the text: In some cases, they can be inserted inline with the text itself. Each type of display should be numbered separately with a section identifier and an element number (for example, "Figure 5-2 shows the suspect's desktop including the wireless router and the attached printer."). Avoid using precise placement terms (preceding, following) because the display element may be repositioned when the report is actually printed.

The key element in report preparation is consistency. Using a template can help you keep your presentation internally consistent, in addition to enforcing consistency across all reports. A very general template might include these sections[17]:

   I. Abstract or summary

   II. Table of contents

  III. Body of report

  IV. Conclusions

   V. References

  VI. Glossary

 VII. Acknowledgments

Sections can be numbered using either a decimal numbering system, such as

  1. Analysis

    1.1. Preliminary analysis

      1.1.1. Research

      1.1.2. Examination plan

    1.2. Onsite Investigation

  2. Conclusions

or a legal-sequential numbering system, such as

I. Analysis

   1. Preliminary analysis

   2. Onsite investigation

II. Conclusions

Your client or your organization may have a preferred style for reporting, and you should use that format unless there is a very good reason not to (and be prepared to support your argument as to why the standard format isn't suitable).

Looking back, we can see that the section labeled as the body of the report contains the important explication of the collection and analysis of the evidence. This section should contain information about methods used to solve the problem, including how the data was collected, special tools or techniques used, statistical methods used, and so on. Refer to any tools used to complete your calculations (MATLAB, for example, or the R statistical package).

The body of the report and the conclusions are the most important sections. Going backwards, a good report will present conclusions that have been supported by the description of collecting the evidence and performing the analysis. Written correctly, your conclusions will flow seamlessly from the presentation of the evidence, creating a story that can only have one ending.

The report body should address how you went about collecting and analyzing the data, including how the data was collected, any special tools or techniques used, statistical methods used, and so on. Make sure to refer to any tools used to complete your calculations (MATLAB, for example, or the R statistical package). Knowing the accuracy and reliability of the tools you've used is crucial to standing up to cross-examination from the opposing attorney. Your report should contain information on error analysis and how certain the results of that tool are. Addressing uncertainty enhances the integrity of your data and your presentation by establishing that you know the limitations of a particular tool. Timestamp analysis, for example, is uncertain because time stamps can be altered. Likewise, document metadata may be inconsistent or confusing (we may have lost the indication of who made the change between version 1 and version 3, for example). Establishing that immediately heightens your credibility because it indicates that you have taken this uncertainty into account while performing your analysis.

Collected evidence are of three kinds. General evidence is the description of who did what to whom, when, and where (that is, the date and time you visited the site, with whom you spoke, and so forth). Physical and demonstrative evidence is the actual digital forensics evidence you collected, and all the records associated with that evidence: what was seized, how it was protected, who had access (chain of custody). Finally, testimonial evidence is the record of your conversations with people: names, date and time, organization, their position within the organization. If you're working with law enforcement, and the interviewee was a suspect, you should include a statement that the person received a Miranda warning.

Before submitting the report, make a final run-through. Only relevant material should be included. Make sure you have used a consistent structure and you haven't repeated yourself. If possible, have someone unfamiliar with the case read the report as a test to determine if it can be understood by an outsider.[18] Pay attention to the mechanics of the report: Check grammar, spelling, punctuation, and readability (most word processing programs can help you with this). Errors in the mechanics can leave the impression that the author is not concerned with details and can arouse suspicions that the investigator may have been less than thorough in the investigation.

Theory into Practice: Generating a Report

All of the digital forensic frameworks that we discussed in previous chapters have a way to generate a report of findings. We'll use an early demo version of AccessData's Forensic Toolkit (FTK) and Technology Pathways's ProDiscover Basic as examples.

ProDiscover Basic's reporting capabilities are very easy to use. The generated report includes all items marked as items of interest, along with any case metadata provided by the investigator. Output formats are text and RTF (Rich Text Format): RTF-formatted files can be incorporated into Microsoft Word or other word processors for additional commentary, or as a separate section of a longer report. Figure 12-2 lists the first page of a report on the Greg Schardt case.

Figure 12-2
ProDiscover
Basic report
output

Evidence Report for Project: Schardt-02

Project Number: 20140209-1

Project Description: Greg Schardt and Mr. Evil

Image Files:
File Name: C:\Users\clbrooks\Downloads\NIST-Hacking\4Dell Latitude CPi.E01
Image File Type: Expert Witness Image
File Number:
Technician Name: Shane Robinson
Date: 09/22/2004
Time: 09:06:04
MD5 Checksum: aee4fcd9301c03b3b054623ca261959a
Checksum Validated: No
Compressed image: No
Time Zone Information:

Time Zone: (GMT-05:00) Bogota, Lima, Quito (SA Pacific Standard Time)
Daylight savings (summertime) was in effect: No
Time Zone information obtained from preferences settings.

Total Drive Information

Total Sectors : 9514260
Total Size : 4757130 KB

Hard Disk: C:
        Volume Name:
        Volume Serial Number : 6CB1-8D9B
        File System : NTFS
        Bytes Per Sector: 512
        Total Clusters: 9510416
        Sectors per cluster: 1
        Total Sectors: 9510416
        Hidden Sectors: 63
        Total Capacity: 4755208 KB
        Start Sector: 63
        End Sector: 9510479

Disks:

Evidence of Interest:

Total Evidence Items of Interest: 6

AccessData's FTK provides the investigator with a report wizard that supports tailoring of a report. Information in the report includes both the investigator and the forensics investigator (assuming they are different individuals). Additional dialog boxes ask the examiner what categories of information should be included and what attributes of that information should be included. Figure 12-3 illustrates the evidence section of a report on the Greg Schardt case and clearly shows how the evidence includes both partitioned (NTFS) and unpartitioned space.

FTK also allows the investigator to include the case log file that records each action taken by the investigator. Figure 12-4 shows a portion of the log when the report was generated. Although not intended for the body of a report (trust me, it's rather dry reading), providing the case log as an appendix would clearly demonstrate the actions of the investigator, and the log also serves as a reminder to the investigator as to exactly when and what was done.

Do's and Don'ts for a DFI

From a professional and ethical standpoint, a DFI is required to abide by a set of guidelines. The American Society of Digital Forensics and Electronic Discovery (ASD-FED) provides a code of ethics for its members (www.asdfed.com/domain3).[19] Since

Evidence List

2/12/2014
Display Name: 4Dell Latitude CPi\Part_1\NONAME-NTFS
Evidence File Name: 4Dell Latitude CPi.E01
Evidence Path: C:\Users\clbrooks\Downloads\NIST-Hacking
Identification Name/Number: Schardt-1-A
Evidence Type: NTFS
Added: 12/14/2013 3:57:59 PM
Children: 4,932
Descendants: 5,000
Comment: Dell Latitude laptop image

Display Name: 4Dell Latitude CPi\UnpartSpace
Evidence File Name: 4Dell Latitude CPi.E01
Evidence Path: C:\Users\clbrooks\Downloads\NIST-Hacking
Identification Name/Number: Schardt-1-A
Evidence Type: Unpartitioned Space
Added: 12/14/2013 4:24:31 PM
Children: 5,000
Descendants: 5,000
Comment: Dell Latitude laptop image

AccessData Forensic Toolkit®

Figure 12-3 Evidence section of an FTK report

```
2/12/2014 10:54:49 AM -- Opening case
2/12/2014 10:54:50 AM -- KFF database being used:  none
2/12/2014 10:54:50 AM -- Examiner's Local Machine Setting is time zone used for file times (create, modify, accessed) in file
2/12/2014 10:54:50 AM --
2/12/2014 10:54:50 AM -- Loading case
2/12/2014 10:54:50 AM -- Building explore path tree
2/12/2014 10:54:51 AM -- Building explore, graphic and email path tree
2/12/2014 10:54:51 AM -- Updating Overview Cache
2/12/2014 10:54:51 AM -- Filtering file list
2/12/2014 10:54:51 AM -- Initializing thumbnail view
2/12/2014 10:54:51 AM -- Resetting search terms list
2/12/2014 10:54:51 AM -- Building the indexed search results tree...
2/12/2014 10:54:51 AM -- Building the live search results tree...
2/12/2014 10:54:51 AM -- Building the bookmark tree
2/12/2014 10:54:51 AM -- Opened case: C:\FTK\Schardt-Hacking\ using FTK version 1.81.2 build 09.01.20
2/12/2014 10:54:51 AM -- Examiner's Local Machine Setting is time zone used for file times (create, modify, accessed) in file
2/12/2014 10:57:13 AM -- Performed Search Query: (Schardt)
       Search Results:  6 Hits in 3 Files
       Search Query: (Schardt)
       Search Results:  6 Hits in 3 Files
2/12/2014 10:57:24 AM -- Displayed Search Results for QUERY: (Schardt)
       4 Hits - [software]   4Dell Latitude CPi\Part_1\NONAME-NTFS\WINDOWS\system32\config\software
       1 Hit - [AppEvent.Evt]   4Dell Latitude CPi\Part_1\NONAME-NTFS\WINDOWS\system32\config\AppEvent.Evt
       1 Hit - [hiberfil.sys_1]   4Dell Latitude CPi\Part_1\NONAME-NTFS\hiberfil.sys_1
```

Figure 12-4   FTK case log output

ASDFED is more closely focused on the forensic examiner, they provide specific guidelines.

Will	Won't
Will diligently work to avoid any conflict of interest	Will not have a financial interest in the outcome of any case
Will present all the facts to the client, without bias and independent of the impact on the case at hand	Will not deliberately obscure or omit evidence that may be either exculpatory or incriminating
Will comply with all applicable laws relating to the practice of digital forensics or e-discovery	Will not accept cases beyond their level of ability to properly perform the work at the highest standard
Will remain neutral and without prejudice in the performance of their duties	Will not misrepresent or overstate their qualifications
Will regularly attend continuing education in their field	Will not reveal confidential information in their care unless ordered by a court of law or permitted by the owner of the confidential information
Will act responsibly in the performance of their duties and in the operation of their practice at all times	Will not make statements about the guilt or innocence of a client in any matter, civil or criminal

These criteria echo several themes that we've addressed earlier in this chapter: maintaining objectivity, presenting all facts to the client, avoiding conflict of interest, and so on. I find one of these admonitions very striking: Never knowingly undertake an assignment beyond your ability. A famous line from "Dirty Harry" Callahan (Clint Eastwood in the film *Magnum Force*) is "A man's got to know his limitations." Although it may be extremely difficult to turn down a high-paying and highly interesting case, acting ethically can contribute to convicting the guilty and exonerating the innocent—as well as bringing justice to the victims.

Resting the Case

After the investigation is complete, you've written the report, and you have provided testimony, you should find a time to reflect on the "lessons learned" from the case, either by yourself or with other colleagues if you're discussing tools and techniques of the investigation itself. In this instance, you might want to discuss some of the following.

 EXAM TIP This material won't be on the exam.

- What improvements can you make in your investigation regarding the gathering of evidence and its analysis?
- Were there particular devices where it was difficult to actually obtain the digital data?
- Are new tools available to increase the speed and accuracy in obtaining the data?
- Are there other sources of corroborating evidence that you discovered, such as logs on remote devices or information stored within the seized evidence (such as new registry fields)?

A second topic for reflection is communicating your results, either via a report or as a witness. Would a different set of topics be more persuasive? Is there corroborating evidence that would make it easier to support a particular interpretation of events? Were there aspects of the presentation that confused your audience?

The ultimate goal of the "lessons learned" exercise is to make you more effective as an investigator. What could you have done differently? How could you have been more efficient (time = money)? How does your new knowledge contribute to preparing and conducting a future investigation? What skills do you need to acquire, and what new tools are available? Did opposing counsel ask questions that you couldn't answer? And so on.

Digital technologies are ever changing and ever increasing. As a DFI, you need to keep current with these technologies, as well as with the laws that affect the collection of digital evidence. Your adversaries are certainly willing and able to take advantage of any changes that would improve their abilities to carry out their (illegal) activities. Standing still is effectively moving backward.

Chapter Review

A DFI can be called as a testimonial or evidentiary witness, in which case their role is to recite the facts of the case regarding access to digital evidence and the results of their analysis. If called as an expert witness, their role is considerably expanded, and they will be able to present conclusions based on the evidence presented and on their own analysis and expertise. Two cases govern when expert witness testimony can be used: *Frye* and *Daubert*. *Frye* presented guidance that is more generic, while *Daubert* provided a checklist to determine if this testimony can be introduced.

Expert witnesses are required to present details of publications for the last ten years, cases in which they've testified/been deposed in the preceding four years, and any previous compensation they have received for testifying. Expert witnesses are also required to prepare and deliver reports. These reports can be formal or informal, verbal or written.

A DFI may testify in court at a trial, at a preliminary hearing, at a deposition, or at a testimony preservation deposition. Regardless of the situation, you should always maintain your composure, stick to the facts of the case, and behave and respond professionally—which may often mean maintaining a professional distance from all other persons involved with the case except for your client.

One measure of a good report is that it is effective in supporting the goals of the investigation and presenting the evidence in a compelling fashion. A good report will create a narrative where the reader or listener will be lead through the evidence discovered and its relevance in supporting the investigation. Conclusions must be supported by the evidence presented. A good report will include only the relevant facts and analysis results in a neutral manner without bias or personal opinion.

Make time after the case is closed (either after your investigation is complete or you have testified) to list the "lessons learned" from the case, whether it be new skills to acquire, new procedures to follow, or different ways of presenting to an audience.

Questions

1. How does an investigative report differ from a threshold report? Choose all that apply.

   A. An investigative report will include all avenues of investigation, including those that led nowhere.

   B. An investigative report contains more details.

   C. An investigative report will include details on victimology.

   D. An investigative report isn't subject to discovery.

2. Which statements illustrate the differences between an expert witness and a technical witness? Choose all that apply.

   A. Expert witnesses can offer an opinion regarding the evidence.

   B. Technical witnesses will usually have been personally involved in the case.

   C. Technical witnesses must always write a report for the court.

   D. Technical witnesses always speak to the nature of the evidence and how it was obtained.

3. A testimony preservation deposition occurs when (choose all that apply):

    A. A witness is not able to be deposed in person

    B. The witness's testimony needs to be preserved

    C. An expert witness may not be able to appear in person at the trial

    D. Testimony requires facilities only available in a particular laboratory environment

4. The National Institute of Standards' (NIST's) efforts to verify the output of various forensics software attempt to address which aspect of the *Daubert* ruling? Choose all that apply.

    A. If the technique has been subject to peer review and publication

    B. Whether the technique or theory can or has been tested

    C. The known or potential error rate of the technique or theory

    D. The existence of standards and controls

5. Which federal statute speaks to stating an opinion on the facts even if the facts are not admissible as testimony?

    A. FRE 705

    B. FRE 702

    C. FRCP 26

    D. FRCP 28

6. What should a CV *not* include?

    A. Specific accomplishments

    B. Justification for a particular trial

    C. Professional education

    D. Professional associations

7. Which critical case resulted in a checklist of qualifications that must be met in order for expert witness testimony to be included?

    A. *Frye*

    B. *Daubert*

    C. *Locard*

    D. *Kumho*

8. An expert witness needs to list the cases where they've been called to testify going back at least _____ years.

    A. Seven

    B. Ten

    C. Four

    D. Three

9. Diagrams, photographs, tables, and so forth should be _____.

    A. Placed in an appendix

    B. Interspersed throughout the report

    C. Included in a separate volume entirely

    D. Preserved from submission if requested by the court

10. What is considered the most important aspect of an investigative report?

    A. Organization

    B. Narrative

    C. Consistency

    D. Coverage

Answers

1. **B.** An investigative report will contain more details than a threshold report.

2. **A, B, C.** All these statements are true. Technical witnesses are not required to write a report.

3. **A, B, C, D.** All these statements are true.

4. **B, C.** NIST tests forensics software to determine if it can detect known issues, thereby killing two birds with one stone.

5. **A.** FRE 705 indicates that expert opinion on the facts is admissible even if the evidence isn't.

6. **B.** A CV should not list the trials at which you've appeared as a witness.

7. **B.** *Daubert* is the case where a checklist for expert testimony was first formulated.

8. **C.** An expert witness needs to list all cases at which they testified in the last four years.

9. **A.** Any demonstrative evidence such as photographs, drawings, maps, and so forth should be in an appendix of the report.

10. **C.** Consistency is the most important element of a report.

References

1. Casey, E. et al., *Digital Evidence and Computer Crime,* 3rd ed. (MA: Elsevier, 2011), pp. 273ff.

2. Casey, p. 273.

3. Casey, p. 266.

4. Retrieved from http://www.daubertontheweb.com/frye_opinion.htm.

5. "Rule 702: Testimony by an Expert Witness." Retrieved from http://www.law .cornell.edu/rules/fre/rule_702.

6. "Rule 705: Disclosing the Fact or Data Underlying an Expert." Retrieved from www.law.cornell.edu/rules/fre/rule_705.

7. Nelson, W. et al., *Guide to Computer Forensics and Investigations,* 4th ed. (MA: Cengage Learning, 2011), p. 544.

8. Nelson, p. 517.

9. Nelson, p. 576.

10. Retrieved from www.eccouncil.org/Support/code-of-ethics.

11. Nelson, W. et al., *Guide to Computer Forensics and Investigations,* 4th (MA: Cengage, 2010), p. 552.

12. Pirsig, R., *Zen and the Art of Motorcycle Maintenance* (NY: William Morrow, 1974), frontispiece.

13. "Rule 26: Duty to Disclose; General Provisions Concerning Discovery." Retrieved from www.law.cornell.edu/rules/frcp/Rule26.htm.

14. EC-Council. *Computer Forensics Investigation Procedures and Responses* (NY: Cengage, 2010), p. 6-2.

15. "Spoliation Law & Legal Definition." Retrieved from definitions.uslegal.com/s/ spoliation/.

16. EC-Council, p. 6-5.

17. Ibid.

18. EC-Council, p. 6:128.

19. "Domain: Ethics and Code of Conduct." Retrieved from www.asdfed.com/ domain3.

Acronyms

Since I collected a set of terms for the glossary from the publications listed here, it seemed only fair that I create a list of acronyms from these documents as well. I've also included terms used in the body of the book.

- SP800-72 Guidelines on PDA Forensics (2004)
- S800-86 Guide to Integrating Forensic Techniques into Incident Response (2006)
- SP800-101r1 Guidelines on Mobile Device Forensics (2014)

5WH   Who, what, when, where, why, and how?

ABA   American Bar Association

ADIA   Appliance for Digital Analysis and Investigation (ADIA)

ADS   alternate data stream

AMA   American Medical Association

AMI   Amazon Machine Instance

AP   access point

APA   American Psychological Association

APDU   application protocol data unit

API   application programming interface

ARIN   American Registry for Internet Numbers

ARP   Address Resolution Protocol

ASCFLD   American Society of Crime Laboratory Directors

ASCII   American Standard Code for Information Interchange

ASDFED   American Society of Digital Forensics and Electronic Discovery

ATA   advanced technology attachment

AWS   Amazon Web Services

BC/DR business continuity/disaster recovery

BCD binary coded decimal

BIOS basic input/output system

BSC base station controller

BTS base transceiver station

CART Computer Analysis and Response Team

CAWFE Certified Advanced Windows Forensic Examiner

CCE Certified Computer Examiner

CCIPS Computer Crime and Intellectual Property Section

CCTV closed-circuit television

CD compact disc

CDFS CD file system

CD-R CD-recordable

CD-ROM CD-read-only memory

CD-RW CD-rewritable

CEH Certified Ethical Hacker

CF compact flash

CFCE Certified Forensic Computer Examiner

CFI computer and financial investigations

CFRDC Computer Forensics Research and Development Center

CFReDS Computer Forensic Resource Data Sets

CFTT Computer Forensics Tool Testing

CFTT Computer Forensics Tool Test

CIDR classless inter-domain routing protocol

CIR consumer infrared

CMOS complementary metal oxide semiconductor

CNIC cellular network isolation card

CODEC coder-decoder

CPA   Certified Public Accountant

CSIM   DMA Subscriber Identity Module

CSIRT   Computer Security Incident Response Team

CSOC   Computer Security Operations Center

CV   curriculum vitae

CVE   common vulnerabilities and exposures

DART   Digital Advanced Response Toolkit

dd   duplicate disk/data dump

DDoS   distributed denial of service

DHCP   Dynamic Host Configuration Protocol

DLL   dynamic link library

DNA   Distributed Network Access

DNS   Domain Name System

DoD   Department of Defense

DoS   denial of service

DVD   digital video disc or digital versatile disc

DVD-R   DVD-recordable

DVD-ROM   DVD-read-only memory

DVD-RW   DVD-rewritable

EAP   Extensible Authentication Protocol

EAP-TLS   EAP with Transport Layer Security

EC2   Elastic Compute Cloud

ECC   error checking and correction

EDGE   Enhanced Data for GSM Evolution

EMS   Enhanced Messenger Service

ES   end system

ESN   electronic serial number

ETSI   European Telecommunications Standards Institute

ESP   encapsulating security payload

ETI   Enterprise Theory of Investigation

eUICC   Embedded Universal Integrated Circuit Card

ext2fs   second extended file system

ext3fs   third extended file system

ext4fs   fourth extended file system

F.I.R.E.   Forensic and Incident Response Environment

FACCI   Florida Association of Computer Crime Investigators

FAT   File Allocation Table

FBI   Federal Bureau of Investigation

FCC ID   Federal Communications Commission Identification Number

FIPS   Federal Information Processing Standards

FISMA   Federal Information Security Management Act

FLETC   Federal Law Enforcement Training Center

FOSS   free and open-source software

FRCP   Federal Rules of Civil Procedure

FRE   Federal Rules of Evidence

FRED   forensic recovery of digital evidence

FRED-L   forensic recovery of digital evidence - laptop

FTP   File Transfer Protocol

GB   gigabyte

GC   garbage collection

GDI   Graphics Device Interface

GPRS   General Packet Radio Service

GPS   global positioning system

GSM   Global System for Mobile Communications

GUI   graphical user interface

GWES   graphics, windowing, and events subsystem

HAL Hardware Abstraction Layer

HFS Hierarchical File System

HIPO hierarchical input-process-output

HKEY HIVE key

HPA host-protected area

HPFS high-performance file system

HTCIA High Technology Crime Investigation Association

HTML Hypertext Markup Language

HTTP Hypertext Transfer Protocol

IaaS Infrastructure as a Service

IACIS International Association of Computer Investigative Specialists

IANA Internet Assigned Numbers Authority

ICCID integrated circuit card identification

ICMP Internet Control Message Protocol

ID identification

IDE integrated drive electronics

iDEN Integrated Digital Enhanced Network

IDS intrusion detection system

IEEE Institute of Electrical and Electronics Engineers

IETF Internet Engineering Task Force

IGMP Internet Group Management Protocol

IIS Internet Information Server

IM instant messaging

IMAP Internet Message Access Protocol

IMEI International Mobile Equipment Identity

IMSI International Mobile Subscriber Identity

IOCE International Organization on Computer Evidence

IOS Internetwork Operating System

IP   Internet Protocol

IPsec   Internet Protocol Security

IR   interagency report

IRC   Internet Relay Chat

IrDA   Infrared Data Association

IRQ   Interrupt Request Line

IS   intermediate system (a router or gateway)

ISFCE   International Society of Forensic Computer Examiners

ISO   International Organization for Standardization

ISP   Internet service provider

IT   information technology

ITL   Information Technology Laboratory

JPEG   Joint Photographic Experts Group

JTAG   Joint Test Action Group

KB   kilobyte

LACNIC   Latin American and Caribbean IP Network Information Centre

LAN   local area network

LBA   logical block addressing

LCD   liquid crystal display

LED   light-emitting diode

LND   last numbers dialed

MAC   modification, access, and creation

MAC   Media Access Control

MACE   modified, accessed, created or entry modified

MAN   metropolitan area network

MATLAB   Mathematics Laboratory

MB   megabyte

MBR   master boot record

MD   Message Digest

MD5   Message Digest 5

MEID   mobile equipment identifier

MFT   Master File Table

MISTI   MIS Training Institute

MMC   multimedia card

MO   magneto-optical

MPE+   Mobile Phone Examiner Plus

MSC   mobile switching center

MS-DOS   Microsoft Disk Operating System

MSISDN   Mobile Subscriber Integrated Services Digital Network

NAS   network accessible storage

NAT   Network Address Translation

NetBIOS   Network BIOS

NFA   Network Forensic Analysis Tool

NFC   near-field communication

NFS   Network File Sharing

NIC   network interface card

NIJ   National Institute of Justice

NIST   National Institute of Standards and Technology

NLECTC-NE   National Law Enforcement and Corrections Technology Center, North East

NNTP   Network News Transport Protocol

NSM   network security monitoring

NSRL   National Software Reference Library

NTFS   Windows NT File System

NTI   New Technologies, Inc.

NTP   Network Time Protocol

NW3C   National White Collar Crime Center

OAL   OEM Adaption Layer

ODBC   Open Database Connectivity

OEM   Original Equipment Manufacturer

OMB   Office of Management and Budget

OS   operating system

OSI   Open Systems Interconnect

OSR2   OEM Service Release 2

PaaS   Platform as a Service

PATA   Parallel ATA

PCMCIA   Personal Computer Memory Card International Association

PDA   personal digital assistant

PEAP   Protected EAP

PIEID   preservation, identification, extraction, interpretation, documentation

PIM   personal information management

POP   Post Office Protocol 3

POSE   Palm Operating System Emulator

PPC   Pocket PC

PPI   pixels per inch

PPTP   Point-to-Point Tunneling Protocol

PRTK   Password Recovery Toolkit

QEMU   Quick EMUlator

RADIUS   Remote Authentication Dial-In User Service

RAID   redundant array of inexpensive disks

RAM   random access memory

RAPI   remote application programming interface

RCFL   Regional Computer Forensic Laboratory

RCS   revision control system

RFC   Request for Comment

RIPE NCC   Réseaux IP Européens Network Coordination Centre

ROM   read-only memory

RSA   Rivest, Shamir, Adelson

RSN   robust security network

S3   simple storage service

SaaS   Software as a Service

SAM   Security Account Manager

SAN   storage area network

SATA   Serial ATA

SCSI   Small Computer System Interface

SD   Secure Digital

SDHC   Secure Digital High Capacity

SDK   Software Development Kit

SDMI   Secure Digital Music Initiative

SEM   Security Event Management

SFTP   Secure FTP

SHA-1   Secure Hash Algorithm 1

SIEM   Security Information and Event Management

SIM   Subscriber Identity Module

SIP   Session Initiation Protocol

SMB   Server Message Block

SME   subject matter expert

SMS   Short Message Service

SMTP   Simple Mail Transfer Protocol

SNMP   Simple Network Management Protocol

SOHO   small office/home office

SOP   standard operational procedure

SP   Special Publication

SPL Search Processing Language

SSD solid-state drive

SSH Secure Shell

SSID Service Set Identifier

SSL Secure Sockets Layer

STA station

SWGDE Scientific Working Group on Digital Evidence

SWGIT Scientific Working Group on Imaging Technologies

TAI International Atomic Time

TB terabyte

TCP Transmission Control Protocol

TCP/IP Transmission Control Protocol/Internet Protocol

TDMA Time Division Multiple Access

TFT thin film transfer

TOR The Onion Router

UART Universal Asynchronous Receiver/Transmitter

UDF Universal Disk Format

UDP User Datagram Protocol

UFS UNIX File System

UICC Universal Integrated Circuit Card

UMTS Universal Mobile Telecommunications System

UPS uninterruptible power supply

URL uniform resource locator

USB universal serial bus

USC United States Code

USIM UMTS Subscriber Identity Module

UTC Universal Coordinated Time

VERIS Vocabulary for Event Recording and Incident Sharing

VLC   VideoLAN client (now just VLC) media player

VMFS   VMware File System

VoIP   Voice over IP

VPN   virtual private network

WAF   web application firewall

WAP   wireless access point

WEP   Wired Equivalent Privacy

Wi-Fi   wireless fidelity

WINCE   Windows CE

WLAN   wireless LAN

WORM   write once, read many

WPA   Wireless Protected Access

WPA2   Wireless Protected Access version 2

XIP   eXecute in Place

About the CD-ROM

The CD-ROM included with this book comes with Total Tester practice exam software with two complete practice exams and a PDF copy of the book.

System Requirements

The software requires Windows XP or higher and 30MB of hard disk space for full installation, in addition to a current or prior major release of Chrome, Firefox, Internet Explorer, or Safari. To run, the screen resolution must be set to 1024 × 768 or higher. The PDF copy of the book requires Adobe Acrobat, Adobe Reader, or Adobe Digital Editions.

Installing and Running Total Tester

From the main screen you may install the Total Tester by clicking the Total Tester Practice Exams button. This will begin the installation process and place an icon on your desktop and in your Start menu. To run Total Tester, navigate to Start | (All) Programs | Total Seminars or double-click the icon on your desktop.

To uninstall the Total Tester software, go to Start | Settings | Control Panel | Add/ Remove Programs (XP) or Programs and Features (Vista/7/8), and then select the Total Tester program. Select Remove and Windows will completely uninstall the software.

Total Tester

Total Tester provides you with a simulation of the live exam. You can also create custom exams from selected certification objectives or chapters. You can further customize the number of questions and time allowed.

The exams can be taken in either Practice Mode or Exam Mode. Practice Mode provides an assistance window with hints, references to the book, explanations of the correct and incorrect answers, and the option to check your answer as you take the test. Exam Mode provides a simulation of the actual exam. The number of questions, the types of questions, and the time allowed are intended to be an accurate representation of the exam environment. Both Practice Mode and Exam Mode provide an overall grade and a grade broken down by certification objectives.

To take a test, launch the program and select the exam suite from the Installed Question Packs list. You can then select Practice Mode, Exam Mode, or Custom Mode. After making your selection, click Start Exam to begin.

PDF Copy of the Book

The entire contents of the book are provided in PDF on the CD-ROM. This file is viewable on your computer and many portable devices. Adobe Acrobat, Adobe Reader, or Adobe Digital Editions is required to view the file on your computer. A link to Adobe's web site, where you can download and install Adobe Reader, has been included on the CD-ROM.

 NOTE For more information on Adobe Reader and to check for the most recent version of the software, visit Adobe's web site at www.adobe.com and search for the free Adobe Reader or look for Adobe Reader on the product page. Adobe Digital Editions can also be downloaded from the Adobe web site.

To view the electronic book on a portable device, copy the PDF file to your computer from the CD-ROM, and then copy the file to your portable device using a USB or other connection. Adobe offers a mobile version of Adobe Reader, the Adobe Reader mobile app, which currently supports iOS and Android. For customers using Adobe Digital Editions and an iPad, you may have to download and install a separate reader program on your device. The Adobe web site has a list of recommended applications, and McGraw-Hill Education recommends the Bluefire Reader.

Technical Support

For questions regarding the Total Tester software or operation of the CD-ROM, visit www.totalsem.com or e-mail support@totalsem.com.

For questions regarding the PDF copy of the book, e-mail techsolutions@mhedu.com or visit http://mhp.softwareassist.com.

For questions regarding book content, please e-mail customer.service@mheducation .com. For customers outside the United States, e-mail international.cs@mheducation.com.

Unlike information security and information assurance, there doesn't seem to be a definitive glossary for digital forensics. I compiled this glossary based on definitions from three NIST special publications:

- SP800-72   Guidelines on PDA Forensics (2004)
- S800-86   Guide to Integrating Forensic Techniques into Incident Response (2006)
- SP800-101r   Guidelines on Mobile Device Forensics (2014)

The most recent definition of a term is the one provided.

acquisition   A process by which digital evidence is duplicated, copied, or imaged.

analysis   The third phase of the computer and network forensic process, which involves using legally justifiable methods and techniques to derive useful information that addresses the questions that were the impetus for performing the collection and examination. The examination of acquired data for its significance and probative value to the case.

anti-forensic   A technique for concealing or destroying data so that others cannot access it.

authentication mechanism   Hardware- or software-based mechanisms that force users to prove their identity before accessing data on a device.

bit-stream imaging   A bit-for-bit copy of the original media, including free space and slack space. Also known as disk imaging.

Bluetooth   A wireless protocol that allows two Bluetooth-enabled devices to communicate with each other within a short distance (e.g., 30 ft.).

brute-force password attack   A method of accessing an obstructed device by attempting multiple combinations of numeric/alphanumeric passwords.

buffer overflow attack   A method of overloading a predefined amount of space in a buffer, which can potentially overwrite and corrupt memory in data.

CDMA Subscriber Identity Module (CSIM)   CSIM is an application to support CDMA2000 phones that runs on a UICC, with a file structure derived from the R-UIM card.

Cellular Network Isolation Card (CNIC)   A SIM card that isolates the device from cell tower connectivity.

chain of custody   A process that tracks the movement of evidence through its collection, safeguarding, and analysis lifecycle by documenting each person who handled the evidence, the date/time it was collected or transferred, and the purpose for the transfer.

closed-source operating system   Source code for an operating system that is not publically available.

cluster   A group of contiguous sectors.

Code Division Multiple Access (CDMA)   A spread-spectrum technology for cellular networks based on the Interim Standard-95 (IS-95) from the Telecommunications Industry Association (TIA).

collection   The first phase of the computer and network forensics process, which involves identifying, labeling, recording, and acquiring data from the possible sources while following guidelines and procedures that preserve the integrity of the data.

compressed file   A file reduced in size through the application of a compression algorithm, commonly performed to save disk space. The act of compressing a file will make it unreadable to most programs until the file is uncompressed. Common compression utilities are PKZIP and WinZip, with an extension of .zip.

cradle   A docking station that creates an interface between a user's PC and PDA and enables communication and battery recharging.

Cyclical Redundancy Check (CRC)   A method to ensure data has not been altered after being sent through a communication channel.

data   Distinct pieces of digital information that have been formatted in a specific way.

deleted file   A file that has been logically, but not necessarily physically, erased from the operating system, perhaps to eliminate potentially incriminating evidence. Deleting files does not always necessarily eliminate the possibility of recovering all or part of the original data.

digital evidence   Electronic information stored or transmitted in binary form.

digital forensics   The application of science to the identification, collection, examination, and analysis of data while preserving the integrity of the information and maintaining a strict chain of custody for the data.

directory   Organizational structures that are used to group files together.

disk imaging   Generating a bit-for-bit copy of the original media, including free space and slack space. Also known as a bit-stream image.

disk-to-disk copy   Copying the contents of one medium directly to another medium.

disk-to-file copy   Copying the contents of media to a single logical data file.

duplicate digital evidence   A duplicate is an accurate digital reproduction of all data objects contained on the original physical item and associated media (e.g., flash memory, RAM, ROM).

electromagnetic interference   An electromagnetic disturbance that interrupts, obstructs, or otherwise degrades or limits the effective performance of electronics/electrical equipment.

electronic evidence   Information and data of investigative value that is stored on or transmitted by an electronic device.

electronic serial number (ESN)   A unique 32-bit number programmed into CDMA phones when they are manufactured.

Enhanced Data for GSM Evolution (EDGE)   An upgrade to GPRS to provide higher data rates by joining multiple time slots.

Enhanced Messaging Service (EMS)   An improved message system for GSM mobile devices allowing picture, sound, animation, and text elements to be conveyed through one or more concatenated SMS messages.

encryption   Any procedure used in cryptography to convert plain text into cipher text to prevent anyone but the intended recipient from reading that data.

examination   The second phase of the computer and network forensics process, which involves forensically processing large amounts of collected data using a combination of automated and manual methods to assess and extract data of particular interest, while preserving the integrity of the data. A technical review that makes the evidence visible and suitable for analysis. Tests performed on the evidence to determine the presence or absence of specific data.

eXecute in Place   A facility that allows code to be executed directly from flash memory without loading the code into RAM.

false negative   Incorrectly classifying malicious activity as benign.

false positive   Incorrectly classifying benign activity as malicious.

feature phone   A mobile device that primarily provides users with simple voice and text messaging services.

file   A collection of information logically grouped into a single entity and referenced by a unique name, such as a filename.

file allocation unit   A group of contiguous sectors; also known as a cluster.

file header   Data within a file that contains identifying information about the file and possibly metadata with information about the file contents.

filename   A unique name used to reference a file.

file signature anomaly A mismatch between the internal file header and its external filename extension; a filename inconsistent with the content of the file (e.g., renaming a graphics file with a nongraphics extension).

file system A method for naming, storing, organizing, and accessing files on logical volumes. A software mechanism that defines the way that files are named, stored, organized, and accessed on logical volumes of partitioned memory.

file slack Space between the logical end of the file and the end of the last allocation unit for that file.

flash ROM Nonvolatile memory that is writable.

forensic copy An accurate bit-for-bit reproduction of the information contained on an electronic device or associated media whose validity and integrity has been verified using an accepted algorithm.

forbidden PLMNs A list of public land mobile networks (PLMNs) maintained on the SIM that the mobile phone cannot automatically contact, usually because service was declined by a foreign provider.

forensic science The application of science to the law.

forensic specialist Someone who locates, identifies, collects, analyzes, and examines data while preserving the integrity and maintaining a strict chain of custody of information discovered.

forensically clean Digital media that is completely wiped of all data, including nonessential and residual data, scanned for malware, and verified before use.

free space An area on media or within memory that is not allocated.

General Packet Radio Service (GPRS) A packet-switching enhancement to GSM and TDMA wireless networks to increase data transmission speeds.

global positioning system A system for determining position by comparing radio signals from several satellites.

hardware driver Applications responsible for establishing communication between hardware and software programs.

hashing The process of using a mathematical algorithm against data to produce a numeric value that is representative of that data.

heap A software data structure used for dynamic allocation of memory.

Hypertext Transfer Protocol (HTTP) A standard method for communication between clients and web servers.

image An exact bit-stream copy of all electronic data on a device, performed in a manner that ensures the information is not altered.

inculpatory evidence   Evidence that tends to increase the likelihood of fault or guilt.

instant messaging (IM)   A facility for exchanging messages in real time with other people over the Internet and tracking the progress of a given conversation.

Integrated Circuit Card ID (ICCID)   The unique serial number assigned to, maintained within, and usually imprinted on the (U)SIM.

Integrated Digital Enhanced Network (iDEN)   A proprietary mobile communications technology developed by Motorola that combines the capabilities of a digital cellular telephone with two-way radio.

International Mobile Equipment Identity (IMEI)   A unique identification number programmed into GSM and UMTS mobile devices.

International Mobile Subscriber Identity (IMSI)   A unique number associated with every GSM mobile phone subscriber, which is maintained on a (U)SIM.

Internet Message Access Protocol (IMAP)   A method of communication used to read electronic messages stored in a remote server.

key chords   Specific hardware keys pressed in a particular sequence on a mobile device.

location information (LOCI)   The location area identifier (LAI) of the phone's current location, continuously maintained on the (C/U)SIM when the phone is active and saved whenever the phone is turned off.

logical backup   A copy of the directories and files of a logical volume.

logical volume   A partition or a collection of partitions acting as a single entity that has been formatted with a file system.

loopback mode   An operating system facility that allows a device to be mounted via a loopback address and viewed logically on the PC.

message digest   A hash that uniquely identifies data. Changing a single bit in the data stream used to generate the message digest will yield a completely different message digest.

metadata   Data about data. For file systems, metadata is data that provides information about a file's contents.

misnamed files   A technique used to disguise a file's content by changing the file's name to something innocuous or altering its extension to a different type of file, forcing the examiner to identify the files by file signature versus file extension. See *file signature anomaly*.

mobile devices   A mobile device is a small handheld device that has a display screen with touch input and/or a QWERTY keyboard, and may provide users with telephony capabilities. Mobile devices are used interchangeably (phones, tablets) throughout this document.

Mobile Subscriber Integrated Services Digital Network (MSISDN) The international telephone number assigned to a cellular subscriber.

Multimedia Messaging Service (MMS) An accepted standard for messaging that lets users send and receive messages formatted with text, graphics, photographs, audio, and video clips.

near-field communication (NFC) A form of contactless, close-proximity radio communications based on radio-frequency identification (RFID) technology.

Network Address Translation The process of mapping addresses on one network to addresses on another network.

network intrusion detection system Software that performs packet sniffing and network traffic analysis to identify suspicious activity and record relevant information.

network traffic Computer network communications that are carried over wired or wireless networks between hosts.

nonvolatile data Data that persists even after a computer is powered down.

normalize The process by which differently formatted data is converted into a standardized format and labeled consistently.

operating system A program that runs on a computer and provides a software platform on which other programs can run.

packet The logical unit of network communications produced by the transport layer.

packet sniffer Software that monitors network traffic on wired or wireless networks and captures packets.

partition A logical portion of a media that functions as though it were physically separate from other logical portions of the media.

password protected The ability to protect a file using a password access control, protecting the data contents from being viewed with the appropriate viewer unless the proper password is entered.

personal digital assistant (PDA) A handheld computer that serves as a tool for reading and conveying documents, electronic mail, and other electronic media over a communications link, and for organizing personal information, such as a database of names and addresses, a to-do list, and an appointment calendar.

personal information management (PIM) applications A core set of applications that provides the electronic equivalents of an agenda, address book, notepad, and business card holder maintained on a device that may be synchronized with another device or to the Cloud.

Post Office Protocol (POP) A standard protocol used to receive electronic mail from a server.

probative data Information that reveals the truth of an allegation.

process An executing program.

protocol analyzer Software that can reassemble streams from individual packets and decode communications that use various protocols.

proxy Software that receives a request from a client then sends a request on the client's behalf to the desired destination.

push-to-talk (PTT) A method of communicating on half-duplex communication lines, including two-way radio, using a "walkie-talkie" button to switch from voice reception to transmit mode.

remote access server Devices such as virtual private network gateways and modem servers that facilitate connections between networks.

Removable User Identity Module (R-UIM) A card developed for cdma-One/CDMA2000 handsets that extends the GSM SIM card to CDMA phones and networks.

reporting The final phase of the computer and network forensic process, which involves reporting the results of the analysis. This may include describing the actions used, explaining how tools and procedures were selected, determining what other actions need to be performed (e.g., forensic examination of additional data sources, securing identified vulnerabilities, improving existing security controls), and providing recommendations for improvement to policies, guidelines, procedures, tools, and other aspects of the forensic process. The formality of the reporting step varies greatly depending on the situation.

sector The smallest unit that can be accessed on media.

security event management software Software that imports security event information from multiple data sources, normalizes the data, and correlates events among the data sources.

Secure Digital eXtended Capacity (SDXC) Supports cards up to 2TB, compared to a limit of 32GB for SDHC cards in the SD 2.0 specification.

slack space The unused space in a file allocation block or memory page that may hold residual data.

Short Message Service (SMS) A cellular network facility that allows users to send and receive text messages of up to 160 alphanumeric characters on their handset.

SMS chat A facility for exchanging messages in real time using SMS text messaging that allows previously exchanged messages to be viewed.

steganography   Embedding data within other data to conceal it. The art and science of communicating in a way that hides the existence of the communication. For example, a child pornography image can be hidden inside another graphic image file, audio file, or other file format.

subdirectory   A directory contained within another directory.

Subscriber Identity Module (SIM)   A smart card chip specialized for use in GSM equipment.

synchronization protocols   Protocols that allow users to view, modify, and transfer/update PDA data from the PC or vice versa. The two most common synchronization protocols are Microsoft's ActiveSync and Palm's HotSync.

thread   A defined group of instructions executing apart from other similarly defined groups, but sharing memory and resources of the process to which they belong.

Universal Integrated Circuit Card   An integrated circuit card that securely stores the International Mobile Subscriber Identity (IMSI) and the related cryptographic key used to identify and authenticate subscribers on mobile devices. A UICC may be referred to as a SIM, USIM, RUIM, or CSIM; these terms can be used interchangeably.

UMTS Subscriber Identity Module (USIM)   A module similar to the SIM in GSM/GPRS networks, but with additional capabilities suited to 3G networks.

Universal Mobile Telecommunications System (UMTS)   A third-generation (3G) mobile phone technology standardized by the 3GPP as the successor to GSM.

universal serial bus (USB)   A hardware interface for low-speed peripherals such as the keyboard, mouse, joystick, scanner, printer, and telephony devices.

volatile data   Data on a live system that is lost after a computer is powered down.

volatile memory   Memory that loses its content when power is turned off or lost.

Wireless Application Protocol (WAP)   A standard that defines the way in which Internet communications and other advanced services are provided on wireless mobile devices.

wireless fidelity (Wi-Fi)   A term describing a wireless local area network that observes the IEEE 802.11 protocol.

wiping   Overwriting media or portions of media with random or constant values to hinder the collection of data.

write-blocker   A tool that prevents all computer storage media connected to a computer from being written to or modified. A device that allows investigators to examine media while preventing data writes from occurring on the subject media.

write protection   Hardware or software methods of preventing data from being written to a disk or other medium.

desktop, 17, 39, 40, 237, 287
environmental impact, 42–44
as evidence, 2
hardening, 250
"instrumentality of the crime," 69
involved in crime scene, 6
laptop, 4, 36, 61, 78–79, 225
networked, 78
portable, 78–79
remote login to, 246
return of, 73
role of, 2
searching/seizing. *See* searching/seizing
   evidence
shutdown procedures, 79
storing, 80
as tool for criminal activities, 6
virtualization platforms, 35
computer-stored records, 19–21
computing investigations, 6. *See also*
   investigations
condensation, 42
confidence, 281
confidentiality, integrity, and availability
   (CIA), 54
conflicts of interest, 282
connectionless protocols, 200
content, 70–72
content address, 21
cookies, 154, 155
Coordinated Universal Time (UTC), 218
corporate investigations, 7–8
corrective controls, 55
court cases. *See also* trials
   case logs, 290
   closing, 47
   postmortem analysis of, 47
   testimony. *See* testimony
   witnesses. *See* witnesses
court orders, 71
covered ciphers, 125
CPU (central processing unit), 112
CPU information, 84
crackers. *See* password cracking
cradle, 312
CRC (cyclic redundancy check), 312
Crime Investigation, 17

crime scene
   computer as part of, 6
   devices at, 78–79
   documenting, 39, 76
   interviews, 75–76
   labeling evidence, 39–40
   managing, 75–76
   photographing, 39, 76
   securing, 39
crime scene report, 80
crime scene tape, 60
crimes
   categories, 15
   vs. cybercrimes, 6
   e-mail-related, 166, 205, 258–259, 267
   victims of, 205, 206, 276
criminal investigations, 7–8
cross-site request forgery (CSRF), 248
cross-site scripting (XSS) attacks, 248
cryptography, 126, 127, 128
CSIM (CDMA Subscriber Identity
   Module), 311
CSIRT (Computer Security Incident Response
   Team), 73
CSRF (cross-site request forgery), 248
The Cuckoo's Egg, 7
curriculum vitae (CV), 279
customer information, 70
CV (curriculum vitae), 279
cyberbullying, 6
cybercrime, 3, 6, 8
cyberstalking, 6
cyclic redundancy check (CRC), 312
cylinder, head, and sector (CHS), 98

D

DARPA (Defense Advanced Research Projects
   Agency), 198
DART (Digital Advanced Response Toolkit), 173
data
   acquisition of. *See* data acquisition
   on archival media, 84
   cellular, 231
   computer-generated vs. computer-stored,
      19–21
   considerations, 8

Stop Hackers in Their Tracks

Hacking Exposed, 7th Edition

Hacking Exposed: Mobile Security

Hacking Exposed: Computer Forensics, 2nd Edition

Hacking Exposed: Wireless, 2nd Edition

Hacking Exposed: Web Applications, 3rd Edition

Hacking Exposed: Malware & Rootkits

IT Auditing, 2nd Edition

IT Security Metrics

Gray Hat Hacking, 3rd Edition

Available in print and ebook formats
 **@MHComputing**